Microsoft®

Building Enterprise Active Directory™ Services

Notes from the Field

PUBLISHED BY
Microsoft Press
A Division of Microsoft Corporation
One Microsoft Way
Redmond, Washington 98052-6399

Library of Congress Cataloging-in-Publication Data
Building Enterprise Active Directory Services / Microsoft Corporation.
     p. cm.
   Includes index.
   ISBN 0-7356-0860-1
     1. Directory services (Computer network technology) I. Microsoft Corporation.

   TK5105.595 .B85 2000
   005.7'1369—dc21   99-057855

Printed and bound in the United States of America.

1 2 3 4 5 6 7 8 9 QMQM 5 4 3 2 1 0

Distributed in Canada by Penguin Books Canada Limited.

A CIP catalogue record for this book is available from the British Library.

Microsoft Press books are available through booksellers and distributors worldwide. For further information about international editions, contact your local Microsoft Corporation office or contact Microsoft Press International directly at fax (425) 936-7329. Visit our Web site at mspress.microsoft.com.

Acquisitions Editor: David Clark
Project Editor: Thom Votteler

Contents

Part 1   Setting the Foundation

Part 2   Migration and Integration Scenarios

Introduction

Welcome to *Building Enterprise Active Directory Services*, seventh volume in the Notes from the Field series. The purpose of this guide is to provide the best practices of those who have implemented successfully Windows 2000 Active Directory in their organizations. The Notes from the Field series is unique in that each guide in the series is developed with the intention of sharing field experiences and real-world implementation scenarios. *Building Enterprise Active Directory Services* could not have been possible without the joint efforts of Microsoft Consulting Services, Microsoft Program Management, and the many customers who have worked with us in implementing Active Directory in their businesses while Windows 2000 was still in development.

Active Directory is considered one of the more integral components of Microsoft's distributed services. Many of the other components will leverage Active Directory for ease of configuration, management, and utilization. Well-planned Active Directory implementations should yield very significant business benefits as it unifies many of the business elements being managed by IT professionals.

Building Enterprise Active Directory Services is intended to be a supplement to the Microsoft Windows 2000 product documentation. Another resource to consider is the *Microsoft Windows 2000 Server Resource Kit* (Microsoft Press, 2000). The Resource Kit provides architectural details and implementation settings in reference to Active Directory and Windows 2000.

What's in This Book

This book contains twelve chapters, divided into three parts.

Part I: Setting the Foundation

Chapter 1, "Windows 2000 Active Directory Design," walks through an Active Directory design for a large distributed enterprise. This chapter provides much detail on the needs assessment, design process, and implementation of Active Directory in the studied environment. The authors of Chapter 1 carefully analyze many of the design criteria such as DNS namespace, Active Directory domains, WAN links, and dial-in configurations.

Chapter 2, "Compaq's Windows 2000 Site Topology Design," is probably the most intuitive and informative document available on Active Directory replication. This chapter describes in full detail the mechanics of Active Directory replication, topology design, and how to choose the correct transport for connected locations in your enterprise. The chapter focuses on Compaq Computer's enterprise design and was written by a Compaq senior consultant who was involved in the company's Joint Development Program.

Chapter 3, "Active Directory Database Sizing," provides an in-depth look at how data is stored in Active Directory and how to properly calculate hardware requirements. This chapter describes how data is physically stored in Active Directory and how the Active Directory store is organized. Information in this chapter will help the reader size domain controllers, size global catalog servers, and design the appropriate creation and placement of Active Directory partitions.

While Chapter 2 describes the details of how replication works, Chapter 4, "Active Directory Replication Traffic Analysis," describes in detail how these replicated data look on the wire—your network infrastructure. The chapter reviews in detail the many aspects of replication as it pertains to bandwidth utilization. This chapter provides the reader information for a solid understanding of Active Directory replication and its potential effects on the enterprise. The chapter also offers details on network ports and how to use NETMON to review replication traffic.

Chapter 5, "Active Directory Client Network Traffic," itemizes the network and directory utilization by Active Directory clients. This topic is as important (if not more so) when designing an Active Directory infrastructure as is replication traffic. Consider that replication traffic occurs when the object is written or modified, while the client traffic may occur each time a user logs into the network or uses an application.

Part II: Migration and Integration Scenarios

Chapter 6, "Domain Migration and Consolidation," provides information about domain upgrades and consolidation strategies. This chapter describes tools and when to use them, and it provides many details on how to take an enterprise from a Windows NT environment to Windows 2000. Additionally, the chapter describes issues pertaining to down-level integration.

Chapter 7, "Integrating Active Directory with a Unix-Based DNS Environment," provides in-depth detail on how to integrate Windows 2000 and Active Directory with Unix platforms and clients. The chapter reviews the tools and methods available and discusses design considerations and their implementations.

Chapter 8, "Integrating Active Directory with Exchange Server," is an important chapter for those implementing Active Directory with existing Exchange infrastructures. The chapter reviews the upgrade process, the integration and synchronization between Exchange and Active Directory, as well as collapsing and restructuring the Exchange environment.

Chapter 9, "Active Directory and Novell NetWare NDS," reviews some of the key architectural differences between Novell's NDS and Active Directory. The chapter then reviews the various ways to synchronize objects between directories in NetWare and Active Directory. This chapter is an excellent introduction to Active Directory for those already familiar with NetWare as the chapter compares the two products from the perspective of an administrative and systems engineer.

Part III: Administration and Security

Chapter 10, "Scripting the Active Directory," is written by one of Microsoft Consulting Services' most experienced implementers of Active Directory. The author describes the scripting environment of Active Directory, including ADSI, ASP, Windows Scripting Host, and WMI.

While Windows 2000 domains can still be used to segment administrative authority within an organization, this technique can be much more expensive administratively than utilizing the administrative delegation feature in Active Directory. Chapter 11, "Delegating Tree/Forest Operations," examines how this feature allows individual domains to be divided into more manageable Organizational Units, whereby selected administrators can be granted privileges.

Chapter 12, "Building a Windows 2000 Public Key Infrastructure," focuses on Public Key Infrastructures (PKI) as a crucial technology for both distributed and heterogeneous computer environments. In such environments, the presence of a rock-solid security system, providing authentication, confidentiality and non-repudiation services, is key. The chapter provides some background information on public key infrastructure, including what you can use it for, how you can implement it as a part of Windows 2000 Active Directory, and what components make up the Windows 2000 PKI.

Icons That Highlight Text

These sidebar icons provide you with simple signposts:

Icon	Description
	Caution or **Warning**. Advises you to take or avoid a specific action to avoid potential damage.
	Note. Emphasizes, supplements, or qualifies points in the text.
	Best Practices or **Guidelines**. Highlights proven practices, techniques, or procedures from MCS real-world experiences.
	Tools. Indicates sample code, Windows NT utilities, or tools provided on the companion CD.

What's on the Companion CD-ROM

On the CD that accompanies this book, you'll find documentation that could not be included in the book due to space considerations, as well as a number of useful tools, scripts, and utilities.

Here's a listing of what you'll find, organized by topic:

Active Directory Namespace Planning

- **Deployment template for Windows 2000.** This template is a Microsoft Project template. It outlines the major planning steps, tasks, and resources necessary to deploy Windows 2000 in a network. Depending on the size of the company, the template will create a project plan including all dependencies, timelines, and milestones. See the folder **Deployment Template** on the CD.

Capacity Planning

- **Tools to populate Active Directory for capacity planning and Active Directory database sizing.** These tools allow customers to re-do the database sizing and replication traffic tests in a lab environment. The toolset creates the important object in a directory (like users, groups, group members, printers, etc.), and comes with scripts and registry files to fully automate incremental tests including defragmentation of the Active Directory database. See the folder **Capacity Planning Tools** on the CD.

- **Tools to generate Exchange 2000 mail- and mailbox-enabled users, groups, and contacts.** Now that your Active Directory is populated, you might want to look into the future when Exchange will move to the Active Directory. After Exchange 2000 is installed in a lab environment, these tools can be used to create mailboxes for users. The effect on the size of the Active Directory can be measured. See the folder **Capacity Planning Tools** on the CD.

- **LDAP tools, scripts, and utilities.** For the network traffic tests, lots of small tools and utilities were used to create typical LDAP search operations. These scripts can be used to re-create our tests in the lab. See the folder **Capacity Planning Tools** on the CD.

- **Replication traffic spreadsheet.** Replication will occur on a daily basis when you install domain controllers. You can use this Microsoft Excel spreadsheet to computer the traffic that traverses your network every day. See the folder **Replication** on the CD.

- **Replication traffic calculation tables.** It is important not only to determine how much replication traffic is generated over your network, but also to assess how long it will take to send the information. These tables help you to do exactly these tasks, whether you operate in a slow-link or high-speed connectivity environment. See the folder **Replication** on the CD.

- **Additional documentation.** There is not enough room in this book to present every single detail of client logon operations, schema changes when Exchange 2000 is installed, and so on. For these topics, you can find detailed papers on the CD, including three chapters from the previous Notes from the Field title, *Optimizing Network Traffic* (Microsoft Press, 1999). See the folder **Documentation** on the CD.

Active Directory Administration

- **Sample Active Server Pages, using ADSI.** The Windows 2000 administration tools give access to all configuration and user information. However, some administrators want more flexibility. The scripting chapter in this book is a tutorial that explains how to create simple but powerful scripts to retrieve all sorts of configuration information from Active Directory, including replication configuration and Global Catalog configuration. For your convenience, a number of ASP pages that use these scripts have been included on the CD. They can be used as they are as powerful monitoring tools. See the folder **DSInfo** on the CD.

- **Tools to tighten security in multi-domain environments.** Large companies often wish to restrict the ability of Domain Administrators to affect forest-wide configuration changes in the schema or configuration container. Chapter 12 in this book explains how to tighten security. We've included a tool (DnProtect.exe) on the CD that allows you to protect individual objects within the various containers. See the folder **DNProtect** on the CD.

How To Use the Companion CD-ROM

To use the companion CD, insert the disc in your CD-ROM drive; a starting menu should appear automatically. If this menu does not appear, run *StartCD.exe* in the root of the CD.

The starting menu provides a launching point for the documents and templates on the CD. It also enables you to install software needed to view the three chapters from *Optimizing Network Traffic* included on the CD. To take full advantage of all the scripts, utilities, and tools we have provided, however, you will want to browse through the folders individually and refer to the appropriate Readme.doc for each folder.

System Requirements

System requirements define the minimum system configuration needed to take advantage of the resources available on the companion CD. The requirements are listed on a page following the Index, near the back of the book.

A Well-Deserved "Thank You"

We would like to take a moment to recognize and thank the customers who assisted Microsoft in the feature evaluation, beta testing, and actual beta implementations of Windows 2000 in their businesses while Windows 2000 was in development. Customers in both the JDP and RDP programs have been critical to Microsoft's understanding of our customers' needs and the software features they require. We consider our customers to be partners in the evolution of our product—partners that make our software better. On behalf of all of us here at Microsoft, thank you for your time, efforts, advice, and dedication to making Windows 2000 a better product.

Some Important Business

The example companies, organizations, products, people, and events depicted in this book are fictitious. No association with any real company, organization, product, person, or event is intended or should be inferred.

Contributors

We dedicate this volume to the authors, contributors, and reviewers who generously gave their time, experience, and vast knowledge to make this title a reality.

Program Manager

Andreas Luther

Senior Technical Editor

Bob Haynie

Assistant Editor

Laurie Dunham

Group Program Manager

Per Vonge Nielsen

Project Managers

Lisa Graham and Abram Spiegelman, EntireNet LLC

Contributors

Micky Balladelli (Compaq), Todd Briley, David A. Clark, Jan DeClerqc (Compaq), Samuel Devasahayam, Tom Dodds, Ken Durigan, Sean Gordon, Johan Grobler, Jim Gross, Dave Heuss (Compaq), Brian Karasawa, Matthias Leibmann, Scott Lengel, Lance Lillie, Andreas Luther, Xavier Minet, Eric Miyadi, David Skinner, Dan Thompson, Rick Varvel, Markus Vilcinskas, Jeff Wagner, Michael Wirth, and Zev Yanovich

Additional Contributors & Technical Reviewers

Richard Ault, David Batterson, Ryan Boone, Frank Callewaert, Andrea Campana, Michael Dennis, Dave Derry, Christoph Felix, Steven Judd, Stuart Kwan, Paul King, Mark Lawrence, Christophe Leroux, Michael Maston, Anthony Milano, Doug Ota, Jeff Parham, Glenn Pittaway, Robert Plesske, John Prichard, Jennifer Seastrom, Thomas Schenkman, Gavin Schiff, Richard Shi, Eric Stadter, and Mark Vodka (Compaq)

Compositors

Elizabeth Hansford, Barb Runyan, Dan Latimer

Indexer

Richard S. Shrout

P A R T   1

Setting the Foundation

This section helps you understand how to set the foundation for a successful Active Directory deployment. It examines the guidelines, special considerations, summaries, and methods required for a large project—information you need to create a design efficiently and effectively. Microsoft Solutions Framework (MSF) aligns business and technology objectives to simplify the design and deployment of technology within an enterprise infrastructure. Much of the material in this book is based on MSF principles and processes, and Chapter 1, "Windows 2000 Active Directory Design," introduces you to a company that used MSF to structure their Windows 2000 project and create a Windows 2000 Active Directory design based on recommendations in the *Microsoft Windows 2000 Server Deployment Planning Guide* (a volume in the *Microsoft Windows 2000 Server Resource Kit*). Chapter 2, "Compaq's Windows 2000 Site Topology Design," looks at how Compaq Computer Corporation designed a replication topology that makes optimum use of Windows 2000 Active Directory functionality—especially the Knowledge Consistency Checker. Chapters 3, 4, and 5 drive deep into the details of how Active Directory provides new ways for businesses to use directory services. Chapter 3, "Active Directory Database Sizing," shows how to determine the server hard disk space required to accommodate directory system growth. Chapter 4, "Active Directory Replication Traffic Analysis," concentrates on how replication affects network traffic. And Chapter 5, "Active Directory Client Network Traffic," looks at how to measure, estimate, and plan for client traffic.

Based on extensive field experience, these chapters describe and explain the fundamental steps for planning and designing the framework for a successful Active Directory implementation.

C H A P T E R   1

Windows 2000 Active Directory Design

By Lance Lillie, Tom Dodds, and Brian Karasawa, Microsoft Corporation

This chapter is about how Woodgrove Bank, a fictional financial institution that is based on the experiences of an actual industry-leading bank, structured their Windows 2000 project using Microsoft Solutions Framework (MSF) and created a Windows 2000 Active Directory design based on the recommendations found in the Windows 2000 deployment guide. The project was accomplished by a design team consisting of members of Microsoft Consulting Services (MCS) and of Woodgrove Bank IT. By aligning business and technology objectives, MSF simplifies the design and deployment of technology within an enterprise infrastructure. It exposes the critical risks, planning assumptions, and interdependencies required to successfully plan, build, and manage a technology infrastructure or a business solution.

What You'll Find in This Chapter

- An introduction to the Microsoft Solutions Framework (MSF) with a discussion of the basic methods and concepts it uses to facilitate and improve system design.

- A thorough discussion of how a design team at fictional company (Woodgrove Bank), consisting of internal members and Microsoft Consulting Services experts, created an Active Directory structure that captured the business structure, met all requirements, improved the original design, and provided a clear path for future development.

- A close examination of the steps, considerations, contingencies, trade-offs, evaluations, and methods required to approach a large project systematically, so that a design can be created efficiently and effectively.

Note   The fictional examples in this chapter use the extension .TLD (top-level domain) in the company domain names rather than .COM to insure that none of the domains are mistaken for those of any actual company or organization.

Overall Design Process at Woodgrove Bank

Stages and Deliverables

The Microsoft Solutions Framework (MSF) breaks the huge job of project design into phases, and this division of labor increases the probability that issues and dependencies are discovered as work progresses—before they become problems. Each phase has a set of deliverables, which helps create a smoother, more controlled approach that allows each stage to build carefully on preceding ones. A complete explanation of MSF is beyond the scope of this chapter, but you can find complete information at http://www.microsoft.com/msf.

Here is an overview of the principal MSF stages:

- **Envisioning.** This is the first stage in the MSF process. During it, Woodgrove Bank worked with MCS to establish the business objectives, technical objectives, executive expectations for the next-generation networking system, risks, team concept, and a concise Vision Statement for the overall project. This process resulted in the delivery of the Vision/Scope document, which established the *unbounded* view of their future Active Directory architecture, assembled the team, established roles and responsibilities, and set the scope of work for phase one of the project. Included within this was a conceptual design that documented the *today* design and the *tomorrow* model using Windows 2000.

- **Planning.** The second major stage completes the planning process. It culminates with the delivery of the master project plan, the draft Functional Specification, and the creation of the development lab. The functional specification describes what the next-generation networking architecture looks like. Rather than try to address all technical issues associated with the deployment of Windows 2000 architecture, it emphasizes the logical design and functionality requirements associated with the next-generation network operating infrastructure.

- **Developing.** When the Functional Specification is approved, it is used as the cornerstone of the Detailed Design and Process Validation phase (lab). As critical assumptions and technology integration needs are validated in the prototype lab and pilot environments, the Functional Specification is frozen— any suggested operational changes to the Windows NT and Windows 2000 system are handled with the formal change control process.

- **Deployment.** The deployment phase of the MSF process is reached when the team agrees that a stable solution has been achieved and is ready for deployment. At this point the core technology is being deployed, the operations team assumes the support role, and documentation is completed. The team is now preparing itself to transition to the next phase of the project.

This chapter is constructed to show how Active Directory was designed, focusing on how the team was organized, how the current Windows NT 4.0 architecture was taken into account, and how the initial Windows 2000 design was completed.

Teams

The MSF team model for infrastructure deployment advocates a small team of peers working in interdependent, multi-disciplinary roles. To develop the Woodgrove Bank solution, several teams were created and charged with development responsibilities. Here are the key roles and responsibilities:

Role	Responsibility
Product Management	Acts as customer advocate to the team
	Acts as team advocate to the customer
	Drives shared project vision/scope
	Manages customer expectations
	Develops, maintains, and executes the business case
	Drives features versus schedule trade-offs
	Develops, maintains, and executes the communications plan
Program Management	Facilitates team communication and negotiation
	Manages resource allocation
	Manages the project schedule and reports project status
	Manages the functional specification
	Drives overall critical trade-off decisions
Development	Selects the specific technology to deploy
	Writes scripts and code to aid installation and deployment
	Builds features to meet the specification and customer expectations
	Participates in design, focusing on physical design
	Estimates time and effort to complete each feature
	Configures and customizes
Test/QA	Develops testing strategy, plans, and scripts to ensure all issues are known
	Manages the build process
	Conducts tests to determine the status of solution development accurately
	Participates in setting the quality bar
Logistics	Acts as team advocate to operations
	Acts as operations advocate to the team
	Plans and manages solution deployment
	Participates in design, focusing on manageability, supportability, and deployability
	Trains operations and help desk personnel for infrastructure release
Training and Education	Acts as team advocate for users
	Acts as user advocate to the team
	Participates in defining user requirements
	Participates in designing features
	Designs, develops performance support systems, and drives usability process

Team members were asked to commit the appropriate hours to meet scheduled deliverable dates for their areas of responsibility. Accountability for one area of responsibility did not preclude members from participating in other project areas. In fact, due to resource issues, Product and Program Management encouraged each member to participate in all areas. This improves the design by getting team members involved in the entire process. It is a good idea, but you should remember that combining particular roles could introduce risks. See the Microsoft Solutions Framework materials for information on which roles can be combined safely, and how.

High-Level Design Goals

The Vision/Scope phase identified the high-level guiding principles considered critical to the successful development and implementation of the next generation network. Here are the major design criteria defined in the project Vision/Scope at Woodgrove Bank:

- Improve user productivity and communication by providing direct connectivity with customers, teammates, and domestic and international employees.
- Provide a mechanism for converting legacy systems and using them in parallel during transition.
- Minimize adverse impact on users.
- Maximize the value delivered by the networking system by minimizing operational costs such as administrator labor, on-going hardware requirements, software and hardware maintenance, and training.
- Minimize the learning curve and its impact on operations associated with implementing the new operating system.
- Lay the foundation for future business needs (global availability of resources).
- Maximize system availability with the goal of 100% up time (minus time required for maintenance).
- Promote information sharing and reuse.
- Support future growth. As the business grows, the networking system must support additional users and locations.
- Be flexible and support personnel movement. The system must be flexible to support the movement of personnel from region to region.
- Provide rapid, timely, reliable, and accurate delivery of all company information.
- Leverage existing IT investments. Woodgrove Bank has adopted the following standards:
  - User desktop: Intel-based machines
  - Primary user operating system: Windows 9x and Windows NT Workstation
  - Office automation tools: Microsoft Office

- Balance functionality with affordability.
- Achieve high quality: information must not be lost and data must not be corrupted.
- Minimize product risk by implementing a system that can evolve to meet new requirements over the next five years.
- Provide varying degrees of security, consistent with Woodgrove Bank, customer, and teammate requirements.

Assessment of the Current Windows NT 4.0 Environment

Current Network Architecture

You have to completely understand your current network infrastructure before you can build a successful Windows 2000 architecture. To do this, MSF builds a user profile that completely documents the current environment. At Woodgrove Bank, the team began by achieving a complete understanding of the existing connectivity and functionality between the Bank and its major hub locations. After interviewing staff, the team created the diagram depicted in Figure 1.1:

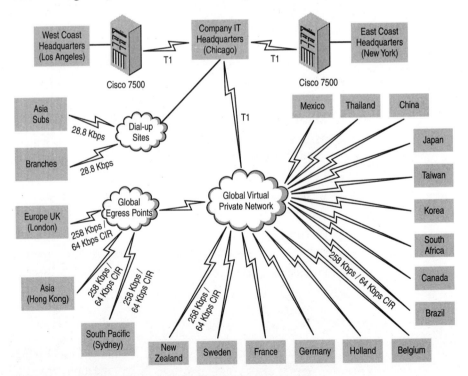

Figure 1.1   Network connectivity at Woodgrove Bank.

The Bank uses T1 links to communicate with the main domestic locations in Chicago, New York, and Los Angeles. Most international locations communicate over 56 K links, although some use 28.8 K dial-up over a VPN network. Sites without direct connectivity are being upgraded in the next three months. All branches still use dial-up links to communicate with corporate headquarters.

Current Domestic Windows NT 4.0 Domain Architecture

The existing Windows NT domain architecture was created when three financial entities merged to form Woodgrove Bank. The corresponding IT organizations also merged, resulting in a composite IT architecture. Each location manages its own domain. When Woodgrove Bank was created by merger, the need to share information required that trust relationships be established to give all users access, and this resulted in the Complete Trust domain architecture, which provides the greatest possible combination of sharing and autonomy for each location. Here is a list of each location and its primary Windows NT domain:

Current Windows NT Account domains at Woodgrove Bank.

Location	Windows NT Domain Name
Los Angeles	LANT
Chicago	CHINT
New York	NYNT
Chicago IT	DataCenterChi

Figure 1.2 is a diagram of the current domain architecture (not including stand-alone international domains).

← → The arrow represents reciprocal trust.

Figure 1.2   Current Domestic fully trusted domain model.

Microsoft presented an option to consolidate the four existing domains. However, because of cost and timing of the recommendation, Woodgrove Bank decided not to attempt consolidation before the Windows 2000 rollout.

Current International Windows NT 4.0 Domain Architecture

The international Windows NT domains are based on a hybrid of the Microsoft multi-master domain architecture. Account domains are mapped to geographical areas with a two-way trust relationship between the regional domain and the corporate IT domains. The trust relationship exists mainly to allow domestic administrators to manage and administer the International domains. Currently, there are domains in Europe, Asia, Australia, and the Americas (Canada and Mexico).

Third-Party Sub-Administration Tools

In its Windows NT 4.0 environment, Woodgrove Bank needed to administer each location individually, regardless of the underlying domain design or amount of available bandwidth. It also needed to perform administrative tasks at the local level, and to limit administration privilege to a given regional office or set of regional offices. The Windows NT 4.0 directory architecture does not provide this level of granular administration, so they turned to third-party tools. These vendors were identified as sources of sub-administration tools and tested in the lab:

- Entevo Corporation
- Mission Critical Software
- FastLane Technologies

Integrating International with the Domestic Domain

Woodgrove Bank does not want to migrate domains from the current trust model in place until the Windows 2000 planning is complete. Figure 1.3 shows the trust relationships between the domestic and International corporate facilities in the current Windows NT 4.0 design:

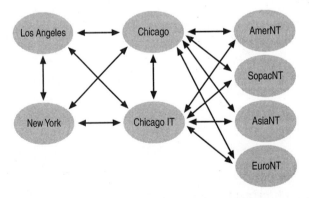

Figure 1.3   Current Domestic and International Trust Relationships

Also, there are many unmanaged domains in the network without any trust relationships. These domains were created by local IT groups and will require special treatment. One option was to create accounts with the same username and password in these separate international domains, thus providing credentials that domestic-domain administrators could use to connect to the international domains. Unfortunately, this broke the single-account model stated in the design criteria, so there was no choice but to continue maintaining these separate account databases until Windows 2000 migrates Woodgrove Bank to a single directory structure. Also, Woodgrove Bank has many disconnected dial-up domains, and these will also be migrated to the single Windows 2000 Active Directory.

Domain Design for Disconnected Sites in the Windows 4.0 Network

Woodgrove Bank uses Routing and Remote Access Services (RRAS) to provide connectivity to some sites that are not permanently connected to the Woodgrove Bank global WAN (see Figure 1.4). The RRAS links support the transfer of:

- NT Domain replication
- Exchange directory replication
- E-mail with attachments
- Remote Administrative access

The RRAS connections use these connection types:

- Analog
- ISDN
- X.25
- Frame relay
- T1

RRAS hardware depends on cost and availability in the specific region of service and on the bandwidth required for acceptable performance. RRAS was configured to dial as follows:

- Direct to regional data center
- To Internet via local ISP using PPTP
- To private network using PPTP

RRAS was chosen because Windows NT 4.0 has no sub-admin facility. The solution incorporated RRAS and third-party sub-admin tools so that Woodgrove Bank did not have to create separate account databases for each dial-up location.

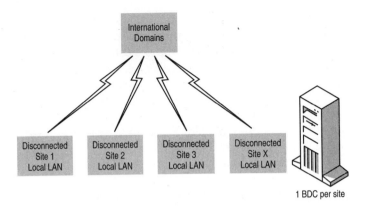

Figure 1.4   Disconnected sites at Woodgrove Bank in Windows NT 4.

Windows 2000 Design

Business Requirements for Active Directory

The original Windows NT 4.0 network outlined above faced challenges that MCS has encountered before: how to do sub-admin within a single domain, how to meet user account scalability requirements, how to properly manage a complete trust domain model, and how to handle sub-admin over slow links. The Woodgrove Bank team found that Windows 2000 was being designed to meet these requirements, and they asked MCS to start an upgrade planning process for the Windows NT 4.0 environment. The first step was to fully understand the business and technical challenges.

Three bank chains merged to form Woodgrove Bank, and this presented integration challenges. They all have Windows NT networks, but they all have different management styles and varied naming schemes. Windows 2000 Active Directory makes it possible to integrate these different approaches and to build a new infrastructure better suited to the new business model. By creating and designing an "ideal" environment with Windows 2000, the design team can rethink network use to get a better idea of what it can deliver and of how to manage it. This sort of brainstorming is recommended when you design for Windows 2000. Companies are familiar with the concept of re-thinking their business; use this as an opportunity to re-think your network.

Woodgrove Bank Active Directory Design

The team undertook these steps to design the Woodgrove Bank Active Directory:

1. Start with a simple design
2. Standardize a naming scheme
3. Create the proper domain architecture

4. Create a forest design
5. Complete site planning
6. Design global catalog and domain controller locations
7. Create proper organization unit and group architecture
8. Define what type of policy is required
9. Look at alternative designs

The design team discovered an effective planning tool: they put up large plastic U.S. and world wall maps and used erasable markers to visualize the Active Directory environment (see Figure 1.7). Active Directory design is an iterative process, and the maps helped designers sketch out and visualize alternatives—which they did many times during design.

The team found that when they considered the worldwide branch offices, *two* designs became attractive. The first created separate domains for all international locations that were regional hubs, and the second created a large international domain for all branches and regional locations. The next sections walk through both designs, explain the design team's thoughts at each decision point, and show how the team came to a recommendation at the end.

Single Domestic and Separate International Domains

Start with a Simple Design

As in most design processes, the first step in designing an Active Directory is to create as simple a model as possible. For example, start with a single forest, tree, domain, and site plan, and then create a good set of criteria for introducing complexity into the design. Be prepared to justify any domain, site, or organizational unit (OU) you want to add: they must be created for a specific, defined purpose because the quantity of objects increases complexity and influences replication, maintenance, and security.

Next, run the proposed scenario through a series of designs. The team at Woodgrove Bank found two designs that met the business, geopolitical, and technical criteria. You never know how many there are going to be, and the more you find, the better your chances of finding the best one—which is to say an iterative design approach is crucial. This is a different design process than was used for Windows NT 4.0. In other words, it's important to not fall into the traps of 4.0 design thinking. The team at Woodgrove Bank got caught in this for a while, flattening the hierarchy using the Windows NT 4.0 trust model, introducing a second forest in the context of a separate domain, and separating security using the Windows NT 4.0 domain model when they should have used the Windows 2000 OU and domain hierarchy model.

The best way to avoid this trap is to start with the MSF *vision* concept and build an *unbounded* view of what the next generation Windows 2000 Active Directory design would look like. You can use MSF to plan a Windows 2000 Active Directory design that meets the needs of any size company. The first deliverable at Woodgrove Bank consisted of:

1. Understanding the business and technical objectives that drive the project.

2. Creating a vision statement that clearly articulates the unrestrained view of why Woodgrove Bank was moving to Windows 2000.

3. Creating an inventory of services currently required by users. For example, authentication, file and print, and service level guarantees (do you guarantee authentication only when the WAN is up? etc.). It also helps if you document the existing WAN architecture, Windows NT 4.0 domain hierarchy and models, list all sites and locations, outline all current resources (printers, routers, file servers, etc.), obtain current organization charts, document the current DNS architecture, obtain any existing standards documents, and understand current operational models—but *do not* let the current Windows NT 4.0 design architecture limit your thinking when it comes to designing the Active Directory.

4. Delivering a solution concept design that is a first pass at designing the directory. The Woodgrove Bank team built the solution concept without modeling it after the Windows NT 4.0 design. Instead, they created a series of best-adapted Active Directory designs, then considered the best ways to migrate the current Windows NT 4.0 networks to the new design.

5. Defining the scope of what the design team will deliver in phase one. MCS and bank staff spent considerable time deciding what was required for phase one of the Windows 2000 rollout. Using MSF, they removed all features not required in phase one and put them in the next phase.

These steps allowed for proper planning and prudent designing based on a detailed understanding of Windows NT 4.0. Neither of the designs presented below is an overlay of the original Windows NT 4.0. The design team sought first to understand the current and future directions of Woodgrove Bank from architectural, business, and political perspectives, and then they built the designs to meet these requirements.

Here is a rough list of the thinking the Woodgrove Bank team used to create a solutions concept and detailed designs for the future:

1. Continually iterate and refine the process throughout the design.

2. Review and compare at least three different models.

3. Consider business growth trends, amount of change in the business, and frequency of change.

4. Start with as simple a model as possible (one domain, one forest, etc.).

5. Move forward in accordance with a set of defined rules.

6. Don't try to create a work of art—focus on building the *right* design.

7. Make sure the design reflects (current and future) business needs, geography, and size.

8. Justify the existence of every site, domain, and organization unit by assessing:
   - Who is creating the DS object
   - What its purpose is
   - Who will administrate the object
   - How long the object will live

9. Don't plan on getting it right the first time.

Next, the team moved into completing the steps required to create a good Active Directory design.

Naming Conventions

Once you understand how you are going to approach the Active Directory design, the next step is to create a first-pass naming scheme. At Woodgrove Bank, the team decided to complete its naming process and adjust it as they went through the design process. You may find it preferable to start your design process, get an understanding of facts such as how many domains you are going to have, and then assign the proper names. Either way, the Active Directory design process can become a way to correct the mistakes of the past and create the optimal naming scheme. The Woodgrove Bank team used these guidelines to standardize the naming scheme:

- Use only standard Internet characters (A–Z, a–z, 0–9 and -). Microsoft DNS supports a wider range of characters, but it does this mainly to help migrate existing Windows NT 4.0 systems that use non-standard Internet characters, so the team decided to use the guidelines outlined in RFC 1123.

- Use names relative to a registered Internet DNS name. Woodgrove Bank used its registered Internet name as a suffix in its Active Directory domain names.

- Never use the same domain name twice. For example, Woodgrove Bank is registered on the Internet as *WGB.tld* and should not create an internal domain called *WGB.tld*.

- Wherever possible, they tried to keep the names short but meaningful. For example, Euro for Europe, SoPac for South Pacific, Corp for Corporate, etc.

- Wherever possible, they used generic naming instead of specific company names. For example, West instead of Los Angeles, Corp instead of Woodgrove Bank, Asia instead Hong Kong for the regional hub location, Central instead of Chicago, etc.

- When forced to use specific names (such as country names for the OUs), they used the International Standards Organization standards for country codes. For example, PL for Poland, UK for United Kingdom, MX for Mexico, etc.

- Wherever possible, the team used generic names for geographic domains and tried to limit them to shorter names. This was more for ease of use than anything else. For example, Intl, Asia, Euro, Dom, SoPac, etc.

Woodgrove Bank used these standards for its naming scheme:

Woodgrove Bank's naming scheme.

Element	Convention	Example(s)
File/Application Servers	All server naming will follow DNS naming guidelines.	WestHub612-4 (West region office in LA, 6th floor server room, rack 12, machine 4)
Printers (Share Name)	Description field to contain additional information about printer and driver type, etc. (Location and Server name fields provide other required information.)	Canon Bubble-Jet BJC6000
Client Computer Names	Machines will be named by Location and Function. First example, the name WestBR2032-TL1 equals West Site, Branch 2032, Teller 1. Second example: West1806-B5 refers to the first machine in the West Site, office 1806, cube B5.	West2032-TL1 West1806-B5 (West Region, Office 1806, Cube B5)
DNS Fully Qualified Domain Name	Adhere to naming standards outlined in RFC 1123. Also, try to make them as understandable as possible.	Dom.Corp.wgb.tld for Domestic and Intl.CORP.WGB.tld for International
User Accounts	Adhere to current standards (proposed Last Name + First Initial + Middle Initial).	SmithJJ
User Full Name	Lastname, Firstname Middle Initial.	Smith, John J
Account Passwords	Minimum six characters and enforce strong passwords.	At least one upper case, one lower case, and symbol characters

When the team got the naming plan in place, they tried to use it to understand how the naming hierarchy might look. Again, they used the Windows 2000 design process as an opportunity to rethink the current naming design. Woodgrove Bank was willing to change the existing architecture to create the optimal Windows 2000 design. With this in mind, the design team started with these namespace design guidelines:

- Decide who owns the root—in this case, corporate IT staff in Chicago.

- Try to use location and functionally accurate names whenever possible.

- Use standards-based naming.

- Fully understand any political, business, or technical challenges.

- Try to limit the number of levels in the tree to three or four. This decision was not based on Windows 2000; it was imposed to keep the design as simple as possible in the first set of iterations.

The design also took into account the internal and external DNS namespaces to decide on root ownership. Networks in enterprises such as Woodgrove Bank have an external (extranet) presence and an internal (intranet) presence. To plan enterprise namespace, you have to decide whether to separate the internal and external namespaces or use one consistent naming convention. Woodgrove Bank decided to join the internal and external networks because this created an architecture that optimized the design by:

- Allowing the design team to create a single namespace that can differentiate between internal and external networks. This is important: if a *WGB.tld* client connects to an intranet and the Internet simultaneously and both have a *WGB.tld*, it would respond to the domain that answered first during the locator search. There would be no way to tell which domain this would be.

- Creating a consistent naming scheme for DNS entries, servers, computers, sites, and services.

- Consolidating the three original DNS systems (one for each of the entities that merged to form Woodgrove Bank) into a new design that treats the three regional locations as business units instead of separate companies.

- Allowing the creation of an Internet-ready infrastructure that will permit on-line banking, outside access to inside information, etc.

In addition to combining external and internal networks, the team decided that designing an "ideal" naming scheme from the ground up would yield continuing benefits that would justify the effort required. One exception: the team did not rename *WGB.tld* because it is the registered external presence for Woodgrove Bank and is already known on the Internet. Starting from the Internet network that is currently identified as *WGB.tld*, the team chose *CORP.WGB.tld* as the start of the naming hierarchy. It was made the root for the entire internal naming scheme to support the Windows 2000 Active Directory as the team built out the forest, trees, and domains, and would also serve as a placeholder domain, which can be useful when:

- A company already has a registered Internet name and they need to differentiate the internal and external namespaces.

- A company wants to use a root placeholder domain as a sterile parent for what normally would have been a set of divisional trees. No "local" administration work is performed in this domain, only enterprise-wide administration work, such as infrastructure/schema changes (FSMOs, etc.) would take place in the CORP domain.

- A company already has registered DNS names.

Thus the Woodgrove Bank DNS hierarchy starts as shown in Figure 1.5:

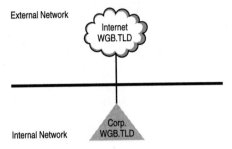

Figure 1.5   Starting point for the Woodgrove Bank DNS hierarchy.

A major advantage of this design was that it allowed Woodgrove Bank to establish a new company-wide IT group to create universal standards. This helped solve a problem they had encountered when they tried to create distributed administration with Windows NT 4.0. As the team moved forward with the Windows 2000 design, it could consolidate the three separate IT organizations. As simple as this sounds, it was difficult to achieve with Windows NT 4.0, technically and politically (corporations often haggle over administrative control in Windows NT 4.0). Active Directory helped solve this problem at Woodgrove Bank because the new CORP domain establishes a centralized set of standards, schema, administrative control, and infrastructure that drives the design. As you look further down in the tree you can see that this was accomplished without any loss of administrative control at the regional locations.

Next, building from the currently registered DNS name *WGB.tld* and the internal name *CORP.WGB.tld*, the team could begin creating the internal DNS structure. Before starting, though, they had to address the redundancy and reliability of *CORP.WGB.tld*. This is the first server they built with the Microsoft DNS service installed in their internal Windows 2000 hierarchy and is the server that hosts the internal name *CORP.WGB.tld*. It is also the owner of the forest root as the first domain controller (DC) in the first tree. The domain cannot be renamed or deleted; the FSMOs can be moved at any time.

The root (top-level) domain is the first domain installed in the forest. It provides two key Flexible Single Master Operations (FSMO) roles to the entire forest. The root domain is essential, so its name should be meaningful to the top level of the organization—for example, the company's name. In Woodgrove Bank's design, CORP.WGB.tld correlates to the root DNS name used for internal services. The root domain is normally active, meaning that it is used like any other domain and that it hosts OUs, users, resources, and other objects. Occasionally, it is dedicated, existing simply as a placeholder in the forest for other child domains and for infrastructure services such as DHCP, DNS, etc. In the deployment planning guide this is referred to as the dedicated forest root domain. The Woodgrove Bank design uses it as a dedicated forest root domain.

Fault tolerance is also important for the unique CORP domain controller. This doesn't necessarily require redundant hardware, but it obviously means that DCs should be designed to assure their reliability and availability. It is also important to make sure to have at least two DCs in every domain.

Thoroughness is important when you create the proper namespace; working too quickly can mean losing time as you go back to square one and start building the design all over again. With a good namespace plan in place, you can often change the design with minimal effort. However, before we can finish the naming hierarchy, we need to complete the partitioning exercise contained in the Domain Planning section to see just how many domains are required.

Determining the Number of Domains

Next, the team followed the deployment guide and the partitioning section to create the proper domain architecture. The team studied the design to determine an appropriate domain structure for the domestic and international business units and how many would be required. Again, the team used a single domain for all international and domestic operations as a starting point. (Remember not to be limited by the current Windows NT 4.0 design, which can include many domains.) The team also kept these factors in mind:

- Domains represent a boundary in Active Directory for security and a scope for replication.

- Windows NT 4.0 resource domains can be migrated into the OU structure of Active Directory.

- Each domain added to the forest increases the management cost of the overall design.

- Security policies and settings (such as administrative rights, security policies, and access control lists) do not cross domains.

- Domains must have a specific purpose before they are created and added to the forest.

Some of the key business objectives driving the domain design included the requirement for a centrally managed yet distributed administration model in both the international and domestic operations, the desire to consolidate all existing domestic domains into a single company account database, and the need to allow all regional international locations to continue to operate autonomously. With these business objectives in mind the team used the criteria outlined in the deployment guide and some of the key business objectives to create a set of criteria that would guide the decision to create a separate domain. These included:

- Weighing the costs of consolidating domains in the first phase and the long-term benefits of having fewer domains.

- The feasibility of consolidating domains in the first phase of the project.

- The need for additional domains based on the administration and policy requirements of each domestic and international location. For example, do some of the international subs need a different security policy than the rest of the company? Is a separate division working on highly sensitive and secure information? In these cases it might make sense to put them in a separate domain.

- Considering replication. Domains are units of replication and to control what information is replicated it may make sense to partition certain business units into their own domains so that administrators can replicate only those required objects to each regional hub.

Using the steps outlined in the deployment guide, the Woodgrove Bank team:

1. Drew out the network topology (see Figure 1.1).

2. Determined the location and placement of domain controllers.

3. Partitioned the forest (created domains) based on inter-domain replication traffic or a new domain's ability to meet the design requirements.

There currently are four domestic domains (ChiNT, NYNT, LANT, DataCenterChi—see Figure 1.2) with explicit two-way trusts. T1 is the fastest link within the Woodgrove Bank environment and the team took this into account when placing DCs in each of the regional locations. The team was careful to avoid limiting its thinking by starting with the current domain architecture.

The home site was identified as Chicago and the first DC was located there. The team did not identify domains at this stage: that comes later. It decided to place DCs in Los Angeles and New York because these locations have many users. It decided *not* to place a DC in each branch: if a link fails users can log on using cached credentials, all server resources are located at corporate, and replicating DC and GC information over their already slow and saturated links would be too costly.

The last issue was to decide whether to partition the forest into separate domains for Los Angeles, Chicago, and New York. The deployment guide suggests partitioning:

1. If the T1s connecting sites cannot handle the replication traffic. Not an issue here. Currently, the average utilization of the Los Angeles-Chicago link is less than 5%, and less than 8% for the New York-Chicago link. If necessary, the Bank can schedule Active Directory replication for idle periods. Further, the Bank's Active Directory is estimated to contain less than 100,000 objects with infrequent changes.

2. If Active Directory traffic competes with other more important business traffic. The team decided to offset this risk by creating an Active Directory replication schedule that minimized the chance of that traffic colliding with other business traffic.

3. If the link will increase business costs on a pay-by-use link. Not an issue for the Bank.

4. If the site is located over an SMTP-only link. Not an issue for the Bank.

So, the team decided to create a single domain called DOM for all domestic operations, and to move the three existing account domains (Los Angeles, Chicago, and New York) to OUs in it. Lower-level domestic regional offices, which are linked to Los Angeles, Chicago, or New York via 56 K links, will also become OUs in DOM, as will all resource domains in the domestic Windows NT 4.0 environment. The plan is to locate as many domain controllers as necessary in each of the three sites and to host at least a single copy of Global Catalog in each regional location, as shown in Figure 1.6.

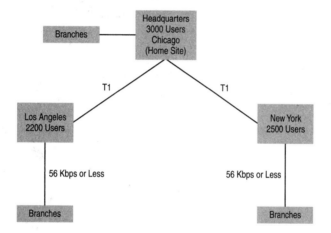

Figure 1.6   The domestic domain (DOM).

Lastly, it was decided not to fold the International network into the domestic domain. The reasons behind separating out the International domain included:

■ **Bandwidth and Replication.** Currently all the international regional hubs in Europe, Asia, the Americas, and the South Pacific are connected by 64 K burst-mode 256K links to corporate. Having a separate international domain allows the Bank to optimize replication traffic by only replicating those objects that are relevant to the International regional hub locations.

■ **Consistency.** The Bank is not ready to consolidate the current Windows NT 4.0 international domains as a part of the phase one Windows 2000 implementation. They understand the advantages of fewer domains and will use the learnings from Windows 2000 domestic implementation to create a plan for consolidating some of the international domains in a later project.

Therefore, for the international network, the team started with a single domain for all international operations called INTL, then used the partitioning exercise to decide if other domains were required. Some reasons to possibly create other domains in INTL were:

1. Currently, these geographies have Windows NT domains and the Bank does not yet want to consolidate them.

2. The current international operations links are slow (56 K CIR or less) or are unreliable in some countries. In some cases no links exist, forcing some regional offices to use 28.8 K modem connections

3. Replication traffic can be consolidated and controlled. Many of the links from the hub locations put a lot of traffic on the wire, and the Bank needs to make sure business traffic is not affected.

The current International domain architecture consists of domains for each regional hub (AsiaNT in Hong Kong, EuroNT in London, SoPacNT in Sydney, and AmerNT in Toronto). The Bank weighed the advantages of physical partitioning and consolidation of existing domains and decided not to attempt it in phase one. Rather than create a single international domain containing all sites, the team decided to have additional domains in Asia, Europe, the South Pacific, and the Americas (Canada, Mexico, and South America). The domestic and international domain hierarchies will have to be structured differently as they are built and included into the tree. The Bank will continue to explore the benefits of a single domain for international, paying particular attention to the DOM consolidation to see what can be learned from the process.

At this point in the design, it became clear that the domain hierarchy from CORP to DOM is one child-domain deep, but the INTL domain has another level of child domains. These four are now grandchild domains to the CORP domain and are structured this way:

- AMERS grandchild domain, *AMERS.INTL.CORP.WGB.tld*, for Canadian, Mexican, and South American non-domestic operations.

- EURO domain, *EURO.INTL.CORP.WGB.tld*, for European, Mediterranean, and African operations.

- SOPAC grandchild domain, *SOPAC.INTL.CORP.WGB.tld*, for Australian and New Zealand operations.

- ASIA grandchild domain, *ASIA.INTL.CORP.WGB.tld*, for Asian operations.

To sum up the design at this point (see Figure 1.7), the Woodgrove Bank Active Directory design now consists of multiple domains consisting of:

- *CORP.WGB.tld* at the root of the tree.

- *DOM.CORP.WGB.tld* as a child domain.

- *INTL.CORP.WGB.tld* as a child domain.

- *ASIA.INTL.CORP.WGB.tld* as a grandchild domain.

- *SOPAC.INTL.CORP.WGB.tld* as a grandchild domain.
- *EURO.INTL.CORP.WGB.tld* as a grandchild domain.
- *AMERS.INTL.CORP.WGB.tld* as a grandchild domain.

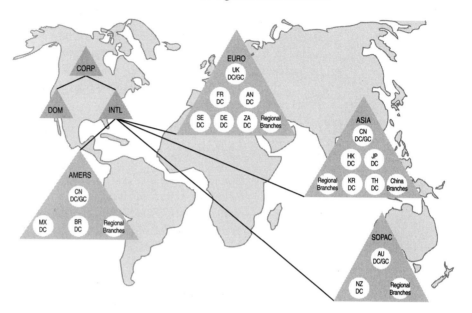

Figure 1.7   Woodgrove Bank architecture.

Forest and Tree Plan

The Woodgrove Bank Active Directory design defined a forest as a set of domains that:

- Have a shared schema
- Share a global catalog
- Are joined by a two-way transitive trust
- Provides for multiple public Internet names (*microsoft.com*, *msnbc.com*, etc.)

Having decided on this forest definition, the Woodgrove Bank team faced complications when planning for a single or multiple forests. Using the concepts outlined early (including "start simple"), the team started with a single forest. But the branch network has traditionally been treated as separate from the corporate network and it could be thought of as a separate forest because it:

- Has a totally separate administration staff
- Would allow the Bank to segment off the replication process completely
- Would allow the Bank to have two totally separate forest-change policies (schema changes, configuration changes and new domain adds would affect only the branch forest)

- Allowed the Bank to separate out security. Users in the branch network could be denied access to corporate resources unless explicit trusts were created.

The disadvantages of separate forests the team considered were:

- The introduction and maintenance of additional domains in a separate forest when consolidation was one of the company goals.
- The maintenance of separate corporate and branch schemas, global catalogs, security, explicit trusts, and domains.
- Lack of a single, consistent, company-wide view of the directory.

The team weighed the advantages and disadvantages, keeping in mind that a core business objective was to create a single company entity out of its current set of multiple companies and branches. It decided to use a single forest because it:

- Allowed users in both the branch and corporate network to have a single view of the directory through a single global catalog. This would overcome the current separateness of the two networks, allowing the Bank to implement a single, common view into the environment to replace the current mix of costly business and administration practices: two admin staffs, separate branch domains with two-way trusts to corporate, separate user account databases, etc.
- Created a single company-wide schema and global catalog. A common forest change control policy would gather up previously separate policies for schema change, configuration, etc. (See the *Microsoft Windows 2000 Deployment Guide* for details.)
- Simplified the management of the Bank's multiple domains. It would alleviate the need to maintain explicit trusts within a single forest; when new domains are added to the forest they are automatically configured with two-way transitive trusts.

The original Windows NT 4 Woodgrove Bank domain model has many multi-master domains and possibly hundreds of resource domains. This model requires a substantial amount of administration overhead and has allowed the formation of separate IT organizations that do not communicate or collaborate enough with the centralized administration group. In practice, the Active Directory designer should always start with the simplest design possible—a single forest and a single tree and a single domain. A single forest design would allow the sharing of a common Active Directory schema and global catalog and combine these resource domains into a single tree in a single forest. This simplifies administration and data sharing, and provides Woodgrove Bank with one common name across the entire enterprise—*CORP.WGB.tld.*

Therefore, the Woodgrove Bank Active Directory design now consists of a single forest, a single tree, and multiple domains consisting of:

- *CORP.WGB.tld* at the root of the tree.
- *DOM.CORP.WGB.tld* as a child domain.
- *INTL.CORP.WGB.tld* as a child domain.

- *ASIA.INTL.CORP.WGB.tld* as a grandchild domain.
- *SOPAC.INTL.CORP.WGB.tld* as a grandchild domain.
- *EURO.INTL.CORP.WGB.tld* as a grandchild domain.
- *AMERS.INTL.CORP.WGB.tld* as a grandchild domain.

Creating the Woodgrove Bank Site Topology

The team now turned its attention to creating a site topology for domestic and international operations. Each forest has its own site topology, and the current Woodgrove Bank design contains only a single forest. The deployment guide defines a site topology as a logical representation of the physical network, and you have to remember this as you create the site topology. To understand Windows 2000 site architecture, you also need to understand some other essential terms:

Site. A site is an area of highly available bandwidth (LAN speed or greater) defined by IP subnets. If a Windows 2000 site has two or more Windows 2000 servers, all members of that site require full availability of bandwidth to carry out conversations with any other servers in that site. This means that traffic between servers within a site cannot be controlled. All intra-site security, logon, and replication is automatic using Remote Procedure Calls and does not require additional configuration. If you have areas of the WAN architecture that do not have good connectivity, you should define them as separate sites. The intra-site replication topology is automatically set up by the Knowledge Consistency Checker (KCC), which achieves a fault-tolerant replication architecture by creating at least two paths to every server in the site. The KCC runs on every DC and constantly checks the replication topology to ensure that everything is running well. It automatically regenerates the optimal topology if a DC fails or a new one is added.

You can also use sites to control authentication. For example, when a user tries to log on to an Active Directory domain, an attempt is made to locate a domain controller within the same site. When creating sites for Woodgrove Bank, the design team had to balance the need for local log on, up-to-date information between sites, and unimpaired performance on the slow links.

Site link. A site link is a representation of connectivity between sites. Site links are used to connect sites that otherwise are connected by low-bandwidth or unreliable links. Site-link options have different feature sets that enable varying degrees of traffic control. An example site-link configuration tested for Woodgrove Bank configured replication between the U.S. and Europe to support compressed TCP/IP as a transport, scheduled replication for low-traffic periods on the network, and scheduled the process to repeat every 12 hours (the default replication schedule for a site link is every 3 hours, 24 hours a day, 7 days a week).

Cost is another important factor when creating site links. By default, Windows 2000 assigns a cost-factor of 100 to every site link created, and the KCC uses cost factors to determine the most efficient path between sites. The design team should assign costs for all site links as part of the design process.

Site Link Bridge. This indicates transitivity between a set of site links. For example, if site link West-to-Central connects Los Angeles and Chicago, and link Central-to-East connects Chicago and New York, and site link bridge X connects them, sites West and East can communicate even though they are not directly connected. Site link bridge X allows domain controllers in site West to create replication connections with domain controllers in site East. If the bridge did not exist (and transitivity was turned off), then DCs in site West and East would attempt to create replication connections only with DCs in site Central, not with each other. See Figure 1.8.

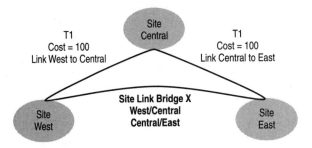

Figure 1.8   Site link bridge.

Next, the team turned to site architecture, which technically always comes down to one thing: bandwidth. Bandwidth affects site design drastically, and it also affects the placement of servers, domain controllers, and global catalogs, and the creation of a replication strategy.

Windows 2000 uses the concept of sites to cope with limited bandwidth or lack of permanent connectivity. The uncontrollable nature of intra-site communication typically drives designers to create a site architecture parallel to geographic locations and the WAN. With site links, inter-site communication is controlled by a connector's feature set.

The Bank's domestic WAN infrastructure provides greater bandwidth (T1), which affords greater flexibility in design options. The international infrastructure, however, has low-speed links (64 KBS/sec CIR are common), and this limits design possibilities. To build the site architecture, the team used these precepts:

- Sites were defined as areas of high bandwidth defined by IP subnets.

- High bandwidth was defined as LAN speed or greater.

- The default intra-site replication schedule uses notifications and occurs every five minutes.

- The default inter-site replication schedule occurs every 3 hours, 24 hours a day, 7 days a week, and will need to be customized based on individual site AD update needs.

- Differences between the domestic and the international environments warranted separate site designs.

Domestic Site Architecture

Referring to the deployment guide and the site topology planning process, the team used these recommended steps to create the site model:

- Define sites and site links using Woodgrove Bank's physical network (Figure 1.1).

- Place servers into the sites (already started in the domain planning section).

- Keep in mind how changes to the domestic or international site topology will affect users.

- Create sites for each set of LANs connected over a backbone.

- Create sites for location not directly connected to the corporate backbone.

- Decide what locations will not have domain controllers and merge those locations into nearby sites.

- For each site created, document its set of constituent IP subnets.

The team found it advantageous to have already completed the partitioning exercise outlined in the domain planning section (above) and could use it as a starting point for site planning. Figure 1.6 shows how this stage looks in the Woodgrove Bank design process; Figure 1.1 shows current infrastructure connectivity. Comparing these and walking through the recommended process outlined in the deployment guide, the team decided to start by creating three sites for the domestic infrastructure (Los Angeles, Chicago, and New York) because:

1. Each location has a high-speed backbone connecting a set of 10- to 100-MB LANs (each with its own registered class B address).

2. The T1s connecting each of the three main locations are not highly utilized (each of the locations maintains an average of approximately 760 Kb/sec of available T1 bandwidth to the WAN hub in Chicago during business hours). Because high bandwidth is defined as LAN-speed, the team decided to separate the three geographies into separate sites to minimize impact on business traffic.

3. All DCs at each site will be centralized in each regional IT location. All downstream locations over the high-speed LAN will be merged into the regional site. Sites over low-speed connections (56K or less) will be placed in separate sites if a DC is available there.

The table below shows the configuration for the first set of domestic site links in the Woodgrove Bank architecture. Note that no site link is created from Los Angeles to New York. This is because site links are transitive and the KCC will automatically allow DCs in Los Angeles to communicate with DCs in New York. The naming scheme shown consists of a generic regional name, a code to identify the location or branch (HQ for regional headquarters, Hub for regional and international hubs, and office number for branches), and a number to identify the link. For example, the link West2939-01 would indicate the first site link in Branch 2939 in the West region.

Site Link	Transport	Cost	Polling Interval	Schedule
CentralHQ-01—WestHub-01	IP	100	2 hours	(always)
CentralHQ-01—EastHub-01	IP	100	2 hours	(always)

This inter-site model provides more flexibility and more control over traffic generated by Windows 2000 on a domestic network connected regionally by T1s. The architecture creates sites at each of the major hub locations (Los Angeles, Chicago, and New York—see Figure 1.9). Each region has many branches that communicate to the regional hub over low-bandwidth connections (56 K or less). Each branch will be placed in its own site, and replication traffic will be scheduled to occur after business hours. For example, the table below adds branches 2939 through 2941 to the table above. Branches 2939 and 2940 communicate with the Los Angeles corporate office via low-speed frame relay, and branch 2941 uses a dial-up only to communicate with Los Angeles.

Site Link	Transport	Cost	Polling Interval	Schedule
CentralHQ-01—WestHub-01	IP	100	2 hours	(always)
CentralHQ-01—EastHub-01	IP	100	2 hours	(always)
WestHub-01—West2939-01	IP	100	30 minutes	2300 to 0500
WestHub-01—West2940-01	IP	100	30 minutes	2300 to 0500
WestHub-01—West2941-01	IP	100		Dial at 2200, and 0400

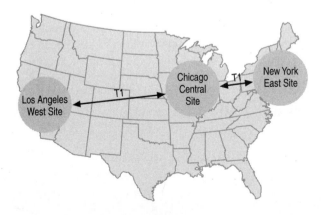

Figure 1.9   Domestic site architecture.

International Site Architecture

The international architecture is complicated by the fact that site architecture is driven by bandwidth: most international locations share slow links (64 Kb/sec CIR, dual-channel ISDN, and analog modems). The deployment guide recommends first documenting all links and connectivity to each international location (see Figure 1.1). Using these results and the results of the domain partitioning exercise completed earlier, the team decided that regional hub locations connected to headquarters by 56 K links would be located in their own sites (Americas, South Pacific, Asia, and Europe).

The rest of the current international architecture contains 25 locations connected with 64 Kb/sec CIR frame relay circuits and is capable of communicating directly with the corporate Chicago location using an international VPN without having to hub through any regional location (See Figure 1.1). Because of these low-speed links between countries and the fact that a DC will be located in each major country location, the design team created separate sites for all countries connected via the 64 Kb/sec frame relay VPN.

For example, consider the site architecture for Europe. All other geographies (Americas, Asia, and South Pacific) have the same site topology. In Europe there are currently five major Bank locations (Holland, Germany, France, Sweden, and the United Kingdom), all of which connect to the United States headquarters in Chicago over 64 Kb/sec links over the company-wide VPN. Because of the current traffic load on these links and the need to control replication traffic, the team decided to place all 64 Kb/sec-based locations in their own sites. Remember that domains and sites are separate and unrelated, and that a domain can have many sites. Figure 1.10 shows this design.

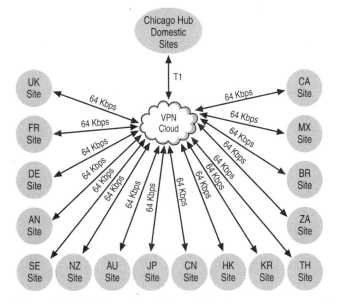

Figure 1.10   International site architecture.

The last site architecture issue is how to handle the dial-up sites. Because the Bank cannot afford to create a connected network for its more than 10,000 branches, it uses polling to upload and download required information throughout the day. In other words, many of these branches are not on the connected network; they use 56 Kb/sec phone lines to upload and download information from the regional and corporate facilities (Figure 1.11).

The decision to create a site at these locations was pretty straightforward. As the deployment guide suggests, a branch becomes a site if a DC is located at it. If no DC is located there it becomes a part of the regional headquarters site.

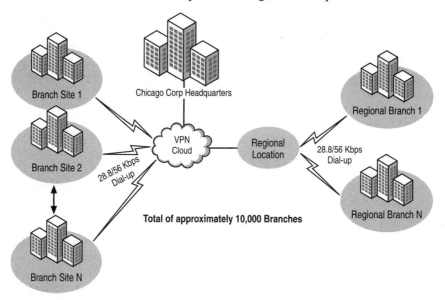

Figure 1.11   Branch network design.

A final step in this phase: the deployment guide suggests that if you have many sites with the same characteristics, it makes sense to connect sites together with a single link. This will be very valuable when the team creates the site links for all the international locations and the connection to corporate headquarters; it can create a single site link that allows connectivity between all locations (see Figure 1.12) rather than creating and managing numerous links.

Figure 1.12   Connecting Sites with a Single Link

Design Global Catalog and Domain Controller Location

The next step was to use the results of the partitioning exercise to design locations for DCs and GCs. To help in this part of the design, the team created a set of rules to determine if a DC or GC would be located in an office or branch.

When did Woodgrove Bank place a DC onsite?

- When fast logon performance was required and the remote location was over a slow link (<T1).

- When a GC was required at a location. A DC is needed to host a GC.

- When it was necessary to satisfy the Bank's need for fault tolerance in the event of a link failure. With a DC onsite, users could still log on to a local DC.

Note   In the event of link failure, access to a GC is required to process a logon request to a native mode domain.

When did Woodgrove Bank place a GC on site?

- When it was desired to improve query performance. A local GC eliminates the need to travel across the links (to the system global catalog) to resolve a query.

Note   Keep in mind that placing a GC locally increases replication traffic.

Domestic Design

In the current domestic design, all three regional hub sites (West, Central, East) have a T1 circuit mesh. This high-speed link will also be used for the regional hub sites serving the DOM domain. The other medium-sized sites run at 56 Kb/sec CIR/256Kb; the other smaller and more isolated sites run at 56 Kb/sec. The presence in the environment of T1s (1.54 MB/sec) makes it advisable to put a domain controller and a global catalog in each of the regions to facilitate logon and speed up network object searching, as shown in Figure 1.13.

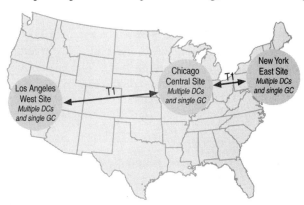

Figure 1.13   Site Model for Domestic with DCs and GCs.

From a tree and domain perspective, the Central site will host the CORP and DOM domains from its location. (It will also host the INTL domain, which will be discussed later.) To minimize replication bandwidth requirements and optimize performance for users at the local level, the team gave each site its own domain controller and global catalog. Thus the Chicago site will host the DOM domain along with the global catalog, and the West and East sites each will have a domain controller and a global catalog server, optimizing local performance speed. Since the domestic WAN connectivity is all high speed, additional global catalog replication traffic was not a concern.

International Design

The international domain has second- and third-level child domains. Logon authentication and network search requests for each domain will be serviced by the domain's DC and GC. In areas with 56 Kb/sec permanent links within the domain, the team decided to put the global catalog at the regional egress point. For example, in the Euro domain, the Poland OU has a dedicated 56 Kb/sec link to the UK egress point, so the design team decided *not* to create a GC in Poland but to have it query the catalog in the UK, as shown in Figure 1.14.

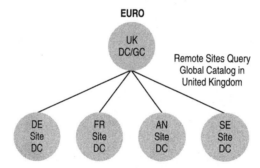

Figure 1.14   Sample remote GC location.

Organizational Units/Groups

The next step is to plan an organizational unit (OU) structure. A Windows 2000 Server Active Directory OU is simply a logical container used to organize domain resources. A filing system on a storage disk allows you to organize files and folders logically, usually by grouping things that are related in some meaningful way. In much the same way, you use OUs to organize items or objects:

- To group objects or resources
- To simplify management of commonly grouped resources
- To allow delegation of administration tasks
- To manage control of the resources through group policy

You can also use OUs to achieve granular administration on resources such as:

- Computers
- Users (called *associates* at Woodgrove Bank)
- Groups
- Printers
- Files shares and volumes
- Applications
- Group policies
- Other OUs

Another advantage is that you can apply group policies to organizational units. In essence, OUs perform a role similar to resource domains in Windows NT 4.0, and the good news at this point in the planning is that you can translate most existing Windows NT 4.0 resource domains to OUs. This reduces the servers required, which simplifies server management, which in turn reduces administrative burden on IT staff by allowing them to delegate administration duties.

Any OU unit structure (and there are many possibilities) must be meaningful to the Administrators and reduce the collective management tasks. To do so, any OU structure should be well thought out and most likely piloted in a lab first. As with any complicated planning, you have to think things through first. A design team can get a lot accomplished with a whiteboard session. Using the deployment guide as a reference, the phrase "organizational unit structure" might start the team thinking about creating a structure that mirrors the business organization, divisions, departments, and projects. Even though this is possible, it could prove difficult and expensive to manage. OUs are for delegating administration, so the structure you create is most likely a reflection of your administrative model. In other words, it might not map exactly to your business organization. They may also reflect one of the following models.

- Geographic location
- Business functional units
- Business organizational structure
- Administrative
- Object-based
- Hybrid of several models

There are others, but these are the common ones. The Woodgrove Bank team realized right off that a mixture of types was indicated. The team also set out to keep the OU structure as flat as possible, rather than create a deeply nested structure (which can reduce query performance). In the early planning and building stages, it is easy to reorganize an OU structure by moving, changing, or deleting OUs. You are not locked in to your first concept. Of course, the further you go into the design, the harder fundamental OU design changes become.

The team set out to create an OU structure that mirrored as closely as possible the Woodgrove Bank functional organization. It was based on the geographic location model because the company spans continents, languages, and political barriers, and was a hybrid version of that model because the regional hub sites require local administration but the branch locations do not.

The designers had an advantage in that the three companies that merged to form Woodgrove Bank share many levels of organized banking structures. They also had a goal to provide more delegation of administration, so to take these things into account the team set up the guidelines below.

Organizational Unit Administration Plan

Local administration is required, particularly in the international sites, so the design will provide OUs for administrative delegation. The Windows 2000 Active Directory allows for more delegation and granularity of management than is currently available in Windows NT 4.0.

Domain administration can be performed anywhere in the CORP domain and its child domains. In addition, by using the Delegation of Administration capability, Woodgrove Bank IT Administrators can assign local user-delegated administration of printers, passwords, selected attributes, or other resources to a specific OU. This design requirement was intended to distribute administrative effort, and to please users, supervisors, and managers who want some authority over their user groups or objects.

You have to be very careful when passing admin responsibility to non-IT personnel. You can increase IT's administration burden rather than lightening it by delegating too much and thus creating support issues. Within the IT group, you can use universal groups to give IT personnel administrator rights across the directory tree without having multiple accounts.

Organizational Unit User Structure

User accounts will exist in the CORP, DOM, and INTL domains. Most of the user accounts will predominately be in either the DOM or INTL domains. OUs will place user accounts in the correct business, functional, or geographic area of the Windows 2000 Active Directory tree, creating the OU structures shown in Figure 1.15 for the CORP domain and child-domains DOM and INTL.

As the design project progresses, the team knows that it will add OUs and make other changes to the OU structure. The team set up a pilot lab to test the working design and its supporting structure so that they could refine OU tactics as they learned to exploit new Windows 2000 Active Directory capabilities. As of the writing of this chapter, the team believed that this part of the design provided a solid infrastructure that will continue to support overall goals as the design progresses.

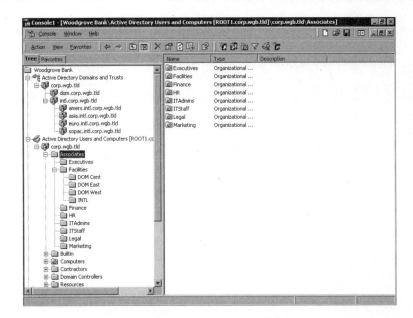

Figure 1.15   CORP, DOM, and INTL users OUs.

The team felt that new Windows 2000 Active Directory features and organizational units justified consolidating users and resources, although having made this decision they still had to decide *where* to create the accounts. To provide for delegation of administration, it seemed obvious that accounts should be created in the organizational unit to which they would belong; unfortunately, this would decentralize the administration model, which the customer team did not want to do. So the team decided to separate the User accounts from the OU structure and put them in an OU called *Associates*. When the User account was created, it was added to the appropriate groups and OU (some of which are nested in other OU's) so that the user accounts can be managed by delegation. In addition to this structure, the customer team wanted to create in each OU a group with the same name. This would simplify tracking group membership and would enhance security within the OU as well as protect users' security permissions within the OU. The customer team figured that if the OU and the group had the same name, it would make it easier to become familiar with the new Windows 2000 Active Directory setup. The design team agreed that this could be a good way to start, but they also realized that things would most likely evolve away from this scheme over time.

The team now had to study the domain model and figure out where to put accounts in the domain structure. Making the account a member of the CORP domain (meaning users in the headquarters business unit) means creating the account in the Associates OU in the CORP domain. Likewise, if a User account is created for a user in the DOM domain, it will be created in the DOM Associates OU, as shown in Figure 1.16.

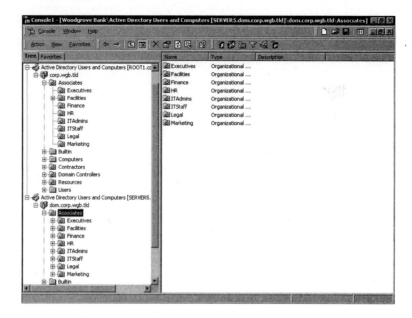

Figure 1.16   DOM and CORP Associates OU.

To define a user's account in the INTL domain requires more specificity. Users who run the INTL domain and the international business unit will be defined in the INTL Associates OU. But the INTL domain also has four child domains. Users created in the INTL domain also have to be placed in the appropriate Associates OU in the corresponding child domain to which they will belong.

Users in the INTL domain exist in an Associates OU but in a much more decentralized model than in the DOM domain. This reflects:

- Geographic and site issues

- Political and language requirements

- Connection link and replication concerns

- Administration requirements

This is another reason why the team ended up with a hybrid design to address the unique needs of the Woodgrove Bank international business units. The domestic operations have many things in common that are not shared by the INTL domain and its child domains. What will be common across both of these domains is the organizational structure for the Associates OUs.

Organizational Unit Resource Plan

As mentioned above, most resources currently in Windows NT 4.0 resource domains can be translated into Windows 2000 Server Active Directory OUs:

- Computers
- Users (called *Associates* at Woodgrove Bank)
- Groups
- Printers
- Files shares and volumes
- Applications
- Group policies
- Additional organizational units

This process required the team to re-think resource deployment to take advantage of OU capabilities. Consider *Delegation of Administration*, which is very different from Windows NT 4.0, in which users have *all* rights or *none*. These delegations are possible in an organizational unit:

- Delegation of administration of all contents in the OU
- Delegation of object-level administration
- Delegation of rights to create, delete, or modify objects
- Delegation of rights to change properties of objects
- Task-specific delegation (reset passwords, etc.)

Delegation of administration, in combination with organizational units, enabled Woodgrove Bank to make several improvements in the new design. For starters, they could reduce the number of domains. When access controls are applied to an OU, a high-level administrator can collectively control the resource as well as define and delegate administration of the object defined in the OU to *users* or *groups of users*—a capacity that has long been sought by Windows NT 4.0 users. It allowed the team to reduce the many original domestic locations to a single domain without having to set up administrators with complete control across entire domains. Users can have administration delegated to them, and can in turn delegate administration of a subset of their objects to another user.

This capability allowed the team to build a management structure based on the company's administrative structure *while* de-centralizing management. This is a significant benefit, but it does require careful planning and may entail training users who will receive delegated authority. In addition to lightening IT administrative loads (when done properly), it also satisfied those users and administrators who have for years wanted to be able to control their printers, file shares, or password re-sets for their group members.

Beyond OUs, you can target selected objects for Delegation of Administration to sites and domains. You have to make sure your planning jibes with the policy for delegation at the more local levels, or the delegation scheme can become confusing (which it did at Woodgrove Bank a couple times) and increase management overhead.

Within OUs, designers establish security structures using *groups* and access controls much the same as with Windows NT 4.0. OUs can contain *any* objects, but groups can contain only *users* and *groups and computers*. Windows 2000 allows you to enable and disable security on groups. This allows you to switch the security status of the group, which in planning means that you are not stuck with your initial decision and can change it later without a lot of rebuilding.

- Security-enabled groups can be used in Access Control Entries to assign permissions and rights to objects, or to individual attributes on an object (a group can contain only users and groups and computers).

- Distribution groups (non-security-enabled) are used for non-security functions such as e-mail distribution lists and contacts. These groups cannot be used to assign permissions and rights.

There are three kinds of groups:

- **Global groups** are used to organize users into administrative units by collecting global groups from the same domain. You can place global groups into global groups in the same domain, universal groups in the same forest, or domain local groups in any trusting domain.

- **Domain local groups** are used to provide access to resources in their domain. They can contain users and global groups from any trusted domain and are available to all machines in the domain if the domain is in native mode.

- **Universal groups** can also contain users and global groups from anywhere in the forest. They are typically used to collect groups from several domains into administrative units, which are then added to domain local groups for use in Access Control Entries (ACEs). Use this type of group sparingly because its membership is replicated to global catalog servers.

Define Policy Model

Also useful is the Group Policy feature—a core component of the Windows 2000 Change and Configuration Management capabilities. You can use group policies to define settings and configurations that can be applied to computers and users in sites, domains, and OUs. You can also apply them to computers and users to include definitions for configuration settings, security, software installation, software or system scripts, and redirections.

Group policies simplify actions that were complex or impossible in Windows NT 4.0. They still can become complex, in that you can apply them at several levels, causing users to inherit settings from several group policies. This can create arrangements that are complex to understand and problems that are even more complex to diagnose. You have to be careful to start simple and proceed slowly so that you can learn their capabilities and remain flexible. Use the pilot lab to determine how much control is *required* as opposed to how much is simply *desired*. Too much control can increase administrative burden and decrease user satisfaction. In the early planning and construction, you can redefine group policies simply without major restructuring.

The design team concentrated on applying group policies to OUs to configure:

- Computer and user settings
- Software installation and maintenance
- Scripts
- Security settings

When creating group policies, the team based its choices on the sites, domains, or OUs that are the intended recipients. You can apply group policies to sites and domains, but it is often more attractive to apply them to OUs and that is where the team concentrated its efforts—to define and enhance the user experience. The effort can also benefit administrators by reducing management tasks and reducing helpdesk call volume.

Woodgrove Bank had tried using Windows NT 4.0 to implement desktop lockdown, but it was impossible to derive sufficient benefit from the effort. As with some of their efforts to reduce TCO by standardizing desktops, IT required so much training and had to handle so many initial support calls that the effort barely broke even. During this effort, they found that there isn't as much computer sharing as they had thought. Woodgrove Bank employees generally don't travel all that much. The new desktop control possible with Active Directory and group policies, however, now makes it possible to achieve a higher degree of control much more easily than was possible with Windows NT 4.0 system policies. Even though you can adapt Windows NT 4.0 system policy templates into group policy templates, the design team started fresh with group policies rather than spend time on adaptation (Figures 1.17 and 1.18).

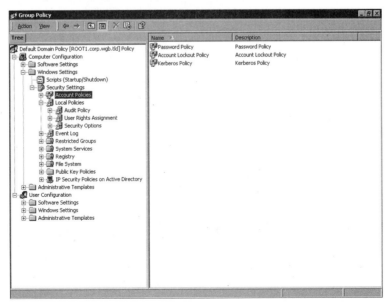

Figure 1.17   Group policy—account policy.

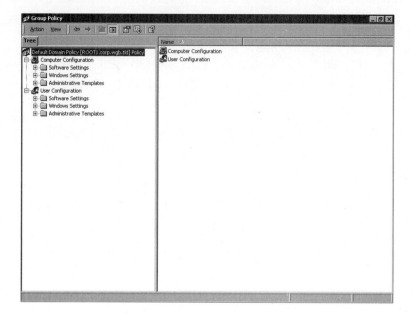

Figure 1.18   Default domain policy.

The team also used the new ability to associate scripts to group policies. The original Windows NT 4.0 implementation allowed only limited efforts with scripts, and many administrators put their interest in the capabilities of the Windows Scripting Host on the back burner. Many business processes in use at Woodgrove Bank involve scripts, and the team now could tie scripts to OUs, create more specific and simpler scripts, and reduce their maintenance and troubleshooting efforts.

The team analyzed helpdesk logs to determine what concerns IT Management would like to address with the roughly 600 possible group policy settings. When the team set out to increase lockdown control, it soon found that this effort was directly tied to the OU structure because the OU structure is initially designed around the business function. For example, the OU for the Accounting group has a finite set of apps and resources that only they use. To define group policies for, say, the Accounting department, the team will search the logs for those users and machines and decide which entries can be addressed by a group policy setting. One decision was to set the option **Hide The Manage Item On The Windows Explorer Context Menu** because users frequently get into configuration trouble when they have access to this capability.

For this reason, the planning stage, which is ongoing throughout the pilot, included minor changes to the OU structure to simplify administration. The team used this effort to improve the OU structure while setting more effective group policies. These features are tightly integrated and a lot of the pilot time was dedicated to understanding and fine-tuning this interaction.

To maximize effectiveness, you should always assign a team to this effort. Organizational unit designs nest OUs within OUs, and the structure can become complex to manage and troubleshoot. If you try to accomplish too much in a group policy, nested OUs can have inheritance problems. The team found that some cases required them to turn on the *Block Inheritance* feature to prevent inheritance of controls. Rather than spend a lot of time troubleshooting later, the team decided early on to change the OU structure. This created checkpoints for the OU design and made many of the group policies simpler to define and manage. It also allowed for simpler group policy definitions that nearly eliminated use of *Block Inheritance*.

Using group policies to create security settings can become complex because there are several levels of complexity in the security settings (Figure 1.19). Start simple, ease into security setting definition, and test them thoroughly in the pilot lab. Before implementing security controls, define and test all of the other aspects of the group policies, and then look at security within them. Some of the features of security that the team used were:

- Account policies
- Local policies
- Event logs
- Restricted groups

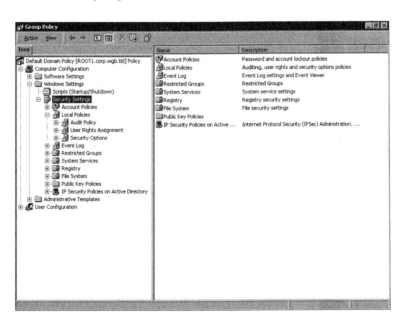

Figure 1.19   Group policy—security settings.

The team found that working with account password settings was much easier in Active Directory than in Windows NT 4.0. It also realized the advantages of being able to create different settings for sites, domains, and OUs, rather than having to impose them for entire domains, as was necessary in Windows NT 4.0. This was especially true of some service accounts.

The team also capitalized on new capabilities for creating local policies settings for computers, in particular, the *User Rights Assignment* and *Security Options* groupings. Windows NT 4.0 requires a lot of manual maintenance to do this. Consider the management of restricted groups. Many users want administrative access to their computer; many administrators do not want them to have it. Under Windows NT 4.0, IT personnel had to visit each machine and configure it. In Active Directory, you can avoid much of this effort by assigning settings to computers.

Changing security options previously required IT per-machine efforts during setup, or later in a support role. The Woodgrove Bank team set to work in the pilot lab to test ways of insuring new security standards on computers, concentrating on using public key policies tied into the current public key infrastructure.

Testing group policies differs from other planning aspects, and when the team found that it needed more than whiteboard discussions it decided to build a simple Active Directory with a single Windows 2000 Server, and then use the Group Policy Reference from the *Microsoft Windows 2000 Server Resource Kit* to study the default group policies. The pilot lab work to define and test group policies was accomplished in three steps chosen to make the process controllable and manageable:

1. Test the group policy default settings selected for the pilot. The team made changes only to *Enable*, *Disable*, or *Configure* in the default group policy settings—it added no files or scripts.

2. Test the scripts and software default settings selected for the pilot. The team used very simple testing scripts and applications so as not to get lost in a diagnosis where it wasn't clear if the problem was the application or the group policy implementation. This was an iterative process that added a component and thoroughly tested it before adding another. This made for efficient diagnosis and troubleshooting and helped the teams learn from the pilot as it progressed.

3. Test the security aspects. As of this writing, this was still under way, but testing showed that security settings had to be thought out when planning the OU structure and the associated group policies. Several times in the pilot testing, the team found it easier to make a small change in the OUs or group policies than try to do too much in one group policy.

The testing procedure changed the group policy default settings, used a client computer to log on, and then evaluated the results. This was repeated until the team had explored all areas of interest. This process led to several lessons:

- Make sure pilot lab machines are fast. Don't use older machines that just happen to be available—this can retard testing.

- Making sure to set the Windows 2000 Server for forced policy acceptance at logon. This ensures that as you make a change you can immediately log on and check the result. Though this is something you probably wouldn't do in a production environment, it makes testing faster and much more efficient.

- Make sure to use small, simple scripts. Once you get them working, move on to more complex ones.

- Make sure, when you start testing software setting and configurations, that you start with small, simple applications. You don't want to go down the rat-hole trying to figure out if it's the application or what you tried to make it do. This testing can be confusing and frustrating if you don't start small then work up to production applications.

- Make sure you use the pilot lab to learn about Windows 2000.

One more lesson: the more willing you are to change the OU structure, the more effectively you will be able to use group policies. You should be able to define group policies that are easy to implement and diagnose within an OU structure that requires minimal administrative and maintenance effort.

Defending Design One

The team created a Design One that has definite advantages and that meets all business requirements. In particular, the global catalog and OU architecture created provide a flexible, reliable, and easy-to-use networking system, because OUs allowed the team to group objects and resources logically. Because users have a local copy of the global catalog, they can access any type of local or remote resource. Design One has zero impact on the existing Windows NT 4.0 environment, maintains full interoperability, and allows for easy migration. Delegated administration decreases the management costs associated with maintaining the Windows 2000 environment, and lays down a foundation on which Woodgrove Bank can create distributed solutions that span the enterprise.

These key strategies were used to create the Design One architecture:

- The design team designed to the company's ideal environment by taking full advantage of new Windows 2000 Active Directory capabilities.

- The namespace design begins with *WGB.tld* and builds a complete contiguous company-wide namespace.

- The site model design gives Woodgrove Bank complete control over the replication architecture.

- Placing domain controllers and global catalogs in each region maximizes authentication performance and resource location while minimizing global network traffic.

- Organizational Units, groups, and group policies were designed to map the business model to the actual network infrastructure, creating a true digital nervous system.

Design One represented the final Woodgrove Bank system architecture, but several discoveries during the process gave the team ideas for a next-generation architecture:

- The company plans to implement a global high-speed network infrastructure. The Design One architecture was based on the in-place low speed network.

- The introduction of multiple seamless access points into the global network via worldwide egress points enabled the team to collapse the INTL child domains into a more elegant international OU structure.

The design team created a future iteration of the architecture; Windows 2000 Active Directory will permit migration to this design with minimal effort.

From the Trenches: Soft Skills Produce Hard Results

As technologists at heart, we always put a strong emphasis on keeping our technology skillsets up-to-date and well-honed. We're always reading technical manuals, attending seminars, pursuing more certification, and seeking advanced training. But as we embarked on our Windows 2000 Active Directory planning project, we found that just having the right technical skills wasn't enough—in fact, this would not even get us to first base in the project. Planning an enterprise directory for an international company is extremely complex and politically challenging. The project touches all parts of a company. If your design does not take into account the entire scope of organizational business requirements, you're going to miss the boat. More importantly, you're going to miss the entire purpose of a global directory implementation. Technology is supposed to enhance productivity and make people more effective at what they do at work, to give companies a competitive advantage in the global marketplace.

We found out that over seventy percent of the time we spent on the Windows 2000 Active Directory project was used interviewing people, understanding the Bank's business, and facilitating internal business groups to work together and make collaborative decisions. As a consulting team, we really had to stretch our consultative diplomacy skills to help people and organizations work toward a common goal (a global directory). The amount of effort dedicated to this process was overwhelming. At times we felt more like counselors than technologists, listening to customer issues, problems, politics, and even problems at home. But in the end we had a very clear understanding of the people at Woodgrove Bank—how they function internally and how they relate externally to *their* customers. We came to understand how they make money, their business dynamics, and how their different business units worked together, or for that matter, didn't work together.

If you plan to embark on such a project, we can't emphasize enough the need for formal consultative *soft* skills training. Learn how to facilitate team communication, how to develop diplomacy, but, most important, understand *yourself*. If you are a consultant or if you are heading up an internal project, you have to know how to read people and work with different personality types. Getting everyone involved and working together to create a global directory is extremely challenging. Not having the soft skills training beforehand makes it even tougher.

We encourage you to seek soft skills training, to put just as much time into building your people skills as you put into building engineering skills. If you do this, you'll become much more effective at what you do, and you'll be a much happier person too. Technological challenges are easy, and, besides, many of them will probably be fixed in the next version of the product. An ability to work effectively with people separates the successful consultants from the rest.

Next Generation INTL Design

The design process considered many alternatives, which resulted in a first phase and a possible future design. With the current slow links, Design One's single domestic and separate international domains is the right design, but as international network bandwidth and reliability improve, Woodgrove Bank could create a more consolidated architecture. To move from Design One to single domestic/single international domain design would require:

- Creating a new OU structure in INTL domain that reflects the design required to move the child domain resources to INTL.
- Moving all resources into the INTL domain.
- Running DCPROMO to collapse and remove the child domains after all resources are removed or reinstalled.
- Rerunning DCPROMO on the former child domain controller and having it join the INTL domain as an additional domain controller.

Although simple in outline, these changes still would require careful planning. They would have the greatest impact on network replication and resource access. The design team would recommend a phased approach with a long-term migration schedule. Without proper planning and testing you run the risk of discovering issues or risks during migration—the wrong time to make this type of discovery. You can find and eliminate many risks by using a complete test model and a phased approach.

The simplified Woodgrove Bank Active Directory design (single INTL and single DOM domains with nested OUs for all international and domestic locations) would look like the design in Figure 1.20:

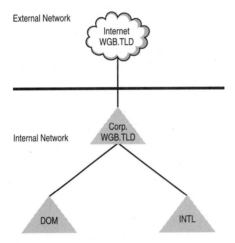

Figure 1.20   Single international and domestic domain design.

Why create a single international domain design?

- Business reasons
  - Many branches do not hub out of the regional locations; they connect to corporate via the VPN and, as such, are really OUs in the INTL domain in both designs.
  - It addresses long-term needs by creating one domestic and one international domain architecture.
- Technical reasons
  - The Active Directory has been tested to support over a million objects and could easily scale to meet the needs of the domestic, international, and branch users in Woodgrove Bank's network.
  - It reduces the complexity of the security model.
  - It simplifies implementations of group policy standards.

Figure 1.21 shows what the simplified architecture looks like using the MMC. Basically, the new model moves all the former domains into the INTL domain as OUs, including all countries that exist as OUs within the international domain. This design addresses both the business and technical requirements outlined for creating a single international domain. This architecture still allows Woodgrove Bank to use sites to control replication and continues to address the sub admin requirement for all regional sites and branches by using OUs.

Figure 1.21   New OU structure for the international domain.

Conclusion

To design an ideal solution with Windows 2000 Active Directory, you have to step back from conventional Windows NT 4.0 thinking. Although you may not get it right the first time (or the second or third), you can achieve a design that provides benefits and solutions. Once you build it in a pilot lab and test it, you will find that it requires some tinkering to make it the most efficient design, the one that truly delivers the benefits you want. The design team discovered that it is crucial to develop iterations and brainstorm your way through each one.

The team found the following to be an effective process:

1. Start with a simple design
2. Standardize a naming scheme
3. Create the proper domain architecture

4. Create a forest design

5. Complete site planning

6. Design global catalog and domain controller locations

7. Create proper organization unit and group architecture

8. Define what type of policy is required

9. Look at alternative designs

At each of these steps, the team took the time to brainstorm and introduce new ideas into the design process. The team started with the simplest possible design and introduced complexity into it only when a business or technical requirement justified it. For example, the current international slow links, language barriers, geopolitical challenges, and administration models forced the design team to introduce domains for each international location. Given greater bandwidth and taking into account the need to create a globally distributed security policy, the architecture could be simplified by moving to a single international domain.

The team learned these key lessons as it moved through the process:

- Align as quickly as possible with all the internal groups that need to be involved in the Active Directory design process. The design will have an impact on all facets of the organization and, as such, the team needs executive sponsorship at the highest levels.

- Don't be trapped by Windows NT 4.0 thinking. Make sure you are completely up to speed on all the facets of designing a Windows 2000 Active Directory.

- Continually refine the process throughout the design. Be willing to test some concepts early to validate further direction.

- Start simple. Add complexity when technical or business requirements demand it. Create a set of rules to prevent unwanted complexity.

- Make sure you completely understand the business rules so that you can build a design that reflects them and that allows for business growth, change, and future requirements.

- Everyone's idea is important. Pursue each team member's design ideas as if they were your own.

- This is an iterative process. Don't plan on getting it right the first time.

C H A P T E R   2

Compaq's Windows 2000 Site Topology Design

By Micky Balladelli, Compaq Computer Corporation

This chapter explains how Compaq Computer Corp. designed a Windows 2000 Active Directory site topology to serve a common network that would take over many of the business responsibilities of three infrastructures incorporated as a result of a merger. It begins by examining the chosen namespace for the domains and the physical network infrastructure, and then looks at the site topology, going into detail on server location. To provide some context, the discussion introduces and explains Active Directory replication terminology, and explains how data is replicated between Windows 2000 servers.

Active Directory replication differs significantly from replication in previous Windows NT versions, in which it was a simple matter of copying information from the primary domain controller (PDC) system to the computers serving as backup domain controllers (BDCs). Windows 2000 uses a multi-master, store and forward replication mechanism—changes made at any domain controller (DC) are copied in a timely, schedulable fashion to all other DCs, no matter how distributed the organization. How quickly this is performed depends on a degree of acceptable latency, CPU efficiency, and available network bandwidth.

Windows 2000 is designed to accommodate the requirements of large enterprises, and the extensible Active Directory can support far more objects than could previous Windows NT versions. Consequently, designers developed a new replication strategy that can sustain many objects in an environment where domains are grouped together to form a global namespace.

One such enterprise environment is in place at Compaq. As a Tier 1 member of the Microsoft Joint Development Program (JDP), Compaq has been a pioneer in the design and deployment of a Windows 2000 system in a production environment. The design discussed in this chapter is based on one created by Dave Heuss, a senior consultant in Compaq's Corporate Information Management department.

What You'll Find in This Chapter

- A discussion of Active Directory replication that explains how it resembles and differs from replication in Windows NT 4. This is important information for understanding how Active Directory structure and functionality affects replication topology design.

- An examination of the basic "design problem" facing Compaq Computer Corporation after acquisitions resulted in three legacy networks. It created a new network infrastructure (GlobalNet), to provide better worldwide connectivity and a base on which to deploy a new Windows 2000 infrastructure, and this required dealing with three internal DNS namespaces—including some Unix-based DNS servers.

- An explanation of how Compaq designed a replication topology that effectively and efficiently uses Windows 2000 Active Directory functionality—especially the Knowledge Consistency Checker.

Fundamentals of Active Directory Replication

Domain Controllers

Windows 2000 domain controllers (DCs) hold a replica of all of the objects belonging to their domain and have full read/write access to these objects. You can perform management operations on any DC, and the changes, because they affect object states or values, must be replicated (propagated) to the other DCs in the domain.

Replication allows all controllers to receive updates and to maintain consistent copies of the Active Directory database. It is not triggered immediately when an object is modified, because this could trigger a flood of replication operations when programs (such as directory synchronization procedures) insert or update many records in the directory in a short time. Instead, replication collects changes for a period of time, and then sends them to other controllers. In normal operation, a controller's Active Directory is in a state of what might be called *loose consistency*—changes may be on the way from other controllers, and when they are received the DCs synchronize. The DCs detect and automatically resolve conflicts caused when different users on separate DCs simultaneously make conflicting changes.

Windows NT 4.0 uses a *single-master replication* model: management operations can be performed only on the primary domain controller (PDC) because it is the only DC with read/write access to the database. PDC operations are replicated to backup domain controllers (BDCs), which maintain a read-only replica of the database that is located physically closer to the users. This allows faster authentication because users do not have to connect to distant DCs over links that may be slow.

Windows NT 4.0 has a *per-object* replication granularity: if a password is modified, the entire user object with all its attributes has to be replicated to all BDCs in the domain. Thus the replication topology is simple: the PDC is linked to all the BDCs in the same domain.

In Windows 2000 every DC maintains a copy of the Active Directory database with full read/write access to all of the objects belonging to the domain. An operation performed on one DC must then be replicated to all other DCs in the domain; if domains are linked to form a forest, some data from each domain must be replicated to the other domains to form a collective view of the forest. To support data copying within the domain (and between domains) Windows 2000 introduces a *multi-master replication* model, and it optimizes Active Directory replication by sending only changed data using *per-attribute* replication granularity. If a user password is changed, only the password (not the complete object) is replicated to other controllers.

Each DC serves as a replication partner for other DCs, and they initiate and perform all replication operations—member servers do not play a role (they do not keep a copy of the database).

Internally, DCs use Globally Unique Identifiers (GUIDs) to reference other DCs or replication partners. GUIDs are generated with an algorithm that ensures their uniqueness even if they are generated at the same time or on the same system. They are more reliable than names because they remain constant even if systems are renamed, ensuring a rename-safe environment. You can move an object from one part of the Active Directory to another without having to delete and recreate it—it will retain the same GUID.

When a DC boots, it stores in the Domain Naming System (DNS) database various service location resource records (SRVs) which identify the services provided by the DC. They allow clients to query DNS for a DC in a particular site. Because the GUIDs associated with DCs are stored in the DNS database as SRV records, DCs can find the IP Address of another DC by issuing a DNS query that includes that DC's GUID. This implies that a well functioning DNS infrastructure, supporting SRV records and preferably dynamic updates, must be in place before you deploy Windows 2000.

Triggering Replication

These operations, which can be performed on objects by users or administrators (depending on permission) trigger replication between DCs:

- **Object creation.** Creating a new object (such as a user) in the directory.
- **Object modification.** Modifying an object attribute—for example, changing a password.
- **Object move.** Moving an object from one container to another. Organizational units (OUs) are special containers that help organize Active Directory objects and often use department names such as **Sales** or **Marketing**. Moving an object from **Sales** to **Marketing** might happen during a reorganization. An object move is performed by modifying the name of the object and therefore is very similar to object modification.
- **Object deletion.** Removing an object from the Active Directory database.

Update Types

Write operations are distinguished according to whether they are performed locally or are performed on a remote DC and replicated locally:

- **Originating write.** This is performed on the same system. For example, if you create a user on the current DC, you perform an originating write to the Active Directory database.
- **Replicated write.** This is issued from an operation that originated on another DC and was replicated to the current DC. For example, if you create a user on DC1 and the operation is replicated to DC2, the DC2 modification is a replicated write.

Information about originating writes is stored in internal tables that are used to detect if an update has been propagated to a DC. This important Active Directory replication feature is called *propagation dampening* and it is key in a multi-master replication environment where DCs may have multiple replication partners that may use different paths to replicate data back to a target DC. The first replication instruction to arrive at the target DC updates the Active Directory, and propagation dampening reduces traffic and eliminates duplication by ensuring that other DCs know when replication operations have already been performed.

Naming Contexts

A naming context (NC) is a tree of objects stored in the Active Directory. There are three types, as shown in Figure 2.1:

- **Configuration NC.** This contains all the objects that represent the structure of the Active Directory in terms of domains, DCs, sites, and other configuration objects.
- **Schema NC.** This contains all the classes and attributes that define the objects and their attributes stored in the Active Directory.
- **Domain NC.** This contains all the other objects of the Active Directory partitioned in a domain: users, groups, OUs, computers, etc.

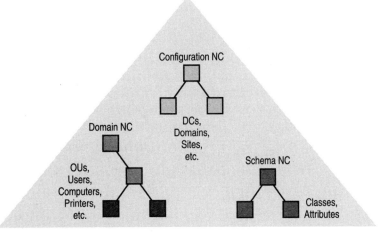

Figure 2.1   Naming contexts.

Domains act as partitions for the Active Directory, but they are not the boundary of replication—that and the replication scope are defined by naming contexts. The boundary of replication indicates how far management operations performed on DCs are replicated to other DCs in the same domain or other DCs in the forest. In other words, naming contexts define how far Active Directory changes are replicated in an organization.

Replication scope in Windows NT is only domain-wide. The wider scope possible in Windows 2000 required developing the concept of naming contexts and two scopes: forest-wide and domain-wide.

The configuration and schema are unique in the entire forest. This means that their NCs must be replicated to all the DCs in every domain in the forest. The configuration NC and schema NC are therefore said to have a forest-wide scope.

Domain objects are replicated only within the domain to which they currently belong. The domain NC has a domain-wide scope: information stored in a domain is confined to an NC and is replicated in the domain itself. There is one exception to this rule: the Global Catalog Server replicates all naming contexts, but in the case of foreign domain naming contexts it replicates only a subset of the information.

Naming contexts contain all the objects of the Active Directory.

Sites

A Windows 2000 site is a collection of IP subnets with good connectivity—in general, servers within a Windows 2000 site should be connected with links of 10 Mbits/sec or better. In this sense, you can compare a site to a LAN. Sites have *locality* in that all systems belonging to the same site can be considered physically close. They benefit from LAN-quality connectivity, and they require it, largely because of how intra-site replication is performed.

The concept of locality extends to workstations because they always attempt to connect to a domain controller in the same site. The Active Directory contains information about sites and their underlying IP subnets and can associate a workstation with a site by comparing the workstation's IP address with the site definitions. As you add servers to a domain, the Active Directory also examines their IP address and tries to place them in the most appropriate site.

When a Windows 2000 server creates a new domain that is the root of a new forest, the Active Directory creates the site *Default-First-Site-Name* and places the DC there. All the DCs joining the domain are added to the default site. Systems continue to be added to the default site until you create a new site.

A domain can span multiple sites (Figure 2.2) and multiple domains can be located in a single site because sites are independent of the domain structure. Domains represent the logical implementation of the Active Directory and sites represent the physical implementation Sites are objects stored in the configuration naming context and therefore site information is replicated to all DCs in the forest.

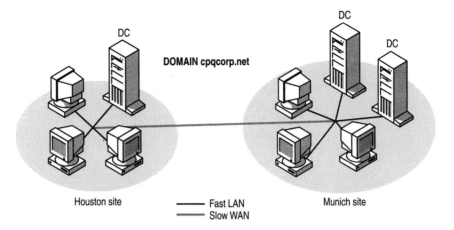

Figure 2.2   **Domain spanning multiple sites.**

Sites serve two roles:

- During workstation logon, they are used to determine the closest DC.
- During Active Directory replication, sites are used to optimize the route and transport of replicated data between sites. This topic is discussed the section "Knowledge Consistency Checker," on page 57.

To make these two functions possible, all DCs in a domain must know about all the sites.

Bridgehead Server

A bridgehead server (BHS) is a DC that performs replication operations with DCs in another site. Each site has one DC (the first DC in the site) that takes the Inter-Site Topology Generator (ISTG) role: it reviews and generates the connection objects for the BHSs in the site, and selects which DCs will serve as BHSs. All DCs in a site are eligible for the ISTG role: to avoid a single point of failure you should not assign this role to a particular DC.

To determine which DCs will become BHSs, the ISTG DC uses an algorithm to evaluate the list of site DCs as defined in the configuration NC, removes any unavailable DCs, orders the remainder by GUID, and then selects the first domain controller at the bottom of the list, or in other words, the oldest DC in the list.

The ISTG will assign one BHS per transport per site and per domain NC. You can, however, create explicit connection objects between DCs located at different sites. By doing this you are implicitly adding more BHSs to the site. If a site contains two DCs belonging to two domains, the ISTG will designate both of them as BHSs. A DC cannot replicate information belonging to another domain, so the two DCs will be assigned to replicate information to DCs in other sites belonging to their respective domains.

If you designate a set of DCs as preferred BHSs, the ISTG will not assign DCs that are not part of the preferred list. If for example a site has five DCs, and two of them are designated as preferred BHSs, the ISTG will use only these two DCs. If both of them are shut down, the ISTG will not use any of the remaining DCs because they are not part of the preferred list. In other words, by defining a preferred list of DCs, you are informing the ISTG that you want inter-site replication to occur only using the DCs in that list.

Replication Transports

Replication occurs between DCs in the same site and between DCs in different sites. Intra-site replication is performed through standard Windows 2000 Remote Procedure Calls (RPCs); inter-site replication can use different transports. The Active Directory holds information about the domain controllers in each site, the connectivity that exists between each site, and the best route over which to replicate. To support network links of varying types, the Active Directory supports two major replication transports:

- DS-RPC (Directory Services RPC)
- ISM-SMTP (Inter-Site Messaging—Simple Mail Transport Protocol)

Replication is based on the assumption that it must occur quickly within a site to minimize directory inconsistencies across all DCs in a site. For this reason, intra-site replication is always RPC-based. Inter-site replication can be performed through RPCs (synchronous) or via special forms of SMTP messages sent between domain controllers (asynchronous). You cannot schedule intra-site replication frequency: when changes occur, each DC sends update notifications to its replication partners after a defined interval. This interval has a 5-minute default, but you can configure it through the system registry. Even if no changes have occurred and replication has not taken place, domain controllers ping each other every hour by broadcasting the latest information about the state of replicated objects to ensure that an update has not been missed. You can configure this by changing the schedule value of the site's NTDS Site Settings object. After a DC receives a notification that an update is available, it makes a connection to the replication partner and initiates replication. Data is not compressed during intra-site replication.

Inter-site replication compresses data larger than 50 KB before sending (to 10-15% of original volume) regardless of the replication transport. Compression and expansion use CPU cycles, but this overhead is more than compensated for by the reduction in network traffic. You *can* schedule inter-site replication to take advantage of compression and timing to offset the fact that inter-site connectivity is usually not so good as intra-site. Replication topologies are normally automatically generated. Sites are created to identify locations connected with WAN links (explained more fully in the section "Connection Objects," below).

When building an enterprise Active Directory implementation, you need to understand how Windows 2000 handles Active Directory replication and the options available to you. During planning, you can combine this understanding with knowledge of the network and the business information (and rules) to reflect your company's needs as you decide how many sites to create, how to connect them, and which transport to use.

Knowledge Consistency Checker

The replication topology is a map of how information replicates between DCs. The Knowledge Consistency Checker (KCC) service, which runs on every DC, generates and maintains the topology, and allows DCs to find other replication partners. If, for example, a DC becomes unavailable because it is shut down, its replication partners change the topology to allow replication over an alternate route.

There is a replication topology per naming context scope: forest-wide or domain-wide. This means that the schema and configuration NCs, which have a forest-wide scope, share the same topology, and that domains in a forest, which by definition have a domain-wide scope, each create their own topology.

The KCC generates and optimizes the replication topology by creating connection objects between DCs. By default, it runs every 15 minutes. You can trigger the KCC manually via the Active Directory Sites and Services snap-in. Use this registry setting to change the check interval for the topology:

```
HKLM\System\CurrentControlSet\Services\NTDS\Parameters\Repl topology
update period (secs)
```

Connection Objects

Connection objects are communication channels used to replicate information between DCs. A connection object's properties include its replication partner, the replication partner's site, the transport it uses (RPC or SMTP), and the schedule for the replication cycle.

A connection object is uni-directional, so there are always two connection objects between DCs in a site. They are normally created by the KCC, but you can create them manually. You can also force immediate replication over a specific connection object by right-clicking the object in the Active Directory Sites and Services snap-in, and clicking the Replicate Now button. You can also force replication by using the Replication Monitor tool (in the resource kit) to synchronize an entire naming context, thus triggering replication between all DCs in it.

The KCC generates the connection objects needed to map, maintain, and optimize the replication topology. If a replication partner becomes unavailable, the KCC maintains a fully functioning replication topology by creating a new temporary connection object with another partner. The KCC will keep the connection object with the failed DC. When the DC becomes available again, the KCC will remove the temporary connection object. The KCC ensures replication between the DCs in a domain or forest; if a DC is shut down, the KCC finds alternate routes to other DCs so that Active Directory data stays synchronized between all DCs.

If you create a connection object, is said to be *explicit*, and the KCC will not manage it. You will have to destroy it. The KCC manages only connection objects that it generates.

The process of replication within a site involves a notification from the source DC to its replication partners. This triggers the replication process. In the event of a missing notification, DCs will use a schedule to trigger replication by themselves. This schedule is defined at the level of the site and you can set it to specify any hour in a week to replicate once per hour, twice per hour, or four times per hour, or you can turn it off. All the connection objects within a site will reflect the schedule defined for the site. This means that if you modify the site schedule, you are affecting all the schedule of connection objects managed by the KCC in the site. If you modify the schedule for a connection object that was generated by the KCC, then the KCC will no longer manage the connection object and you will need to manage it. If that is the case, the connection object schedule takes precedence over the site schedule.

Connection objects are the most important components in a replication topology because they enable information transfer from a DC to its replication partners. Connection objects show when replication happens (storing this information in the replication schedule) and they regulate the consistency of the Active Directory.

Global Catalog Replication

A global catalog (GC) is a special type of DC that holds read-only subsets of information about objects from all other domains in the forest. Because a GC is also a DC in its own domain, it replicates all the objects and all the attributes from DCs or GCs of the same domain. This means that GCs must replicate partial domain NC information from all the domains in the forest, and must replicate the entire domain NC from their own domain. The KCC creates additional connection objects to allow domain NC information to reach GCs belonging to other domains, and to replicate domain information across domain boundaries. Replication to GCs in the forest occurs in the same manner as replication of domain NC information between DCs, except that the domain NC replication to GCs can be performed using either RPC or (better over slow links) SMTP. When replicating domain NC between GCs or DCs belonging to the same domain, RPC must be used. Replication of domain NC information between GCs belonging to different domains can benefit from the SMTP transport. The difference is that DCs or GCs of the same domain replicate writeable data of the domain NC. GCs belonging to different domains replicate read-only data of partial domain NCs. SMTP replication is allowed only for read-only domain NC data.

For replication, this relationship exists between a DC and a GC:

- A DC replicates three naming contexts: the configuration NC, the schema NC, and the domain NC in which the DC resides. The equation below shows that the replication involving a domain controller is affected by changes in any of these three naming contexts:

$$R_{dc} = NC_{domain} + NC_{schema} + NC_{config}$$

- Global catalog replication equates to the replication of a DC in the same domain, because a GC is also a DC in its own domain. However, for all other domains in the forest, each GC also replicates partial domain NCs, which contain all the objects in a domain NC but only a subset of each object's attributes. You can select which attributes are replicated to all GCs by setting the *isMemberOfPartialAttributeSet* property, which is set in the schema. The equation below shows GC replication, and you can see how it differs from DC replication:

$$R_{gc} = R_{dc} + NC_{partial\ domain} * (n - 1)$$

Where n = the number of domains in the forest

If a forest has only one domain, it does not increase traffic to set all DCs as GCs because each controller in a domain replicates the full set of attributes for all objects anyway.

If a site contains a GC, then all the DCs in that site can also be GCs. It is not costly to promote all DCs to GCs in that site because the site's only bridgehead server will perform inter-site replication and the site's other DCs will use intra-site replication. GC replication with all GCs in the same site is always performed over RPCs because a site represents a well-connected set of networks.

DCs can replicate the schema and configuration NCs from GCs. They can replicate the domain NC from GCs in the same domain but not from GCs in other domains. This is because GCs contain read-only replicas from other domains and thus are not authoritative on these objects.

Compaq's Corporate Namespace

When Compaq acquired Tandem and Digital Equipment Company, it inherited three legacy networks. They are currently bridged to allow connectivity between the companies and to allow applications such as Microsoft Exchange to be used throughout Compaq. To replace these legacy networks, Compaq has introduced a new network infrastructure (GlobalNet), which provides better world-wide connectivity and is the base on which they will deploy the new Windows 2000 infrastructure.

The three current internal DNS namespaces (*compaq.com*, *tandem.com*, and *dec.com*) will be replaced in the new infrastructure with a new one (*cpqcorp.net*). The new network is used by several network operating system infrastructures, and a portion of it is dedicated to Windows 2000.

UNIX-based DNS servers are authoritative for the *cpqcorp.net* zone and for child DNS domains that are not used by the Windows 2000 infrastructure. Dynamic updates to the DNS database are not allowed in those domains. Dynamic addresses for Windows 2000-based systems and SRV resource record generation are authorized only in the DNS zones dedicated to Windows 2000 domains. Every Windows 2000 domain has a matching DNS zone and uses Windows 2000 DNS servers. The Windows 2000 zones are integrated into the Active Directory to increase security.

The Windows 2000 domain structure (Figure 2.3) has four major domains—the root domain (*cpqcorp.net*, which holds the forest-wide FSMO role owners) and one child domain for each geography:

- *americas.cpqcorp.net*, covering North and South America.
- *emea.cpqcorp.net,* covering Europe, the Middle East, and Africa
- *asiapacific.cpqcorp.net,* covering Asia, Australia, and the Far East

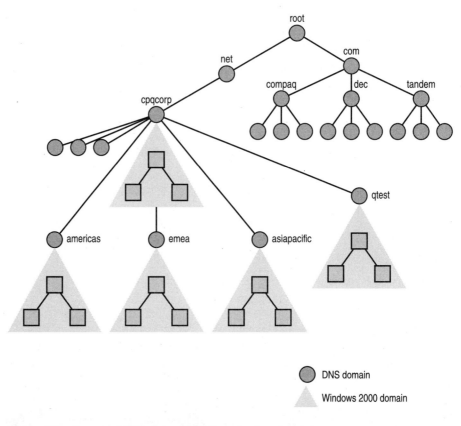

Figure 2.3 Compaq's Windows 2000 domain structure.

The design has tried to minimize creation of other Windows 2000 domains in the production environment. Compaq started with 13 Windows NT 4.0 account domains and about 1700 resource domains. All objects in these domains will gradually be consolidated into one of the four Windows 2000 domains.

The Compaq Services business unit runs a parallel Windows 2000 infrastructure. They use this forest to test new releases (of Windows 2000 and of associated layered products such as Exchange 2000), to simulate customer problems, and to train the internal technical community. They do not use it for production purposes such as corporate authentication and e-mail, however it is connected to Compaq's network infrastructure and Compaq's corporate DNS servers have delegated name servers for these zones.

Network Infrastructure

This section reviews the legacy networks' implementation and constraints, and the new physical infrastructure design.

GlobalNet

GlobalNet is the unified corporate network that is replacing the Compaq, Digital, and Tandem legacy networks, which are shown in Figure 2.4. Its structure is based on a set of core locations (called Ring 1) linked by a fast ATM backbone. Other locations are connected by slower links to the core sites.

There are seven core locations:

- Houston, TX
- Littleton, MA
- Cupertino, CA
- Munich, Germany
- Reading, England
- Tokyo, Japan
- Singapore

To increase network availability, two different vendors provide the connectivity between each site. Additional backbones are connected to the core sites to reduce risks of core ATM backbone failure. European and Asia Pacific networks are connected to two other backbone sites; United States networks are connected to three other sites each.

Every site has a LAN, some of which were designed specifically for existing data center requirements, others of which were adapted to the requirements of the Windows 2000 servers that run the Windows 2000 infrastructure: domain controllers, global catalogs, DNS servers, WINS servers, DHCP servers, etc.

A collection of OSPF routing areas (called Ring 2) is attached to the Ring 1 network. These areas are the hubs for the second-level networks that are specifically designed to address country or regional requirements. Some hubs are dually connected to the Ring 1 backbone for redundancy. The host countries finance these networks, so they are not all of the same kind or quality. The site topology design took this into consideration, scheduling replication in some cases to reduce costs. Site-link scheduling details are discussed in the section "Site Links," on page 69.

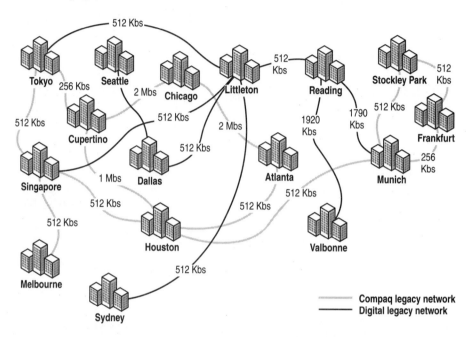

Figure 2.4   A simplified version of the Compaq and Digital legacy networks.

Networks expanding into countries and regions beyond Ring 2 are called Ring 3. Their bandwidths vary with country and user population size.

The legacy networks still used by Compaq, Digital, and Tandem locations are gradually being replaced with GlobalNet Ring 3 networks, but it may take a while to replace the Digital network because some of its systems run the DECnet protocol, which GlobalNet does not support.

Addressing Considerations

GlobalNet uses a Class A address space divided into sub-networks based on a 22-bit subnet mask (255.255.252.0) to allow at least 1024 addresses for each physical location. Additional subnets are allocated for locations that require more addresses because they have more users or have users running multiple systems. Sites with no more than 50 people are allocated the 23-bit subnet mask 255.255.254.0, which provides 512 possible addresses.

These subnets are further subdivided into logical class C networks for address allocation purposes. For example, a location that is allocated a 22-bit subnet, based at 16.30.0.0 can use the class C networks 16.30.0.0, 16.30.1.0, 16.30.2.0 and 16.30.3.0. This makes it possible to divide the address space between systems that use Windows 2000 DNS and systems that use UNIX BIND name service. How many logical class C networks are assigned to each name service depends on how many systems are Windows-based and how many run UNIX or OpenVMS. Routing is done at the 22-bit subnet level.

Another reason to divide the address space further is that each name service must have control of the address-dependant reverse lookup zones it uses to translate IP addresses back to a host name. When a Windows 2000 system is dynamically registered with Windows 2000 DNS, the name and reverse lookup entries are created automatically, so the Windows 2000 DNS server must be able to write updates to the reverse lookup zones. When using a dynamic address provided by a DHCP server there are two basic cases:

- A Windows 2000 system receives the address from the DHCP server. Windows 2000 dynamically updates the forward lookup zone with its own address record (called an **A record**), and the DHCP server updates the reverse lookup zone with the equivalent pointer record (**PTR**).

- A down-level client receives the dynamic address from a DHCP server. The DHCP server updates the A record and the PTR record in the DNS database.

Because dynamic IP address updates are not implemented for OpenVMS and UNIX-based systems, the DHCP servers serve only the Windows-based systems, so it is safe to allow Windows 2000 DNS servers to own the reverse lookup zones.

Windows 2000 sites are configured to contain all their assigned IP subnets and not just the class C subnets reserved for the Windows 2000 systems. This is done:

- To allow misconfigured systems to use locally defined services. If a Windows 2000 system is accidentally configured with an IP address reserved to the UNIX/OpenVMS subnets, it still needs to access local resources such as a DC and a GC. Misconfigured systems will use local Windows 2000 services regardless of which IP subnet they belong to, *if* all the IP subnets at a facility belong to the same site. This is quite important because it allows a Windows 2000 system to be authenticated using a local domain controller and to access other local resources such as a GC server for searches and lookups. If the system cannot do this, it will request the DNS server for a service such as a DC for a domain, but because the system does not belong to any specific site, it may end-up using a remote server and thus be penalized by a slow network link. In this case, reverse address registration will fail for the system, but its address records will be properly registered and it will be given the correct local domain controller for logon.

- To allow logical class C subnet allocations to be flexibly adjusted without affecting the definition of sites and site links in the site topology.

- To better allow the sites and site link definitions to reflect the actual network topology rather than its management structure.

You can assign WAN IP subnets that can be used by network devices that control the WAN. You probably will use a different address assignment strategy than you use for facility-based LANs, but this does not affect the site topology design because a Windows 2000 infrastructure is not implemented in these subnets.

Legacy Networks

Compaq's legacy networks will shrink as facilities are converted to GlobalNet and connected to their OSPF routing hub. The *dec.com* network for Compaq legacy users will be re-addressed, because its current class A network will be used for GlobalNet.

GlobalNet interconnects with the legacy networks from various core sites. The Digital legacy network connects at Tokyo, Singapore, Cupertino, Littleton, and Reading. The Compaq legacy network connects at Munich, Stockley Park (from Reading), Houston, Cupertino, Tokyo, and Singapore.

Site Topology Design

A Windows 2000 site topology is a logical model layered on top of a physical network. Windows 2000 does not communicate with network routers to retrieve OSPF table information about the network and its characteristics. Rather than trying to detect the physical network, the KCC relies on the site topology for the information (on network availability and replication cost) it uses to generate the best replication path between DCs.

The three layers in Figure 2.5 are produced by three distinct designs, but each relies on information defined in the layers below:

- The bottom layer is the physical network.

- The middle layer is the Window 2000 site model, which is based on and reflects the physical network.

- The top layer is the Windows 2000 domain structure, which is affected by a number of political and business constraints. And because domains rely on the site topology for replication, their design uses the site model to determine and conform to replication constraints. Replication restrictions may require that you split domains; the physical network may restrict how you configure replication.

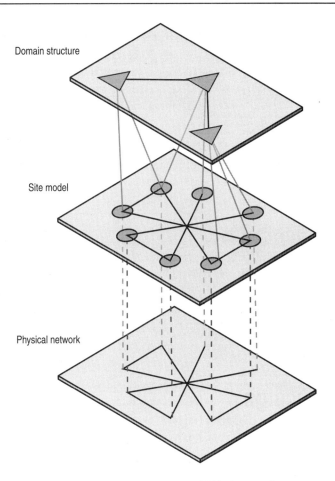

Domain structure

Site model

Physical network

Figure 2.5   Three-layer Windows 2000 site topology.

There is an important distinction between domain structure design and site topology design. Domains contain objects; sites reflect the location of user communities. A domain is mapped to a site by placing a replica of the domain into the site. A site does not contain a portion of a domain—it contains the entire domain. Sites contain DCs and these are replicas of a domain. If you place a GC in a site, the entire Active Directory becomes available to that site; if you place no DCs or GCs in a site, it is useless because no objects are available within it.

Site topology can affect domain structure because it determines the bandwidth available for replication. Active Directory scalability makes it possible for most companies to deploy just one domain in their enterprise, but there usually are reasons to split domains, and the network bandwidth used for Active Directory replication is one of them, especially if the Active Directory has many objects that change frequently. You can tune the site topology to reduce replication traffic.

Intra-Site vs. Inter-Site Replication

Intra-site and inter-site replication differ in some important ways. The table below shows how:

	Intra-site	Inter-site
Transport	RPC	RPC or SMTP (see note below)
Topology	Ring	Spanning tree
Replication Model	Notify and pull	Pull
Compression	None	Full beyond 50 KB

Note SMTP replication is available only for the schema and configuration naming contexts, and for a domain naming context that is replicated to global catalog servers. SMTP replication cannot be used to replicate a domain NC between two domain controllers of the same domain.

Intra-site replication characteristics:

■ Transport must be RPC over IP.

■ The generated replication topology is a ring between domain controllers. If a DC cannot reach another DC in the same site within three hops, it generates additional connection objects. This means that if there are seven DCs in a site, a simple ring connecting all DCs is generated because all DCs can reach all the other DCs within the three hops limit. If there are more than seven DCs, additional connection objects are created and the topology looks like a ring containing a star.

■ The replication period (5-minute default) is configurable via registry settings.

■ Replication is based on a *notify and pull* model. A DC notifies its immediate replication partners about the need to replicate information, the partners provide necessary information to allow the DC to prepare the information, then the DCs pull the information for local processing.

■ Data is never compressed, because bandwidth is always available within a site.

Inter-site replication characteristics:

■ The transport can be RPC or SMTP (*if* replicating the configuration and schema naming contexts, *or* when replicating from a domain NC to a GC in another domain).

■ The topology generated is a spanning tree, which by definition avoids loops.

■ The availability schedule controls when data is replicated. The frequency can be customized. The default frequency is 3 hours, and this interval is customizable to a minimum of 15 minutes or to a maximum of 10080 minutes (one week).

- Replication is based on a *scheduled pull* model. A DC pulls information from a replication partner, then processes it locally. A second DC in turn pulls the information from that DC. The process involves no notification, however the pull operation is scheduled.

- Compression is enabled for data over 50 KB.

Creating Replication Topologies

You can use either of these basic approaches to create a replication topology:

- Turn off the KCC and manually create the connection objects between the various DCs. This gives you total control, but if a server goes down, the KCC will not try to find an alternate route and you will have to create a replacement connection object.

- Let the KCC do everything. You create the sites and the site links (as you would for a complete mesh network) then let the KCC use the cost and the replication defined for each site link to compute the best replication routes. Give the KCC information about the underlying network and create a set of site links and site link bridges (these concepts are explained in sections below). This method, which allows you to reflect physical network constraints and enforce particular routes, is the most flexible and powerful because it allows you to tune and optimize replication. It does, however, require a meticulous site topology design. Compaq chose this approach.

Site Topology

One of Compaq's primary considerations for the Windows 2000 site design was to compartmentalize the network to reflect the basic GlobalNet topology. The design was based on the assumption that "the network is always available." Although this certainly is subject to local funding and implementation decisions, it does reflect a bias towards maximizing available bandwidth.

GlobalNet falls into three concentric rings, representing connectivity and bandwidth patterns; the site model logically follows.

Core Sites

The ATM core comprises seven locations. Each node must have a LAN that hosts enterprise infrastructure servers. Windows 2000 servers (DCs, GCs, DNS, DHCP, and WINS servers) are placed in these LANs. The nodes also have additional systems belonging to other network operating infrastructures.

The core sites constitute independent, interconnected Windows 2000 sites, which provide most Windows 2000 services. The IP subnets for networks connected to the core sites are associated to the equivalent Windows 2000 site. Creating single sites increases the redundancy and therefore the availability of the Windows 2000 servers. GlobalNet has such high bandwidth and availability that it can easily handle replication traffic for Active Directory objects. The nature of intra-site replication reduces latency for replicated objects. Within a site, replication frequency is five minutes; operations requiring urgent replication (such as disabled accounts and RID pool changes) are triggered immediately and automatically.

The Windows 2000 server placement strategy locates most types of infrastructure servers at the core sites only, unless a facility is either very large, running business critical operations, or at the end of a very unreliable WAN link. This approach, which uses fewer but larger servers, is used because:

- It reduces remote management of core servers by using more centrally located servers.
- It reduces replication traffic across WAN links, reducing the bandwidth required for the Windows 2000 infrastructure.

GlobalNet's high network availability makes this a workable strategy.

Ring 2 and Ring 3 Sites

Windows 2000 services for most facilities are provided from the core site to which they connect. If the routing area connects to two core sites, one is chosen to provide services.

Some locations outside the core sites also require that DCs and DNS servers be available locally to increase authentication speed and object lookup. Some facilities within an OSPF routing area require a DC because of their business importance or because they have an unreliable network connection. Future deployment of products such as Exchange 2000 or Systems Management Server V2.0 may also require more replication sites within OSPF routing areas.

Because individual countries or regions implemented the OSPF routing area design of Ring 2 and Ring 3 networks, the site topology design took into account the requirements and constraints of these country-level networks. The design created a specific site for each of these facilities, containing all subnets for that location and including the appropriate site links (explained below) to connect a Ring 2 site to the core site. In some cases Ring 3 sites are connected to the Ring 2 locations instead of directly to the core sites, to optimize distribution of the replication topology.

The design defines a site link to connect any site that is created within an OSPF routing area to either the core site that the area connects to or to another site within the same OSPF routing area, if that connection reflects the actual network topology.

Site Links

Inter-site replication requires an explicit *site link* network connection between two sites.

A site is a collection of IP subnets with good connectivity, and can be considered a LAN. Site links are logical connections between sites. They must mimic the network and should be viewed as having similar characteristics to the underlying connection between the sites—in other words, you can think of them as WAN links.

There is an important distinction between connection objects and site links. Connection objects connect DCs; they are generated by the KCC or you can manually create them. Site links are used by the KCC to determine the cost and availability of a network for performing replication between two sites; you *must* create site links manually.

A site link has an associated cost. The KCC uses the cost factor and the site link availability schedule to determine which connection objects must be created between DCs to enable replication, and then creates a spanning tree of connection objects (which avoids looping) between DCs at different sites.

The site link's cost factor is a number between 1 and 32767 (default 100) that indicates the cost of replicating information from one site to another. The smaller a link's value, the better its network connectivity, and the easier it is to replicate information across it. You *must* define cost factor values during the design phase. By itself the cost doesn't mean anything: it simply represents a logical cost of replicating information between two sites. Compaq decided to choose three values: 10, 50, 100. A value of 10 represents a link between core sites; 50 represents a link between a core site and a Ring 2 site; 100 represents a link between a Ring 2 and Ring 3 site. The KCC computes inter-site replication costs by adding the cost of every site link between two sites and comparing numbers to determine the best (least expensive) route.

You can add multiple sites that have identical costs and availability schedules in the same site link. The KCC treats these sites equally when creating and managing resource objects.

The Compaq core sites are connected via site links that match the ATM circuit connections and are assigned a cost value of 10, which is the lowest connection value in the enterprise. Costs that reflect primary paths from a site to the core are valued at 50, as illustrated in Figure 2.6. The Compaq design allows the creation of additional site links between sites (either within an OSPF routing area or a core site) if there are corresponding physical network connections, but it stipulates that any site links representing backup or secondary network connections should be valued at 100 or greater. This is because the costing scheme should encourage replication traffic to travel across the preferred network connections and to move from the spokes of the network to the hub, around the hub, and then back out the spokes. This is the most efficient use of a network such as GlobalNet.

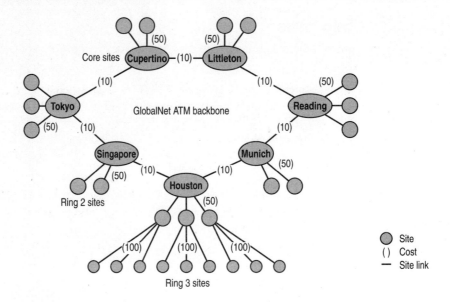

Figure 2.6   Sites and their costs.

The initial design did not schedule replication because it was believed that the network would have relatively high bandwidth and availability. But in the final implementation, network utilization costs required replication tuning in some countries. Canada, for instance, charges a tariff on data that moves across the border, so to reduce costs, replication out of Canada is scheduled for specific hours during each day. India also requires a special site link because network bandwidth there is very small and very unstable at certain times of the day. Replication topology optimization is an ongoing process. Other cases requiring further tuning may yet be discovered.

Site Link Bridges

A *site link bridge* connects two site links to form a bridge in more or less the same way a router connects two networks. It creates a transitive and logical link between two sites that don't have an explicit site link.

In the example shown in Figure 2.7, there are four sites. Littleton does not have an explicit site link to Atlanta. Placing a site link bridge between the two site links enables the Littleton DC to generate the connection objects needed for replication to the Atlanta DC.

In Windows 2000, site link bridges are seldom necessary because site links are transitive by default, so for most small to medium Windows 2000 deployments it is acceptable and recommended to allow the KCC to find alternate DCs on any available site.

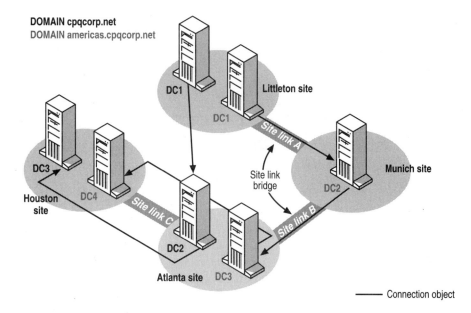

Figure 2.7   Site Link Bridge enabling transitivity.

Transitivity affects all site links: if you turn it off, none of them is transitive and you must create explicit site link bridges. Some designers turn it off so that they can fine-tune the generation of the replication topology, which assumes that they have a well-defined cost structure. You should carefully consider your situation before turning off site link transitivity. It is usually advisable only in large implementations that have multiple replication paths with the same total cost. If you want to avoid a particular path, for example to avoid a firewall, then you can tune the replication topology by creating an explicit site link bridge that controls the visibility of specific site links from a site. You can turn on site link transitivity by clicking on the *Bridge all site links* check box in the **Properties** dialog on the selected replication transport. The ability to select site link transitivity on a per transport basis allows more flexibility. Asynchronous transports such as SMTP can be selected for slow or unreliable links and it may be a wise choice to leave site link transitivity on. Synchronous transports such as RPC require a more stable network connection, so these transports may need a finer setting.

The cost scheme implemented in Compaq's site topology provides the KCC with enough information to generate an optimum replication topology, but the design leaves site link transitivity on to prevent outages and to increase replication availability. All site links are bridged, and this provides DCs with the site visibility they need when looking for alternate replication partners.

Server Location

Each core site contains a DC server for the *cpqcorp.net* domain, a DC server for the geography domain in which the core site resides (*americas.cpqcorp.net*, *emea.cpqcorp.net*, or *asiapacific.cpqcorp.net*), and a global catalog server for the core site's local geography. All DC servers are configured as DNS servers. Others, such as WINS servers, are also placed in the core sites. When Exchange 2000 is deployed, more Global Catalog Servers will have to be deployed into sites within the OSPF routing areas, because Exchange 2000 uses the Global Catalog to replace Exchange's Global Address List. Placement and purchase of those additional Global Catalog Servers is deferred until the Exchange 2000 project.

FSMO Roles

Windows 2000 supports multi-master replication of directory data—any DC in the domain can be used to modify the values of an object, then the changes are replicated between all DCs. When update conflicts ensue (as they may with any complex model) the conflicting attributes version numbers are evaluated; if they are the same the writer with the most recent time stamp wins.

Some objects in the directory, such as the schema itself, cannot be resolved with such methods, because two versions of the schema may generate instances of objects using different properties and it would be hard to resolve such conflicts without losing data. To avoid schema conflicts, a special DC (called the Schema Master) performs a single-master replication mechanism. This is a *Flexible Single-Master Operation* (FSMO, pronounced *Fizmo*) role implemented in a single-master replication model. There are five FISMO roles:

Schema Master

The Schema Master is unique in the forest. It alone can create new classes or attributes, which are then replicated as updates to all domains in the forest.

Domain Naming Master

The Domain Naming Master, which manages the names of every domain in the forest, is also unique in the forest. It alone can add and remove domains in the tree or forest to avoid naming conflicts. In future releases, the Domain Naming Master will allow domain *moves* within the forest.

PDC Emulator

The PDC Emulator is unique in the domain. It provides backward compatibility to down-level clients and servers by:

- Providing down-level clients support for password updates.
- Performing replication to down-level BDCs.
- Acting as the Master Domain Browser, if the Windows NT Browser service is enabled.

- Synchronizing time between systems belonging to the same forest. The PDC emulators in a forest synchronize time between themselves across domains, and spread this synchronization to member servers and workstations. The source for this synchronization is the PDC emulator of the root domain. The PDC in the root domain can be synchronized with an external time source.

Windows 2000 DCs replicate password changes to the PDC first. Each time a DC fails to authenticate a password, it contacts its PDC to see if it can authenticate the password there, perhaps as a result of a change that has not yet been replicated.

RID Master

The RID Master is unique in the domain. When a security principal (such as a user or group) is created, it receives a domain-wide *Security ID* (SID) that is composed of a Domain ID, and a domain-wide unique *Relative ID* (RID). Every Windows 2000 DC receives a pool of RIDs it can use. The RID Master manages assignment of these pools to ensure that these IDs remain unique on every DC.

Infrastructure Master

The Infrastructure Master is unique in the domain. When an object from another domain is referenced, the reference contains the GUID, the SID, and the DN of that object. If the referenced object moves:

- The object GUID does not change. (GUIDs never change.)
- The object SID changes if the move is cross-domain (to receive a SID from the new domain).
- The object DN always changes.

The Infrastructure Master DC in a domain updates the SIDs and DNs in cross-domain object references in that domain.

FSMO Placement

Compaq placed the FSMO roles at headquarters core sites (shown in Figure 2.8): Houston (Compaq HQ), Munich (Europe HQ), and Singapore (Asia Pacific HQ). The enterprise FSMO roles are owned by DCs belonging to the *cpqcorp.net* domain.

The FSMOs for the domains are placed this way:

- The schema and the domain naming masters for the enterprise run on the same DC, which is dedicated to these roles.
- The DC server in Houston is the RID, Infrastructure, and PDC FSMO for *cpqcorp.net.*
- The *americas.cpqcorp.net* DC server in Houston is the RID, Infrastructure, and PDC FSMO.
- The DC server in Munich is the RID, Infrastructure, and PDC FSMO for *emea.cpqcorp.net.*

- The DC server in Singapore is the RID, Infrastructure, and PDC FSMO for *asiapacific.cpqcorp.net*.

- The FSMOs for the geography domains fail over to the DCs in Littleton, Reading, and Tokyo. The FSMO for *cpqcorp.net* fails over to the root DC in Littleton, MA. The Forest FSMOs also fail over to the root DC in Littleton.

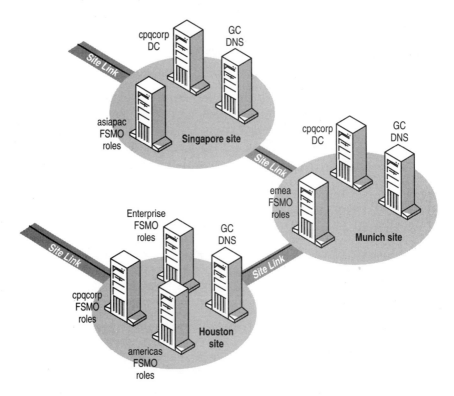

Figure 2.8   FSMO role placement for Compaq.

Domain Controllers and Global Catalog Servers

The DCs for the *cpqcorp.net* domain are at the headquarters core sites, one at each geographical location: Houston, Singapore, and Munich.

A GC server configured as a DNS server is also at every core site. GC placement will be reviewed for the Exchange 2000 deployment.

The DCs for each geography domain (*EMEA, Americas, and AsiaPacific*) are placed in their respective core sites. Core sites do not host a DC from another geography because:

- It reduces costs to have fewer, larger servers at each core site.

- The ATM backbone has enough bandwidth for acceptable authentication speeds.

- Every core site has a GC that can be used for queries and lookups of information residing in other geography domains.
- Roaming user traffic is not considered to be high.

If authentication performance becomes an issue, they can place a domain DC at the core site headquarters locations in Houston, Munich, and Singapore.

From the Trenches:
Fine-Tuning Replication for Large Active Directory Stores

At Compaq we like "midnight" projects—the kind that generally get started by discussions between technical people—and one of these was to generate a large Active Directory store. By large, we mean 40 million users and contacts, well beyond a "normal" number of objects; the kind of huge directory service that might be required by organizations such as telecommunications companies, Internet service providers, or government agencies.

We started out thinking about size and speed. We wrote a C++ application on top of ADSI and this multi-threaded application is well adapted to LSASS. Running in the LSASS multi-threaded environment, the application generates objects faster by an order of magnitude than a comparable single-threaded Visual Basic version.

From there, it was simply a matter of populating the store, which we did. Before long we had 40,000,000 objects, and, this part of the project being complete, we started considering real-world issues. The first of these was the most obvious: however much information you hold, you have a single point of failure if you hold it in a single system. We decided to create a replica on a second system, and this is where the size of the store became a problem.

We installed Windows 2000 on a second server, configured it to mirror the first system, and started running DCPROMO—the wizard-based tool that promotes a Windows 2000 server into a domain controller—to instruct the second system to join the domain containing the 40,000,000 objects as a domain replica. We let the DCPROMO process run intensively for five days, but we pulled the plug when we realized that although the Configuration and Schema naming contexts replicate fairly quickly, the 40 million objects reside in the Domain NC, which takes forever to replicate. Once we thought about it, it was obvious: a domain controller sends 100 objects to its replication partner and waits a couple seconds for the partner to process the objects. This works well enough under "normal" circumstances, but when you are trying to move as many objects as we were, you are looking at a long-range project.

When replicating large number of objects, speed of replication is quite important, and you should shoot for speeds as fast as the network connection allows. But you can help things along by fine-tuning replication. To solve our 40-million-object problem, we went into the registry key:

HKEY_LOCAL_MACHINE\SYSTEM\CurrentControlSet\Services\NTDS\Parameters

The following keys can be used to modify the default behavior of Active Directory replication:

- Control the priority used by the replication thread. This is more interesting in a multi-CPU environment where a CPU could be dedicated to processing replication data:

  - Replication thread priority high set to 1. If not set or set to 0, this gives the replication thread a low priority.

  - Replication thread priority low set to 0. By default this value is set to −1 which simply means that the key should be ignored.

- Tune packet sizes and number of objects per packet for each type of replication: intra-site RPC, inter-site RPC, and inter-site SMTP. The values are:

  - Replicator intra site packet size (objects)

  - Replicator intra site packet size (bytes)

  - Replicator inter site packet size (objects)

  - Replicator inter site packet size (bytes)

  - Replicator async inter site packet size (objects)

  - Replicator async inter site packet size (bytes)

Synchronous replication computes packet size dynamically, to best use available system memory. Objects/packet starts at 100 for a 100 MB or smaller server and increases to 1000 for servers of a 1 GB or more. Servers of 100 MB or smaller send 1 MB; 1 GB or larger servers send 10 MB. Asynchronous packets are fixed at 100 objects and 1 MB.

Adjust latency. The values are:

- **Replicator notify pause after modify (secs)** to control the number of seconds to wait after a modification occurs on a DC before notifying the first replication partner.

- **Replicator notify pause between DSAs (secs)** to control how much time the replication partner will wait to notify the next replication partners in the replication topology.

Conclusion

The design of a fine-tuned replication topology is key to a large-enterprise Windows 2000-based infrastructure. Because Windows 2000 and many applications depend on the Active Directory, you must carefully plan the replication topology to provide the foundations for disseminating amounts of information that may be very large. Applications that already depend on the Active Directory include:

- The version of DNS provided with Windows 2000, which optionally uses the Active Directory to store its data and uses the replication mechanism to ensure that other DNS servers receive updates.

- Microsoft Exchange 2000 uses the Active Directory to store information about mailboxes and servers.

- You can create solutions that integrate your data with the Active Directory. Applications enabled for Active Directory can modify the schema to add their own object classes, instances of which will replicate using the replication topology already in place.

C H A P T E R   3

Active Directory Database Sizing

By Matthias Leibmann and Andreas Luther, Microsoft Enterprise Services

The Microsoft Windows 2000 Active Directory provides new ways for businesses to use directory services. Previous versions of Windows NT restricted directory use in some functions such as administrating users and user groups. The Windows 2000 Active Directory extends these functions and other capabilities, and opens the use of the directory as a data store and as a means for network services or directory-enabled applications to publish information in an enterprise-wide network.

The Active Directory uses a database as the information store and the same database engine that is used in Microsoft Exchange Server 5.5. The Active Directory is an enterprise-level directory service, meaning that the system scales for deployment across an enterprise-wide network, integrates with existing directories through synchronization, and supports enterprise-class applications. To keep the Active Directory database up to date, domain controllers generate replication network traffic.

For network administrators, this brings up two questions: How do you size server hard-disk space needed by growth of the directory service? And how does the replication and client traffic affect overall network performance? This chapter addresses the first question. Chapter 4 covers replication traffic; Chapter 5 covers client logon and LDAP traffic.

What You'll Find in This Chapter

■ A discussion of the concepts of Active Directory structure and components—an introduction to the basics you need to understand before you can begin planning.

■ Results of sizing tests on single-object changes of all types, on a sample company (to provide a more realistic look at the sorts of quantities and scales involved), on global catalogs, and on Exchange 2000, which is enabled for Active Directory. Results are presented in tables and graphs, and observations are offered on trends and characteristics.

■ Summaries, special considerations, guidelines, and recommendations.

Active Directory Database Architecture and Components

Besides network administration, you can use Active Directory as a back-end for applications. To take advantage of this, some applications that used to use proprietary directories (such as Microsoft Exchange 2000 and SAP's R3 business applications) will move their directory-related information to the Active Directory in new versions.

To understand the impact on hard disk sizing, you have to know how the database manages information storage. The explanation below begins with a brief overview of the database's architecture, then presents statistics on the directory database size.

General Structure

The Windows 2000 Active Directory service runs in the protected trusted domain as part of the Local Security Authority process (LSASS.EXE), which manages authentication packages and authenticates users and services. Running within LSASS.EXE allows Active Directory to manage sensitive information such as account passwords securely.

The Active Directory implementation has three layers: Core Directory Service Agent (DSA), Database Layer (DB), and Extensible Storage Engine (ESE) (Figure 3.1). Additional components on top of these layers provide communication with other internal or external services. The LDAP interface (which conforms to RFC 2222) provides access for LDAP clients such as Windows 2000 workstations or Windows 9*x* workstations with the Active Directory client package. The replication interface provides directory replication with other Active Directory domain controllers. The SAM interface provides security services.

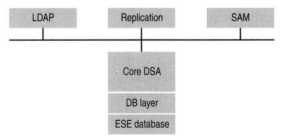

Figure 3.1   Active Directory functional layers.

The core DSA enforces directory semantics, maintains the schema, guarantees and maintains object identity, and enforces data types on attributes. It is also responsible for the class structural and semantic rules, including class inheritance (from abstract and structural classes), auxiliary classes, and enforcement of mandatory properties. All access control routines are implemented as part of the DSA.

Because the ESE database is flat, with no hierarchical namespace, the database layer provides it with the abstraction of an object hierarchy.

A directory object is named by a *distinguished name* (DN) that contains the components of the domain naming system (DNS) name of the domain where the object resides. The *relative distinguished name* (RDN) of an object is the object's name relative to its parent. Each database object has an ObjectGUID (Global Unique Identifier) that is globally unique and cannot be changed after the object is created.

The LDAP interface exposes objects through their distinguished names. Some attributes contain references to other Active Directory objects, such as a user's *manager* attribute. Internally, the value of these attributes is the ObjectGUID of the object they reference. This ensures that a reference always points to the same object, even if that object is renamed or moved. The LDAP interface automatically converts these references to the distinguished name, so when an LDAP client reads these attributes it gets back a distinguished name, not an ObjectGUID.

The ESE database consists of the data table and the link table. The data table contains a relatively small number of *fixed* columns where storage is allocated for the column on every row, and a large number of *tagged* columns, meaning that storage is allocated only if a value is present. The fixed columns are used to maintain the structure of the directory and are generally invisible to clients; the tagged columns contain the attributes that clients see and care about.

Database Structure

The Active Directory Database (NTDS.DIT) contains two tables:

- **Link table**, containing data that represents linked attributes, which contain values referring to other objects in the Active Directory (for example the *MemberOf* attribute on a user object, which contains values that reference groups to which the user belongs). It also is far smaller than the data table and is not discussed further in this chapter.

- **Data table**, containing the rest of the information in the Active Directory: users, groups, application-specific data, and any other data stored in the Active Directory after its installation. In most installations this is far larger than the link and schema tables, so it is discussed in detail in this chapter.

The data table can be thought of as having rows (each representing an instance of an object, such as a *user*) and columns (each representing an attribute in the schema, such as *GivenName*). For each attribute in the schema, the table contains a column, also called a *field*. Field sizes can be *fixed* or *variable*. Fixed-size fields contain an integer or long integer as data type; variable-size fields typically hold string types (for example, Unicode strings). The database allocates only as much space as a variable-size field needs—16 bits for a 1-character Unicode string, 160 bits for a 10-character Unicode string, and so on.

The database space used to store an object depends on the number of attributes for which values are set and the size of the values. For instance, if the administrator creates two user objects (User1 and User2) and sets only the minimum attributes on them, then later adds a 10-character description to User2, the User2 space ends up around 80 bytes bigger than the User1 space (20 bytes for the 10 characters plus metadata on the newly generated attribute).

Database records cannot span database pages, so each object is limited to 8 KB. However, some attribute values of an object don't count fully against this limit. Long, variable-length values can be stored on a different page than the object record, leaving behind only a 9-byte reference. In this way, an object and all its attribute values can be much larger than 8 KB.

Changes to the Database

The Active Directory database is stored in a file named NTDS.DIT. When the directory service needs to access data, LSASS.EXE loads pages from the database file into memory. It reserves a pool of memory for these operations and moves the pages between the database and the pool on a *least recently used* (LRU) basis. Some pages in the memory and in the database file get out of synch whenever the DSA performs a write operation on an object. To correct this condition, all pages in the memory are flushed to the database file every time the database shuts down. The domain controller also swaps pages from the memory back to the hard disk (in the background) whenever it is in an idle or low-load state.

Changes are made to in-memory copies of objects. The act of committing a transaction is what writes the changes to the log file first. Writing the changes to the log file is much faster than writing them to the database and this helps make sure that the change operation is recorded and not lost if the database crashes at that moment. As part of its background work, the database engine continually updates the database file with recently committed changes, getting them from memory directly (not from the log files).

When you perform bulk load operations in the directory (for instance, for performance or scalability tests), you will see that the LSASS.EXE process grows bigger and bigger. This is caused by the database system's memory buffer allocation. The database continues to allocate more memory until the operating system prevents making more buffers available. This can happen when the system approaches 50% of its physical memory limitations. But in order to operate as fast as possible, the database tries to get as much memory as it can. When the database is updated later, the memory buffers are released again, and LSASS.EXE shrinks.

If the domain controller cannot shut down in an orderly fashion (which usually means a power failure) the database is left out-of-date because the most recent in-memory pages could not be written to the disk. Transaction logs are used to recover the database. Any change made to the database is also appended to the current log file, and its disk image is always kept up to date. The database change process is (see Figure 3.2):

1. LSASS.EXE writes the change to the log file
2. LSASS.EXE writes the change to a database page in the memory buffer
3. LSASS.EXE confirms the transaction
4. The change is written to the disk (at shutdown, or at idle time)

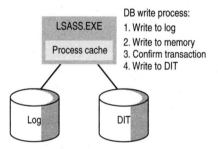

Figure 3.2   Database change process.

If a directory service halt prevents the database file from being successfully flushed to disk, the database performs a recovery on the next restart. Essentially, the database reads through the log files in order and reapplies changes until the database is once again consistent and up-to-date.

The ESE maintains transaction logging in a circular mode. That means every time the log-file *edb.log* is filled with transactional data, it is renamed to *edbXXXXX.log* and a new 10-MB *edb.log* file is created. Old log files are numbered sequentially and log files are always 10 MB regardless of how many transactions have been recorded in them. ESE does not maintain all previous transaction log files. Instead the Garbage Collection Process (explained below) deletes old log files during its housekeeping run, freeing up disc space again.

Note   This differs from Microsoft Exchange Server, which allows you to use non-circular database transaction logging, which deletes old log-files and thus allows you to implement differential and incremental backups.

Active Directory runs full-backups, so you don't have to keep old log files. Exchange stores private database information on one Exchange server, but Active Directory replicates all information to all domain controllers in the same domain—when you restore domain controllers you can always back-fill them from their replication partners. The backup process saves the directory database file along with the current log files. If you recover later, transactions that happened during the time between the last full backup and the restore are lost.

To enhance performance on domain controllers that must handle high request rates, you should hold the Windows 2000 operating system on one hard drive, the Active Directory database file on a second, and the log files on a third. Always use mirrored drives on domain controllers to prevent data loss from a hard-drive crash.

Garbage Collection

Garbage collection is a housekeeping process that runs on every domain controller, deleting objects and files no longer needed by the directory service. It runs 15 minutes after a DC reboot, then after every 12 hours of continuous operation. It deletes unneeded log files deletes tombstones, and defragments the database.

Deleting Unneeded Log Files

A log file is unneeded once all changes (and all previous log files) have been written to the database file.

Deleting Tombstones

Rather than physically delete objects from the database, the directory service removes most attributes and tags the object as being in the *tombstone* state; this alerts replication partners that the object was deleted. The database removes tombstones after an interval (the *tombstone lifetime*). The default is 60 days and you should not change it: tombstones are used to replicate object deletions. If you restore a directory server from a backup tape older than the tombstone lifetime, the server does not learn of some deletions, leading to inconsistencies between domain controllers. (The *Restore* utility tries to prevent this, but it can't prevent you from changing tombstone lifetime.) To accommodate occasional disruption of replication due to communication failures, keep tombstone lifetime substantially longer than the expected replication latency.

Database Defragmentation

To update the database file, the database system uses the quickest way, which is not always the most efficient way to fill database pages. Defragmentation rearranges how the data is written in the database. Online defragmentation does not reduce database file size, but it makes more space available for new objects.

You can also defragment the database file offline. Take the domain controller offline, boot it into directory services repair mode (use the F8 key at system start-up), and use NTDSUTIL.EXE. This creates a second, defragmented version of the database file that is considerably smaller than the original database file. You can at this point choose which database file you want to use on the domain controller.

Note   NTDSUTIL reads parameters from the command line. In that way it's very easy to automate specific tasks by writing command files. You can use multiple strings separated by spaces in one NTDSUTIL parameter, but put the expression in quotes so NTDSUTIL parses the commands correctly. For example, you can compact a database with:

```
ntdsutil.exe files "compact to e:\" q q
```

This runs NTDSUTIL, defragments the database, and quits NTDSUTIL again.

Recommendation: Use offline defragmentation only when you know database contents have shrunk considerably (for instance, when a global catalog server becomes a normal domain controller) and you need to reclaim space for other uses. Keep the original NTDS.DIT file until the domain controller has restarted with the defragmented file. Once you have no doubts that the directory database is in a consistent state, you can delete the original (fragmented) database file.

To test how the database grows when a specific set of objects is loaded, you have to remember:

1. When the directory is loaded with objects, the database is in a fragmented state, making it impossible to tell how much space the objects really consume in the database file.

2. Online defragmentation makes space available, but does not shrink the database file. It optimizes performance by freeing up inefficiently used database pages for reuse.

3. Only offline defragmentation gives you a clear picture of the space consumption.

In a production environment, you should always select online defragmentation: it leads to the same results as the offline process and does not require taking the machine offline. For database growth testing, however, you should defragment the directory database offline after a bulk load of objects, because only the offline defragmented version of the directory database allows you to assess how much space is consumed. To stress these differences, some of the following database load tests show results for both the fragmented and the offline defragmented versions of the database file.

Active Directory Database Sizing Tests—Single Objects

This section shows the results of tests that load objects into the Active Directory. In general, two different kinds of tests were performed. The first series loaded the database with a large number of identical objects to show how the database grows when objects are loaded, and how much space is consumed for these object types. For a more real-life approach, the second series created a blueprint of a company with user objects, group objects and files shares. It was designed to show how the database grows for small, medium, and large companies.

Most of the tests used several steps for the object load operation. The empty database size was recorded, then the first set of objects was loaded. An offline defragmentation was performed, then the fragmented and the defragmented versions of the database were measured. The fragmented version was used when the next set of objects was loaded.

The test procedures were automated as much as possible. Command scripts and Visual Basic applications were written to populate the directory, add attributes to objects in the directory, reboot the machine in repair mode, and write the results to .CSV files. All of those tools and a description of how they work and should be set up (a README file) are included on the CD that accompanies this book, in the *Capacity Planning Tools* folder.

Calculating Growth and Object Sizes

For each table the Object Size based on the growth of the DIT was calculated this way:

```
(Compressed DIT size [KBytes] - Compressed DIT Start [KBytes]) / Number
Of Objects x 1024 = Object Size [bytes]
```

Single Object Type Loads

The single object load tests concentrated on finding out how database size increases relative to increases in attribute value size. As pointed out above, the database engine consumes space only for attributes for which values are set, so the number of attributes that have values for an object makes a big difference in that object's size. The tests for user and organizational unit (OU) objects set only mandatory attributes—those that must contain value(s) so that the directory service can create the object. Later tests show how adding attributes to an object affects object size.

User Objects

Obviously, user objects play a big role in any directory deployment, so if you want to know how big the database will grow you need know how big these objects are. The test loaded the database (**DB** in the table columns) with up to 1,000,000 users, in increments of 100,000 (see Figure 3.3 and the table that follows).

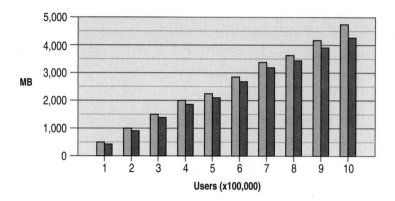

MB

Users (x100,000)

Figure 3. 3   Database file growth as function of user objects.

Users	Fragmented database			Defragmented database		
	Kbytes/DB	Growth	Bytes/User	Kbytes/DB	Growth	Bytes/User
0	10,256			10,256		
100,000	559,120	548,864	5,620	436,240	425,984	4,362
200,000	1,095,696	536,576	5,557	864,272	428,032	4,373
300,000	1,576,976	481,280	5,348	1,290,256	425,984	4,369
400,000	2,021,392	444,416	5,149	1,716,240	425,984	4,367
500,000	2,353,168	331,776	4,798	2,142,224	425,984	4,366
600,000	2,897,936	544,768	4,928	2,568,208	425,984	4,366
700,000	3,407,888	509,952	4,970	2,994,192	425,984	4,365
800,000	3,809,296	401,408	4,863	3,420,176	425,984	4,365
900,000	4,282,384	473,088	4,861	3,848,208	428,032	4,367
1,000,000	4,823,056	540,672	4,928	4,274,192	425,984	4,366

The database file growth pattern is linear. The growth between two load operations is always almost identical: approximately 425,000 Kbytes in the defragmented version. However the fragmented growth varies between 331,000 and 548,000.

This shows very well how the online defragmentation works. The tests were conducted over a few days: a load iteration would be performed and the resulting file size was checked the next day, by which time online defragmentation had kicked in and rearranged the objects in the database. This did not shrink the database file size, but it made space available for new objects. Therefore, the file is sometimes bigger for the fragmented version. After online defragmentation and the next set of objects was loaded, the database file space freed up by the defragmentation could be used, so the additional growth is not much different from the growth of the defragmented database version.

Loading 1,000,000 users (with only mandatory attributes set) in the Active Directory takes about 4 GB. To compute the size of one user object, subtract the size of an empty store, and then divide the store size by the number of users. In this case, one user object is 4,366 bytes.

Adding Attributes

The next series of tests enlarged the user objects with 1 to 30 additional attributes defined in the schema as string value attributes. Each string was filled with 10 characters.

The test began with a store containing 100,000 user objects with only the mandatory attributes set. The server was demoted to a non-domain controller, promoted back, and loaded with 100,000 user objects again, this time with one additional attribute. This was repeated with two attributes and so on.

Additional attributes with user object results table.

# ExtAttr.	Kbytes/DB	Bytes/User	DB/Defrag	Bytes/User	Bytes/Attr.
0	10,256		10,256		
1	540,688	5,432	430,080	4,404	38
2	561,168	5,641	434,176	4,446	40
3	561,168	5,641	434,176	4,446	27
4	565,264	5,683	438,272	4,488	30
5	567,312	5,704	442,368	4,530	33
6	571,408	5,746	442,368	4,530	27
7	489,488	4,907	448,512	4,593	32
8	499,728	5,012	448,512	4,593	28
9	499,728	5,012	454,656	4,656	32
10	583,696	5,872	540,672	5,536	117
11	591,888	5,956	540,672	5,536	106
12	591,888	5,956	548,864	5,620	105
13	1,007,632	10,213	548,864	5,620	96
14	602,128	6,061	559,104	5,725	97
15	602,128	6,061	559,104	5,725	91
16	604,176	6,082	559,104	5,725	85
17	606,224	6,103	561,152	5,746	81
18	626,704	6,312	571,392	5,851	83
19	618,512	6,229	571,392	5,851	78

(continued)

# ExtAttr.	Kbytes/DB	Bytes/User	DB/Defrag	Bytes/User	Bytes/Attr.
20	618,512	6,229	571,392	5,851	74
21	616,464	6,208	571,392	5,851	71
22	616,464	6,208	573,440	5,872	68
23	720,912	7,277	587,776	6,019	72
24	630,800	6,354	587,776	6,019	69
25	630,800	6,354	587,776	6,019	66
26	630,800	6,354	587,776	6,019	64
27	630,800	6,354	587,776	6,019	61
28	1,200,144	12,184	747,520	7,655	117
29	1,138,704	11,555	749,568	7,676	114
30	1,200,144	12,184	749,568	7,676	110

The fragmented version of the database performs big jumps in size at some steps, and smaller jumps at others. This is because instead of storing data efficiently right away, the ESE database writes the data out as fast as possible, which leads to database fragmentation and optimizes space consumption in single database pages as part of the online database defragmentation process. This process will free up space in the database. The growth of the defragmented database is very linear. On average, an additional 10-character string attribute adds approximately 100 bytes to the object size (Figure 3.4).

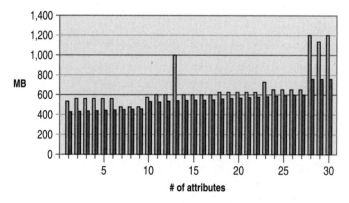

Figure 3.4   Adding attributes to user objects.

Organizational Units

User objects in the Active Directory are larger than most other objects because they contain many mandatory attributes.

Information in the Active Directory is organized in a hierarchy using organizational units (OUs). The table below illustrates the effect of OU objects on database size and shows that the growth pattern again is very linear. The size of one organizational unit is 1,992 Bytes.

OU test results table.

#OUs	Fragmented database			Defragmented database		
	Kbytes/DB	Growth	Bytes/Ou	Kbytes/DB	Growth	Bytes/Ou
0	10,256			10,256		
1,000	12,304	2,048	2,097	12,304	2,048	2,097
2,000	14,352	2,048	2,097	14,352	2,048	2,097
3,000	16,400	2,048	2,097	14,352	0	1,398
4,000	18,448	2,048	2,097	16,400	2,048	1,573
5,000	20,496	2,048	2,097	18,448	2,048	1,678
6,000	22,544	2,048	2,097	22,544	4,096	2,097
7,000	24,592	2,048	2,097	24,592	2,048	2,097
8,000	26,640	2,048	2,097	26,640	2,048	2,097
9,000	28,688	2,048	2,097	26,640	0	1,864
10,000	30,736	2,048	2,097	28,688	2,048	1,887
11,000	32,784	2,048	2,097	30,736	2,048	1,907
12,000	34,832	2,048	2,097	32,784	2,048	1,922
13,000	36,880	2,048	2,097	34,832	2,048	1,936
14,000	38,928	2,048	2,097	36,880	2,048	1,947
15,000	40,976	2,048	2,097	38,928	2,048	1,957
16,000	43,024	2,048	2,097	40,976	2,048	1,966
17,000	45,072	2,048	2,097	43,024	2,048	1,974
18,000	49,168	4,096	2,214	45,072	2,048	1,981
19,000	49,168	0	2,097	47,120	2,048	1,987
20,000	51,216	2,048	2,097	49,168	2,048	1,992

Groups

Groups represent a flexible management mechanism in Active Directory. Two types are implemented: *security groups,* which are used to grant permissions to resources, and *distribution groups*, which are used to build sets of related users for organizational purposes without implementing security (for example, to build distribution lists in messaging environments).

At first look, you would think the types differ significantly when it comes to sizing, but this is not the case. It's true that security groups are used to grant or deny access to resources, and that they must therefore implement a SID attribute in the object. But distribution groups also implement the SID attribute when they are created; this allows administrators to change the status of groups. For instance, you can create a security group then change it to a distribution group. If you later changed it back to a security group, it must carry the same SID as before. Size is not affected by group scope (universal, global, or local) either, because scope is implemented as a single attribute that simply flags the group as belonging to one of the three categories.

Empty Security Groups sizing

Tests for measuring security group sizing first created a store with 100,000 users (only mandatory attributes set). Then several iterations created global security groups with differing numbers of members, so that overhead per group member could be calculated. After each iteration the directory was reset with the 100,000 users store. The tests began by creating 10,000 empty groups, to get the size of the group object itself. Size of one security group object: 2,097 bytes.

Empty global security groups

Groups	Fragmented database			Defragmented database		
	DB/KBytes	Growth	Bytes/Group	DB/KBytes	Growth	Bytes/Group
0	559,120			436,240		
1,000	561,168	2,048	2,097	438,288	2,048	2,097
2,000	563,216	2,048	2,097	440,336	2,048	2,097
3,000	563,216	0	1,398	442,384	2,048	2,097
4,000	565,264	2,048	1,573	444,432	2,048	2,097
5,000	567,312	2,048	1,678	448,528	4,096	2,517
6,000	569,360	2,048	1,748	450,576	2,048	2,447
7,000	571,408	2,048	1,798	452,624	2,048	2,397
8,000	573,456	2,048	1,835	454,720	2,096	2,365
9,000	577,552	4,096	2,097	456,720	2,000	2,330
10,000	579,600	2,048	2,097	456,720	0	2,097

Adding Members to Groups

Members of a group are stored in the group object as a single multi-valued attribute. To get the overhead for adding members to a group, the test created from 1,000 to 5,000 groups, adding from 10 to 500 users per group.

The table below shows results in Kbytes of the compressed database: 100,000 users with mandatory attributes included, which is compressed to 436,240 Kbytes.

Members added per group	1,000 Groups	2000 Groups	3,000 Groups	4000 Groups	5,000 Groups
10	440,336	442,384	446,480	448,528	452,624
20	440,336	444,432	448,528	452,624	456,720
30	440,336	444,432	450,576	454,672	458,768
40	442,384	446,480	452,624	456,720	462,864
50	442,384	448,528	454,672	460,816	466,960
60	442,384	450,576	456,720	462,864	471,056
70	444,432	450,576	458,768	464,912	473,104
80	444,432	452,624	460,816	469,008	477,200
90	444,432	454,672	462,864	471,056	481,296
100	446,480	454,672	464,912	475,152	485,392
250	454,672	473,104	491,536	509,968	528,400
500					608,272

Here are the details for the 5000 Groups column:

	Fragmented database		Defragmented database		
Members	DB/KBytes	Bytes/Member	DB/KBytes	Growth	Bytes/Member
0	559,120		436,240		
10	559,120	na	452,624	16,384	336
20	575,504	na	456,720	4,096	210
30	569,360	na	458,768	2,048	154
40	585,744	na	462,864	4,096	136
50	589,840	na	466,960	4,096	126
60	598,032	na	471,056	4,096	119
70	587,792	na	473,104	2,048	108
80	604,176	115	477,200	4,096	105
90	608,272	112	481,296	4,096	103
100	616,464	117	485,392	4,096	101
250	663,568	86	528,400	43,008	75
500	768,448	86	608,272	79,872	70

The overhead for each additional member depends on the number of group members. For small groups with approximately 20 members, 200 bytes is a good ballpark figure. For larger groups, the number goes down to 70 bytes.

Note The tests were run on different machines, so sizing for the fragmented database varies because of different Jet table fillings and garbage collection intervals. When the databases on the different machines are defragmented again, the results again become predictable.

Empty Distribution Groups Sizing

Distribution group sizing was tested using pretty much the same method. A store with 100,000 contacts was created, then distribution groups with 100, 200, and 300 contacts as members were created. As expected, the results show no differences in group size or overhead per member, because all group objects are instantiated from the same object class, and membership is a multi-valued attribute for all group objects. Overhead per distribution group is 2,097 bytes.

	Fragmented database			Defragmented database		
DLs	DB/Kbytes	Growth	Bytes/DL	DB/Kbytes	Growth	Bytes/DL
0	192,528			174,096		
1,000	194,576	2,048	2,097	176,144	2,048	2,097
2,000	198,672	4,096	3,146	178,192	2,048	2,097
3,000	200,720	2,048	2,796	180,240	2,048	2,097
4,000	202,768	2,048	2,621	182,288	2,048	2,097
5,000	204,816	2,048	2,517	184,336	2,048	2,097
6,000	206,864	2,048	2,447	186,384	2,048	2,097
7,000	208,912	2,048	2,397	190,480	4,096	2,397
8,000	213,008	4,096	2,621	190,480	0	2,097
9,000	215,056	2,048	2,563	194,576	4,096	2,330
10,000	217,104	2,048	2,517	194,576	0	2,097

Adding Members to Distribution Group

100 members per distribution group

	Fragmented database			Defragmented database		
Number of DLs	DB/Kbytes	Growth	Bytes/ Member	DB/Kbytes	Growth	Bytes/ Member
0	192,528			174,096		
1,000	204,816	12,288	126	182,288	8,192	84
2,000	217,104	12,288	126	192,528	10,240	94

(continued)

Number of DLs	Fragmented database			Defragmented database		
	DB/Kbytes	Growth	Bytes/Member	DB/Kbytes	Growth	Bytes/Member
3,000	229,392	12,288	126	202,768	10,240	98
4,000	241,680	12,288	126	213,008	10,240	100
5,000	253,968	12,288	126	223,248	10,240	101
6,000	264,208	10,240	122	233,488	10,240	101
7,000	276,496	12,288	123	241,680	8,192	99
8,000	288,784	12,288	123	251,920	10,240	100
9,000	301,072	12,288	123	262,160	10,240	100
10,000	313,360	12,288	124	272,400	10,240	101

200 members per distribution group

Number of DLs	Fragmented database			Defragmented database		
	DB/Kbytes	Growth	Bytes/Member	DB/Kbytes	Growth	Bytes/Member
0	192,528			174,096		
1,000	213,008	20,480	105	190,480	16,384	84
2,000	235,536	22,528	110	206,864	16,384	84
3,000	256,016	20,480	108	225,296	18,432	87
4,000	278,544	22,528	110	241,680	16,384	87
5,000	299,024	20,480	109	260,112	18,432	88
6,000	319,504	20,480	108	276,496	16,384	87
7,000	339,984	20,480	108	292,880	16,384	87
8,000	362,512	22,528	109	309,264	16,384	87
9,000	385,040	22,528	110	327,696	18,432	87
10,000	405,520	20,480	109	344,080	16,384	87

300 members per distribution group

Number of DLs	Fragmented database			Defragmented database		
	DB/Kbytes	Growth	Bytes/ Member	DB/Kbytes	Growth	Bytes/ Member
0	192,528			174,096		
1,000	221,200	28,672	98	196,624	22,528	77
2,000	249,872	28,672	98	217,104	20,480	73
3,000	280,592	30,720	100	239,632	22,528	75
4,000	309,264	28,672	100	262,160	22,528	75
5,000	337,936	28,672	99	284,688	22,528	75
6,000	366,608	28,672	99	307,216	22,528	76
7,000	397,328	30,720	100	329,744	22,528	76
8,000	426,000	28,672	100	350,224	20,480	75
9,000	454,672	28,672	99	372,752	22,528	75
10,000	485,392	30,720	100	395,280	22,528	75

Contacts

Contacts (such as lists of external partners or customers) are another important object for enterprise directories. Contacts are not security principals, so they have a smaller footprint than users. To test contact sizing, 100,000 contacts with only mandatory attributes were created. Then, for each attribute added, bytes were added based on the overhead/attribute table above. The results show linear scaling of the Active Directory database. Size per contact is 1,678 bytes. (See Figure 3.5.)

# of Contacts	Fragmented database			Defragmented database		
	DB/KBytes	Growth	Bytes/ Contact	DB/KBytes	Growth	Bytes/ Contact
0	10,256			10,256		
10,000	28,688	18,432	1,887	26,640	16,384	1,678
20,000	47,120	18,432	1,887	43,024	16,384	1,678
30,000	63,504	16,384	1,818	59,408	16,384	1,678
40,000	81,936	18,432	1,835	75,792	16,384	1,678
50,000	98,320	16,384	1,804	92,176	16,384	1,678
60,000	116,752	18,432	1,818	108,560	16,384	1,678
70,000	135,184	18,432	1,828	124,944	16,384	1,678
80,000	153,616	18,432	1,835	141,328	16,384	1,678
90,000	170,000	16,384	1,818	157,712	16,384	1,678
100,000	188,432	18,432	1,825	174,096	16,384	1,678

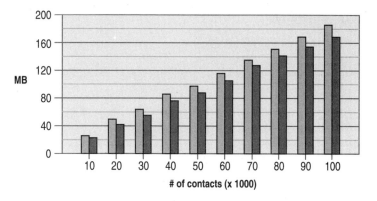

Figure 3.5   Adding attributes to contacts.

Storing Public Key Certificates in the Active Directory

Many users will want to use public key certificates for authentication and secure e-mail. Public keys are often much larger than any other attribute in the directory and it is not unusual to find users with more than one public key, each serving a different purpose (one for e-mail, another for authentication, etc.). For this reason, it is very important to consider public key support in determining database size in your enterprise.

The next test shows how much bigger user objects grow when public keys are deployed. For this test a store was loaded with 100,000 users, then three X.509 v3 certificates were deployed in three steps. The store size before and after the deployment is shown. A Windows 2000 Certificate Server issued this certificate; the size of the certificate stored as a file is 1,294 bytes. The growth of the user object per certificate is bigger than the size of the certificate is 2,181 bytes.

Objects used to test growth with public keys.

# Certificates	0	1	2	3
DB/Kbytes	555,024	647,184	860,176	1,071,120
Growth		92,160	212,992	210,944
Bytes/ User	5,578	6,522	8,703	10,863
Growth/User		944	2,181	2,160
DB/Kbytes	434,192	577,552	790,544	1,003,536
Growth		143,360	212,992	212,992
Bytes/ User	4,341	5,809	7,990	10,171
Growth/User		1,468	2,181	2,181

Printers and Volumes

The final single-object test measured the effect of printer and volume objects on Active Directory Database size. The test created 20,000 printers then created volume objects in 20 steps. The two tables below show the results. Size per printer object is 2,412 bytes. Size per volume object is 1,573 bytes. Again, the tables show a linear scaling in the Active Directory.

Printers.

	Fragmented database			Defragmented database		
# Printers	DB/Kbytes	Growth	Bytes/ Printer	DB/Kbytes	Growth	Bytes/ Printer
0	10,256			10,256		
1,000	12,304	2,048	2,097	10,256	0	0
2,000	14,352	2,048	2,097	14,352	4,096	2,097
3,000	18,448	4,096	2,796	16,400	2,048	2,097
4,000	20,496	2,048	2,621	18,448	2,048	2,097
5,000	22,544	2,048	2,517	20,496	2,048	2,097
6,000	24,592	2,048	2,447	22,544	2,048	2,097
7,000	28,688	4,096	2,696	26,640	4,096	2,397
8,000	30,736	2,048	2,621	28,688	2,048	2,359
9,000	32,784	2,048	2,563	30,736	2,048	2,330
10,000	36,880	4,096	2,726	32,784	2,048	2,307
11,000	38,928	2,048	2,669	34,832	2,048	2,288
12,000	40,976	2,048	2,621	36,880	2,048	2,272
13,000	43,024	2,048	2,581	38,928	2,048	2,258
14,000	45,072	2,048	2,547	43,024	4,096	2,397
15,000	49,168	4,096	2,656	45,072	2,048	2,377
16,000	51,216	2,048	2,621	47,120	2,048	2,359
17,000	53,264	2,048	2,591	49,168	2,048	2,344
18,000	57,360	4,096	2,680	51,216	2,048	2,330
19,000	59,408	2,048	2,649	55,312	4,096	2,428
20,000	61,456	2,048	2,621	57,360	2,048	2,412

Volumes.

# of Volumes	Fragmented database			Defragmented database		
	DB/Kbytes	Growth	Bytes/ Volume	DB/Kbytes	Growth	Bytes/ Volume
0	10,256			10,256		
1,000	10,256	0	0	10,256	0	0
2,000	12,304	2,048	1,049	12,304	2,048	1,049
3,000	14,352	2,048	1,398	12,304	0	699
4,000	16,400	2,048	1,573	14,352	2,048	1,049
5,000	18,448	2,048	1,678	16,400	2,048	1,258
6,000	20,496	2,048	1,748	18,448	2,048	1,398
7,000	22,544	2,048	1,798	20,496	2,048	1,498
8,000	24,592	2,048	1,835	22,544	2,048	1,573
9,000	26,640	2,048	1,864	22,544	0	1,398
10,000	28,688	2,048	1,887	24,592	2,048	1,468
11,000	28,688	0	1,716	26,640	2,048	1,525
12,000	30,736	2,048	1,748	28,688	2,048	1,573
13,000	32,784	2,048	1,775	30,736	2,048	1,613
14,000	34,832	2,048	1,798	30,736	0	1,498
15,000	36,880	2,048	1,818	32,784	2,048	1,538
16,000	38,928	2,048	1,835	34,832	2,048	1,573
17,000	40,976	2,048	1,850	36,880	2,048	1,604
18,000	40,976	0	1,748	36,880	0	1,515
19,000	43,024	2,048	1,766	38,928	2,048	1,545
20,000	45,072	2,048	1,783	40,976	2,048	1,573

Storing BLOBS in the Active Directory

Binary objects (such as bitmaps of photos) can also be represented within the Active Directory. To test their impact on database size, a 100,000-user store with mandatory attributes was created, then a 16.0-K bitmap (a realistic size for a photograph) was imported to every user (Figure 3.6). Growth of user object was 26,068 bytes. Subtracting the 16.9 K (the bitmap) from the 21,726 bytes (21.2 K) shows an additional overhead of 4.3 K, or approximately 25% per binary blob.

Figure 3.6   Bitmap imported to 100,000 users.

Binary data object growth with bitmaps.

	Fragmented database			
# Pictures	DB/Kbytes	Growth	Bytes/User	Growth/User
0	550,928		5,536	
1	3,051,536	2,500,608	25,606	20,070

	Defragmented database			
# Pictures	DB/Kbytes	Growth	Bytes/User	Growth/User
0	434,192		4,341	
1	2,979,856	2,545,664	26,068	21,726

Active Directory Database Sizing Tests—Sample Company

Modeling a customer database provides a more realistic look at how these changes affect database size. Tests were conducted on a sample company consisting of the directory objects and quantities shown below:

Sample company objects.

User	100,000
Computers	100,000
Groups	10,000
Items per group	25
Printers	10,000
Volumes	10,000

The objects were first loaded with mandatory attributes, then with additional attributes in subsequent tests. The attributes were assigned 10 characters.

Sample Company with Minimum Properties

The first test looked at the growth pattern as attributes were loaded in stages representing 10% of the original sample (10% represents 10,000 users, 10,000 workstation accounts, 1,000 groups with 25 members each, 1,000 printers, and 1,000 volumes).

Minimum properties growth test results.

% Sample Company	Fragmented database		Defragmented database	
	DB/Kbytes	Growth	DB/Kbytes	Growth
0	10,256		10,256	
10%	114,704	104,448	98,320	88,064
20%	217,104	102,400	184,336	86,016
30%	305,168	88,064	272,400	88,064
40%	397,328	92,160	360,464	88,064
50%	495,632	98,304	448,528	88,064
60%	591,888	96,256	534,544	86,016
70%	686,096	94,208	622,608	88,064
80%	782,352	96,256	708,624	86,016
90%	876,560	94,208	798,736	90,112
100%	978,960	102,400	884,752	86,016

Again, database growth is linear and thus predictable. In the fragmented state, the growth for a 10% increase is around 102,400 K. In the defragmented state, it is around slightly below the high of 90,112 K in most cases.

Sample Company with Custom Attributes

The next table shows the effect of adding attributes. For user objects, 30 attributes were chosen (first name, last name, office number, phone number, and so on); for workstations, 8 attributes were added; for groups and volumes, 4; for printers, 15. All attributes were filled with 10-character strings. For a complete list of the attributes used, see the document SampleCompanyAttributeSet.doc on the CD that accompanies this book.

Custom properties results.

% Sample Company	Fragmented database		Defragmented database	
	DB/Kbytes	**Growth**	**DB/Kbytes**	**Growth**
0	10,256		10,256	
10%	198,672	188,416	139,280	129,024
20%	325,648	126,976	268,304	129,024
30%	462,864	137,216	397,328	129,024
40%	602,128	139,264	526,352	129,024
50%	731,152	129,024	655,376	129,024
60%	870,416	139,264	784,400	129,024
70%	1,011,728	141,312	913,424	129,024
80%	1,150,992	139,264	1,042,448	129,024
90%	1,286,160	135,168	1,171,472	129,024
100%	1,423,376	137,216	1,300,496	129,024

Again: linear growth—no database explosion. In the graphic representation in Figure 3.7, the left bar in each pair shows the database size in Kb; the smaller bar shows database growth from step to step.

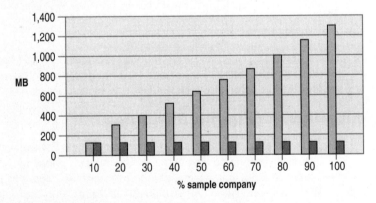

Figure 3.7　Custom properties results graph.

Access Control Entries

The Active Directory uses *static inheritance* for access control entries. This means that every object contains the access control list (ACL) that applies to it. When a new set of access control entries (ACEs) or deny ACEs are set on a container level, they are pushed from the container level down to all child objects that are configured to inherit ACEs from their parent. This is done because it obviously is much faster to get access rights from the object itself than to traverse a whole tree but it does cause objects to take up slightly more space in the directory.

A good practice is to delegate access rights on directory objects only to *user groups* and not to *single users*. This way only a single ACE is written to objects that inherit from their parent. When more users need to receive the same rights on children of an OU, the users are added to the group that already has the necessary rights—no additional ACE is written to the children of the OU.

For the following tests, a domain controller was loaded with 10 OUs, and 100,000 users (each OU has 10,000 users). Next, full access control on all objects in the whole domain was granted to one group and the resulting size of the database was noted. In the next step, the same delegation was repeated, this time to a different group, and so on. The tests went up to 20 access control entries. The table below shows a subset of the results:

Access control entry growth results (extract).

| Number of ACEs | DB/Kbytes | | Bytes/Users | Bytes/ACE |
	Fragmented database	Defragmented database		
0			4,362	
1	667,664	436,240	4,467	105
2	677,904	440,336	4,509	74
3	677,904	440,336	4,509	49
4	677,904	440,336	4,509	37
5	677,904	440,336	4,509	29
6	677,904	481,296	4,928	94
7	677,904	481,296	4,928	81
8	677,904	481,296	4,928	71
9	677,904	481,296	4,928	63
10	677,904	481,296	4,928	57
11	677,904	483,344	4,949	53
12	677,904	483,344	4,949	49
13	677,904	483,344	4,949	45
14	677,904	483,344	4,949	42
15	677,904	483,344	4,949	39
16	677,904	552,976	5,662	81
17	677,904	552,976	5,662	76

(continued)

| Number of ACEs | DB/Kbytes | | Bytes/Users | Bytes/ACE |
	Fragmented database	Defragmented database		
18	677,904	552,976	5,662	72
19	677,904	552,976	5,662	68
20	677,904	552,976	5,662	65
21	677,904	552,976	5,662	62
22	677,904	552,976	5,662	59
23	677,904	552,976	5,662	57
24	677,904	552,976	5,662	54
25	677,904	552,976	5,662	52

The defragmented version of the database shows that user object growth averaged about 60 bytes/ACE. This is less than 5% of the size of a user object that is filled with mandatory attributes only. Adding even one attribute requires more space (100 bytes).

Reclaiming Space in the Database

As pointed out above, when objects are deleted in the directory service, the data is not released from the database immediately; instead the deleted object is transformed into a tombstone. When tombstones expire (after the tombstone lifetime), the space can be reused. Although online defragmentation makes the space available again, the database size still does not shrink unless offline defragmentation is used.

The next test examined how space is made available for new objects again. It began with database loaded with a full copy of the sample company, then went through three steps:

1. 50% of the company was deleted
2. The database was loaded again in 10% steps until it reached the original size
3. An additional 10% was loaded

In parallel, the test also measured the effect of tombstones on a GC that is a domain controller in a different domain.

Note   To speed up tombstone deletion, you can set two attributes with ADSIEDIT (part of the *Microsoft Windows 2000 Resource Kit*) under this object in the Configuration-naming context:

```
cn=directory service, cn=windows nt, cn=services
    tombstoneLifetime
    garbageColPeriod
```

The first (tombstoneLifetime) determines how long tombstones will reside in the Active Directory before the Garbage Collector removes them physically from the store. The default setting is 60 days, and for this test it was set to its minimum—2 days. Then the date was set to the third day after the day of the test, in case the machines rebooted. The second (garbageColPeriod) determines the interval after which the Garbage Collector activates. Because these tests were run over night, there was no need to set this attribute. (See Figure 3.8 on the following page.)

Note   Do not take changing tombstone lifetime lightly. Tombstones are used to replicate the fact that objects have been deleted, and the removal of tombstones before they are replicated can create inconsistencies in the databases of replication partners. Domain controller backup schedules are especially important. The lifetime of a backup tape should equal tombstone lifetime. If backup tapes are older than the configured tombstone lifetime you should not use those tapes to restore a domain controller. It is good practice not to change the tombstone lifetime in production environments, although it is acceptable in a lab during testing.

Reclaimed space results.

% of Sample Company	Child Domain Controller		Growth
	DIT fragmented/Kbytes	DIT defragmented/Kbytes	
0	10,256	10,256	
100%	1,570,832	**1,300,496**	1,290,240
50% & tombstones	1,601,552	1,134,608	-165,888
50% & NO tombstones	1,601,552	655,376	-479,232
60%	1,601,552	784,400	129,024
70%	1,601,552	913,424	129,024
80%	1,601,552	1,042,448	129,024
90%	1,601,552	1,171,472	129,024
100%	1,601,552	**1,300,496**	129,024
110%	1,601,552	1,429,520	129,024

% of Sample Company	Root Domain Controller (Global Catalog)		Growth
	DIT fragmented/Kbytes	DIT defragmented/Kbytes	
0	10,256	10,256	
100%	770,064	**710,672**	700,416
50% & tombstones	774,160	614,416	-96,256

(continued)

% of Sample Company	Root Domain Controller (Global Catalog)		Growth
	DIT fragmented/Kbytes	DIT defragmented/Kbytes	
50% & NO tombstones	774,160	362,512	-251,904
60%	774,160	430,096	67,584
70%	774,160	501,776	71,680
80%	774,160	569,360	67,584
90%	774,160	641,040	71,680
100%	774,160	**710,672**	69,632
110%	845,840	780,304	69,632

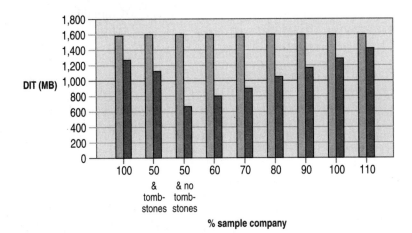

Figure 3.8   Reclaimed space test results.

After the objects were deleted, the size of the defragmented database was measured twice: right after the delete and after the tombstone lifetime had expired. The first size indicates how much space is regained when the objects still exist as tombstones but some attributes have already been deleted. The results show that after the delete operation, the database retains its size even though a huge number of objects are loaded again. There is only a small growth before the original size is reached again.

The defragmented version of the database shrinks by 50% percent after the delete, then grows following the same pattern as for the original load. When more loads are performed over 100%, space is consumed in the same manner.

What does this mean for directory service administrators? In a domain controller's first 60 days (60 is the default tombstone lifetime), the database will only grow, even if a large number of objects are deleted. After 60 days, the database will either stay the same size or grow slightly. The fact that the file doesn't shrink after objects are deleted does not mean, however, that new space has not been made available.

Summary of Database Sizing Tests

Guidelines for assessing Active Directory database size:

1. In the chart, find your company's size and database size.

2. Compare the objects you want to use and the number of objects used in the tests. If you have additional objects that are security principals, add 4,400 bytes for each; if they are not security principals (such as OUs) add 2,000 bytes.

3. Compare the number of attributes you set on the objects with the test numbers. For additional attributes, add 100 bytes per attribute. For binary data, such as bitmaps, add the file size plus a spare buffer of 25% of the file size.

4. To be prepared for additional objects in the future and for tombstones, at least *double* your estimate now. In fact, if you are thinking about deploying applications in the future that use the Active Directory as a data store, 3 – 4 times as much is a more appropriate factor. Remember, adding a certificate to users adds 2,181 bytes. Some messaging applications might add SMIME certificates. Buying more server hardware up front might be expensive, but adding hardware later can be even more painful.

5. Access control entries add around 60 bytes per entry to each object. Consider using groups for access delegation, then add users only to the predefined groups.

Active Directory Database Sizing Tests—Global Catalog Servers

This test investigates the additional storage resources a domain controller requires when it serves as a global catalog (GC) server—a domain controller that holds a partial replica of all domain naming contexts in the enterprise, in addition to the standard Schema, Configuration, and full Domain naming context of the domain it belongs to. The schema defines what attributes are included in a global catalog server.

Any domain controller can be promoted to a global catalog server. Although it makes no real difference which domain or site the GC server belongs to, deploying them along site boundaries supports faster search and logon operations.

To investigate GC and non-GC server growth, a test environment was used consisting of a small domain tree with a child domain with one domain controller, and a parent domain with one domain controller, which is a GC server. For the tests, the child domain was loaded with the objects in several steps. The size of the DC Active Directory database size and the GC DIT size were measured after each step, waiting for a full replication of the GC attributes.

Global Catalog Servers with Sample Company

Again, the tests used a sample company with additional custom attributes (see previous tests with the sample company) and the usual increments. All groups are global domain groups.

The results show a size comparison based on percentages: by what percentage is a global catalog server larger than a normal domain controller? In other words: what percentage of its Domain naming context does a domain controller replicate to a global catalog server in another domain? The results again show a constant behavior: global catalog growth of approximately 55%.

GC servers with child domain results: fragmented and defragmented database.

	Child domain fragmented	Child domain defragmented	GC	GC defragmented
Empty	10,256	10,256	10,256	10,256
10%	196,624	139,280	88,080	81,936
20%	327,696	268,304	163,856	151,568
30%	460,816	397,328	239,632	221,200
40%	598,032	526,352	315,408	290,832
50%	731,152	655,376	391,184	362,512
60%	868,368	784,400	466,960	430,096
70%	1,003,536	913,424	542,736	501,776
80%	1,140,752	1,042,448	618,512	569,360
90%	1,273,872	1,171,472	694,288	641,040
100%	1,409,040	1,300,496	770,064	710,672

GC servers results: percentage of defragmented database.

	Child domain	Global Catalog groups	Percentage
Empty	10,256	10,256	0.00
10%	139,280	81,936	59%
20%	268,304	151,568	56%
30%	397,328	221,200	56%
40%	526,352	290,832	55%
50%	655,376	362,512	55%
60%	784,400	430,096	55%
70%	913,424	501,776	55%
80%	1,042,448	569,360	55%
90%	1,171,472	641,040	55%
100%	1,300,496	710,672	55%

Global Catalog Servers and Sample Company with Universal Groups

Universal groups publish the group memberships in the global catalog, so their use highly affects the additional load on GC servers. Global groups and local domain groups replicate only their existence to the global catalog (like any other object in the Active Directory), not their group memberships. To compare the first numbers with a more realistic sample company scenario, the same tests were done, but with 9 global domain groups for each universal group.

The results compare size for the 100% sample company with 100% global domain groups, with the sample company with 90% global domain groups and 10% universal groups.

GC servers with child domain, 10% universal groups results.

	Child domain	CD defragmented	GC	GC defragmented
Empty	10,256	10,256	10,256	10,256
90% Global Groups	1,269,776	1,171,472	694,288	641,040
100%	1,398,800	1,300,496	772,112	712,720

GC servers with 10% Universal Groups results table.

	Child domain	Global Catalog groups	Percentage
Empty	10,256	10,256	0.00
90% Global Groups	1,171,472	641,040	55%
100%	1,300,496	712,720	55%

Based on 100 bytes per member and the 25 members per group (1000 groups) in that test, the expected result for additional GC size would be:

```
(100 bytes x 25 x 1000)/1024 = 2441 Kbytes
```

Calculating the measured numbers from both tests

```
100% global groups: 710,672
90% global, 10% universal: 712,720
```

results in 2048 Kbytes, which essentially matches the calculated size.

Note   Verify these numbers carefully before using them in your own calculations. These tests set additional custom attributes and results can be influenced by which attributes are marked for global catalog server replication.

Also note that the child domain has all the objects loaded. In realistic scenarios the child domain should have a smaller number of objects. So the additional load on the global catalog would obviously be much less significant assuming the GCs are located in the parent domains. Remember that from a planning perspective GCs depend not on Domain namespace planning, but on the physical site they reside in.

Global Catalog Sizing with Individual Objects

The next step in testing GC database sizing is to isolate and determine the different object types. The tests were done with 100,000 users (full attributes), 10,000 groups (mandatory attributes) and 10,000 contacts (mandatory attributes).

User Objects and the GC

GC servers with child domain results:
users with 30 additional attributes, absolute numbers difference GC/DC.

	Child domain	CD defragmented	GC	GC defragmented
Empty	10,256	10,256	10,256	10,256
100,000	129,040	86,032	49,168	47,120
200,000	202,768	159,760	88,080	81,936
300,000	280,592	235,536	124,944	116,752
400,000	356,368	309,264	163,856	151,568
500,000	436,240	382,992	200,720	186,384
600,000	512,016	458,768	239,632	221,200
700,000	589,840	534,544	276,496	256,016
800,000	669,712	608,272	315,408	292,880
900,000	743,440	682,000	352,272	325,648
1,000,000	825,360	757,776	391,184	362,512

GC servers with child domain results:
users with 30 additional attributes, percentage difference GC/DC.

	Child domain	Global Catalog groups	Percentage
Empty	10,256	10,256	0.00
100,000	86,032	47,120	55%
200,000	159,760	81,936	51%
300,000	235,536	116,752	50%

	Child domain	Global Catalog groups	Percentage
400,000	309,264	151,568	49%
500,000	382,992	186,384	49%
600,000	458,768	221,200	48%
700,000	534,544	256,016	48%
800,000	608,272	292,880	48%
900,000	682,000	325,648	48%
1,000,000	757,776	362,512	48%

The results shown are linear and scaleable. A global catalog grows about 48% when a user object is created with 30 attributes, 8 of which are marked for global catalog replication.

Global Domain Group Objects and the GC

GC servers with child domain results; Global domain groups, no members.

	Child domain	CD defragmented	GC	GC defragmented	Percentage
Empty	10,256	10,256	10,256	10,256	
100,000	34,832	30,736	34,832	30,736	100%
200,000	57,360	53,264	57,360	51,216	96%
300,000	79,888	71,696	79,888	71,696	100%
400,000	102,416	92,176	102,416	92,176	100%
500,000	124,944	112,656	124,944	112,656	100%
600,000	149,520	133,136	149,520	133,136	100%
700,000	172,048	153,616	172,048	153,616	100%
800,000	194,576	176,144	194,576	176,144	100%
900,000	217,104	194,576	217,104	194,576	100%
1,000,000	239,632	215,056	239,632	215,056	100%

Contact Objects and the GC

GC servers with child domain results: Contacts, mandatory attributes.

	Child domain	CD defragmented	GC	GC defragmented	Percentage
Empty	10,256	10,256	10,256	10,256	
100,000	28,688	26,640	28,688	26,640	100%
200,000	47,120	43,024	47,120	43,024	100%
300,000	63,504	59,408	63,504	59,408	100%
400,000	81,936	75,792	81,936	75,792	100%
500,000	98,320	92,176	100,368	92,176	100%
600,000	116,752	108,560	116,752	108,560	100%
700,000	135,184	124,944	135,184	124,944	100%
800,000	153,616	141,328	153,616	141,328	100%
900,000	170,000	157,712	172,048	157,712	100%
1,000,000	188,432	174,096	188,432	174,096	100%

This presents an interesting case in that groups (no members, mandatory attributes) and contacts (mandatory attributes) are the same size in the domain controller and global catalog. This indicates that no attributes are marked for GC replication with the mandatory attribute set: only the object itself is replicated. Again, the scaling is linear.

Global Catalog Summary

These results indicate only *generally* what happens in a real case. Many factors determine the additional load on global catalogs:

- Are universal groups the most commonly used group type?
- Are global groups the most commonly used group type?
- How many group members are included in universal groups, if universal groups are used?
- How many additional attributes are loaded (besides the mandatory attributes, which won't be replicated to the GC)?
- Is the schema changed to include attributes in partial replication?
- Are applications installed that change the schema in order to extend partial replication?

There are only a few guidelines for the use of the global catalog server:

- Use universal groups or global groups for enterprise-wide access-right operations (granting or denying access to globally available resources, such as Active Directory objects).

- Keep the number of group members in universal groups as low as possible. Typically, all members of universal groups should be global groups.

- Keep changes in the universal groups as infrequent as possible. You can do this by requiring all members of universal groups to be global groups, and making individual membership changes in the global groups.

- Before replicating additional attributes to GC servers, evaluate thoroughly whether the additional load on the GC is required or just "nice to have."

- When deciding on GC hardware, keep future applications that use the GC in mind. Upgrading servers later is more expensive than investing in more hardware when machines are first selected.

Adding Microsoft Exchange 2000

Exchange 2000 fully integrates with the Active Directory, helping to create a single object store for user, messaging, and network administration and management. All Exchange directory related information (especially for core messaging and collaboration services) will reside in the Active Directory.

This will affect Active Directory database sizing as Exchange 2000 adds the information it needs to run services in the directory. This can be as simple as a user's e-mail address, or as complex as configuration related information (messaging stores, etc.) needed to maintain the messaging environment

The tests in this section concentrate on enabling user, contact, and group objects for Exchange 2000 services such as messaging and real-time collaboration features. The tests assess the impact of extending the standard Active Directory schema with additional classes and attributes, adding those to the directory objects and comparing the objects without Exchange 2000 installed. This should give you some insight on how a large directory-enabled application influences the Active Directory.

Extending the Schema with Exchange 2000

Exchange 2000 adds its own classes and attributes to the Active Directory, extending the schema and consuming Active Directory database space. The schema simply describes how objects inside the directory are built, providing a template or description: extending it does not add overhead to objects right away. What grows immediately is the Schema naming context where the object descriptions are stored (the physical location in the directory database).

Several tests of schema extension effects used the Exchange 2000 Beta 3 setup with the *schemaonly* switch. The first was for the sample company with custom attributes.

Exchange 2000 Beta 3 Schema extension on sample company.

	Fragmented DB/Kbytes	Defragmented DB/Kbytes
10% Sample company before installing Exchange 2000:	194,576	139,280
10% Sample company after installing Exchange 2000:	194,576	143,376
Database growth Exchange 2000 schema extension:	0	4,096

To extend the Active Directory schema with Exchange 2000, without setting up other components you can run *setup /schemaonly* from the Exchange 2000 CD.

This example shows that schema extensions resemble "normal" object loads in the database. The fragmented version did not grow because database pages weren't filled, so it was not necessary to allocate extra space for the schema. However offline defragmenting, which compacts the database, shows how this extension affected the database size.

The same tests were done with an empty Active Directory after running DCPROMO. The initial database size showed a 4 MB growth right away.

Exchange 2000 Beta 3 will add to the Active Directory:

Number of Classes	155
Number of Attributes	818
Number of Attributes of those marked for GC replication	275

Note   Although 4 MB is not a significant increase in the database size, you should remember schema extensions are cost intensive, especially when setting additional GC attributes. They set the replication USNs for partial naming contexts (Domain naming contexts of domains where the GC is not a member) to 0 on every global catalog server, forcing a full replication of the global catalog throughout the Active Directory forest. When directory-enabled applications come with their own schema extensions, consider implementing them *before* you deploy the directory in the production environment, or try to batch changes.

Adding Mailboxes to Users

The next test creates 10,000 users (in 10 steps) with minimum attributes. After each step the users were Exchange 2000 mailbox-enabled and the database size was measured. Size per mailbox-enabled user is 7,969 bytes.

#Users	Fragmented database			Defragmented database		
	DB/Kbytes	Growth	Bytes/User	DB/Kbytes	Growth	Bytes/User
0	14,352			14,352		
1,000	26,640	12,288	12,583	20,496	6,144	6,291
2,000	36,880	10,240	11,534	28,688	8,192	7,340
3,000	47,120	10,240	11,185	36,880	8,192	7,690
4,000	55,312	8,192	10,486	45,072	8,192	7,864
5,000	65,552	10,240	10,486	55,312	10,240	8,389
6,000	75,792	10,240	10,486	61,456	6,144	8,039
7,000	83,984	8,192	10,186	69,648	8,192	8,089
8,000	92,176	8,192	9,961	75,792	6,144	7,864
9,000	102,416	10,240	10,020	83,984	8,192	7,923
10,000	110,608	8,192	9,857	92,176	8,192	7,969

Exchange 2000 Attributes for Users

This table shows the attributes set for mail-box enabling users for Exchange 2000, and whether they are marked for global catalog (GC) and indexing (IN) in the Active Directory schema.

Attributes set for a User Object	Schema Properties	Attributes set for a Mailbox enabled User Object	Schema Properties	Exists already in AD
accountExpires		accountExpires		yes
badPasswordTime		badPasswordTime		yes
badPwdCount		badPwdCount		yes
cn	GC+IN	cn	GC+IN	yes
codePage		codePage		yes
countryCode		countryCode		yes
displayName	GC+IN	displayName	GC+IN	yes
distinguishedName	GC	distinguishedName	GC	yes
givenName	GC+IN	givenName	GC+IN	yes
instanceType	GC	homeMDB	GC	no
lastLogoff		homeMTA	GC	no
lastLogon		instanceType	GC	yes
logonCount		lastLogoff		yes
name	GC+IN	lastLogon		yes

(continued)

Attributes set for a User Object	Schema Properties	Attributes set for a Mailbox enabled User Object	Schema Properties	Exists already in AD
objectCategory	GC+IN	legacyExchangeDN	GC+IN	yes
objectClass	GC	logonCount		yes
objectGUID	GC+IN	mail	GC+IN	yes
objectSid	GC+IN	mailNickname	GC+IN	no
primaryGroupID	GC+IN	mDBUseDefaults	GC	no
pwdLastSet		msExchALObjectVersion		no
sAMAccountName	GC+IN	msExchFBURL	GC+IN	no
sAMAccountType	GC+IN	msExchHomeServerName	GC	no
userAccountControl	GC+IN	msExchMailboxSecurityDescriptor	GC	no
userPrincipalName	GC+IN	name	GC+IN	yes
uSNChanged	GC+IN	objectCategory	GC+IN	yes
uSNCreated	GC+IN	objectClass	GC	yes
whenChanged	GC	objectGUID	GC+IN	yes
WhenCreated	GC	objectSid	GC+IN	yes
		primaryGroupID	GC+IN	yes
		proxyAddresses	GC+IN	yes
		pwdLastSet		yes
		sAMAccountName	GC+IN	yes
		sAMAccountType	GC+IN	yes
		showInAddressBook	GC	yes
		textEncodedORAddress	GC+IN	yes
		userAccountControl	GC+IN	yes
		userPrincipalName	GC+IN	yes
		uSNChanged	GC+IN	yes
		uSNCreated	GC+IN	yes
		whenChanged	GC	yes
		whenCreated	GC	yes

Adding Voice Mail

Enabling voice mail for the user adds only one attribute:

Additional Attribute to Enable Voice Mail	Schema Properties	Exists already in AD
msExchVoiceMailEnabled		no

Adding Instant Messaging

Enabling instant messaging adds these attributes:

Additional Attributes to Enable Instant Messaging	Schema Properties	Exists already in AD
msExchIMACL	GC	no
msExchIMMetaPhysicalURL	GC	no
msExchIMPhysicalURL	GC	no

Mail-Enabling Groups

Again 100,000 object of type global domain group with mandatory attributes were created in 10 steps. Size per mail-enabled group is 3,418 bytes. (See Figure 3.9.)

Mail enabling group objects for Exchange 2000.

#Groups	Fragmented database			Defragmented database		
	DB/KBytes	Growth	Bytes/Group	DB/KBytes	Growth	Bytes/Group
0	14,352			14,352		
10,000	71,696	57,344	5,872	51,216	36,864	3,775
20,000	116,752	45,056	5,243	83,984	32,768	3,565
30,000	157,712	40,960	4,893	118,800	34,816	3,565
40,000	198,672	40,960	4,719	151,568	32,768	3,513
50,000	237,584	38,912	4,572	184,336	32,768	3,481
60,000	276,496	38,912	4,474	217,104	32,768	3,460
70,000	319,504	43,008	4,464	251,920	34,816	3,475
80,000	358,416	38,912	4,404	284,688	32,768	3,460
90,000	393,232	34,816	4,311	315,408	30,720	3,425
100,000	432,144	38,912	4,278	348,176	32,768	3,418

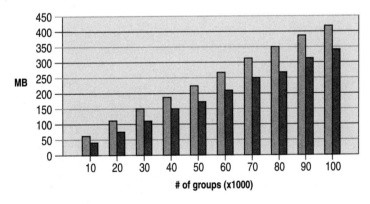

Figure 3.9   Mail enabling group objects for Exchange 2000.

This table shows the attributes set for mail enabling groups for Exchange 2000, and whether they are marked for global catalog (GC) and indexing (IN) in the Active Directory schema.

Attributes Set for a Group	Schema Properties	Attributes Set for a Mail Enabled Group	Schema Properties	Exists already in AD
cn	GC+IN	cn	GC+IN	yes
distinguishedName	GC	displayName	GC+IN	yes
groupType	GC+IN	distinguishedName	GC	yes
instanceType	GC	groupType	GC+IN	yes
name	GC+IN	instanceType		yes
objectCategory	GC+IN	legacyExchangeDN	GC+IN	yes
objectClass	GC	mail	GC+IN	yes
objectGUID	GC+IN	mailNickname	GC+IN	no
objectSid	GC+IN	msExchALObjectVersion		no
sAMAccountName	GC+IN	name	GC+IN	yes
sAMAccountType	GC+IN	objectCategory	GC+IN	yes
uSNChanged	GC+IN	objectClass	GC	yes
uSNCreated	GC+IN	objectGUID	GC+IN	yes
whenChanged	GC	objectSid	GC+IN	yes
whenCreated	GC	proxyAddresses	GC+IN	yes
		sAMAccountName	GC+IN	yes
		sAMAccountType	GC+IN	yes
		showInAddressBook	GC	yes
		textEncodedORAddress	GC+IN	yes
		uSNChanged	GC+IN	yes
		uSNCreated	GC+IN	yes
		whenChanged	GC	yes
		whenCreated	GC	yes

Mail-Enabling Contacts

As with groups, mail-enabling contacts creates no mailboxes, only directory entries. The effect of mail-enabling 100,000 contacts with mandatory attributes on Active Directory size is shown in the following table. Size per contact is 4,907 bytes.

# of Contacts	Fragmented database			Defragmented database		
	DB/KBytes	Growth	Bytes/Contact	DB/KBytes	Growth	Bytes/Contact
0	14,352			14,352		
10,000	75,792	61,440	6,291	61,456	47,104	4,823
20,000	135,184	59,392	6,187	110,608	49,152	4,928
30,000	194,576	59,392	6,152	159,760	49,152	4,963
40,000	253,968	59,392	6,134	204,816	45,056	4,876
50,000	313,360	59,392	6,124	253,968	49,152	4,907
60,000	370,704	57,344	6,082	301,072	47,104	4,893
70,000	432,144	61,440	6,112	350,224	49,152	4,913
80,000	491,536	59,392	6,108	397,328	47,104	4,902
90,000	548,880	57,344	6,082	446,480	49,152	4,917
100,000	608,272	59,392	6,082	493,584	47,104	4,907

This table shows the attributes set for mail enabling contacts for Exchange 2000, and whether they are marked for global catalog (GC) and indexing (IN) in the Active Directory schema.

Attributes set for a Contact Object	Schema Properties	Attributes set for a Mail Enabled Contact	Schema Properties	Exists already in AD
cn	GC+IN	cn	GC+IN	yes
displayName	GC+IN	displayName	GC+IN	yes
distinguishedName	GC	distinguishedName	GC	yes
givenName	GC+IN	givenName	GC+IN	yes
instanceType	GC	instanceType	GC	yes
name	GC+IN	internetEncoding	GC	no
objectCategory	GC+IN	legacyExchangeDN	GC+IN	yes
objectClass	GC	mail	GC+IN	yes
objectGUID	GC+IN	mailNickname	GC+IN	no
uSNChanged	GC+IN	msExchALObjectVersion		no
uSNCreated	GC+IN	name	GC+IN	yes
whenChanged	GC	objectCategory	GC+IN	yes

(continued)

Attributes set for a Contact Object	Schema Properties	Attributes set for a Mail Enabled Contact	Schema Properties	Exists already in AD
whenCreated	GC	objectClass	GC	yes
		objectGUID	GC+IN	yes
		proxyAddresses	GC+IN	yes
		showInAddressBook	GC	yes
		targetAddress	GC	no
		textEncodedORAddress	GC+IN	yes
		uSNChanged	GC+IN	yes
		uSNCreated	GC+IN	yes
		whenChanged	GC	yes
		whenCreated	GC	yes

Adding Voice Mail functionality to the contact adds only one attribute.

Additional Attribute Enable Voice Mail	Schema Properties	Exists already in AD
msExchVoiceMailEnabled		no

Sample Company with Exchange 2000

The final test mail-enabled the sample company users and groups with custom attributes.

Sample Company with custom properties results.

% Sample Company	Fragmented database		Defragmented database	
	DB/Kbytes	Growth	DB/Kbytes	Growth
0	14,352		14,352	
10%	247,824	233,472	196,624	182,272
20%	456,720	208,896	382,992	186,368
30%	661,520	204,800	567,312	184,320
40%	870,416	208,896	751,632	184,320
50%	1,071,120	200,704	931,856	180,224
60%	1,282,064	210,944	1,118,224	186,368
70%	1,474,576	192,512	1,271,824	153,600
80%	1,654,800	180,224	1,425,424	153,600
90%	1,818,640	163,840	1,581,072	155,648
100%	1,994,768	176,128	1,736,720	155,648

Overall, Figure 3.10 shows consistent behavior, but notice that after 60% the growth decreased by about 20%, then again became consistent. This behavior was not understood, and no errors were found in the log files of the tools used (included on the CD ROM that comes with this book) or by several spot checks on mail enabled objects. The results show consistent global catalog growth of about 61%.

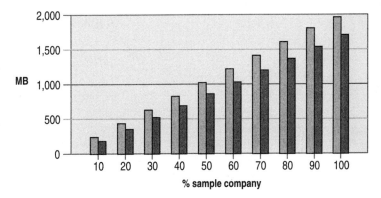

Figure 3.10   **Mail-enabling sample company users and groups with custom attributes.**

GC servers with child domain results.

	Child domain	CD defragmented	GC	GC defragmented
Empty	14,352	14,352	14,352	14,352
247,824	196,624	176,144	120,848	247,824
456,720	382,992	303,120	227,344	456,720
661,520	567,312	426,000	333,840	661,520
870,416	751,632	552,976	440,336	870,416
1,071,120	931,856	675,856	544,784	1,071,120
1,282,064	1,118,224	800,784	651,280	1,282,064
1,474,576	1,271,824	923,664	755,728	1,474,576
1,654,800	1,425,424	1,048,592	858,128	1,654,800
1,818,640	1,581,072	1,165,328	962,576	1,818,640
1,994,768	1,736,720	1,286,160	1,067,024	1,994,768

GC servers with global domain groups results.

	Child domain	Global Catalog groups	Percentage
Empty	14,352	14,352	0.00
10%	196,624	120,848	61%
20%	382,992	227,344	59%

(continued)

	Child domain	Global Catalog groups	Percentage
30%	567,312	333,840	59%
40%	751,632	440,336	59%
50%	931,856	544,784	58%
60%	1,118,224	651,280	58%
70%	1,271,824	755,728	59%
80%	1,425,424	858,128	60%
90%	1,581,072	962,576	61%
100%	1,736,720	1,067,024	61%

Summary Active Directory Objects with and without Exchange 2000

Here are the differences found by testing mail-enabled objects and non-mail-enabled Active Directory objects.

Object	Without Exchange 2000	With Exchange 2000	Percentage changed
Users (bytes)	4,366	7,969	82%
Groups (bytes)	2,097	3,418	63%
Contacts (bytes)	1,678	4,907	192%
Sample Company (Kbytes)	90,112	186,368	107%

The numbers for the users, groups and contacts are based on only the mandatory attribute set for Active Directory and for Exchange 2000. The numbers for the sample company show the amount that the database grows on each 10-percent step of the sample company with custom properties.

Caution   This calculation is theoretical, in that all objects are based solely on the mandatory attribute set. A more realistic picture would be to profile the objects based on the company's object attribute set. This will add attributes to the existing mandatory ones (decreasing the overall object overhead ratio) and you can then compare the results with overhead figures for Exchange 2000 additions. For example, if you do this for the 30 attributes set for a user, the numbers would look like this:

User object, 30 attributes, without Exchange 2000: 7676 bytes

User object, 30 attributes, with Exchange 2000: 11297 bytes

Growth: 47%

By mail-enabling the preceding objects, Exchange 2000 adds:

- 13 attributes to user objects
- 8 attributes to groups
- 9 attributes to contacts

Note   For a list of all Exchange 2000 attributes and how they change the Windows 2000 schema, see the documents "Exchange 2000 Attributes.doc" and "GC with Exchange 2000.doc" on the CD that accompanies this book.

Conclusion

The storage requirements of the Active Directory database are very predictable. Many companies may not achieve a 100,000-user directory for some time, so it is appropriate to note that (from the perspective of disk-space usage) domain controller hardware requirements are not breathtaking—in most cases the directory database remains significantly below 1 GB. However, in order to lower cost of ownership of these systems in the future, you should plan on 3 to 4 times the expected size of the database.

Directory-enabled applications such as Exchange 2000 require space in the Active Directory although how much depends on which attributes are set on Exchange objects. Keep in mind that if an application uses the Active Directory and extends the schema, its impact on replication can be significant even when database schema changes are small.

Some additional recommendations: use mirrored drives to protect against the loss of a hard-disk device, and for big domain controllers or GCs hold the database and the log files on separate hard drives to isolate them from the operating system partition.

C H A P T E R   4

Active Directory Replication Traffic Analysis

By Andreas Luther, Microsoft Enterprise Services, and Xavier Minet, Microsoft Consulting Services, Belgium

Chapter 2 of this book covered the architecture of the Active Directory replication in great detail. This chapter concentrates on the traffic implications of replication on the network. The discussion assumes that you are already familiar with:

- Naming contexts
- Connection objects
- The Knowledge Consistency Checker (KCC)
- Sites
- Replication topologies (intra-site and inter-site)
- Site links
- Site link bridges
- Notifications

If you need a refresher course, see Chapter 2 or the white paper "Active Directory Architecture" (ADArch.doc) on the CD that accompanies this book.

What You'll Find in This Chapter

- A discussion of the general concepts relevant to assessing Active Directory replication traffic.

- An introduction to basic planning.

- Results of extensive tests that measured Active Directory replication: results are tabulated and presented graphically, and (when possible) formulas for predicting traffic volumes are derived.

- Analysis of test results and recommendations based on traffic characteristics and patterns.

Why Measure Replication Traffic?

Network traffic always costs money. Sometimes, as in a LAN, the costs are reasonable; in other cases, the total costs of purchasing equipment, lease costs of transfer media (such as satellites) and maintenance are a huge part of a company's IT budget.

Most enterprises today live in a distributed environment, using LANs intra-site and WANs inter-site to connect factories, headquarters, and branches. The variety of network scenarios is vast; clients in the field always seem to have specific requirements for network operating systems and all applications that cause network traffic.

Active Directory replication traffic is a trade-off. Data should be as up-to-date as possible on all domain controllers, which means that latency should be as small as possible, which means fast updates, which means frequent replication. On the other hand, replication frequency does not always equal efficiency. Not all data has to appear in all branches at the same time. Printers that are installed in Singapore don't need to be visible in Cairo ten minutes later, if they need to be visible there at all.

Replication trade-off factors:

- Cost of replication (= data volume)
- Replication efficiency (= batching changes together)
- Replication latency (= availability of changes)

These factors affect two important components of the planning process for an Active Directory: the site structure, and the domain structure.

As explained in Chapter 2, replication works differently between sites (or geographical locations) than it does within a site. Intra-site replication uses a notification mechanism to keep replication latency as low as possible; inter-site replication uses compression to reduce traffic volumes, and to schedule when and how often replication happens.

When it comes to deciding whether a network connection can support connectivity between domain controllers, an Active Directory designer basically has four choices:

- Replicate intra-site (assumes great network connectivity)
- Replicate inter-site (adds scheduling and compression)
- Partition the namespace and replicate only schema/configuration and global catalog information
- Partition the namespace, and replicate schema/configuration information only

Option number 1 is different from the others in that it assumes a very well connected environment, where the cost of transferring data between machines is not a major concern. LAN connectivity is usually 10 Mb/sec or higher. Compression is not used because it takes up CPU cycles, and domain controller cycles should serve clients for logon operations and searches, not be spent compressing data. The decision to partition the namespace into multiple domains or even forests is not based on network bandwidth constraints, but on issues such as business units, company politics, etc.

Not so the other three scenarios, which are based on an assumed slower connection between locations. Granted, these connections can be fast—T-1 lines—but they can just as likely be challenging—9600 Kb/sec satellite connections with long round-trip times. If good connectivity is available, it can be reasonable to spread domains over multiple sites and replicate the Domain naming context over these links. However, other operations within a domain also generate network traffic. One example is password optimization, in which the PDC FSMO role owner is updated with password changes immediately. This sort of network traffic must be taken into account along with replication traffic.

As network connections become slower, it becomes more reasonable to partition the namespace into multiple domains drops. Domain size is only one factor in this calculation; change frequency is even more important. If a domain is huge but its content is fairly static, you can still spread the domain over several locations and have acceptable latency. You can create domain controllers in a headquarters and ship the computers out to subsidiaries. This avoids the relatively large replication traffic needed to initially replicate the directory to the new domain controller, and after the DC is installed only changes have to be sent over the slow links. Even a slow connection (56Kb/sec RAS, for instance) is sufficient if changes are rare. But if employee turnover is brisk and group memberships change frequently, even a medium-sized domain might use up considerable bandwidth on a 128 Kb/sec link.

When connectivity gets really slow or unreliable, you must partition the name-space, but you still have to decide if you should replicate a global catalog over the network. The global catalog is used for directory operations such as logons and forest-wide searches, but you can limit how much it is used or not use it at all.

Your network does not determine your domain structure, but it does constrain it. Ask these questions:

- Does the physical network support the ideal namespace?
- Are the costs of the WAN traffic created by the Active Directory justified?

If the answer to one of these questions is *no*, you should evaluate a more partitioned namespace.

Types of Replication Traffic

To assess the replication network traffic between two Active Directory domain controllers, ask two questions:

- What information is replicated?
- How is it replicated?

Question number 1 concerns the common naming contexts for these two domain controllers. The Schema and Configuration naming contexts are replicated to all domain controllers. In addition, every Active Directory forest has at least one Domain naming context and may have many. Domain controllers in the same domain replicate the full Domain naming context to each other; they normally never replicate objects that reside in the Domain naming context to domain controllers of other domains. The exception to this rule is the global catalog, which replicates all objects from all Domain naming contexts, but only a subset of the attributes (also referred to as a *partial replication*). A GC can source from a domain controller of another domain to get the desired objects or it can source another GC, whatever has lower replication costs.

This results in three types of replication:

- Schema/Configuration replication
- Domain replication (objects with full attribute set)
- Global catalog replication (objects with attribute subset)

The second question, how information is replicated, relates to sites. Within a site (intra-site) replication is driven by the occurrence of directory changes. Five minutes after a change is made in the database, the domain controller that received an update notifies its replication partners, which then pull the changes. Inter-site replication can be, and usually is, controlled: the administrator can define a schedule window when replication is allowed, and define how often replication should happen if the window is open. And domain controllers compress data before sending it over links presumed to be slow.

Two protocols are available for inter-site replication: RPCs (also used intra-site) and SMTP (which can be used only for Schema/Configuration and global catalog server replication, not for Domain naming contexts between domain controllers in the same domain).

To summarize, you have to measure the structure of these replication types:

1. Intra-site replication
   a. Domain replication
   b. Schema/Configuration replication
   c. Global catalog server replication
2. Inter-site replication
   a. RPC based replication
      i.   Domain replication
      ii. Schema/Configuration replication
      iii. Global catalog server replication

  b. SMTP based replication

   i. Schema/Configuration replication

   ii. Global catalog server replication

Replication Scenarios

With a test setup of only four domain controllers you can test and measure all types of replication traffic (Figure 4.1):

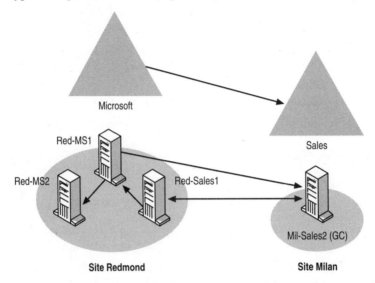

Figure 4.1   Replication traffic test setup with four domain controllers.

This small environment consists of two domains: *Microsoft.com* and *Sales.Microsoft.com*. Each has two domain controllers. *Microsoft.com* has Red-MS1 and Red-MS2: *Sales.Microsoft.com* has Red-Sales1 and Mil-Sales2.

The network is distributed over two sites: Redmond (headquarters) and Milan. Both sites have one global catalog: Red-MS1 for Redmond, Mil-Sales2 (the only domain in Milan) for Milan.

This covers all replication cases.

■ Between two domain controllers that belong to the same domain, both intra-site (Red-MS1 and Red-MS2) and inter-site (Red-Sales1 and Mil-Sales2) replication occurs

■ Partial global catalog server replication, both intra-site (Red-MS1 and Red-Sales1) and inter-site (Red-MS1 and Mil-Sales2). Replication between Red-MS1 and Mil-Sales2 can use either the RPC or the SMTP transport.

How To Measure Replication Traffic

This seems obvious: make the desired changes in the directory on one domain controller, and then measure the network traffic used to replicate the change. However, your result will vary depending on the method you use. There are three ways to capture replication traffic:

- Wait until the scheduled replication happens.
- Use the Sites and Services MMC snap-in, select the desired connection object, and force replication.
- Use the resource kit application *repadmin.exe* to force replication.

Two factors affect the network traffic for replication:

- What tool was used to force replication.
- On which domain controller the tool runs (the DC where the change was made, or its replication partner).

To compare lab results with the traffic that is created in real life, you have to understand the impact of these factors.

Intra-Site Replication

Intra-site replication uses a notification mechanism. The normal process is:

1. The administrator makes a change on one domain controller.
2. The domain controller waits a specified interval (five minutes by default), and then sends a notification to its replication partners.
3. The replication partner pulls the changes.

The notification is an RPC call that contains (among other things) which naming context changed. The partners use this knowledge to request only the changes for the affected context.

If there are two domain controllers in the same domain, DC1 and DC2, and the administrator adds a new user on DC1, the replication sequence is:

1. DC1 notifies DC2 of the change (1 RPC call plus 1 RPC acknowledgement).
2. DC2 pulls the changes from DC1 (1 RPC call plus 1 RPC acknowledgment, including the data; if the size of the data is bigger than what fits in the RPC response, additional TCP packets are sent from DC1 to DC2).

As part of the change notification, DC1 identifies which naming context changed (when a new user object is added the Domain naming context changes).

Replication partners in the same site usually replicate frequently. Once a session is established between the domain controllers, it usually stays alive until the next replication happens, although a new session is established when no replication calls come before a timeout interval (Inter-site, after 5 minutes of inactivity, Intra-site never) or when a domain controller boots up and starts the first replication call.

The Active Directory uses dynamic port mapping for RPC-based replication. Clients of replication calls simply establish a session, they do not know of or request a specific TCP port. Instead, every Windows 2000 computer maintains a port mapper service that keeps a list of services that use TCP or UDP ports, listens on port 135, and assigns port numbers to services that use dynamic ports. Setting the following registry key can overwrite dynamic port mapping:

```
HKEY_LOCAL_MACHINE\CurrentControlSet\Services\NTDS\Parameters\TCP/IP
Port
```

You can set this to 1349 (decimal), for example, to make 1349 the IP port, then find all replication-related packets by filtering on that port with Network Monitor.

This is also very useful when you deal with VPNs and firewalls.

Here is the complete traffic pattern for establishing a new session between a replication client and a server:

1. The replication client (in this example DC1—it wants to send the notification and is therefore a client) binds to the RPC port mapper service on the replication server DC2 (1 RPC call), and the replication server acknowledges the successful bind operation (1 RPC call return).

2. The replication client queries the port mapper for the port number used by the replication service (1 RPC call, plus 1 RPC answer packet).

3. The replication client unbinds from the port mapper interface on the server (1 RPC packet, plus 1 RPC acknowledgment).

4. The replication client binds to the replication interface (1 RPC call, plus 1 RPC acknowledgment).

5. The client notifies the server of the change (1 RPC call plus 1 RPC acknowledgement).

6. The server pulls the changes (1 RPC call plus 1 RPC acknowledgment, including the data; if the size of the data is bigger than what fits in the RPC response, additional TCP packets are sent from DC1 to DC2).

Steps 1 – 4 create additional network traffic. This pattern changes when you use one of the tools described above to force replication.

RepAdmin

Repadmin.exe is a command-line tool that ships with the *Microsoft Windows 2000 Resource Kit.* You can use it to perform several replication functions, including specifying a single naming context for replication.

During testing, this command line was used to force replication:

```
repadmin /sync dc=haybuv,dc=tld dc2 <server UUID >, where
```

- /sync defines that the requested operation is the synchronization of a naming context
- dc=haybuv,dc=tld defines the naming context (in this case, the domain haybuv.tld)
- dc2 defines the machine name of the destination domain controller
- the *<server GUID >* is the GUID that the source domain controller registered in DNS

You can see the GUIDs of a domain controller (objectGUID) and all its replication partners when you run RepAdmin with the parameter */showreps* on a domain controller.

```
C:\Tools>repadmin /showreps
Redmond\DC1
DSA Options : IS_GC
objectGuid  : 2d172f6c-6656-4284-aff9-f291d3f03be9
invocationID: 578595c6-b318-4450-82c2-4b35c0a8a46d

==== INBOUND NEIGHBORS =======================================

CN=Schema,CN=Configuration,DC=haybuv,DC=tld
    London\DC1 via RPC
        objectGuid: 76613fc0-baac-419e-9a6f-4cc084e49650
        Last attempt @ 1999-11-06 00:08.06 was successful.

CN=Configuration, DC=haybuv,DC=tld
    London\DC1 via RPC
        objectGuid: 76613fc0-baac-419e-9a6f-4cc084e49650
        Last attempt @ 1999-11-06 00:07.50 was successful.

DC=haybuv,DC=tld
    London\DC1 via RPC
        objectGuid: 76613fc0-baac-419e-9a6f-4cc084e49650
        Last attempt @ 1999-11-06 00:08.29 was successful.

==== OUTBOUND NEIGHBORS FOR CHANGE NOTIFICATIONS ============

CN=Schema,CN=Configuration, DC=haybuv,DC=tld
    London\DC4 via RPC
        objectGuid: 76613fc0-baac-419e-9a6f-4cc084e49650
```

When you use RepAdmin to force replication and run it on the destination compuer, the traffic pattern differs slightly from that of scheduled replication. In that case, the notification call, which is directed to the same machine, is looped back and therefore not visible on the network. In this case, the traffic pattern outlined on page 132 is missing step 5 (two RPC calls) when you use RepAdmin.

MMC Forced Replication

You can also use the Active Directory Sites and Services MMC snap-in to force replication (Figure 4.2). Open the NTDS-Settings container of a domain controller and select the connection object that defines an incoming replication connection. Right-click the connection object and select **Replicate Now** from the menu.

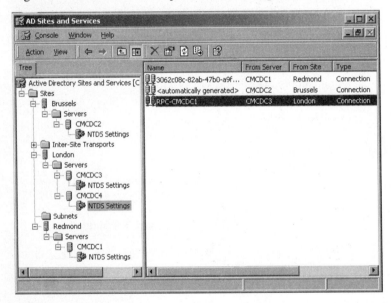

Figure 4.2   Forcing replication through the NTDS Settings container.

This example selects the incoming connection object to CMCDC4 from CMCDC1 and replicates changes from CMCDC1 to CMCDC4. The MMC snap-in does not allow you to specify which naming context should be replicated: it replicates all naming contexts common to these two domain controllers. For domain controllers in the same domain, these are the Schema, Configuration, and Domain. Global catalogs might have more.

Replication of each naming context consists of one notification call (1 RPC call, plus 1 RPC response) and the pulling of information (1 RPC call, 1 RPC response plus additional data packets). This means that in the traffic pattern outlined above, steps 5 and 6 happen three times, which creates additional traffic.

Summary of Replication Options

All intra-site figures presented in this chapter were derived using scheduled Active Directory replication. This was done because the other two methods generate different amounts of overhead and data, depending on whether they are used to trigger replication from the server that is the source of the change or the server that will receive the updated object information when replication occurs.

For example, if there are two Windows 2000 domain controllers (DC1 and DC2) in the same domain and site, and you add a user to DC2 and directory replication is triggered from DC2 using the Sites and Services MMC snap-in, **16,568** bytes (12,949 of overhead plus 3,619 data) of traffic are generated. If you add a user to DC2 but this time directory replication is triggered from DC1 using the MMC snap-in, **9,256** (5,637 of overhead plus 3,619 data) bytes of traffic are generated.

Note The byte count you see on the wire depends on the length of distinguished names of domain controllers and the lengths of the naming context names. The same applies in the replication tests below. If users have long names, numbers will be slightly higher. The error should be below 1% of the test data.

The difference is attributable to the amount of overhead created during the session setup. The amount of data is about the same in either case, but DC1-to-DC2 requires only 7 frames of overhead and DC2-to-DC1 requires 41. Normal Active Directory replication is unaffected by this overhead. This is why it was chosen as the replication method for the traffic tests in this chapter.

Calculating replication traffic is not an exact science, but by using an isolated test network with little activity and forcing replication on a scheduled basis you can produce predictable results. Session overhead traffic is always the same, but variation in how data is transferred from the buffer onto the wire causes slight variation in the number of frames and the amount of data contained in them. Also, the more data transferred, the higher the risk of packet fragmentation, which is why you can't assume that the traffic generated by adding 100 users simply equals 100 times the traffic generated by adding one user. To account for this variation, all directory and global catalog replication traffic presented in this section averages five tests for each activity being measured.

If you want to calculate your own replication traffic, use the table below to adjust your results. For example, the table shows that traffic generated by adding a single user can vary from 6,082 bytes (2,076 overhead plus 4,006 data) to 16,568 bytes (12,949 overhead and 3,619 data) depending on the method used to trigger replication and where it is triggered from. It also shows that in scheduled Active Directory replication, the location where replication originates is not a factor, because it always originates at the server where the change occurs.

- If you use the MMC snap-in to schedule replication and you trigger it from the machine where the change occurred, you should subtract **10,486 bytes** (16,568 – 6082) from your figure to determine how much replication traffic would be generated using scheduled Active Directory replication.

- If you use RepAdmin to schedule replication and you trigger it from the machine where the change occurred, you should subtract **5,978 bytes** (12,060 – 6,082) from your figure to determine how much replication traffic would be generated using scheduled Active Directory replication.

Note   All tests used scheduled Active Directory replication and all numbers include associated overhead traffic.

Comparison of replication traffic generated by the three triggering methods.

Replication Method	Where replication was initiated	Session overhead		Data		Total (Session + Data)	
		# of Frames	# of Bytes	# of Frames	# of Bytes	# of Frames	# of Bytes
Scheduled	1 user	4	2076	5	4006	9	6082
	100 users	4	2076	423	395537	427	397613
RepAdmin	Initiated on DC2 (1 user)	2	1981	5	3619	7	5600
	Initiated on DC2 (100 users)	2	1981	412	395005	414	396986
	Initiated on DC1 (1 user)	32	8441	5	3619	37	12060
	Initiated on DC1 (100 users)	32	8441	417	395258	449	403699
MMC	Initiated on DC2 (1 user)	7	5637	5	3619	12	9256
	Initiated on DC2 (100 users)	7	5637	310	388911	317	394548
	Initiated on DC1 (1 user)	41	12949	5	3619	46	16568
	Initiated on DC1 (100 users)	41	12949	325	391470	366	404419

Modeling Replication Traffic

For single variables (such as adding users) you can model replication traffic by using linear (of the form $y=mx+c$) curve fitting techniques on the measured data. For multiple variables (such as adding users with different attributes) modeling requires more advanced curve fitting, resulting in the three-dimensional (3D) graphs that begin on page 142.

The models generated from the measured data give an idea of the data traffic expected in the different replication scenarios.

The factors that impact data modeling are:

- Network fragmentation, which creates a new packet and increases overhead
- Compression of inter-site traffic above a threshold of 32KB of data. This is based on the compression buffer size. Data in the compression buffer is encapsulated with the TCP and IP headers and translates to an observed traffic size of around 38 KB.

The test results described in this chapter were subjected to non-linear regression curve fitting to produce equations that are either linear approximations for replication traffic for single variables or more complex approximations for multiple variables.

Global Catalog and Intra-Domain vs. Inter-Domain Replication

When a domain controller replicates its Domain naming context to a global catalog, there is a difference in replication traffic between the domain controller and the global catalog based on the domain controllers being of the same domain (intra-domain replication), or the domain controllers being in different domains (inter-domain replication).

If the domain controller is in the same domain as the global catalog, the full Domain naming context is replicated; if it is in a different domain than the global catalog, only a partial replication occurs. Partial replication includes all objects but only those attributes defined in the schema for GC replication. When groups are present, intra-domain replication includes all groups and all group memberships.

Inter-domain replication replicates all groups but only group memberships for universal groups. The table below shows the details:

Intra- and inter-domain group replication.

Catalog types	Intra-domain	Inter-domain
Global groups	Replicated	Replicated to GC
Global group members	Replicated	
Local domain groups	Replicated	Replicated to GC
Local domain members	Replicated	
Universal groups	Replicated	Replicated to GC
Universal group members	Replicated	Replicated to GC
User object and published attributes	Replicated	Replicated to GC
Volumes	Replicated	Replicated to GC
Printers	Replicated	Replicated to GC

Intra domain traffic is the same for all three group types (local domain, global, and universal). The groups are based on the same object class and only an attribute setting differentiates the group types, so intra domain traffic can be modeled for all three groups using one group type. Inter domain traffic is different as illustrated for the replication of group members for global and local domain groups for GCs in different domains. Replicating global groups between GC servers in different domain does not increase replication traffic as group membership increases because group membership details are not replicated. Universal groups on the other hand experience a steady rise in traffic as the additional group membership details are replicated to the GC in the second domain.

Single Attribute Changes

The Windows 2000 Active Directory has a replication granularity of one attribute: if only one attribute changes, only that one new value is sent over the network.

To examine this, the tests looked at two areas: how efficient single-property replication is when compared to whole-object replication, and how replication traffic grows with attribute size. The tests use string-data attributes taken from the user object because these affect traffic growth clearly.

The table below lists bytes of traffic generated when adding a specific number of users in combination with zero or more attributes. All values in this table and all tables in this chapter include the overhead associated with establishing a connection between two domain controllers. At the end of the data is a formula you can use to approximate the amount of replication traffic outlined in the associated table. Each set of tables also includes a brief explanation the numbers.

Replication of one attribute with number of characters ranging from 1 – 33.

Character	Bytes	Diff	Character	Bytes	Diff	Character	Bytes	Diff
1	2,487	0	12	2,503	0	23	2,649	0
2	2,487	0	13	2,519	16	24	2,649	0
3	2,487	0	14	2,519	0	25	2,649	0
4	2,487	0	15	2,519	0	26	2,649	0
5	2,503	16	16	2,519	0	27	2,649	0
6	2,503	0	17	2,519	0	28	2,649	0
7	2,503	0	18	2,519	0	29	2,665	16
8	2,503	0	19	2,519	0	30	2,665	0
9	2,503	0	20	2,519	0	31	2,665	0
10	2,503	0	21	2,649	130	32	2,665	0
11	2,503	0	22	2,649	0	33	2,665	0

Replication of one attribute with number of characters ranging from 34 – 66.

Character	Bytes	Diff	Character	Bytes	Diff	Character	Bytes	Diff
34	2,665	0	45	2,697	16	56	2,713	0
35	2,665	0	46	2,697	0	57	2,713	0
36	2,665	0	47	2,697	0	58	2,713	0
37	2,681	16	48	2,697	0	59	2,713	0
38	2,681	0	49	2,697	0	60	2,713	0
39	2,681	0	50	2,697	0	61	2,729	16
40	2,681	0	51	2,697	0	62	2,729	0
41	2,681	0	52	2,697	0	63	2,729	0
42	2,681	0	53	2,713	16	64	2,729	0
43	2,681	0	54	2,713	0	65	2,729	0
44	2,681	0	55	2,713	0	66	2,729	0

Replication of one attribute with number of characters ranging from 67 – 99.

Character	Bytes	Diff	Character	Bytes	Diff	Character	Bytes	Diff
67	2,729	0	78	2,761	0	89	2,777	0
68	2,729	0	79	2,761	0	90	2,777	0
69	2,745	16	80	2,761	0	91	2,777	0
70	2,745	0	81	2,761	0	92	2,777	0
71	2,745	0	82	2,761	0	93	2,793	16
72	2,745	0	83	2,761	0	94	2,793	0
73	2,745	0	84	2,761	0	95	2,793	0
74	2,745	0	85	2,777	16	96	2,793	0
75	2,745	0	86	2,777	0	97	2,793	0
76	2,745	0	87	2,777	0	98	2,793	0
77	2,761	16	88	2,777	0	99	2,793	0

Following is the formula for approximating traffic generated by replication of one attribute with number of characters ranging from 1 to 99:

```
Bytes =(3.12 x C ) + 2521.13 where C is the number of characters in the
attribute
```

The first table above shows that replicating a 1-character string property causes 2,487 bytes of traffic. Increasing the string size to 4 characters does not change the value. From 5 to 13 characters the traffic increases by 16 bytes. This is a common increment because the Active Directory uses Unicode to store strings in the database. Each Unicode character is 2 bytes, so for every 8 characters a 16-byte buffer is created. From the 20th to the 21st character is a big jump of 130 bytes. This was caused by network fragmentation; the packet that contained the changed value reached its maximum size of 1,500 bytes and a new packet had to be created (causing overhead for an empty packet). After this jump, the 8-character/16-byte pattern resumes.

The next table shows how replication traffic grows when multiple attributes are changed on multiple objects at the same time. The test added the same attributes (something like address information or phone numbers) to user groups from 1 to 10,000. The table below shows the traffic when multiple user objects are changed as well as the use of 1 to 10 attributes. The test used 10-character string-based attributes.

Replication of multiple attributes and user objects.

# User Objects	Plus 1 Attributes	Plus 2 Attributes	Plus 3 Attributes	Plus 4 Attributes	Plus 5 Attributes
1	2,602	2,698	2,778	2,874	2,954
2	2,954	3,130	3,306	3,482	3,658
3	3,306	3,578	3,834	4,160	4,416
4	3,658	4,010	4,416	4,828	5,180
5	4,026	4,512	5,020	5,452	5,954
10	5,954	6,834	7,905	8,839	9,719
20	9,719	11,593	13,538	15,412	17,286
30	13,538	16,292	19,160	22,045	24,853
40	17,226	21,165	24,853	28,678	32,497
50	21,045	25,864	30,486	35,305	40,061
100	40,064	49,505	58,963	68,464	77,802
200	79,442	98,417	117,420	136,455	154,918
300	118,716	147,176	174,573	203,813	232,290
400	158,170	195,488	234,066	272,044	307,982
500	196,148	243,387	291,123	338,182	384,832
1,000	391,582	484,845	579,186	675,509	768,866
5,000	1,951,359	2,417,524	2,887,525	3,359,402	3,763,213
10,000	3,896,415	4,843,056	5,776,456	6,716,534	7,645,915

# User Objects	Plus 6 Attributes	Plus 7 Attributes	Plus 8 Attributes	Plus 9 Attributes	Plus 10 Attributes
1	3,050	3,130	3,226	3,306	3,402
2	3,834	4,010	4,240	4,416	4,592
3	4,688	4,944	5,276	5,532	5,858
4	5,472	5,938	6,290	6,642	6,994
5	6,386	6,834	7,397	7,845	8,277

# User Objects	Plus 6 Attributes	Plus 7 Attributes	Plus 8 Attributes	Plus 9 Attributes	Plus 10 Attributes
10	10,653	11,533	12,527	13,598	14,418
20	19,220	21,165	22,979	24,853	26,804
30	27,798	30,900	33,437	36,185	39,130
40	36,185	40,064	43,812	47,631	51,336
50	44,823	49,565	54,084	58,783	63,662
100	87,363	97,139	106,142	116,014	125,172
200	174,193	192,776	212,285	230,988	249,303
300	260,408	287,127	317,993	343,908	373,472
400	346,560	383,818	420,278	460,094	494,134
500	429,568	481,531	524,885	570,282	617,874
1,000	856,979	953,386	1,047,081	1,141,071	1,233,311
5,000	4,216,675	4,763,315	5,227,246	5,695,456	6,155,913
10,000	8,566,961	9,506,368	10,435,762	11,369,540	12,301,583

Again, network traffic is predictable. Changing 10 attributes on 1,000 users creates approximately 10 times the traffic as changing 10 attributes on 100 user objects (1,233,311 bytes vs. 125,172 bytes).

The graph in Figure 4.3 demonstrates the linear nature of traffic growth:

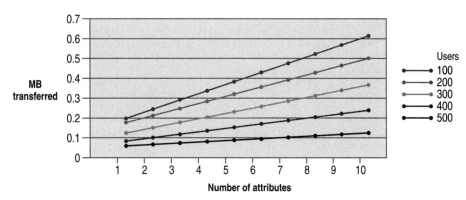

Figure 4.3   **Changing attributes on variously sized user groups.**

Because replicating single attributes causes little network traffic, it is not useful to research the behavior in different domain/site scenarios. The relationship between user objects, attributes, and replication bytes is represented in the 3D diagram (Figure 4.4).

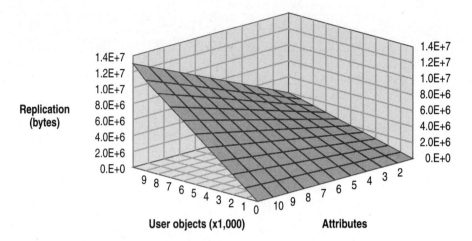

Figure 4.4   Model of user objects, attributes, and replication in bytes.

Intra-Site Domain Object Replication

Intra-site replication assumes fast and reliable network connections—a 10-Mb/sec Ethernet network or something comparable—so it does not compress data, saving domain controller CPU cycles for other tasks, such as client logon, search operations, etc.

In the sample tested, both the global and the universal groups had no members. For all objects, only the mandatory attributes were set. The table below shows how many bytes were created when objects were sent between replication partners:

Objects created between replication partners.

# of Objects	Users	Global Groups	Universal Groups	Volumes	Printers
1	6,082	4,224	4,224	3,881	5,477
2	10,082	6,258	6,258	5,655	9,084
3	13,985	8,309	8,309	7,377	12,500
4	17,817	10,397	10,397	9,154	15,993
5	21,900	12,431	12,431	10,748	19,409
10	41,573	22,819	23,463	19,275	36,904
20	80,825	43,392	43,392	36,654	71,914
30	121,080	64,102	64,102	53,919	106,978
40	159,580	84,789	84,789	71,124	141,905
50	199,023	105,362	105,362	88,389	176,855

# of Objects	Users	Global Groups	Universal Groups	Volumes	Printers
100	397,228	208,729	208,729	176,097	351,787
200	793,284	417,368	417,728	350,939	706,374
300	1,189,340	626,841	626,841	525,505	1,056,234
400	1,580,970	836,495	836,075	700,407	1,408,354
500	1,986,291	1,044,511	1,044,126	875,021	1,759,155
1,000	3,978,845	2,087,954	2,087,714	1,748,749	3,518,453

The growth pattern is again linear, as the graph in Figure 4.5 demonstrates:

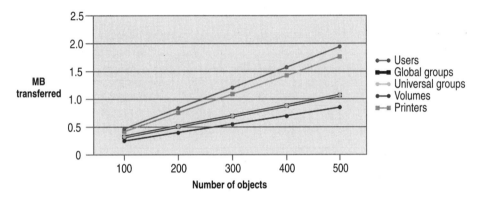

Figure 4.5   Traffic growth when objects are replicated intra-site.

Because the traffic is linear, you can apply these formulas:

Formula for calculating traffic generated by adding Users, Groups, Volumes and Printers:

- **Users**: 3973 x U + 624, where U is the number of users you are adding
- **Global Groups**: 2086 x GG + 1547, where GG is the number of global groups you are adding
- **Universal Groups**: 2086 x UG + 1547, where UG is the number of universal groups you are adding
- **Volumes**: 1747 x V + 1736, where V is the number of volumes you are adding
- **Printers**: 3517 x P + 1614, where P is the number of printers you are adding

The multiplication factors used with the number of objects show the size of the object on the wire. Although the test used only the mandatory attribute set (required by the directory service to create an object), the traffic varies depending on the type of the object. Volumes, or file shares, are small. Users and printers are on the high side. The factors for global groups and universal groups are almost identical. This is not surprising, because the Active Directory schema has only one group class: group type is defined by setting a value on an attribute.

The next test examines replication of additional attributes. User objects were created and filled with different sets of attributes. In the first test, mandatory attributes only; for the next, one attribute was added to the mandatory attributes; for the next test, three; for the last test, five. The test used 10-character string attributes. See Figure 4.6.

Replication of additional attributes.

User objects	Mandatory attributes	Plus 1 attribute	Plus 2 attributes	Plus 3 attributes	Plus 4 attributes	Plus 5 attributes
1	6,082	6,193	6,289	6,321	6,417	6,497
2	10,082	10,198	10,428	10,508	10,684	10,860
3	13,985	14,241	14,513	14,745	15,011	15,267
4	17,817	18,283	18,635	18,795	19,147	19,499
5	21,900	22,272	22,834	22,966	23,414	23,846
10	41,573	42,453	43,387	43,727	44,738	45,618
20	80,825	82,776	84,704	85,504	87,318	89,323
30	121,080	123,076	125,907	127,161	129,969	132,854
40	159,580	163,399	167,087	168,878	172,620	176,385
50	199,023	203,645	208,404	210,458	215,271	219,970
100	397,228	406,686	416,067	420,426	429,944	439,265

User objects	Mandatory attributes	Plus 6 attributes	Plus 7 attributes	Plus 8 attributes	Plus 9 attributes	Plus 10 attributes
1	6,082	6,593	6,673	6,769	6,849	6,945
2	10,082	11,036	11,212	11,388	11,564	11,740
3	13,985	15,539	15,795	16,187	16,323	16,649
4	17,817	19,982	20,154	20,686	21,038	21,504
5	21,900	24,408	24,840	25,258	25,851	26,299
10	41,573	46,672	47,606	48,546	49,420	50,356
20	80,825	91,197	93,011	94,962	96,830	98,704
30	121,080	135,662	138,547	141,301	144,126	146,994
40	159,580	180,069	183,952	187,717	191,459	195,224
50	199,023	224,675	229,297	234,110	238,749	243,622
100	397,228	448,663	458,158	467,616	476,997	486,455

Packet fragmentation prevents the derivation of a formula for calculating these small differences. Generally, the increase per 10-character string attribute is between 77 and 97 bytes; 85 bytes is a good ballpark figure.

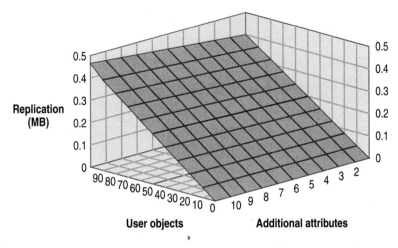

Figure 4.6   Model of user objects, additional attributes, and replication in bytes.

The next test concentrates on *group replication*, showing how many bytes of overhead are created per group member. To replicate 1 group with 100 members, this is: (20,234bytes – 4,222 bytes)/100 = 160 bytes. The tests used global domain groups.

Blank fields represent tests that were not run because they would have taken too much time and because the results are so predictable (overhead per group member is around 163 bytes) that there was no point in taking the time to test the obvious.

Group replication.

Groups	No Members	10 Members per group	Overhead per member	100 Members per group	Overhead per member	500 Members per group	Overhead per member	1000 Members per group	Overhead per member	5000 Members per group	Overhead per member
1	4,224	5,889	167	20,234	160	85,392	162	167,451	163	822,537	164
2	6,258	9,634	169	38,110	159	168,574	162	331,474	163	1,639,895	163
3	8,309	13,202	163	56,117	159	251,733	162	496,085	163	2,449,992	163
4	10,397	17,041	166	74,124	159	335,629	163	660,613	163	3,278,489	163
5	12,431	20,666	165	92,077	159	417,960	162	825,164	163	4,080,005	163
10	22,819	39,165	163	181,998	159	847,369	165	1,663,643	164	8,175,569	163
20	43,392	76,123	164	361,655	159	1,665,163	162	3,343,534	165	16,361,759	163
30	64,102	116,409	174	541,300	159	2,492,464	162	4,933,807	162	24,521,897	163
40	84,789	150,039	163	741,377	164	3,333,755	162	6,579,795	162	32,723,283	163
50	105,362	186,997	163	911,552	161	4,080,028	159	8,231,192	163	40,919,890	163
100	208,729	373,367	165	1,822,367	161	8,327,929	162	16,487,484	163	81,760,221	163
200	417,368	745,953	164	3,598,999	159	16,641,588	162	32,950,740	163	163,538,758	163
300	626,841	1,121,249	165	5,410,110	159	24,982,448	162	49,442,089	163		
400	836,495	1,509,972	168	7,202,374	159	33,288,387	162	65,938,115	163		
500	1,044,511	1,879,715	167	8,999,594	159	41,580,622	162	82,349,704	163		
1,000	2,087,954	3,678,276	159	17,997,865	159	83,290,525	162	164,710,700	163		
5,000	10,252,818	18,420,929	163								
10,000	20,516,840	36,865,529	163								

The results are modeled in the 3D chart in Figure 4.7.

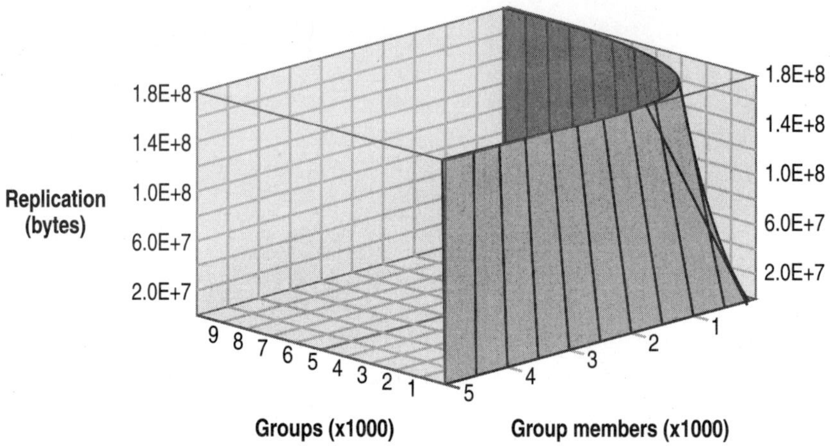

Figure 4.7   Group replication—bytes of overhead created per group member.

As a reality check, compare universal group and global group replication traffic:

Groups	No members	10 Members/group
1	4,224	5,889
2	6,258	9,634
3	8,309	13,182
4	10,397	16,921
5	12,431	20,606
10	23,463	39,165
20	43,392	76,123
30	64,102	113,081
40	84,789	150,039
50	105,362	187,051

The traffic is identical to the global domain groups, because all group types are based on the same class.

To summarize: intra-site domain replication is very predictable; replicating more objects or attributes increases network traffic by direct ratio.

Intra-Site GC Replication

Intra-site global catalog replication involves two domain controllers (one of which is a global catalog) that belong to different domains. Because the global catalog holds only a subset of Domain-naming context attributes, this is also called *partial replication*. See Figure 4.8.

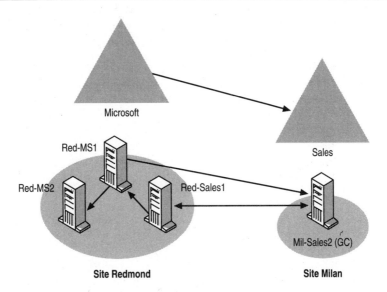

Figure 4.8   Intra-site global catalog replication.

This scenario examines the traffic between Red-Sales1 (domain controller in *Sales.Microsoft.com*) and Red-MS1 (domain controller in *Microsoft.com*), which is a global catalog server.

The first test examines the traffic generated for objects. Except for domain replication, group type plays a role in global catalog server replication. Universal groups publish the group memberships in the GCs, but global groups do not, so more replication traffic is expected for universal groups than for global groups. The table shows the bytes/object. The numbers in *italics* are the domain replication numbers for comparison.

Intra-site GC replication of objects.

Objects	Users	Global groups	Universal groups	Volumes	Printers
1	5,194	4,346	4,346	4,004	4,732
	6,082	*4,224*	*4,224*	*3,881*	*5,477*
2	8,255	6,428	6,428	5,852	7,425
	10,082	*6,258*	*6,258*	*5,655*	*9,084*
3	11,283	8,511	8,511	7,647	9,987
	13,985	*8,309*	*8,309*	*7,377*	*12,500*
4	14,224	10,647	10,767	9,501	12,543
	17,817	*10,397*	*10,397*	*9,154*	*15,993*
5	17,192	12,713	12,773	11,219	15,176
	21,900	*12,431*	*12,431*	*10,748*	*19,409*

(continued)

Objects	Users	Global groups	Universal groups	Volumes	Printers
10	32,191	23,129	23,369	20,305	28,258
	41,573	*22,819*	*23,463*	*19,275*	*36,904*
20	62,565	44,253	44,853	38,273	54,964
	80,825	*43,392*	*43,392*	*36,654*	*71,914*
30	92,170	65,786	65,966	56,312	80,530
	121,080	*64,102*	*64,102*	*53,919*	*106,978*
40	122,981	86,893	88,778	74,171	107,127
	159,580	*84,789*	*84,789*	*71,124*	*141,905*
50	152,046	107,057	109,962	91,850	133,653
	199,023	*105,362*	*105,362*	*88,389*	*176,855*
100	301,046	212,756	216,716	182,251	265,331
	397,228	*208,729*	*208,729*	*176,097*	*351,787*
200	604,881	425,650	430,030	362,960	528,331
	793,284	*417,368*	*417,728*	*350,939*	*706,374*
300	913,574	637,704	643,944	544,569	792,028
	1,189,340	*626,841*	*626,841*	*525,505*	*1,056,234*
400	1,211,034	832,894	832,894	725,278	1,057,821
	1,580,970	*836,495*	*836,075*	*700,407*	*1,408,354*
500	1,508,494	1,040,885	1,041,497	905,567	1,320,179
	1,986,291	*1,044,511*	*1,044,126*	*875,021*	*1,759,155*

The graph in Figure 4.9 shows again the linear growth pattern of the replication traffic:

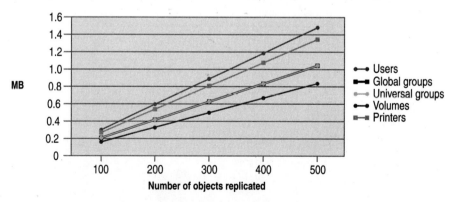

Figure 4.9   Intra-site GC replication of objects.

For each object type you can apply a formula. Following is the formula for calculating global catalog traffic generated by adding users, groups, volumes, and printers:

- **Users:** 3020 x U +1953, where U is the number of users added
- **Global Groups:** 2084 x GG +3295, where GG is the number of global groups added
- **Universal Groups:** 2088 x UG +4306, where UG is the number of universal groups added
- **Volumes:** 1807 x V + 2046, where V is the number of volumes added
- **Printers:** 2637 x P + 1857, where P is the number of printers added

The test shows that the replicated objects for GC replication are smaller than for domain replication. For user objects, the difference is noticeable. For group objects, there is no big difference when groups without members and no additional attributes are replicated. In order to compare object sizes, use the factors from the formula as baseline. Thus, for user replication intra-domain, the formula is:

```
3973 x U + 624
```

So a baseline of 3,973 bytes for the size of one user object is used:

Object type	Domain replication	GC replication
Users	3,973	3,020
Global Domain Groups	2,086	2086
Universal Groups	2,086	2086
Volumes	1,747	1,807
Printers	3,517	2,637

The table compares objects that were created with only the mandatory attribute set. Most companies will supplement the basic objects with information such as users' phone numbers and descriptions of groups and printers. Global catalog replication should not be affected by these additional attributes, as the table below shows. The numbers in *italics* are intra-site domain replication for comparison.

Intra-site GC replication of users with additional 10 character attributes (default schema)

# of User Objects	Mandatory attributes	Plus 1 attributes	Plus 2 attributes	Plus 3 attributes	Plus 4 attributes	Plus 5 attributes
1	5,068	5,068	5,068	5,068	5,068	5,068
	6,082	*6,193*	*6,289*	*6,321*	*6,417*	*6,497*
10	31,861	31,861	31,861	31,861	31,861	31,861
	41,573	*42,453*	*43,387*	*43,727*	*44,738*	*45,618*
100	299,401	299,282	299,282	299,282	299,282	299,282
	397,228	*406,686*	*416,067*	*420,426*	*429,944*	*439,265*

(continued)

# of User Objects	Mandatory attributes	Plus 6 attributes	Plus 7 attributes	Plus 8 attributes	Plus 9 attributes	Plus 10 attributes
1	5,068	5,068	5,068	5,068	5,068	5,068
	6,082	*6,593*	*6,673*	*6,769*	*6,849*	*6,945*
10	31,861	31,861	31,861	31,861	31,861	31,861
	41,573	*46,672*	*47,606*	*48,546*	*49,420*	*50,356*
100	299,401	299,401	299,401	299,401	299,282	299,401
	397,228	*448,663*	*458,158*	*467,616*	*476,997*	*486,455*

Replicating 100 users with mandatory attributes or 10 additional attributes creates the same replication traffic. Comparing the numbers for 10 attributes shows that this makes a significant difference for domain replication but not GC replication. At this point, only string-based attributes, which are relatively small by nature, were used. Using larger attributes such as pictures will add substantially to domain replication, but won't affect global catalog replication. To add more attributes to global catalog server replication, you have to change the schema.

Universal and global groups are the same size because they were created with no members. The next two tables compare global and universal groups.

Global groups.

# of Groups	No members	10 members	20 members	100 members
1	4,298	4,298	4,244	4,244
10	23,529	24,061	23,093	22,797
100	209,981	209,981	209,921	210,653
500	1,044,923	1,044,929	1,044,809	1,045,601
1,000	2,088,614	2,088,494	2,106,753	

The amount of data does not change if members are added to the group because global groups do not replicate members to the GC.

Universal groups.

# of Groups	No members	10 members	20 members	100 members
1	4,244	5,888	7,507	20,149
10	23,121	39,198	55,070	181,815
100	209,981	374,300	532,487	1,799,822
500	1,045,661	1,866,362	2,657,983	8,995,963
1,000	2,106,507	3,732,598	5,315,585	
Formulas	2103 x UG + 286	3730 x UG + 1676	5313 x UG + 1685	1533 x UG + 1705478

In the formulas, UG is the number of Universal Groups being added. This is represented in 3D in Figure 4.10.

Universal group replication traffic depends heavily on the number of group members. Replicating 500 universal groups of 100 members each creates 9 times as much traffic as for a comparable global group.

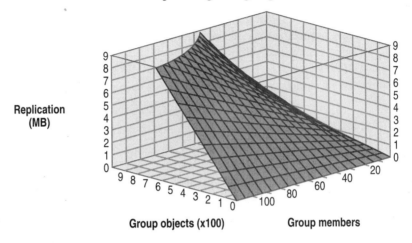

Figure 4.10   Universal group replication.

Intra-site GC replication is predictable. Objects replicated within a site to GCs are smaller than when replicated to a domain controller of the same domain. The difference is not big if only the mandatory attribute set is used on objects. If additional attributes are used, they won't be replicated to the global catalog, so the ratio goes down. However, if you change the schema so that attributes are added to partial replication, or if applications (such as messaging systems) add them, global catalog server replication traffic increases. Group type is also relevant for the traffic to the global catalog, because universal groups replicate their group members.

Inter-Site Replication

Inter-site and intra-site replication differ. Intra-site replication uses a notification process, but inter-site replication is usually scheduled. You can define when the window for replication opens and closes, and how often per hour replication should happen when the window is open. This frequency cannot be higher than 15 minutes and can be as infrequent as once a week at a specific time. Obviously, the more changes that can be batched together, the fewer replications can be configured, and the more efficient replication will be. Compression minimizes the amount of traffic. That is good, but the more infrequently replication takes place, the higher the latency. Once again, you have to assess and balance trade-offs to achieve acceptable efficiency.

Because inter-site replication does not use notifications, requesting domain controllers cannot know which naming contexts have changed and must request changes for all naming contexts.

The flow for two domain controllers in the same domain, which are *not* global catalogs, looks like this:

1. The replication client (say, DC1) binds to the RPC port mapper service on the replication server DC2 (1 RPC call), and the replication server acknowledges the successful bind operation (1 RPC call return).

2. The replication client queries the port mapper for the port number used by the replication service (1 RPC call, plus 1 RPC answer packet).

3. The replication client unbinds from the port mapper interface on the server (1 RPC packet, plus 1 RPC acknowledgment).

4. The replication client binds to the replication interface (1 RPC call, plus 1 RPC acknowledgment).

5. The client requests changes for the Schema naming context (1 RPC call plus 1 RPC acknowledgment, including the data). If there is too much data to fit in the RPC response, additional TCP packets are sent from DC2 to DC1.

6. The client requests changes for the Configuration naming context.

7. The client requests changes for the Domain naming context.

Requesting changes for all naming contexts increases the initial traffic, but if there are more than 32 KB of data compression kicks in and decreases traffic to around 8% to 10% of the uncompressed volume.

To measure replication traffic between sites, you can use the MMC Active Directory Sites and Services snap-in to perform the same actions performed by scheduled inter-site replication. Other than for intra-site replication, the MMC snap-in creates exactly the same traffic as scheduled inter-site replication.

Inter-Site Domain Replication

This test examines inter-site domain replication, which involves two domain controllers in different sites within the same domain. These serve as *bridgehead servers* and are the only domain controllers of this particular domain that replicate over a WAN link. Once they receive updated information, they distribute it to the other domain controllers in their site.

This scenario examines replication between Red-Sales1 and Mil-Sales2. Both domain controllers are in the *Sales.Microsoft.com* domain, but in different sites (Redmond and Milan) (Figure 4.11).

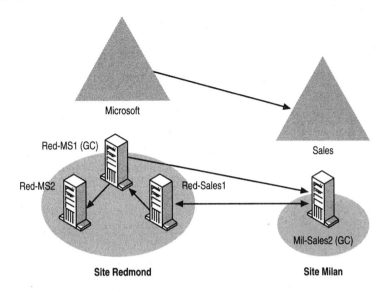

Figure 4.11   **Inter-site domain replication.**

The test measured only object creation. Changing the number of group members is not a factor because group members are *always* replicated between domain controllers of the same domain.

Here is the object creation traffic:

Users	Bytes replicated when adding users	Bytes replicated when adding global groups	Bytes replicated when adding volumes	Bytes replicated when adding printers
1	12,222	13,124	10,006	10,488
2	16,239	12,382	14,494	12,634
3	20,234	14,553	13,661	14,781
4	24,228	16,597	15,363	16,981
5	28,169	18,571	17,185	19,051
10	10,820	29,051	26,083	30,111
20	12,970	11,712	11,076	11,898
30	15,215	13,485	12,442	14,875
40	17,617	15,039	13,929	15,407
50	20,230	17,165	15,260	17,217
100	33,681	25,232	22,344	26,351
200	53,052	43,530	38,054	45,956
300	74,079	62,447	54,212	65,341
400	124,930	86,786	71,679	87,146
500	135,937	98,159	83,479	102,965

(continued)

Users	Bytes replicated when adding users	Bytes replicated when adding global groups	Bytes replicated when adding volumes	Bytes replicated when adding printers
1,000	264,003	188,283	160,255	199,188
5,000	1,295,294			
7,500	1,941,285			
10,000	2,602,976			
20,000	5,243,967			
25,000	6,453,716			

The table shows when compression kicks in. For user objects, it happens between 5 and 10 objects, for groups, printers and volumes (which are smaller) between 10 and 20 objects. Once compression reduces the traffic, the growth for more objects becomes predictable again. The graph in Figure 4.12 shows the pattern between 10 and 50 objects in each category:

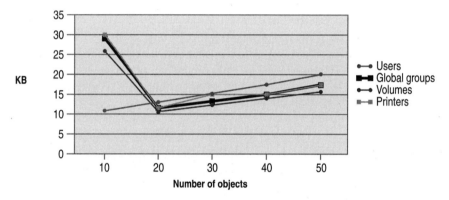

Figure 4.12   Inter-site domain replication.

To evaluate the efficiency of the compression, compare the numbers directly:

Users	Bytes replicated when adding users		Bytes replicated when adding global groups		Bytes replicated when adding printers		Bytes replicated when adding volumes	
	Inter-site	Intra-site	Inter-site	Intra-site	Inter-site	Intra-site	Inter-site	Intra-site
1	12,222	6,082	13,124	4,239	10,488	5,477	10,006	3,881
2	16,239	10,082	12,382	6,316	12,634	9,084	14,494	5,655
3	20,234	13,985	14,553	8,302	14,781	12,500	13,661	7,377
4	24,228	17,817	16,597	10,364	16,981	15,993	15,363	9,154

Users	Bytes replicated when adding users		Bytes replicated when adding global groups		Bytes replicated when adding printers		Bytes replicated when adding volumes	
	Inter-site	Intra-site	Inter-site	Intra-site	Inter-site	Intra-site	Inter-site	Intra-site
5	28,169	21,900	18,571	12,382	19,051	19,409	17,185	10,748
10	10,820	41,573	29,051	22,620	30,111	36,904	26,083	19,275
20	12,970	80,825	11,712	43,147	11,898	71,914	11,076	36,654
30	15,215	121,080	13,485	63,697	14,875	106,978	12,442	53,919
40	17,617	159,580	15,039	85,323	15,407	141,905	13,929	71,124
50	20,230	199,023	17,165	104,697	17,217	176,855	15,260	88,389
100	33,681	397,228	25,232	208,670	26,351	351,787	22,344	176,097
200	53,052	793,284	43,530	415,917	45,956	706,374	38,054	350,939
300	74,079	1,189,340	62,447	632,738	65,341	1,056,234	54,212	525,505
400	124,930	1,580,970	86,786	836,243	87,146	1,408,354	71,679	700,407
500	135,937	1,986,291	98,159	1,030,714	102,965	1,759,155	83,479	875,021
1,000	264,003	3,978,845	188,283	2,073,080	199,188	3,518,453	160,255	1,748,749

This is even more impressive when you look at charts for the single object types, shown in Figures 4.13, 4.14, and 4.15:

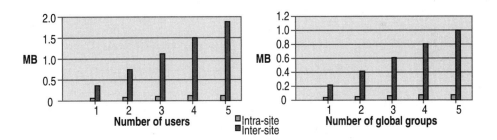

Figure 4.13   Inter-site domain replication.

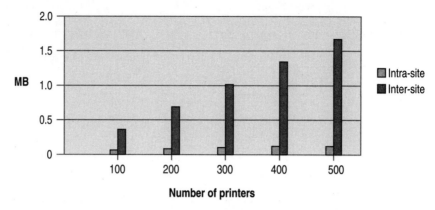

Figure 4.14   Inter-site domain replication.

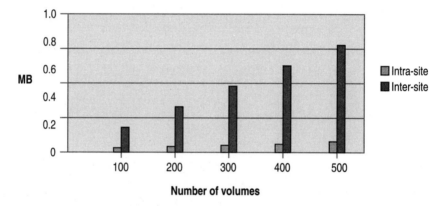

Figure 4.15   Inter-site domain replication.

Inter-site formula for calculating global catalog traffic generated by adding users, groups, volumes, and printers:

- **Users:** 10,433 + (259 x U), where U is the number of users added
- **Global Groups:** 12,606 + (174 x GG), where GG is the number of global groups added
- **Volumes:** 11,849 + (146 x V), where V is the number of volumes added
- **Printers:** 12,483+ (184 x P), where P is the number of printers added

For groups, it also matters how many members are added to the group when it is created. In the table above, the groups had no members. The table below illustrates the impact on group replication when members are added:

Univ. groups	No members	10 members	50 members
100	25,312	33,372	57,425
300	62,447	86,195	161,025
500	104,571	140,730	253,167

Creating new objects generates network traffic, and so does *removing* objects from the Active Directory. Deleting an object converts the object into a tombstone, which is replicated to all other domain controllers.

This table compares the traffic for the creation and deletion of user objects:

Users	Bytes replicated when adding users	Bytes replicated when removing users
1	12,222	9,858
2	16,239	11,444
3	20,234	13,014
4	24,228	14,601
5	28,169	16,111
10	10,820	21,164
20	12,970	33,910
30	15,215	12,490
40	17,617	14,073
50	20,230	15,391
100	33,681	22,492
200	53,052	38,792
300	74,079	54,824
400	124,930	72,643
500	135,937	85,275
1,000	264,003	164,196
5,000	1,295,294	795,941
Formulas	259 x U + 10433	157 x U + 11563

Even though tombstones are much smaller than full objects, tombstone replication creates considerable network traffic.

Adding User Attributes

Although the main operation in directory services is retrieving data, there are also frequent updates such as manipulating existing attributes or adding values to empty attributes (filling in information about users, such as street address, employee ID, etc.).

The test to measure replication traffic used a VB script that creates a 10-character string for a certain number of attributes. It was used on objects that already existed in the directory.

```
DSOU= "LDAP://OU=TestOU,DC=parent,DC=com"

set MyOU = GetObject(DSOU)
MyString = "klcdef1234"


for each MyUser in MyOU

    MyUser.put ("streetAddress"), MyString
    MyUser.put ("company"),MyString
    MyUser.put ("department"),MyString
    MyUser.put ("description"), MyString
    MyUser.put ("displayName"), MyString
    MyUser.put ("employeeID"), MyString
    MyUser.put ("comment"), MyString
    MyUser.put ("division"), MyString
    MyUser.put ("mail"), MyString
    MyUser.put ("mobile"), MyString
    MyUser.setinfo
next

wscript.echo "done"
```

The table shows the results:

Users	+1 Attr.	+2 Attr.	+3 Attr.	+4 Attr.	+5 Attr.
1	8,710	8,790	9,126	8,966	9,062
2	9,062	9,238	9,414	9,590	9,766
3	9,414	9,666	9,942	10,312	10,584
4	9,766	10,118	10,584	10,936	11,288
5	10,118	10,664	11,112	11,544	12,046
10	11,188	12,926	13,997	14,931	15,811
20	15,947	17,825	19,770	21,644	23,518
30	19,910	22,718	25,412	28,293	31,105
40	23,678	27,497	31,185	35,064	12,330
50	27,577	32,336	36,958	12,842	13,545
100	14,329	15,455	16,255	17,681	18,727
200	22,860	24,157	26,098	29,067	30,961
500	43,300	48,896	56,852	61,381	65,942
1,000	102,107	90,747	100,544	115,741	125,301
5,000	393,598	428,144	473,190	550,346	598,291

Users	+6 Attr.	+7 Attr.	+8 Attr.	+9 Attr.	+10 Attr.
1	9,142	9,238	9,318	9,414	9,490
2	9,942	10,118	10,408	10,644	10,760
3	10,836	11,112	11,368	11,640	11,946
4	11,640	12,046	12,398	12,750	13,102
5	12,478	13,469	13,549	13,997	14,429
10	16,805	17,685	18,619	19,690	20,570
20	25,332	27,337	29,211	31,025	32,976
30	33,990	11,850	12,218	12,570	12,906
40	12,730	13,062	13,753	14,249	14,649
50	14,073	14,441	15,087	15,679	16,207
100	20,162	20,850	21,944	23,466	24,404
200	33,359	34,935	37,414	40,194	42,312
500	72,422	76,314	82,427	89,315	94,751
1,000	137,808	145,455	158,088	171,984	185,168
5,000	664,032	700,817	764,980	831,957	892,102

The table demonstrates again when compression kicks in. For example, replicating 10 changed attributes to 20 users generates more network traffic than the same operation on 30 or 100 users. This shows that it is good practice to let changes accumulate before replicating them, which means that reducing replication frequency probably also reduces network traffic.

The data can be represented by the 3D diagram and equation in Figure 4.16.

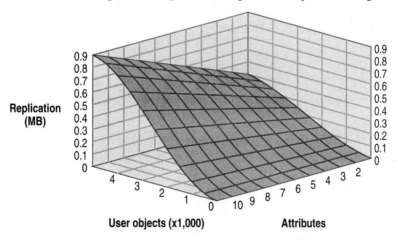

Figure 4.16   Effect of compression on replication traffic.

As seen in the table, the compression threshold is around 38 KB. The model approximates the impact of compression and the percentage of error decreases on either side of the compression threshold.

Replication of Password Changes

User and workstation passwords are just attributes, but they differ from string-based attributes in that passwords are always encrypted—in storage and replication. Data encryption reduces the efficiency of any compression algorithm because encryption scrambles the recurring patterns that can usually be found in strings or in non-compressed pictures. Therefore, password change replication creates more traffic than normal attribute replication.

You can use this VB script to change passwords on existing user objects:

```
DSOU= "LDAP://OU=TestOU,DC=parent,DC=com"
set MyOU = GetObject(DSOU)

MyPassword = "Reset"
MyCounter = 0

for each MyUser in MyOU
    MyUser.SetPassword MyPassword
    MyUser.setinfo
next

wscript.echo "done"
```

The table below compares replication for passwords and normal string based attributes:

Changes	Passwords	String attributes
1	17,936	8,710
2	30,849	9,062
3	34,042	9,414
4	27,613	9,766
5	35,720	10,118
10	43,707	11,188
20	44,842	15,947
30	68,158	19,910
40	67,097	23,678
50	68,079	27,577

Changes	Passwords	String attributes
100	120,296	14,329
200	232,768	22,860
500	505,725	43,300
1,000	967,816	102,107

Password replication traffic is considerably higher. You can calculate it with this formula:

If **P** is the number of simultaneous password changes, the number of bytes replicated is:

```
943 x P + 29,345
```

The change of a single string based attribute is 77 x U + 12,558, where U is the number of users for which the attribute was changed.

Thus replicating 1000 passwords causes more traffic than creating 1000 users. This is worth keeping in mind if your system includes large numbers of users who have to change their passwords at the same time. For example, in domain migration projects, it is common to create a new domain containing new accounts. You get everything set up over the weekend, then on Monday morning users have to log on to the new domain. Usually, they have to change their passwords the first time they log in. If there are 1,000 users in one site using the new domain, more than 950 KB of replication traffic is generated. It is buffered and is not replicated until the replication window (which you probably have specified via the schedule on the site link) opens up.

Don't confuse password replication with "urgent" DC to PDC FSMO password transmission. An updated password is sent intra-site or inter-site (configurable) to the PDC FSMO role owner separate from normal replication between DCs. An urgent password change is additional traffic to the replication between DCs.

Changing Group Memberships

Along with password changes, another frequent administrative operation is group membership changes such as addition of members to or removal of members from a group.

The Active Directory implements group memberships as a multi-valued attribute on the group. Replication in Active Directory happens on a per-attribute level, so changes to a multi-valued attribute require that the attribute be replicated. Because the entire multi-valued attribute must be replicated, group membership changes require replicating all group members. Thus traffic is determined by the size of the group after the change, *not* by the number of changes.

In Active Directory, group membership is restricted to 5,000. To test and measure group change replication traffic, groups with 1 to 5,000 members were created, then one member was removed from the group. Here are the results:

Initial number of members	Bytes replicated
10	10,054
20	11,834
30	13,533
40	15,196
50	16,821
100	25,540
200	42,839
300	16,897
400	19,766
500	22,524
1,000	36,650
2,000	65,107
5,000	150,451

Compression kicks in between 200 and 300 group memberships in a single group. Note, however, that in a production environment, the membership change will not be the only operation that is replicated. If, for example, users are created and then added to groups, all data is collected before the compression algorithm is applied. If **M** is the number of members in a group, the number of bytes replicated when a member is deleted from the group is: $16,000 + (27 \times M)$

Administrative Operations

So far, all tests concerned the addition of users, groups, and other objects that are typically stored in a directory service. Other administrative information (such as subnet and site data) also has to be stored in the Active Directory, and information such as DNS data can be stored in the Active Directory or elsewhere. The next tests were designed to show how changes to this type of information affect inter-site or WAN traffic.

Dynamic DNS information

Microsoft's DNS server and Active Directory allow you to store DNS information in the directory database and replicate it from there. This usually is more advantageous than using standard zone transfer: DNS servers that are also Active Directory domain controllers are *primary* DNS servers, which means they can accept Dynamic DNS update requests from clients. And this means you can create one replication topology for Active Directory and DNS, saving you the trouble of maintaining a separate topology for the DNS zone transfer. Active Directory DNS integrated zones also allow you to use secure DNS.

The next test looks at how directory integrated DNS zones affect network traffic. The test used the *dnscmd.exe* tool (from the *Microsoft Windows 2000 Resource Kit*) to add records to DNS. When directory integrated DNS zones are used, these records are stored in the Domain naming context.

This batch file was used to add groups of entries in DNS:

```
echo off
dnscmd 10.10.1.3 /RecordADD parent.com dummy1    10.10.10.1
dnscmd 10.10.1.3 /RecordADD parent.com dummy2    10.10.10.2
dnscmd 10.10.1.3 /RecordADD parent.com dummy3    10.10.10.3
dnscmd 10.10.1.3 /RecordADD parent.com dummy4    10.10.10.4
dnscmd 10.10.1.3 /RecordADD parent.com dummy5    10.10.10.5
dnscmd 10.10.1.3 /RecordADD parent.com dummy6    10.10.10.6
dnscmd 10.10.1.3 /RecordADD parent.com dummy7    10.10.10.7
dnscmd 10.10.1.3 /RecordADD parent.com dummy8    10.10.10.8
dnscmd 10.10.1.3 /RecordADD parent.com dummy9    10.10.10.9
dnscmd 10.10.1.3 /RecordADD parent.com dummy10   10.10.10.10
```

Here are the results:

Records	Bytes replicated
10	12,746
20	31,585
30	36,104
40	40,563
50	12,602
100	18,951
200	31,161
300	39,099
400	48,729
500	53,307
1,000	124,069

The traffic is predictable, according to this formula:

If **R** is the number of records added to an Active Directory integrated DDNS, the number of bytes replicated is: $94 \times R + 18{,}214$.

Modifying Security on Active Directory Objects

In Active Directory, security can be applied on any directory object, even on a single attribute. When you change security on a container object, you can specify that the changes be pushed down to all objects and child-containers within the container. This allows you flexibility when setting up security. For example, you can easily specify that only members of the HR group can access the *Salary* attribute on any user objects in the entire forest. Or you can administer specific objects (printers, etc.) or attributes (passwords, etc.) or you can delegate administration to users or groups on the level of one or multiple organizational units (OUs).

When an access control change on a container should be applied to all objects within the container, the domain controller actually manipulates all access control entries on all objects in the container. This ensures that when somebody wants to access an object, the directory service can check access rights only on this object—it does not have to walk up the tree and check on all containers. This speeds up access checks, but extends the time needed to apply the change.

When access control entries are manipulated on multiple objects, the effect on replication depends on whether the change is applied on the container then sent down to all objects, or applied on multiple objects directly. In real life, most people tend to apply the change on the container when, for example, they want to delegate the right to reset user passwords on all user objects in one OU.

You can make changes in access control either with the delegation wizard in the Active Directory Users and Workstations MMC-snap-in or by selecting the object or container object of interest and selecting the **Security** tab from the **Properties** dialog box. You can also use VB scripting.

Here are the results of a test on network traffic generated by replication on a single OU:

Objects in OU	Bytes replicated when OU re-ACLed	Bytes replicated when 1 ACE added	Bytes replicated when 2 ACEs added
10	9,570	27,357	15,579
20	9,570	9,938	9,954
30	9,570	10,772	10,884
40	9,570	11,540	11,617
50	9,570	12,282	12,330
100	9,570	16,347	16,379
200	9,570	26,050	
300	9,570	35,526	
400	9,570	46,952	
500	9,570	52,958	

Objects in OU	Bytes replicated when OU re-ACLed	Bytes replicated when 1 ACE added	Bytes replicated when 2 ACEs added
1,000	9,570	99,484	
2,000	9,570	205,071	
5,000	9,570	471,518	

The first column shows the number of objects (users in this case) in the OU. The second column is bytes of network traffic generated when the change was made on the container (the OU) itself, and then inherited by the objects in the container. You can see that the number of objects in the container does not affect network traffic. This is because only the *change* on the container is replicated. Note that this number depends entirely on the size of the security descriptor. The security descriptor is just an attribute: the more ACEs are set on the container, the bigger this number will be. The third column shows the traffic when the changes are applied on the objects directly instead of using the container. This time, traffic grows when the number of manipulated objects gets bigger, and that is why this operation is not the better option. Still, you can use this formula to calculate the results:

If **R** is the number of objects where you add one ACE, the number of bytes replicated is: 94 x R + 18,214. Note again that this number changes if you add Access Control Entries to the defaults.

Modifying the Configuration (Subnets, Sites, and Site Links)

Modifying configuration information such as subnets, sites, and site links is of special interest because the Configuration container is replicated to all domain controllers. You can decide through partitioning and GC placement whether Domain naming context information, either within the domain or through partial replication to global catalogs, is replicated to a specific site. Not so Configuration and Schema information: these are always replicated to all domain controllers. Schema and Configuration naming context information can be replicated either with RPC-based or SMTP transport. The next test added the traffic for both transports to the configuration tables. For more information on subnets, sites and site links, See Chapter 2, "Compaq's Windows 2000 Site Topology Design."

You can use scripts to create configuration objects. The CD that comes with this book includes the sample script *CreateSites.vbs* (see the Replication folder on the CD). When you add sites, remember that the *iteration* argument allows you to run the script several times without having to delete (and synchronize) the sites created on a previous run.

The following three tables display the results:

New sites	Replicated bytes (RPC)	Replicated bytes (SMTP)
1	18,068	31,890
2	19,781	41,094
3	25,202	50,578
4	30,815	59,734
5	36,374	69,000
10	14,071	30,114
20	19,744	45,164
30	25,086	44,888
40	32,637	68,893
50	38,128	76,451
100	71,311	162,440
200	133,808	297,912
300	196,277	419,849
400	259,051	551,128
500	322,650	683,145
1000	635,230	1,259,917

New subnets	Replicated bytes (RPC)	Replicated bytes (SMTP)
1	10,246	23,247
2	11,960	26,131
3	13,675	29,073
4	15,329	31,485
5	17,027	34,727
10	25,462	49,151
20	11,266	24,177
30	12,696	26,307
40	14,231	34,427
50	15,789	30,379
100	23,480	40,715
200	40,492	77,376
300	57,501	114,061
400	76,487	154,000
500	89,989	171,862
1000	174,009	304,104

New site links	Replicated bytes (RPC)	Replicated bytes (SMTP)
1	10,838	24,177
2	13,068	28,105
3	15,505	31,919
4	17,795	35,787
5	20,232	39,599
10	32,106	59,059
20	11,848	25,047
30	13,591	27,165
40	15,229	29,561
50	17,211	32,129
100	26,557	44,605
200	46,338	84,582
300	66,123	124,853
400	88,612	169,072
500	104,386	189,488
1000	201,978	374,872

Note that the traffic for the SMTP transport is higher than the RPC transport. This is discussed at length in the section below on global catalog server replication.

Again, the network traffic pattern is linear and can be calculated with these formulas:

If **Nsites** is the number of sites added to the configuration, the number of bytes replicated is:

```
Nsites x 616 + 14,748 ) over RPC
Nsites x 1,246 + 35,685 over SMTP
```

If **Nsubnets** is the number of subnets added to the configuration, the number of bytes replicated is:

```
Nsubnets x 160 + 11403 over RPC
Nsubnets x 284 + 25938 ) over SMTP
```

If **Nsitelinks** is the number of site links added to the configuration, the number of bytes replicated is:

```
Nsitelinks x 186 + 12787 over RPC
Nsitelinks x 343 + 25352 over SMTP
```

Schema Changes

Schema information also is replicated to all domain controllers regardless of domain membership. The schema defines what classes of objects can be created in the Active Directory and what attributes can or must be set on them.

You can use this script to define new attributes:

```
dim oRootDSE
dim oSchema
dim oAttribute
dim MyOID
dim MyCounter
dim MyNumberofAttrib
dim MyAttribute


MyCounter=1
MyNumberofAttrib=2 'to increment at each run
MyNewOID="1.2.840.113556.1.4.7000.18" 'to increment at each run
MyNewAttribute="test4" 'to increment at each run

set oRootDSE = getobject("LDAP://RootDSE")
set oSchema = getobject("LDAP://"&oRootDSE.get("schemaNamingContext"))

for x = MyCounter to MyNumberofAttrib

    MyOID = MyNewOID & cstr(x)
    MyAttribute = MyNewAttribute & cstr(x)
wscript.echo MyAttribute
wscript.echo MyOID
    set oAttribute = oSchema.create("attributeSchema","cn=" &
MyAttribute)
        oAttribute.put "cn", MyAttribute
        oAttribute.put "attributeId", MyOID
        oAttribute.put "oMSyntax",2
        oAttribute.put "attributeSyntax","2.5.5.9"
        oAttribute.put "isSingleValued",True
        oAttribute.setinfo
Next

wscript.echo "done"
```

You can use this script to define new classes:

```
dim oRootDSE
dim oSchema
dim oAttribute
dim MyOID
dim MyCounter
dim MyNumberofAttrib
dim Myclass
```

```
MyCounter=1
MyNumberofClasses=2 'to increment at each run
MyNewOID="1.2.840.113556.1.5.7000.13" 'to increment at each run
MyNewClass="ClassToReplicate" 'to increment at each run

set oRootDSE = getobject("LDAP://RootDSE")
set oSchema = getobject("LDAP://"&oRootDSE.get("schemaNamingContext"))

for x = MyCounter to MyNumberofClasses

    MyOID =  MyNewOID  & cstr(x)
    MyClass = MyNewClass  & cstr(x)

wscript.echo MyClass
wscript.echo MyOID
    set oClass = oSchema.create("classSchema","cn=" & MyClass)

    oClass.put "cn", Myclass
    oClass.put "governsId", MyOID
    oClass.put "objectClassCategory",1 ' 1 = Structural Class

    oClass.setinfo

Next

wscript.echo "done"
```

You can use this script to associate attributes to classes:

```
const ADS_PROPERTY_APPEND          = &H3

dim oRootDSE
dim oSchema
dim oClass

MyCounter=1
MyNumberofClasses=1 'to increment at each run
MyNumberofAttributes=1 'to increment at each run
MyNewClassOID="1.2.840.113556.1.5.7000.13" 'to increment at each run
MyNewAttribOID="1.2.840.113556.1.4.7000.18" 'to increment at each run
MyNewClass="ClassToReplicate"
MyArray = MyNewAttribOID  & cstr(MyCounter)

set oRootDSE = getobject("LDAP://RootDSE")
set oSchema = getobject("LDAP://"&oRootDSE.get("schemaNamingContext"))

for x = MyCounter to MyNumberofClasses

    'MyClassOID =  MyNewClassOID  & cstr(x)
    MyClass = MyNewClass  & cstr(x)
```

```
wscript.echo MyClass

    for Y = MyCounter to MyNumberofAttributes
        MyArray = MyArray &"," & MyNewAttribOID  & cstr(y+1)
        wscript.echo MyArray
    Next

  set oRootDSE = getobject("LDAP://RootDSE")
set oSchema = getobject("LDAP://"&oRootDSE.get("schemaNamingContext"))

set oClass = oSchema.getobject("classSchema","cn=" & Myclass)

oClass.putex ADS_PROPERTY_APPEND,"mayContain",Array(MyArray)

  oClass.setinfo

next

wscript.echo "done"
```

You must execute these scripts in the order they are presented above: create attributes first, then classes, and then associate classes and users.

New attributes	Bytes replicated (RPC)	Bytes replicated (SMTP)
1	10,546	24,653
2	12,188	27,703
3	14,087	30,805
4	15,729	34,195
5	17,551	37,345
10	26,609	53,649
20	11,976	25,809
30	13,927	28,769
40	16,073	31,935
50	18,225	34,835
100	29,925	49,321

New classes	Bytes replicated (RPC)	Bytes replicated (SMTP)
1	11,154	25,427
2	13,463	29,421
3	15,505	33,179
4	17,743	37,113
5	24,370	40,991
10	31,119	60,735

New classes	Bytes replicated (RPC)	Bytes replicated (SMTP)
20	13,220	27,219
30	15,689	30,509
40	18,273	34,033
50	20,784	37,451
100	37,628	55,048

Additional existing attributes in an existing class	Bytes replicated (RPC)	Bytes replicated (SMTP)
1	13,266	24,436
2	9,408	
3	9,364	24,642
4	9,380	24,668
5		24,657
10	13,470	25,060
20	10,482	25,430
30	9,742	26,086
50	10,231	27,318

Linear regression, when compression is used, yields these formulas:

If **A** is the number of new **attributes** added the schema, the number of bytes replicated is:

```
130 x A + 13 840 x A over RPC
134 x A + 31220 over SMTP
```

If **C** is the number of new **classes** added the schema, the number of bytes replicated is:

```
172 x C + 15748 over RPC
157 x C + 33596 over SMTP
```

Global Catalog Server Replication

Inter-site GC replication involves two domain controllers (one a GC) that belong to different domains and are replicating Schema, Configuration, and the partial Domain naming context. This type of replication can use RPC-over-IP or the SMTP transport. The tests examine both transports, as shown in Figure 4.17.

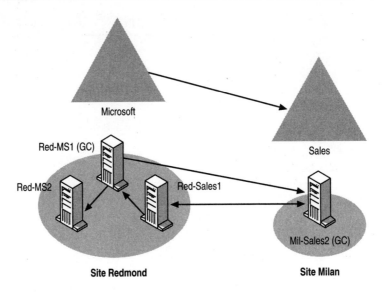

Figure 4.17   Inter-site global catalog replication.

In the example, Mil-Sales2 (a GC in *Sales.Microsoft.com*) replicates partial *Microsoft.com* information from Red-MS1. Note that Red-MS1, which is also a GC, would not use Mil-Sales2 as a source for the *Sales.Microsoft.com* Naming context, because Red-MS1 can find a closer domain controller in *Sales.Microsoft.com* (in this case, Red-Sales1 is in the same site).

For this replication set, three factors are of interest: how partial inter-site replication compares to partial intra-site replication, how group membership affects the overall picture, and how the RPC and the SMTP based transports compare to each other in terms of traffic generated.

Adding User Objects

For this test, user objects were created on one Domain naming context and then replicated to a GC. The table shows both transports. For comparison, the table shows the domain replication traffic between two domain controllers in the same domain:

	Global catalog replication		Domain replication	
Users	**Bytes (RPC)**	**Bytes (SMTP)**	**Users**	**Bytes (RPC)**
1	11,240	29,758	1	12,222
2	14,269	33,869	2	16,239
3	17,221	37,980	3	20,234
4	20,250	41,104	4	24,228
5	23,202	46,202	5	28,169

	Global catalog replication		Domain replication	
Users	Bytes (RPC)	Bytes (SMTP)	Users	Bytes (RPC)
10	38,253	76,378	10	10,820
20	12,314	27,640	20	12,970
30	18,025	30,222	30	15,215
40	16,031	32,876	40	17,617
50	21,392	39,298	50	20,230
100	28,129	49,182	100	33,681
200	49,396	91,705	200	53,052
300	70,831	133,942	300	74,079
400	95,160	188,581	400	124,930
500	112,045	203,347	500	135,937
1,000	217,484	407,269	1,000	264,003

The tests show that GC replication causes less traffic than intra-domain replication using the RPC transport. For instance, for 1,000 users domain replication is 264,003 bytes and GC replication is 217,484 bytes. The tests used only the mandatory attribute set on users: in a real production environment, users generally have other information added. This affects domain replication (as shown above) but not GC replication, which changes only if the schema is altered to replicate more existing attributes or new attributes to GCs.

SMTP creates considerably more traffic than RPC because the headers that the SMTP system has to create for the messages cannot be compressed. Compression efficiency naturally goes down. To choose a transport for inter-site GC replication:

- If your network is fast, or slow but reliable, choose the RPC transport
- If your network is unreliable (many retries) or connected through a messaging system, choose the SMTP transport

In any case, keep in mind that you can use SMTP only for Schema, Configuration, and GC replication, not for Domain replication. Whenever domain controllers in different sites are connected through a WAN link, you must use the RPC transport for replication, so you should configure *all* replication traffic to use RPC.

From the traffic pattern you can derive these formulas:

If **U** is the number of users added, the number of bytes generated for replicating the GC is:

```
198 x U + 14681 over RPC
385 x U + 20699 over SMTP
```

Replicating Groups

All group types are replicated to the GCs (as are all objects). Only universal groups publish group memberships to the global catalog—global domain groups and local domain groups do not—so while planning you need to find out:

- What traffic is generated when empty groups (of any type) are created
- How group membership changes the traffic for universal groups

The second of these is especially important because replication happens every time universal group membership changes; global domain groups and domain local groups remain static in the GCs after the group is generated.

Since group type does not affect traffic significantly when empty groups are created, the next tests measured only global domain groups:

Global groups	Bytes (RPC)	Bytes (SMTP)
1	10,380	25,752
2	12,422	31,132
3	14,493	36,512
4	16,641	41,892
5	18,631	47,274
10	29,051	57,278
20	11,732	26,934
30	13,529	29,090
40	15,103	31,496
50	16,081	33,720
100	25,296	49,486
200	43,913	84,403
300	62,479	130,366
400	83,069	172,363
500	97,993	192,412
1,000	189,659	370,884

The numbers can be used to derive this formula:

If **G** is the number of global groups added to the directory, the number of bytes generated for replicating the GC is:

```
174xGG+12136 over RPC
342 x GG + 26377 over SMTP
```

Group replication traffic for GCs is similar to domain replication when only the mandatory attribute set is used. For example, inter-site domain replication for 100 GG is 25,312 and the inter-site GC replication for 100 GG is 25,296 using RPC. Nevertheless, whether groups are replicated inside a domain or to a GC affects traffic because the bulk of the replication traffic is generated by the group membership, which is not replicated to GCs for domain local groups or domain global groups.

The next test demonstrates this. It measured the traffic caused by the creation of universal groups with group members:

Objects	Universal groups (10 members) (RPC)	Universal groups (10 members) SMTP)	Universal groups (50 members) (RPC)	Universal groups (50 members) (SMTP)
1	12,218	28,318	19,766	38,138
2	16,163		30,917	
3	20,234		36,275	
4	24,152		11,476	
5	28,169	52,500	11,930	27,072
10	11,092	25,888	14,233	30,262
20	13,609	29,188	18,723	36,316
30	15,852	32,412	23,274	42,354
40	18,247	35,546	27,825	48,384
50	20,818	39,188	32,412	54,718
100	33,148	57,242	54,265	85,766
Formulas	124 x UG +16436	219 x UG + 30544	316 x UG +17938	560 x UG + 27467

The traffic models for RPC and SMTP GC replication are shown in the 3D diagrams in Figure 4.18.

With RPC transport, you can calculate the overhead per group member this way:

```
Overhead/member = (Traffic for 50 members - Traffic for 10
members)/Number of members
```

For 1 universal group using data in the table above.

```
= (19,766 - 12,218)/40 for a single universal group increased from 10 to
50 members
= 189 bytes per member per group
```

This includes the overhead to initiate the replication and does not account for replication. To minimize the overhead associated with replication and include the impact of compression, choose a larger number of groups. So for 100 universal groups:

```
(Traffic for 50 members - Traffic for 10 members)/(Number of Groups x
Number of Users)
```

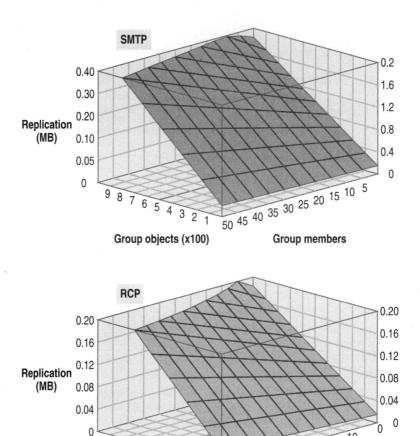

Figure 4.18 Traffic models for RPC and SMTP GC replication.

Taking two data points to compensate for compression, you can see that the overhead is a lot less than for a single universal group:

At 10 universal groups

```
= (14,233-11,092)/(10x40)
= 9 bytes per member per group
```

At 100 universal groups

```
= (54,265-33148)/(100x40)
= 6 bytes per member per group
```

So although the maximum traffic per member per universal group is 189 bytes, a planning figure of 8 bytes is a realistic figure with which to account for implemented universal group sizes and for replication compression.

For SMTP, the overhead is higher—about 12 bytes per member per group.

Printers and Volumes

To complete the picture, here are the numbers for printers and file volumes.

Printers.

Printers	Bytes replicated (RPC)	Bytes replicated (SMTP)
1	10,520	25,790
2	12,622	29,396
3	14,931	33,204
4	17,093	36,608
5	19,201	40,214
10	30,325	58,382
20	11,930	27,068
30	13,737	29,446
40	15,455	32,002
50	17,297	34,558
100	26,351	46,794
200	46,132	87,189
300	65,741	127,628
400	87,578	171,335
500	103,493	192,393
1,000	200,208	378,373

The resulting traffic formula is:

If **P** is the number of printers added to the directory, the number of bytes generated for replicating the GC is:

- 185 x P + 12439 over RPC
- 349 x P + 25015 over SMTP

Volumes.

Volumes	Bytes replicated (RPC)	Bytes replicated (SMTP)
1	10,006	25,094
2	11,822	27,902
3	13,673	30,710
4	15,379	33,518
5	17,157	36,328
10	26,103	50,318
20	11,108	25,936
30	12,458	27,778
40	13,929	29,776
50	15,231	31,690
100	22,216	41,186
200	37,894	75,773
300	53,508	110,356
400	70,929	147,699
500	83,319	163,903
1,000	159,930	321,001

If **V** is the number of volumes added to the directory, the number of bytes generated for replicating the GC is:

- 146 x V+11569 over RPC
- 293 x V + 23655 over SMTP

Tuning SMTP Replication

The next test created 200 sites, and showed this SMTP-related network traffic pattern (assuming the sites were created on a DC in site A):

```
Site B        6K      > Site A
Wait up to 15 seconds
Site B <   30K         Site A
Wait up to 15 seconds

Site B        6K       > Site A
Wait up to 15 seconds
Site B <   30K         Site A
Wait up to 15 seconds
```

```
Site B      6K       > Site A
Wait up to 15 seconds
Site B <    30K        Site A
Wait up to 15 seconds

Site B      6K         Site A
Wait up to 15 seconds
Site B <    30K        Site A
Wait up to 15 seconds

Site B      6K       > Site A
Wait up to 15 seconds
Site B <    30K        Site A
Wait up to 15 seconds

Site B      6K       > Site A
Wait up to 15 seconds
Site B <    30K        Site A
Wait up to 15 seconds

Site B      6K       > Site A
Wait up to 15 seconds
Site B <    24K        Site A
Wait up to 15 seconds
```

The bridgehead server in site B asks the bridgehead server in site A for changes (this is the 6 K packet). Site A sends the data (the 30 K packets). Site B then asks for more change (the 2nd 6 K packet), etc.

Where do these 30 K packets come from? By default, packet sizes are computed on the basis of memory size (the test used DCs with 128 MB memory) unless you have more than 1 gigabyte (GB) or less than 100 megabytes (MB). You can override these memory-based values in the registry and adjust the default size of the packets used to transport Active Directory replication data. Modify or add entries to this registry path with the REG_DWORD data type:

```
HKEY_LOCAL_MACHINE\System\CurrentControlSet\Services\NTDS\Parameters.
```

These entries determine the maximum number of objects per packet and maximum size of the packets.

For SMTP replication between sites:

- **Replicator async inter site packet size (objects)**

  Range: >=1

- **Replicator async inter site packet size (bytes)**

  Range: >=10 KB

If you do not set these registry entries, the system limits the packet size this way:

- The packet sizes in bytes is 1/100th the size of RAM with a minimum of 1 MB and a maximum of 10 MB.
- The packet size in objects is 1/1,000,000th the size of RAM, with a minimum of 100 objects and a maximum of 1,000 objects.

There is one exception: the value of the **Replicator async inter site packet size (bytes)** entry is always 1 MB. Many mail systems limit the amount of data that can be sent in a mail message (2 MB to 4 MB is common), although most Windows-based mail systems can handle large 10-MB mail messages.

Even though the destination requests an initial size, it can be constrained by the source's memory size. If this happens, you need to adapt the registry key described above on the source *and* destination DCs.

Here are some default sizes of data packets (assuming 100 objects/packet) when the domain controllers have 128 MB memory:

Element	Data packet size
Site	30 K
User	40 K
Global group	35 K
Printer	37 K
Volume	30 K
Subnet	33 K
Site Link	37 K

Depending on your network, you might want to avoid sending several 6-K request packets to obtain 30-K answer packets. The table below shows how network traffic might change depending on the value of the Replicator async inter-site packet size (objects) registry key. The test repeated operations such as adding 200 sites, adding 500 users, with different values of the mentioned registry key (default, 200, 500, and 1000).

Value of "Replicator async inter-site packet size (objects)."

# New Objects	Default (128MB)		200		500		1000	
	Packet size	Bytes	Packet size	Bytes	Packet size	Bytes	Packet size	Bytes
200 Sites	30K	297,912	42K	234,996	95K	189,161	147K	173,998
500 Global groups	35K	192,412	49K	169,567	115K	156,695	116K	140,052

# New Objects	Default (128MB)		200		500		1000	
	Packet size	Bytes	Packet size	Bytes	Packet size	Bytes	Packet size	Bytes
500 Users	40K	203,347	56K	188,586	133K	175,109	133K	158,712
500 Printers	37K	192,393	52K	175,348	121K	161,955	121K	145,680
500 Volumes	30K	163,903	41K	147,716	94K	133,437	95K	117,550
500 Subnets	33K	171,862	45K	158,814	105K	145,663	105K	128,578
500 Site links	37K	189,488	52K	177,412	123K	164,711	123K	147,922

The grayed cells did not hit the limit on the number of objects. But if you take the line for adding 200 sites, you can see that by changing the *Replicator async inter site packet size (objects)* registry value from its default (internally computed on a 128 MB system) to 1000, you can reduce the traffic by 40% for sites, 28% for global groups, 28% for users, 25% for printers, 29% for volumes, 26% for subnets and 22% for site links.

Inter-Site Traffic Calculation Tables

As shown above, you can approximate Active Directory and global catalog replication traffic using formulas derived from the test results. On the CD that accompanies this book, the document *Inter Site Traffic Calculation Tables.do*c uses the formulas to build some network traffic reference tables. The tables also show the time it takes to replicate the information over various types of networks.

Slow Link Replication

The tests in this section show some numbers of real replication tests over slow links. Domain controllers in different sites were connected by a high-class WAN simulator called *null-modem cable*. Sites were connected by two dial-on-demand RAS servers connected by a serial cable (Figure 4.19). Line speed was simulated by configuring the speed on the modem connection.

This table shows traffic volumes and replication times using line speeds between 115,200 and 2,400 bps:

Inter-site replication using WAN emulator at different speeds.

Speed (bps)	Users	Total frame size (bytes)	Number of frames	Replication time (seconds)
115,200	1000	273,689	309	45.223675
57,600	1	9,316	13	1.862883
	10	7,810	11	1.902945
	100	32,072	47	7.561703
	1000	280,047	418	67.975198
38,400	1000	284,036	428	93.385213
19,200	1000	285,852	457	161.704132
9,600	1000	283,130	405	298.570392
2,400	1000	306,083	536	1589.207628

Another test examined replication stability over very slow links. RPC-based replication was stable (without optimizations) on 19,200 bps connections, but began to encounter time-outs at 9,600 and 2,400 bps. Optimizations such as increasing the window size for TCP/IP, etc., helped to stabilize RPC replication for all line speeds. For tuning explanations and procedures, see the files chapt01.pdf, chapt02.pdf, and chapt03.pdf in the folder OptChaps on the CD that accompanies this book. (These files are electronic versions of three chapters that appear in a previous Notes from the Field volume, *Optimizing Network Traffic*.)

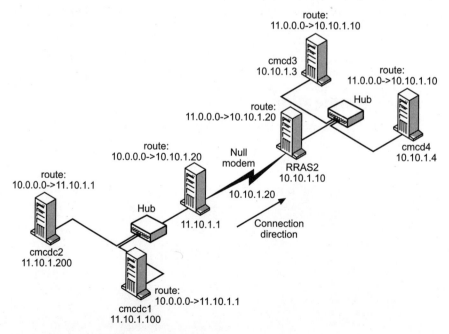

Figure 4.19   Site link test environment.

Tests were performed in a lab environment, where 100% of the network bandwidth was available for replication. Because this is seldom the case in real-world environments, the tests added load on the network by copying files at the same time. At 9,600 bps, replication was still stable after optimizations, although the time required for replication was significantly higher:

Replication and File Copy at 9600 bps

Users	File size	Total frame size (bytes)	Number of frames	Replication time (seconds)
1000	242,688	593,027	1050	665.557114

To put these figures in perspective, consider that most companies don't have more than 1,000 changes per replication sequence. Even so, the tests show that replication of 1,000 user objects took only 11 minutes over a low-speed 9,600 bps connection that could give up 50% for the directory service.

Conclusion

Some replication observations and recommendations:

- Intra-site replication assumes good network connectivity so domain controllers can save CPU cycles (for client logons, search operations etc.) by not compressing data for intra-site replication.

- Replication traffic is predictable. Use the tables in this chapter to find the data for your objects. If you set additional attributes on objects, add 85 - 100 bytes per attribute for string sizes up to 10 characters.

- Partial replication (global catalog replication) is smaller than normal replication. As more attributes are set on objects, the size difference increases.

- Inter-site replication adds compression. If there is a slow link between domain controllers be sure they are in separate sites.

- You can schedule inter-site replication to reduce communication between domain controllers or avoid network contention during peak hours.

- The SMTP transport creates more network traffic than the RPC Site connector. Use RPCs between sites whenever possible. For very slow links, tune SMTP replication according to your hardware platform.

To choose between RPC and SMTP inter-site transports:

- If good network connectivity is available and you want fast client logon—use one site.

- If you want to reduce network traffic and the connection between domain controllers is fairly reliable—use multiple sites and the RPC-over-IP replication connector.

- If the network connection is so unreliable that RPC-based replication doesn't work, or domain controllers have no direct network connection (connected only through a messaging system)—use the SMTP replication connector. Remember that you can use it only for Schema, Configuration, and partial replication, *not* for replication between two domain controllers in the same domain.

C H A P T E R   5

Active Directory Client Network Traffic

By Markus Vilcinskas, Matthias Leibmann, Andreas Luther, Microsoft Enterprise Services; Johan Grobler, Microsoft Consulting Services; and Dan Thompson, Microsoft Corporation

The directory service and replication, as the previous two chapters have shown, create network traffic. Clients generate traffic as well. This chapter shows how to measure and account for client traffic. It can be a significant planning factor: you may base a decision to partition the Active Directory namespace on a comparison of expected client traffic and replication traffic. For example, a primary design goal is to minimize WAN traffic. Suppose that your network has branch offices connected through slow links to headquarters and that you can easily add local domain controllers. If the daily logon and directory lookup traffic of five users already causes more network traffic than replicating all company data to the branch, you could consider five users to be the threshold for adding a DC in a branch.

This is a very simple example. This chapter goes into more detail to help you make these sorts of decisions. Many companies have an environment mixing Windows NT 4 servers and workstations plus Windows 2000 Active Directory domain controllers plus Windows 2000 Professional Workstations. The discussion takes this into account, examining the major types of logon traffic: Windows NT 4 workstations to Windows NT 4 servers, Windows 2000 Professional to Windows NT 4, and Windows NT 4 workstations to Active Directory domain controllers.

To examine the subject in detail, the chapter describes tests of:

- Windows NT 4 client logon traffic
- Windows 2000 client logon traffic
- LDAP search operations

What You'll Find in This Chapter

■ Discussions of logon traffic for Windows NT 4.0 and Windows 2000 that explain the differences between them by examining basic processes and types of traffic.

■ A detailed functional discussion of the Lightweight Directory Access Protocol (LDAP), elaborated by traffic testing for common LDAP functions performed with a variety of tools.

Note   The fictional examples in this chapter use the extension .tld (top level domain) in the company domain names rather than .com to insure that none of the domains are mistaken for those of any actual company or organization.

Windows NT 4 Client Logon Traffic

Overview

The domain model introduced in Microsoft Windows NT was designed to provide a centralized account database that would, among other things, reduce network administrative overhead. Centralized account management provides numerous advantages, but it also produces network traffic when you log on at a computer that is not a controller in a domain environment.

This section analyzes the logon traffic between a client and a controller in a domain environment under different conditions. The first part explains Windows NT 4.0 logon communication, and the second examines the traffic it puts on the wire.

Logon Procedure

When you log on to the console of a Windows NT 4 client, you are not logging on to every computer in the domain, only to those on which you are accessing network resources. If you are logged on to a remote computer, then a NetBIOS session has been successfully established. When two Microsoft network systems communicate over a network, they use a high-level protocol called server message block (SMB), commands for which fit into four categories:

- Session control
- File commands
- Print commands
- Message commands

The local machine sends an SMB in the form of a *Session Setup & X* request along with the credentials of the account that wants to establish the session to the target, and receives a positive acknowledgement if the specified account is a valid domain account.

Remember: in this context, *account* refers to users *and* computers. Each computer belonging to a domain has an account in the domain's database. Logging on is a special procedure. The first logon to a domain occurs before any user can use the console of a workstation to get in—it is performed by the workstation during the Windows NT boot process. The *netlogon* service is responsible for maintaining NetBIOS sessions: during its life on a workstation, it keeps available a session to the validating controller or reestablishes one, if necessary. When someone logs on, the session transfers user-specific information between the workstation and the server. See Figure 5.1.

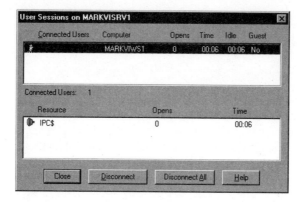

Figure 5.1   Sessions on a server.

NetBIOS Sessions

A NetBIOS connection is based on a session with the remote system. The client
tries to initialize a session with a *Session Setup & X* request and specifies the share
to which it wants to be connected. If the credentials passed by the client are valid,
the server creates a new user session and adds it to the table of local user sessions.
An index of the session is added as a parameter in the response frame and to all
frames that the client issues on the opened share, so that the server can load the
proper user context.

The SMB protocol can also be used as a vehicle for RPC requests, which are
preferred on remote systems. This is also referred to as *Named Pipe* transport and
is shown in Figure 5.2.

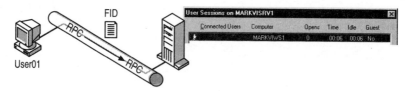

Figure 5.2   Named Pipe (RPC-based) transport.

Security

Windows NT uses a secured channel to transmit user credentials safely over the
network. The client and server validate each other's identity during the
workstation boot process and use a session-specific key to encrypt critical
information. When the validation process succeeds, the client sends a challenge (a
16-byte value used only once during the lifetime of a Windows NT installation) to
the server and the server responds.

Passwords are stored as hash values created with a one-way function in the
domain controller's Security Account Manager (SAM) database.

Workstation Boot Process

The workstation boot process consists of:

- TCP/IP initialization
- Domain logon

This section describes the packet flow that you can monitor during a typical boot process for a workstation that is a member of a domain.

Note   You should consider most packet sizes used in this section as *guidelines*. Factors such as workstation, server, and domain names affect packet size, causing them to differ slightly in different environments.

TCP/IP Initialization

DHCP Process

The DHCP configuration determines the process's initial steps. The DHCP process consists of four network frames:

- DHCPDiscover
- DHCPOffer
- DHCPRequest
- DHCPAck

A workstation sends a DHCPDiscover frame if it has no knowledge of a DHCP server or if it could not extend a previous configuration after 87.5% of the lease duration has expired. Any server with a valid configuration can make a DHCPOffer. The client selects the first arriving offer, and tries to request it with a DHCPRequest. The server has to confirm the lease with a DHCPAck frame.

Each frame contains about 342 bytes (the exact number depends on the number of options specified). Each frame has a target address of 255.255.255.255.

If a workstation already has a valid configuration, it tries to extend the lease each time the workstation boots, starting the DHCP process with a DHCPRequest frame to the client's DHCP server (Figure 5.3).

Src MAC Addr	Dst MAC Addr	Protocol	Description
HB-ACCT-WS1	*BROADCAST	DHCP	Discover
00105A68069E	*BROADCAST	DHCP	Offer
HB-ACCT-WS1	*BROADCAST	DHCP	Request
00105A68069E	*BROADCAST	DHCP	ACK

Figure 5.3   DHCP process frames.

Avoiding TCP/IP Conflicts

The workstation sends three ICMP echo requests (pings) to avoid address conflicts with other clients (Figure 5.4). Each frame contains 60 bytes. If there is no answer, the workstation continues initializing.

Src MAC Addr	Dst MAC Addr	Protocol	Description
HB-ACCT-WS1	*BROADCAST	ARP_RARP	ARP: Request, Target IP: 192.168.45.150
HB-ACCT-WS1	*BROADCAST	ARP_RARP	ARP: Request, Target IP: 192.168.45.150
HB-ACCT-WS1	*BROADCAST	ARP_RARP	ARP: Request, Target IP: 192.168.45.150

Figure 5.4   ICMP echo requests (pings).

Registering Names

A workstation with a valid TCP/IP configuration tries to register its workstation and domain (or workgroup) name with a WINS server or by using a broadcast message, depending on the configuration (Figure 5.5). Using WINS doesn't reduce the number of frames send by the client, but it does reduce the number of broadcast messages and it increases the availability of a workstation's name in a segmented network. Each registration frame contains 104 bytes.

Src MAC Addr	Dst MAC Addr	Protocol	Description
HB-ACCT-WS1	00105A68069E	NBT	NS: Registration req. for HB-ACCT-WS1 <00>
00105A68069E	HB-ACCT-WS1	NBT	NS: Registration (Node Status) resp. for HB-ACCT-WS1
HB-ACCT-WS1	00105A68069E	NBT	NS: Registration req. for HB-ACCT <00>
00105A68069E	HB-ACCT-WS1	NBT	NS: Registration (Node Status) resp. for HB-ACCT

Figure 5.5   Name registration.

Domain Logon

Locating Controllers

Each workstation must establish a session with a controller of its domain. The logon process starts with the determination of at least one domain controller. The workstation can either query the WINS server for all <1C> entries or it can send this frame as a local subnet broadcast. The query frame contains about 92 bytes (its exact length depends on domain name length) (Figure 5.6).

Src MAC Addr	Dst MAC Addr	Protocol	Description
HB-ACCT-WS1	00105A68069E	NBT	NS: Query req. for HB-ACCT <1C>
00105A68069E	HB-ACCT-WS1	NBT	NS: Query (Node Status) resp. for HB-ACCT <1C>, Success

Figure 5.6   Session establishment.

The WINS server replies to this request with up to 25 controller IP addresses. The reply first returns addresses owned by the queried WINS server, sorted by registration date and time. The answer has at least 104 bytes (if only one controller is returned).

Logon Request

If the query was successful, the workstation selects the first controller from the list and sends a SAM LOGON request in the form of a local subnet broadcast and then as frames directed to the list of controllers the workstation retrieved from the previous

<1C> query (Figure 5.7). This frame contains about 336 bytes (its exact length depends on the length of the workstation's name). First, the Address Resolution Protocol (ARP) is used to resolve each controller's MAC address. A successful ARP request consists of 60 bytes (the request) plus 42 bytes (the answer).

Each controller that receives such a request sends a SAM response of 296 bytes.

Src MAC Addr	Dst MAC Addr	Protocol	Description
HB-ACCT-WS1	*BROADCAST	Netlogon	SAM LOGON request from client
HB-ACCT-WS1	*BROADCAST	ARP_RARP	ARP: Request, Target IP: 192.168.45.100
HB-ACCT-DC1	HB-ACCT-WS1	ARP_RARP	ARP: Reply, Target IP: 192.168.45.150 Target Hdwr Addr: 00E04C390D2B
HB-ACCT-WS1	HB-ACCT-DC1	Netlogon	SAM LOGON request from client
HB-ACCT-WS1	HB-ACCT-DC1	Netlogon	SAM LOGON request from client
HB-ACCT-DC1	HB-ACCT-WS1	Netlogon	SAM Response to SAM LOGON request

Figure 5.7   SAM LOGON request.

Logon to a Controller

Name Resolution

The workstation then resolves the name of the first answering controller, either by querying WINS or by broadcast. The query has 92 bytes and the answer has about 90 bytes (its exact length depends on the length of the requested name) (Figure 5.8).

Src MAC Addr	Dst MAC Addr	Protocol	Description
HB-ACCT-WS1	00105A68069E	NBT	NS: Query req. for HB-ACCT-DC1
00105A68069E	HB-ACCT-WS1	NBT	NS: Query (Node Status) resp. for HB-ACCT-DC1, Success

Figure 5.8   Name resolution.

Session Request

Now the workstation uses a three-way TCP handshake to try to establish a NetBIOS session with the controller. The session request has 112 bytes and the answer has 58 bytes (its exact length depends on the length of the NetBIOS names) (Figure 5.9).

Src MAC Addr	Dst MAC Addr	Protocol	Description
HB-ACCT-WS1	HB-ACCT-DC1	NBT	SS: Session Request, Dest: HB-ACCT-DC1 , Source: HB-ACCT-WS1 <00>
HB-ACCT-WS1	HB-ACCT-DC1	TCP	.A...., len: 0, seq: 28974-28974, ack: 14007075, win: 8760
HB-ACCT-DC1	HB-ACCT-WS1	NBT	SS: Positive Session Response, Len: 0
HB-ACCT-DC1	HB-ACCT-WS1	TCP	.A...., len: 0, seq: 14007079-14007079, ack: 29046, win: 8688

Figure 5.9   Session request.

Protocol Negotiation

The SMB protocol has undergone many revisions and extensions since its release in 1984, so both sides have to negotiate the latest dialect they can use for communication. The request has 228 bytes and the response has 151 bytes. The client then tries to establish a tree connection with the server's IPC$ share. The session setup request has 244 bytes and the response has 200 bytes (Figure 5.10).

Src MAC Addr	Dst MAC Addr	Protocol	Description
HB-ACCT-WS1	HB-ACCT-DC1	SMB	C negotiate, Dialect =
HB-ACCT-DC1	HB-ACCT-WS1	SMB	R negotiate, Dialect # = 7
HB-ACCT-WS1	HB-ACCT-DC1	SMB	C session setup & X, Username = , and C tree connect & X, Share = \\HB-ACCT-DC1\IPC$
HB-ACCT-DC1	HB-ACCT-WS1	SMB	R session setup & X, and R tree connect & X, Type = IPC

Figure 5.10   Protocol negotiation.

Retrieving Trusted Domains

After a successful logon the client initiates an RPC request for a list of trusted domains. This sequence's frames total about 2000 bytes (the exact length depends on the number of trusted domains) (Figure 5.11).

Src MAC Addr	Dst MAC Addr	Protocol	Description
HB-ACCT-WS1	HB-ACCT-DC1	SMB	C NT create & X, File = \lsarpc
HB-ACCT-DC1	HB-ACCT-WS1	SMB	R NT create & X, FID = 0x800
HB-ACCT-WS1	HB-ACCT-DC1	MSRPC	c/o RPC Bind: UUID 12345778-1234-ABCD-EF00-0123456789AB call 0x...
HB-ACCT-DC1	HB-ACCT-WS1	MSRPC	c/o RPC Bind Ack: call 0x5 assoc grp 0x6D58 xmit 0x1630 recv 0x1630
HB-ACCT-WS1	HB-ACCT-DC1	R_LSARPC	RPC Client call lsarpc:LsarOpenPolicy2(..)
HB-ACCT-DC1	HB-ACCT-WS1	R_LSARPC	RPC Server response lsarpc:LsarOpenPolicy2(..)
HB-ACCT-WS1	HB-ACCT-DC1	R_LSARPC	RPC Client call lsarpc:LsarEnumerateTrustedDomains(..)
HB-ACCT-DC1	HB-ACCT-WS1	R_LSARPC	RPC Server response lsarpc:LsarEnumerateTrustedDomains(..)
HB-ACCT-WS1	HB-ACCT-DC1	R_LSARPC	RPC Client call lsarpc:LsarClose(..)
HB-ACCT-DC1	HB-ACCT-WS1	R_LSARPC	RPC Server response lsarpc:LsarClose(..)
HB-ACCT-WS1	HB-ACCT-DC1	SMB	C close file, FID = 0x800
HB-ACCT-DC1	HB-ACCT-WS1	SMB	R close file

Figure 5.11   Retrieving trusted domains.

Secure Channel Setup

The workstation then establishes a secure channel with the controller. This channel will be used every time a client needs to have its user account validated or to retrieve user information from the controller. Eight frames are used, totaling 1500 bytes (Figure 5.12).

Src MAC Addr	Dst MAC Addr	Protocol	Description
HB-ACCT-WS1	HB-ACCT-DC1	SMB	C NT create & X, File = \NETLOGON
HB-ACCT-DC1	HB-ACCT-WS1	SMB	R NT create & X, FID = 0x801
HB-ACCT-WS1	HB-ACCT-DC1	MSRPC	c/o RPC Bind: UUID 12345678-1234-ABCD-EF00-01...
HB-ACCT-DC1	HB-ACCT-WS1	MSRPC	c/o RPC Bind Ack: call 0x0 assoc grp 0x6FF6 xmi...
HB-ACCT-WS1	HB-ACCT-DC1	R_LOGON	RPC Client call logon:NetrServerReqChallenge(..)
HB-ACCT-DC1	HB-ACCT-WS1	R_LOGON	RPC Server response logon:NetrServerReqChallenge(..)
HB-ACCT-WS1	HB-ACCT-DC1	R_LOGON	RPC Client call logon:NetrServerAuthenticate2(..)
HB-ACCT-DC1	HB-ACCT-WS1	R_LOGON	RPC Server response logon:NetrServerAuthenticate2(..)

Figure 5.12   Secure channel setup.

Registering Names

The workstation then registers its name for additional services such as the Messenger Service and the browser service if the client is at least a potential browser. Six frames are used, totaling 640 bytes (Figure 5.13).

Src MAC Addr	Dst MAC Addr	Protocol	Description
HB-ACCT-WS1	3COM 68069E	NBT	NS: Registration req. for HB-ACCT-WS1 <03>
3COM 68069E	HB-ACCT-WS1	NBT	NS: Registration (Node Status) resp. for HB-ACCT-WS1
HB-ACCT-WS1	3COM 68069E	NBT	NS: Registration req. for HB-ACCT-WS1
3COM 68069E	HB-ACCT-WS1	NBT	NS: Registration (Node Status) resp. for HB-ACCT-WS1,
HB-ACCT-WS1	3COM 68069E	NBT	NS: Registration req. for HB-ACCT <1E>
3COM 68069E	HB-ACCT-WS1	NBT	NS: Registration (Node Status) resp. for HB-ACCT

Figure 5.13   Name registration.

User Logon

A user logon does more than validate the user's credentials: a controller also has to pass user-specific information such as group membership back to the client if the user was validated.

Each user is validated twice. The operating system first passes the user's credentials over the secure channel to the controller to validate the user and to retrieve all the information needed to create the user's access token. The RPC call used for this purpose is *NetrLogonSamLogon*. If the server can validate the user, it includes the group membership information in the response to that call (Figure 5.14).

```
Src MAC Addr  Dst MAC Addr  Protocol  Description
INVENT00028F  LOCAL         SMB       C NT create & X, File = \NETLOGON
LOCAL         INVENT00028F  SMB       R NT create & X, FID = 0x803
INVENT00028F  LOCAL         MSRPC     c/o RPC Bind:          UUID 12345678-1234-AB...
LOCAL         INVENT00028F  MSRPC     c/o RPC Bind Ack:      call 0x3  assoc grp 0...
INVENT00028F  LOCAL         R_LOGON   RPC Client call logon:NetrLogonSamLogon(..)
LOCAL         INVENT00028F  R_LOGON   RPC Server response logon:NetrLogonSamLogon...
```

Figure 5.14   Client validation.

This sequence uses about 1700 bytes if the account belongs only to the Domain Users group. Only two frames (operation number 0x2) are used for each additional user logon sequence (Figure 5.15).

```
Src MAC Addr  Dst MAC Addr  Protocol  Description
INVENT00028F  LOCAL         MSRPC     c/o RPC Request:      call 0xC  opnum 0x2  ...
LOCAL         INVENT00028F  MSRPC     c/o RPC Response:     call 0xC  context 0x0...
```

Figure 5.15   Name registration.

Network packet size depends on how many groups the user belongs to—each user-defined group a user belongs to consumes 8 bytes if a user is a member of at least one of them. The table below shows that the jump from 0 to 1 groups is 24 bytes. Packet size does not depend on group name length because Windows NT transfers the group's SID rather than its name.

User defined groups	Size (bytes)
0	506
1	530
2	538
3	546
4	554
5	562
10	602
20	682
30	762
50	922

Next, the logon sequence sets up a user session with the controller (Figure 5.16), which is needed to retrieve the contents of a policy file and a logon script if they are available. The packets needed for this process total about 800 bytes if no logon script or system policy file is available. If one of these files is available you'll have to add some more bytes depending on the file size.

```
Src MAC Addr  Dst MAC Addr  Protocol  Description
MARKVIWKS1    LOCAL         SMB       C session setup & X, Username = user00, and C tree connect & X,...
LOCAL         MARKVIWKS1    SMB       R session setup & X, and R tree connect & X, Type = A:
MARKVIWKS1    LOCAL         SMB       C NT create & X, File = \ntconfig.pol
LOCAL         MARKVIWKS1    SMB       R NT create & X - NT error, System, Error, Code = (52) STATUS_O...
```

Figure 5.16   User session setup.

Logon Scripts and Policy Files

To transfer a file over the network, the client first needs to request the information about the file system on which the file is stored and about the file's properties. This is returned in an SMB frame, and if its header and data exceed the TCP or UTD packet maximum the datagram is fragmented for transmission. The rest of the data is sent in *session message continuous* frames and reassembled on receipt. Login scripts are user-specific. If a user has been assigned a logon script, the operating system copies its contents over the network to make it locally available. The same happens if a policy file (consisting of computer- and user-specific data) is used in a given network. The operating system checks to see if a policy file is available during the workstation boot process and during each user logon (Figure 5.17).

Src MAC Addr	Dst MAC Addr	Protocol	Description
INVENT00028F	LOCAL	SMB	C NT create & X, File = \ntconfig.pol
LOCAL	INVENT00028F	SMB	R NT create & X, FID = 0x80a
INVENT00028F	LOCAL	SMB	C transact2 Query file system info
LOCAL	INVENT00028F	SMB	R transact2 Query file system info (respons...
INVENT00028F	LOCAL	SMB	C close file, FID = 0x80a
LOCAL	INVENT00028F	SMB	R close file
INVENT00028F	LOCAL	SMB	C NT create & X, File = \ntconfig.pol
LOCAL	INVENT00028F	SMB	R NT create & X, FID = 0x80c
INVENT00028F	LOCAL	SMB	C transact2 Query file info, FID = 0x80c
LOCAL	INVENT00028F	SMB	R transact2 Query file info (response to fr...
INVENT00028F	LOCAL	SMB	C read & X, FID = 0x80c, Read 0x2000 at 0x0...
LOCAL	INVENT00028F	SMB	R read & X, Read 0x2000
LOCAL	INVENT00028F	NBT	SS: Session Message Cont., 1460 Bytes

Figure 5.17   Client file-transfer over the network.

Accessing Resources on a Member Server

To access a resource located on a member server that is a member of the client's domain, the user must establish a user session on that computer. The process uses the same sorts of network packets used for a user's local domain logon (Figure 5.18).

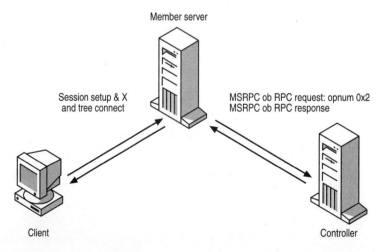

Member server

Session setup & X
and tree connect

MSRPC ob RPC request: opnum 0x2
MSRPC ob RPC response

Client

Controller

Figure 5.18   Accessing resources on a member server.

Logon from a Resource Domain

The domain model allows you to establish communication links (called *trusted relationships*) between domains and to distribute administrative authorities. You can use trusted relationships to group the administration of network resources in a separate domain (called a *resource domain*) but maintain all user accounts in a master domain (called an *account domain*).

A user on a computer that is a member of the resource domain can logon its account from the account domain: the resource domain controller simply passes the user's credentials through to an account domain controller. This process requires establishing more NetBIOS sessions:

- One session between client and the resource domain server
- One session between the domains' controllers
- One session between the resource domain workstation and the account domain server

Windows 2000 Professional Logon Traffic to Active Directory

This section provides an overview of the logon traffic generated between a Windows 2000 Professional workstation and Active Directory. This combination provides new features such as IntelliMirror technology, which allows users to roam between computers and still have all documents available, and enable controlled Policy-based management.

Rather than deploy all features right away, most organizations use a phased approach to get the deployment up and running first, then add features gradually. The sections below start with a workstation boot process, move on to user logons, and then discuss how specific features affect network traffic.

It has to be understood that client logon references both logical objects under the Active Directory, as well as physical object (files). An example of the distinction would be that although restrictions on the logon (like permitted hours of logon— say 8 A.M. to 5 P.M.), are stored as part of the object (properties) in the Active Directory, other settings (like desktop appearance restrictions) are stored in Group Policy, which consists of physical files.

In order to measure the effect that different settings would have on client logon traffic, one would have to modify and measure the results from both settings that affect physical objects (such as files), as well as settings that are affected on logical objects (such as properties of Active Directory objects).

The logical objects involved in the client logon process would be:

- Properties set on objects in the Active Directory – e.g. Minimum Password Length.
- Security settings on the specific Active Directory objects – e.g. The group membership property of specific object (ACLs).
- Security settings on the physical objects – e.g. The ACLs on the GPO files.

Where as the physical objects (files) involved in the logon process would be:

- Group Policy objects, which include
  - Registry settings
  - Security settings
  - Scripts (like logon/logoff scripts)
- User data – e.g. Files located in offline folders.

Thus, the tests that are covered in this paper can be divided into two major categories. (i) The results of modifications that were made to the physical file objects (GPO/registry settings) and (ii) modifications that were made to logical objects i.e. the security settings of these files.

(i) The following tests were made with reference to the ACLs of certain objects:

- Security Settings – In this batch of tests, the effect of changing the ACLs on the Group Policy objects were investigated.
- Group Membership

(ii) These were done with respect to changes in the physical objects e.g. the size of the GPO files:

- Group Policy – Here the effect of the number of GPO files that affected the logon were tested.
- Group Policy settings – Here the effect of the change in size of the GPOs was tested. The more options within the Administrative Templates are enabled on the GPO, the larger the resultant file (registry.pol.).
- Security settings – These are saved in an .inf file.
- Roaming profiles and offline folders – Testing results on size of offline folders for example.

Scripts or executables not stored as part of Group Policy were not tested, as the resulting traffic depends on the size of these files.

This section discusses lab tests of the effects of various settings and Group Policy settings on client logon traffic: group memberships, Group Policy settings, security settings, and roaming user profiles. The results are summarized in the following table:

Object	Effect on traffic generated
Group Policy (number of Group Policy options)	Linear. Depends on number of GPOs. Ballpark: increases 10–50 Kb under normal conditions. Affects traffic during machine startup, initial logon, potentially every 90 minutes, but by default thereafter only for changes.
Group Policy Settings (administrative templates)	Linear. (Ballpark: increases 10–30 Kb under normal conditions.
Group Policy Settings (security settings)	Insignificant. Increase in traffic more due to group memberships.
Group membership	Linear. Depends on number of groups. Ballpark: increases 5–20 Kb under normal conditions.
Roaming profiles	Constant once roaming profiles are enabled. Logon traffic increases to ± 250 Kb (110 Kb without roaming profiles), logoff traffic increased to 650 Kb.
Offline folders	Fairly insignificant, except during synchronization. Depends on size of offline folders.

Note   Normal logon traffic in a clean environment with no options enabled generates about 100–120 Kbytes of network traffic.

A few recommendations based on the results:

- Keep the number of GPOs to a realistic minimum, to avoid complexity (auditing, etc.) and to keep client network logon traffic in check.

- Keep bandwidth in mind when you deploy IntelliMirror technology. The effect of 1000's of clients logging off at the end of the day can significantly affect network performance.

Test Harness Setup

The test harness consisted of four single-processor, Windows 2000 machines (all running RC2) set up this way:

- 1 Windows 2000 Professional Workstation (WS1)
- 2 Domain controllers (DC1 and DC2).
- 1 DHCP server and 1 DNS server.

The network traffic was traced using Network Monitor v2.943. All packets to and from the workstation (including DNS traffic) were reported.

Effect of Group Membership on Logon Traffic

Creating groups and group memberships reduces the administrative overhead of managing large numbers of users, but it also affects client logon traffic. Windows 2000 (by default) use the Kerberos authentication protocol. During authentication and logon, the client is provided with a Kerberos ticket, which contains, among other information, the SIDs of the groups to which the user belongs. The information in the Kerberos ticket is called the PAC (the Privilege Attribute Certificate). Microsoft extended the base Kerberos protocol to include authorization data, so a Windows 2000 ticket and TGT both contain a special field called the PAC. As a user is given membership in more groups, the size of the Kerberos ticket (the PAC) grows.

In the first test, the user is made a member of multiple universal groups to test the effect on logon traffic.

Flat Structure (User Is a Member of Multiple Groups)

To test the effect of universal group membership on logon traffic, the user was added to a number of groups. Groups were not nested: that is, User1 was a member of group1, group2, group3 ...... groupx; no groups were members of other groups.

# of Groups	WS startup traffic (Kb/s)	Interactive logon traffic (Kb/s)
1	56	44
5	56	46
10	56	48
20	56	55

Figure 5.19 shows the effect on traffic. Workstation *startup* traffic remained constant because group membership was applied only to the user account. A linear regression derives a formula you can use to extrapolate the data:

$X = Y \times 0.89 + 96$

where X = data in Kbytes/sec and Y = the amount of group members

To find the figure for a user with 100 group memberships:

X = 100 x 0.89 +96 = 89+96 = 185 Kbytes/sec of client logon traffic can be expected, all other parameters being constant.

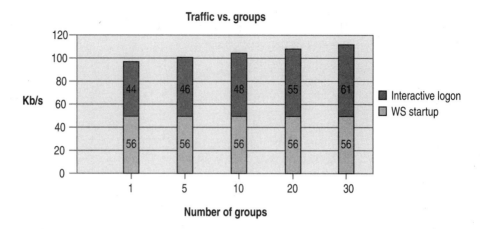

Figure 5.19   Flat structure test.

Hierarchical Structure
(User Is a Member of Multiple Nested Groups)

To test the effect of universal group membership on logon traffic, the user was added to a number of nested groups (Figure 5.20). User1 was a member of group1, which in turn was a member of group2, which in turn was a member of group3, which in turn was a member of group4 .... which in turn was a member of groupx.

Groups	WS startup traffic (Kb)	Interactive logon traffic (Kb)
1	56	45
5	56	46
10	56	49
20	56	54

Linear regression yields this formula:

$X = Y x 0.89 + 96$

where **X** = data in Kbytes/sec and **Y** = the amount of group members.

To find the figure for a user with 100 nested-group memberships:

$X = 100 x 0.89 + 96 = 89 + 96 = 185 \ Kbytes/sec$

(Tested under lab conditions this equaled 135 Kbytes.)

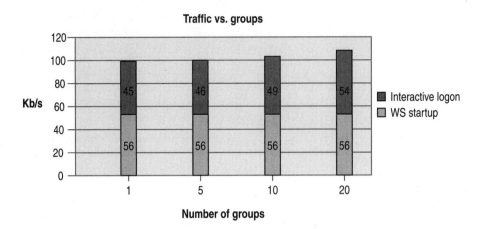

Figure 5.20   Hierarchical structure test.

So traffic increases linearly with group memberships, but there is very little difference between nesting memberships or a flat structure. The increase in traffic can be ascribed to the Kerberos PAC part of the authentication traffic, which grows to include the SIDs of all the groups. From the packet traces, you can see that for 100 groups, the Kerberos tickets grows from 2 Kbytes/ticket, to almost 8 Kbytes/ticket.

Effect of Group Policy on Logon Traffic

Enhancing the concept from NT 4.0, Windows 2000 expands Group Policy technology to include virtually every desktop and user-settable option or restriction, enabling the administrator to manage desktop and user settings from a central point.

The administrator can, for example, control the appearance of desktops throughout the company by specifying a certain bitmap as the desktop wallpaper.

As mentioned in the introduction, Group Policy objects (GPO) consist of physical files. For Administrative Templates those are registry settings that are applied to the desktop and are located under SYSVOL/domain.com/sysvol/ Policies/{C0f080-xxxx...}/registry.pol). These files are downloaded and applied to the desktops on changes as part of the logon process. This means that both the amount of files and the size of the files would affect traffic to the desktop.

The secondary effect on logon traffic would be the security settings (ACLs) that are set on these files. Theoretically, traversing a long list of ACLs (and resolution under the Active Directory) while applying these files, could affect the amount of traffic generated during the logon process.

The effect of Group Policy on client logon traffic will vary according to:

- The amount of options or restrictions that has been enabled/disabled. This results in changes in the physical size of the files contained in a GPO (more options = larger files).

- The number of GPOs that are set up. So for example one can set up a GPO for the site, or for the domain, and one for the OU under which the User Object is located. This will result in 3 GPO files being applied or downloaded to the desktop.
- The security settings on these files. The ACLs on the GPOs can be modified so that certain GPOs only apply to certain groups or users.
- The policies can be nested or presented in a flat structure.

The first test modified Group Policy settings and applied them at both the computer and user levels. The test examined the difference between applying policies in nested and flat structures.

The results show the effect of the initial policy download after changes have been applied and the normal day-to-day traffic that occurs after the policy download (that is, with no download of GPOs).

Flat Structure (Policies Applied at Domain Level)

This test applied Group Policy settings at the domain level only (GPOs were not nested). The results show a full policy download on initial setup and thereafter on changes. The traffic was measured for workstation startup traffic, during which computer account policies and computer GPOs are downloaded, and interactive user logon traffic, during which user Group Policy settings are downloaded.

For the tests on the GPOs, the settings were set on both the USER and the MACHINE part of the GPOs.

- The USER settings modifications register changes in the registry.pol file.
- Changes under the MACHINE sections are applied to the GptTmpl.INF file.

Tests were done on changes to both the MACHINE and USER changes under the GPOs.

The settings were chosen for their single value properties instead of string or multivalued properties, which could vary according to string length. Thus only settings which required a simple ENABLE/DISABLE were modified e.g. "Disable Logoff" = "Enabled".

The following settings were changed in the GPOs:

For the MACHINE part:

Under Computer Configuration/Windows Settings/Security settings/Account Policies/Password polices:

1. Password History
2. Password age
3. Password length
4. Password complexity

Under Computer Configuration/Windows Settings/Security settings/Local Policies/User Rights:

1. Change System Time
2. Force shutdown
3. Log on locally
4. Shut Down

For the USER part:

Under User Configuration/Admin Templates/System Templates/Logon/Logoff:

1. Disable lock computer
2. Disable Logoff
3. Disable Run once list

User Configuration/Admin Templates/System Templates/Start Menu & Taskbar:

1. Remove Favorites from Start menu
2. Remove Run form Start menu
3. Disable Logoff
4. Remove Search from Start menu
5. Remove Help from Start menu
6. Disable changes to taskbar

The data in the table and in Figure 5.21 show a fairly linear response curve. This is to be expected because GPOs are downloaded as files (SMB traffic), so adding Group Policy objects increases SMB packet traffic moving to the client computer. The files are downloaded from the domain controller's *sysvol* directory, for example:

```
SMB: C NT create & X, File = \domain.com\Policies\{31B2F340-016D-11D2-
945F-00C04FB984F9}\
```

Note again that additional file transfers like software installation and scripts saved on file shares are exceptions here, because the network traffic depends on the size of these files.

GPOs	WS startup traffic (Kb)	Interactive logon traffic (Kb)
0	56	46
1	61	61
5	72	69
10	85	76

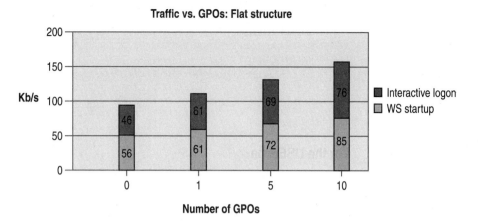

Figure 5.21   Flat structure test.

Traffic increases only when there are changes to a Group Policy. Once a GPO is downloaded and applied on the client, subsequent logons carry less traffic.

The test showed that changes in any GPO or in the user's group membership resulted in another complete download of the GPO.

The data in Figure 5.21 and in the table above represent the data for the full Group Policy object download, established for this system. After this initial download, network logon traffic is still affected by the number of GPOs present on the system, because the data returned from queries for relevant policies (LDAP, RPC calls, etc.) is larger than the policy files, which are not downloaded.

Here are the results for data without the Group Policy downloads—the situation users will experience most of the time:

Group Policy objects	Groups	WS startup traffic (Kbytes)	Interactive logon traffic (Kbytes)	Total client traffic (Kbytes)
1	1	55	36	91
1	50	55	65	120
1	100	55	98	153
5	1	61	38	99
5	50	61	72	133
5	100	61	98	159
10	1	67	45	112
10	50	67	77	144
10	100	67	98	165
20	1	77	59	136
20	50	77	77	154
20	100	77	98	175

Figure 5.22 shows a graph of the results:

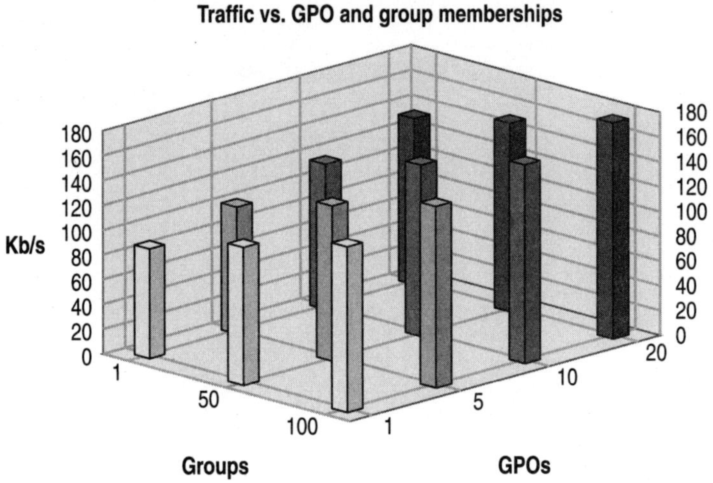

Traffic vs. GPO and group memberships

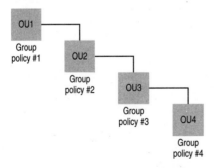

Kb/s

Groups   GPOs

Figure 5.22   Data download without policy files.

Regression analysis on these results yields this formula for client logon traffic:

Kbytes logon traffic = 86 + 2.33 x **GPO** + 0.6 x **Groups**

where **GPO** = The number of Group Policy objects in effect, and **Groups** = the number of groups the user belongs to.

Hierarchical Structure (Policy Objects Applied at OU Level)

This test nested Group Policy objects in OUs. The results in Figure 5.23 show a trend comparable to that of the previous test, again because the policy settings tested exist as files that are downloaded to the workstation.

```
OU1
Group
policy #1    OU2
             Group
             policy #2    OU3
                          Group
                          policy #3    OU4
                                       Group
                                       policy #4
```

Figure 5.23   Hierarchical structure with policies at OU level.

LDAP query responses grow larger as Group Policy objects are added, but the Group Policy objects are downloaded only when there are changes. Thus, there is an increase in traffic during the first logon after any change (to group memberships, etc.) has been applied in the Active Directory; traffic then drops to normal levels, with a slight increase due to LDAP query growth of 5% -10%, as shown in Figure 5.24.

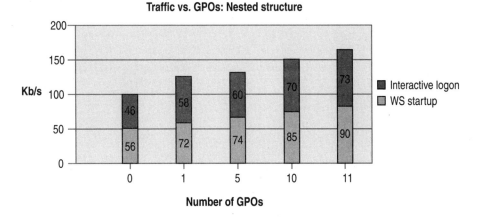

Figure 5.24   Hierarchical structure results.

Linear regression yields this formula:

$$X = 4.3 \times Y + 113$$

where **X**= traffic in Kbytes and **Y** = amount of Group Policy objects.

For example, 20 Group Policy objects should yield: X = 10 x 4.3 + 103 = 156 Kbytes of traffic.

Enabling Multiple Group Policy Options

The next test examined the effect on traffic of enabling multiple options within a GPO. An example would be to *Add Logoff to Start Menu* under the USER profile options, then check the amount of network traffic.

Policy options	WS startup traffic (Kbytes)	User logon traffic (Kbytes)
1	69	124
10	70	125
20	74	129
30	76	131
40	79	134

Figure 5.25 shows a graph of the trend:

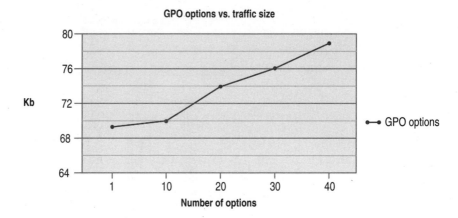

Figure 5.25   Multiple policy options results graph.

Setting Security on Group Policy Objects

The Group Policy architecture in Windows 2000 allows using access control rights on the files that store settings to specify whether a Group Policy should apply to a user or a workstation. The next test shows what happens when a user, who has initially no right on a file, is made a member of a group, which was granted a certain set of permissions on one or more policies (in other words, the ACL on the GPO files were modified). The changes were again tested for the registry files (USER or registry.pol) settings, and on the GPTtmpl.INF file (for control purposes). Changes are downloaded to the machine once changes have been applied.

Policy Settings	Security changes	WS startup traffic (Kbytes)	User logon traffic (Kbytes)
1	0	63	35
1	1	64	34
1	5	65	34
1	10	64	34
2	1	68	35
2	5	66	36
2	15	65	36
2	25	65	35

Changing the various security settings on a policy does not significantly alter client-server traffic, except when group memberships and policies are added.

Increasing Both Group Policy Objects and Group Memberships

The combined effect of increasing the number of Group Policy objects and group membership on client logon traffic was tested. Figure 5.26 shows an almost linear increase in client logon traffic.

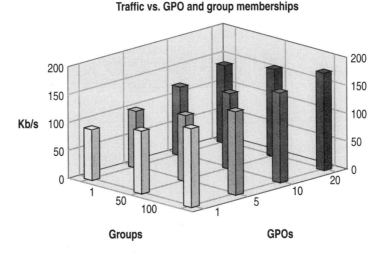

Figure 5.26   Increasing Group Policy and group memberships results.

IntelliMirror Technology

Microsoft IntelliMirror technology allows you to use various computers and not see any difference between the services they provide to you: access to data files, hyperlinks, and applications. At this stage, IntelliMirror's main components are *roaming user profiles, redirected folders, offline folders, software installation, desktop operating system installation and registry,* and *security based settings.* The user's exposure to the IntelliMirror features is transparent, there is no Start menu item called IntelliMirror. On the other hand, the administrator does need to perform certain configuration tasks to implement the IntelliMirror-based user data and user settings management.

Roaming User Profiles

By default, Roaming User Profiles store user preferences for hyperlinks, start menu items, system and application settings as well as all user documents located in the **My Documents** folder and its subfolders on the server. When a user logs on, the server-stored profile is merged with the local cached copy of the user profile, if there is one. If the user logs on to the computer for the first time, all the profile information, including any Start Menu customizations and the **My Documents** folder are copied to the local hard drive. If the user does not have a pre-existing profile on the server, a default profile is created locally, which is then copied to the server at logoff for use on subsequent logons. Temporary and certain local computer information will not roam with the user. The following items belong to this category:

- **Temp.** The user's personal **Temp** directory. By default, temporary files created during the user session are stored here.

- **Temporary Internet Files.** All temporary files created by Internet Explorer during a browsing session. To provide faster access to Web pages some pages are stored in this folder.

- **Application Data.** Here applications can store specific local files that do not have to travel with the user to another computer.

- **History.** A list of recently accessed Web pages.

Windows 2000 improves on Windows NT's implementation of roaming user profiles with support for merging user profiles (at the file level) and support for last-writer-wins. The merge algorithm decides whether the information on the roaming profile share or the local cached copy is more recent. Figure 5.27 identifies all the directories and files that are stored on the server.

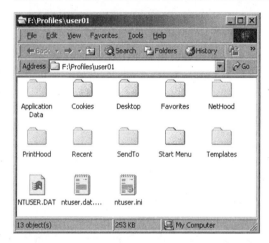

Figure 5.27   Files and directories stored on the server for roaming profiles with no additional applications installed.

The user-specific section of the registry (HKEY_CURRENT_USER) is saved into a file (NTUSER.DAT) and synchronized as part of the logon/logoff process. (When only local profiles exist, these files and directories are stored on the client computer in the default directory's *Documents and Settings* subdirectory. You can change this setting through an unattended setup.)

Note   Since all user-specific sections of the registry are stored in a single file, the whole file is always copied at logoff to server when at least one setting was changed. Synchronization does not mean that single registry keys or values are updated, but that the file is updated when it changed.

When roaming profiles are enabled, the settings represented by these files and folders are applied during client logon. The merging algorithm decides which files to load and synchronizes them with the server copy when the client logs off.

Using the default settings for roaming profiles may create significant logon/logoff traffic. However, an administrator has a number of options available that can significantly reduce this traffic. Administrator's can use Group Policy to define non-roaming folders, to set quotas for user profile size, and to manage user settings centrally. A highly recommended method is to redirect the **My Documents** folder and make it available offline (see "Folder Redirection" later in this chapter).

Client traffic test results are shown in the following table. (Tests of this logon/logoff traffic used a typical initial profile under Windows 2000 Professional.)

Situation	Profile size (Kbytes)	Logon traffic (Kbytes)	Logoff traffic (Kbytes)
Regular logon, local user profile	391	90	1
Regular logon, roaming user profile	391	289	744

By far the greatest amount of traffic is directed from the workstation to the server that stores the profiles. The logon traffic to the domain controller does not increase. As always, one should balance the increased manageability, reliability, and convenience of enabling these features against the network traffic they will generate.

As can be expected, the size of a user's profile is dependent on the number of applications installed, and the amount of user data in their profile. The more applications and data they have, the larger the profile will be. While the merging algorithm ensures that only changed files are synchronized between the server and workstation at logon/logoff, remember that a user logging into a new workstation for the first time will have their complete profile, including all user data in the **My Documents** folder (unless you are redirecting), copied over the network.

Also, bear in mind that due to the overhead of synchronization, logon and logoff traffic are typically higher than might be expected from the profile size. This is especially true of logoff traffic.

The following table illustrates the difference between profile size, and actual traffic:

Situation	Profile size (Kbytes)	Logon traffic (Kbytes)	Logoff traffic (Kbytes)
Regular logon	391	289	742
Roam to new machine (no profile)	391	1,014	741
Roam to new machine (profile existing)	391	596	741

Numbers based only on logon and logoff traffic: no changes were made in configuration or user data.

When users work mostly at the same computer (the typical case) logoff traffic increases because the changed local profile files are synchronized with the server profiles. If users roam to other computers, the logon traffic always increases and logoff traffic increases if the users change data.

The following table shows some data from our test environment using a profile that contains two 1-MB files:

Situation	Profile size (Kbytes)	Logon traffic (Kbytes)	Logoff traffic (Kbytes)
Logon, change 2 files (1MB each), logoff	2481	285	2992
Synchronize changed user data (2 files, 1 MB each) to new computer (roam), user data not changed during session ·	391 at logon 2481 at logoff	2820	772

An important point to remember is that typically, a new user's profile will increase in size with every session as configuration and application data is accumulated (window sizes and positions, personalized menus, favorites, cookies, application data, etc.). However this is usually trivial compared to the increase in traffic caused by the user data that accumulates in My Documents. Fortunately, Windows 2000 administrators have several options for handling profile size. Administrators can use Group Policy to define non-roaming folders and set quotas for user profile size. The most elegant method is to use folder redirection and redirect the **My Documents** folder and make it available offline.

Folder Redirection

This new Windows 2000 feature (Professional and Server) allows users and administrators to redirect the path of a folder to a new location such as a folder on the local computer or a directory on a network share.

The following folders can be redirected:

- My Documents
- The My Pictures folder under My Documents
- Application Data
- Desktop
- Start Menu

The redirection is transparent to the user and can be configured via Group Policy or by the user.

For roaming user profiles, it is strongly recommended that you redirect the **My Documents** folder to a shared network folder because it simplifies the back up of user documents redirected to the appropriate server folders, and will help to decrease logon/logoff client traffic. You can leave the redirected folder online, which means that it is only available when the workstation is connected to the server. Another way is taking it offline, which will be covered in the next section.. Basically, this increases availability of user data because even when the network connection to the server share is broken users can access and work on the local cached copy, which is synchronized with the server copy when the network connection is restored.

With redirected folders, logon and logoff traffic depend solely on the amount of user configuration data stored in the profile, not on the growth of user data. But as long as the user data is stored on a network share, all access to it creates network traffic. Traffic peaks at logon and logoff hours can be made less painful for the end user experience, but you still have to make sure the network can handle permanent user accesses, and this means you have to study user data access patterns and decide whether to redirect the **My Documents** folder.

Situation	Profile size (Kbytes)	Logon traffic (Kbytes)	Logoff traffic (Kbytes)
Logon, change 2 files (1MB each), logoff	396	276	768
Roam to new computer, user data not changed during session	396 at logon 396 at logoff	283	763

Offline Folders

Offline folders allow you to make data that's normally located on a fileserver available to offline users (workers traveling with a notebook, when the server is offline for maintenance, etc.). If the user accesses a shared folder on a server (for example, \\server\data1) then moves offline, this data remains available without apparent change (transparently). Files and folders, which are made available offline by the user or by the administrator, are copied to a special area on the user's hard drive, the **Offline Files** folder.

Combined with roaming user profiles and folder redirection, offline folders enhance the user experience. The **My Documents** folder is available under almost all circumstances. Synchronization occurs by default at logoff, but this is configurable via Group Policy. Alternatively, synchronization can be started manually at any time. Network access is optimized so that locally available data is not retrieved from the network share. All changes are instantly committed to the network share version of the file. The folder synchronization at logon and logoff ensures that files are always synced. The resulting network traffic is very similar to the redirected folders scenario without offline folders.

Situation	Profile size (Kbytes)	Logon traffic (Kbytes)	Logoff traffic (Kbytes)
Logon, change 2 files (1MB each), logoff	396	288	767
Roam to new computer, user data not changed during session	396 at logon 396 at logoff	283	763

Group Policy is the best way to configure folder redirection and offline availability of redirected folders. Enabling offline folders is a machine-wide setting and requires a reboot to become effective.

The main traffic occurs during the regular user session, not on logon or logoff. A slightly increased load for the local hard drive can be expected, because every changed version of a networked file must also be written to the local cache, i.e. the Offline Files Folder.

Network traffic does not increase in comparison to the traffic on file open and file save operations to legacy file shares.

Legacy network operation:

Action	Kbytes
Copy 1MB text file from c:\temp to U:\ (home dir on share)	1,149
Open 1MB text file on U:\ (home dir on share), with WordPad	1,157
Change and save 1MB text file on U:\ (home dir on share)	1,114

Working with redirected folders, which are available offline:

Action	Kbytes
Copy 1MB text file from c:\temp to MyDocs (redirected and available offline)	1,141
Open 1MB text file from MyDocs (redirected and available offline), with WordPad	37
Change and save 1MB text file in MyDocs (redirected and available offline)	1,132

NetBIOS Traffic

The NetBIOS interface and protocol is still available in Windows 2000 for backward compatibility with older applications, although you can disable it. A test comparing the effect on client network traffic of enabling and disabling the protocol showed that disabling NetBIOS prevents the generation of NetBIOS network traffic: all traffic occurs over the IP protocol.

Enabling NETBIOS or the *Obtain settings from the DHCP server* setting on the client, created little pure NetBIOS traffic—specifically, NetBIOS name registration requests.

```
UDP: Src Port: NETBIOS Name Service, (137); Dst Port: NETBIOS Name
Service (137); Length = 76 (0x4C)
NBT: NS: Registration req. for WS1          <00>
NBT: NS: Registration req. for WS1          <03>
NBT: NS: Registration req. for WS1
NBT: NS: Registration req. for DOMAIN    <1E>
```

In each case the client machine broadcasts a name registration request four times for every NetBIOS service (<00>, <03>, etc.) Each packet was 110 bytes, so the total was 4 x 110 x 4 = 1.8 Kbytes per client machine, which is less than 2% of the network traffic generated.

Detailed Description of the Windows 2000 Professional Workstation Logon Traffic

The document *Win2000ClientLogon.doc* on the CD that accompanies this book describes client boot and logon traffic on a packet level.

LDAP Concepts, Operations, Traffic, and Capacity Planning for Active Directory

The Lightweight Directory Access Protocol (LDAP) was designed to locate and access resources in a distributed computing environment. A directory access and manipulation protocol that is highly functional but relatively simple, it allows you to query and manipulate information in the Directory Information Tree (DIT)—Microsoft's implementation of which is the Active Directory—which can include data on users (e-mail addresses or phone numbers) or on other resources such as printers, distributed file system shares, or SQL Server databases.

Because LDAP is the primary interface to the Active Directory, its operations are involved whenever objects in the Active Directory are accessed or manipulated, either through Windows 2000 administrative tools or Windows 2000 end-user interfaces. Developing applications for Active Directory implies using either native LDAP APIs or higher-level APIs such as those in the Active Directory Service Interface (ADSI). To plan for capacity, infrastructure designers and administrators need to understand how much LDAP traffic is generated when operating against Active Directory; application developers need to be aware of LDAP behavior in order to use LDAP APIs efficiently. To help you plan and implement the infrastructure for Windows 2000 and Active Directory, this section provides some insights on LDAP operations that occur when accessing Active Directory and the resulting network traffic patterns.

A directory access protocol must be able to authenticate, query, and manipulate directories and LDAP is an IETF (Internet Engineering Task Force) standard. (The IETF has also developed standards for DNS, POP, SMTP, and HTTP.) The APIs, which are distinct from the protocol, were defined in RFC 1823.

Key aspects of LDAP:

- Protocol elements are carried directly over IP, as either TCP or UDP.
- Many protocol data elements are encoded as ordinary strings.
- A lightweight BER encoding is used to encode all protocol elements.

LDAP is described by a combination of four models:

- **Informational.** Describes the structure of information in a DIT.
- **Naming.** Describes how information is organized and referenced.
- **Functional.** Describes what can be done with the information.
- **Security.** Describes how information is protected in the DIT.

Informational Model

Derived from the ISO X.500 standard for creating enterprise-level directories, the informational model describes entries and attributes as defined in RFC 1777 "Lightweight Directory Access Protocol" and RFC 2251 "Lightweight Directory Access Protocol (v3)." Information on schemas and entries follows.

Schema

A schema acts as a blueprint or a template for the directory by listing the classes and attributes from which all entries are derived. To exist in the DIT, an entry or attribute must adhere to the definitions described in the schema, which determine the available classes, attribute type definitions, and syntaxes from which an entry can be derived.

A class is a category of objects that share a set of characteristics. Each object in the directory is an instance of one or more classes in the schema. Object classes are defined in X.501 (as per RFC 2252 section 4.4). In general, every entry contains an abstract class (*top* or *alias*), at least one structural object class, and zero or more auxiliary object classes. Some DITs use the alias class as a pointer when objects have been moved.

Note   Microsoft does not implement the abstract class *alias* because it is not necessary within the Microsoft DIT, which attaches a globally unique identifier (GUID) to each object so that it can be safely renamed. A GUID is a 128-bit (16-byte) number generated by an algorithm designed to ensure its uniqueness. This algorithm is part of the Open Software Foundation (OSF) Distributed Computing Environment (DCE), a set of standards for distributed computing.

Abstract classes serve as templates for structural classes and must not exist in the DSA as entries. Structural classes, which are derived from abstract classes, can exist in DSA as entries. Structural classes inherent all attributes associated with parent abstract classes. Auxiliary classes allow an entry to inherent a specific set of attributes; they work like *include* files. The *88* classes were defined before the 1993 X.500 standard and as such are a legacy. If you look at the attribute *ObjectClass* for an entry you can determine what classes were used to derive it. For example, the *ObjectClass* attribute of a user entry enumerates the classes *top*, *person*, *organizationalPerson*, and *user*. Top, person, and organizationalPerson are all abstract classes. User is the structural class from which the entry was actually created.

Attributes are data items used to describe the classes defined in the schema. Because they are defined in the schema separately from the classes, one attribute definition can be applied to many classes. The attribute type is identified by a short descriptive name and an object identifier (OID). Attributes are defined in *RFC 2252 Lightweight Directory Access Protocol (v3): Attribute Syntax Definitions*. Some of the attributes defined in RFC 2256 LDAPv3 schema are:

- **Common Name:** CN (2.5.4.3)
- **Organizational Unit:** OU (2.5.4.11)
- **ObjectClass:** (2.5.4.0)

The syntax for an attribute defines the storage representation, byte ordering, and matching rules for comparisons of property types. This includes whether the attribute value must be a string, a number, a unit of time, etc. Every attribute of every object is associated with only one syntax. *RFC 2252 Lightweight Directory Access Protocol (v3): Attribute Syntax Definitions* defines well-known syntaxes. Syntaxes for use with LDAP are named by OIDs. Examples:

- **Distinguished Name:** (1.3.6.1.4.1.1466.115.121.1.12)
- **UTC time:** (1.3.6.1.4.1.1466.115.121.1.53)
- **Object Class Description:** (1.3.6.1.4.1.1466.115.121.1.37)

Entry

An entry is either a container or leaf object of a specific structural class. An entry is composed of various attributes that are defined in the schema for the class from which it was derived. Entries must have a relative distinguished name (RDN) that is unique among its siblings, and the concatenation of the RDNs or Distinguished Names (DNs) must be unique in the DIT.

Note   Microsoft documentation often refers to directory entries as *objects*.

Attributes

Containers and leaf entries can have attributes, which are defined in the schema and must obey the schema's definition. Attributes are composed of a name, an OID, and a value. The syntax for the attribute is defined in the schema. Attributes are classified as *must* or *may*. *Must* attributes are mandatory, meaning that the entry must have the attribute to exist; *may* attributes are optional. Attributes can be either single- or multi-value.

Note   Microsoft documentation often refers to attributes as *properties*.

Naming Model

The OSI directory model uses an object's Distinguished Name (DN) as the primary key for directory entries. The naming model is outlined briefly in RFC 1777 and RFC 2251. The LDAP naming model was further enumerated in RFC 1779 *A String Representation of Distinguished Names* and RFC 2253 *Lightweight Directory Access Protocol (v3): UTF-8 String Representation of Distinguished Names*.

Distinguished Name

Entries are arranged in the DIT based on their Distinguished Name, which serve as the primary keys for DIT objects. The DN is composed of a series of Relative Distinguished Names (RDNs). Each naming component represents a branch in the DIT. A DN is analogous to the absolute path name to a file in the Windows file system. Some examples:

```
cn=seven,dc=rainiersoft,dc=tld
cn=nine,dc=rainiersoft,dc=tld
```

Relative Distinguished Name

Each component of the DN is a Relative Distinguished Name that is unique within its container. The RDN—analogous to a file name or directory in a file system—is composed of an attribute type and a value, and is formatted: <rdncomp> :== <attr> '=' <value>. Examples of RDNs:

```
cn= Dan
ou= sales
dc= rainiersoft
```

where *cn* = common name, *OU* = organizational unit, and *dc* = domain component.

Functional Model

The functional model has three areas: authentication, interrogation, and update. Authentication allows the client to prove its identity to the DSA, interrogation provides a method for the client to search the DIT, and update defines a mechanism with which the client can add or modify DIT information.

Authentication

The authentication model consists of three operations: bind, unbind, and abandon. The bind command initiates a protocol session to the DSA; once it is established a method of authentication is negotiated between the DSA and the client, and, when authentication succeeds, the DSA returns a bind response to the client. The unbind command terminates an LDAP session between the client and the DSA. The abandon command cancels the session; the client can issue it to, for instance, cancel a lengthy search operation before it completes.

Interrogation

The interrogation model consists of two operations: search and compare. The search operation selects entries from a specific region of the DIT based on customized criteria (a search filter) and uses these arguments:

- A search *base* (the DN of the search base object) defines the location in the directory from which to begin searching.
- A search *scope* defines how deep to search within the search base.
  - *Base* (or zero-level) searches the base object only.
  - *One-level* searches objects immediately subordinate to the base object but not including the base object itself.
  - *Subtree* searches the entire subtree of which the base DN is the topmost object, including the base object.
- A *filter* that allows certain entries in the subtree and excludes others.
- A *selection* that indicates what attributes to return from objects that match the filter.
- Optional controls that affect how the search is processed.

LDAP search filters as defined in RFC 2254 allow you to define search criteria so that you can achieve more effective and efficient searches. For example, you can use filters to find all the users whose surname is *Smith* or who report to manager *Mary Jones*. Search filters are represented by UTF-8 strings. The *compare* operation returns a Boolean response based on a comparison of an entry's attribute value.

LDAP filter operator	Description
=	Equal
~=	Approximately equal
<=	Less than or equal to
>=	Greater than or equal to
&	AND
|	OR
!	NOT

Update

The update model consists of four operations: add, modify, modify RDN, and delete. The add command creates an object in the DIT based on information provided by the client to the DSA. This information must meet any conditions imposed on entry creation by the classes defined in the schema. The modify command allows the client to modify (create, change, or delete) an entry's attributes. The modify RDN command provides a mechanism with which an entry can be moved in the DIT. Modifying the RDN components of an entry effectively moves it to a new DIT container. To succeed, an entry modification must satisfy the schema's constraints and be within the client's access permission. The delete command allows a client to remove an entry from the DIT.

Additional Concepts

Ports

LDAP uses either a TCP or UDP to connect from the client to the DSA. The connection occurs over a socket and uses these end points:

Function	Port
LDAP	389
LDAP Secure Sockets Layer (SSL)	636

Note Microsoft implements two more LDAP ports to access additional directory services provided by the global catalog. For details on the global catalog, see Chapter 4, "Active Directory Replication Traffic Analysis."

Function	Port
Global catalog (GC)	3268
Global catalog Secure Sockets Layer	3269

Synchronous vs. Asynchronous Operations

Most LDAP operations can be performed either synchronously or asynchronously. Synchronous function calls must return an indication of the outcome of the operation, or another LDAP error code if the call fails, before the client application can continue executing. Synchronous LDAP APIs have an *s* appended to the function name, as in *ldap_search_s*.

Asynchronous functions allows the client to continue performing other tasks, including making new requests to the server or processing search results. Synchronous *and* asynchronous functions return a message ID for the initiated operation, but an asynchronous function uses the message ID to request the results.

RootDSE

The RootDSE is a standard attribute defined in the LDAP 3.0 specification. It contains information about the directory server, including its capabilities and configuration. A search response contains a standard set of information that is defined in the RFC 2251 Lightweight Directory Access Protocol (v3). The LDAP protocol assumes there are one or more servers that jointly provide access to a DIT. At the root of the DIT is a DSA-specific entry (the RootDSE) that is not part of any naming context. Each server has different attribute values in the RootDSE.

You can retrieve RootDSE datafrom an LDAPv3 server by doing a base-level search with a null BaseDN and with filter *ObjectClass=*. The RootDSE publishes information about the LDAP server including which LDAP versions, SASL mechanisms, and controls it supports, and the DN for its subschemaSubentry. Operational attributes can be exposed to extend administration functionality.

Section 5.2 of RFC 2252 defines a set of RootDSE attributes that should be published by LDAPv3 servers that support them, and Section 3.4 of RFC 2251 adds the subschemaSubentry, for a total of seven standard attributes published in the RootDSE section of an LDAPv3 server. These core attributes are:

- **namingContexts.** Values correspond to naming contexts that this server masters or shadows. If the server believes it contains the entire directory, the attribute has a single value that is the empty string (indicating the null DN of the root). A client can use this attribute to choose suitable base objects for searching when it has contacted a server.

- **subschemaSubentry.** This value is the name of a subschema entry (or subentry if the server is based on X.500(93)) in which the server makes available attributes that specify the schema. Supported attributes are exposed in the attributeTypes property and supported classes in the objectClasses property. The subschemaSubentry property and subschema are defined in LDAPv3 (RFC 2251).

- **altServer.** Values are URLs of other servers that can be contacted when this server becomes unavailable. If the server does not know of any other servers that can be used, this attribute is absent. Clients can cache this information to use if their preferred LDAP server later becomes unavailable.

- **supportedExtension.** Values are object identifiers (OIDs) identifying the supported extended operations the server supports. If the server does not support any extensions, this attribute is absent.

- **supportedControl.** Values are the object identifiers (OIDs) identifying controls the server supports. If the server does not support any controls, this attribute is absent.

- **supportedSASLMechanisms.** Values are the names of supported SASL mechanisms the server supports. If the server does not support any mechanisms, this attribute is absent. By default, GSSAPI is supported.

- **supportedLDAPVersion.** Values are the LDAP protocol versions the server implements.

Active Directory also supports these *informational* attributes:

- **currentTime.** Based on Zulu time in the format: xxxx(year)xx(month)xx(day)xxxxxx.x(hours,minutes,seconds military time)'Z'.

- **dsServiceName.** NTDS settings.

- **defaultNamingContext.** The default NC for a particular server. By default, this is the DN for the domain of which this directory server is a member.

- **schemaNamingContext.** DN for the enterprise Schema naming context.

- **configurationNamingContext.** DN enterprise Configuration naming context.

- **rootDomainNamingContext.** DN for the root of the domain for which this server is a DC.

- **supportedLDAPPolicies.** Supported LDAP management policies.

- **highestCommittedUSN.** Highest USN committed to the database on this server.

- **dnsHostName.** DNS name of this DC.

- **ldapServiceName.** Service principal name (SPN) for the LDAP server. Used for mutual authentication.

- **serverName.** DN for the server object for this directory server as defined in the Configuration container.

- **supportedCapabilities.** Values are object identifiers (OIDs) identifying the server's supported capabilities.

Administrative Limits and Query Policy

Support for LDAPv3 extensions for querying, paging, and sorting, places demands on the memory and computational resources of the Active Directory server. Before deploying LDAP servers, you should load-balance test them to develop baseline measurements on which to base adjustments.

You can set limits on the server resources available to clients requesting LDAP queries, paged result sets, and sorted result sets. These limits constitute the LDAP query policy, and are stored as a multi-value attribute on query policy objects. Because server workload and resources vary, the query policy is configurable at the server level. Query policy applies to these LDAP query-related operations:

- **Search.** The basic query operation. An LDAP search might cover a small part of a single directory service store or span every directory service store in the forest (and beyond, through support for virtual containers). A search can generate a significant amount of disk activity, take a long time, and return a large volume of data.

- **Search with paged results.** Because a search can return a large volume of data, the client can ask the server to hold the result set and return it in "pages." (See "Paging Search Results" on page 225.) The server must hold the result set until the client releases it or unbinds.

- **Search with sorted results.** A client can request a result set in a particular order. Sorting requires storage and CPU cycles at the server. (See "Sorting Search Results" on page 226.) The resources consumed are directly proportional to the size of the result set.

- **Search with replication.** You can specify the maximum number of attribute values that can be returned per request.

- **Change notify.** A client can request change notification on particular objects in the directory. A change notify request is posted with an asynchronous LDAP query.

Note You can use NTDSUTIL (provided by Microsoft for performing low-level administrative tasks against the Active Directory) to view or modify a DC's query policy. You can use the Active Directory Sites and Services MMC snap-in to assign query policies to domain controllers but not to sites. You can use the MODIFYLDAP.VBS script to create, delete, assign, or modify query policy objects. Query policy objects are stored in the container cn=Query-Policies, cn=Directory Service,cn=Windows NT,cn=Services in the Configuration partition. All DCs use the default query policy if none other is assigned. If a site policy is assigned, the DC uses it. A specific policy assigned to a domain controller takes precedence over any site policy.

You can use the NTDSUTIL command-line tool to see the administrative limits and values. The table below shows the administrative limits in effect for the default query policy.

Default query policy settings in Windows 2000 Active Directory table

LDAP administrative limits	Default values	Description/search behavior
InitRecvTimeout	120	Initial Receive Timeout. The maximum number of seconds the server waits for the initial request before the connection closes. If a connection is idle for more than this limit, the LDAP server returns an LDAP disconnect notification and closes the connection.
MaxConnections	5000	Maximum Connections. The maximum concurrent LDAP connections allowed on the server. If this limit is reached, the LDAP server returns an LDAP disconnect notification and closes the connection.
MaxConnIdleTime	900	Maximum Connection Idle Time. The maximum number of seconds that the client is allowed to be idle before the connection is closed. If a connection is idle for more than this limit, the LDAP server returns an LDAP disconnect notification and closes the connection.
MaxActiveQueries	20	Maximum Active Queries. The maximum concurrent search operations allowed on the server. When this limit is reached, the LDAP server returns a busy notification.
MaxNotificationPerConn	5	Maximum Notifications per Connection. The maximum concurrent notification requests allowed per connection on the server. When the stated limit is reached, the server returns a busy notification.
MaxPageSize	1000	Maximum Page Size. The largest page size allowed by the server. The server returns the number of rows specified by MaxPageSize. If the paged results were requested, the client can retrieve additional pages until all results are returned.
MaxQueryDuration	120	Maximum Query Duration. The maximum number of seconds allowed for a query to complete. If paged results are requested, the client can continue the query if the timer expires before the query completes. When this limit is reached, the server returns the timeLimitExceeded error.

LDAP administrative limits	Default values	Description/search behavior
MaxTempTableSize	10000	Maximum Temporary Table Size. The upper limit, in candidate objects, on the temporary table. If the temporary table maximum limit is reached by an OR query optimization, the optimization is abandoned and replaced with a direct table scan.
MaxResultSetSize	262144	Maximum Result Set Storage. The maximum storage that the server can hold for all paged result sets. If the stated limit is reached, the oldest result sets are discarded.
MaxPoolThreads	4	Per Processor Asynchronous Thread Queue (ATQ) Threads. The number of threads allocated by ATQ per processor. This value is sent as an advisory notification to ATQ, which decides whether to use it. **Note:** If it takes a long time to bind, increase the count to 6 or 8.
MaxDatagramRecvSize	1024	Maximum Receive Datagram Size. The maximum size of datagrams the server can receive. The server pre-allocates datagram buffers and cannot receive larger datagrams.

LDAP Controls

RFC 1823, which defines the LDAP API for LDAP v3, is being updated to include support for new LDAP v3 controls. Windows 2000 supports several new controls that extend the functionality of the LDAP protocol. The LDAP API supports server controls, which can be sent to a server or returned to the client with any LDAP message, and client controls, which affect the behavior of the LDAP API only, are never sent to a server.

If you know the control object identifier (OID) you can use the LDP.EXE utility to implement these controls. You can view all supported controls and their OIDs by reading the *supportedControls* property on the RootDSE for the domain controller LDP.exe. The OIDs for each control are designated in LDAP as the control type (controlType).

Tree Delete (controlType 1.2.840.113556.1.4.805)

When used with a delete request (DelRequest) message, this allows a client to delete an entire subtree of a container object. When this control is invoked, the server checks to see that the user has permission to invoke it. Other restraints on containers can override an attempt to delete it. For example, a deletion cannot cross a directory partition (or naming context) boundary.

Directory Synchronization (controlType 1.2.840.113556.1.4.841)

This enables the Active Directory Read Provider to extract the latest changes from the Active Directory replication module. The LDAP-based Active Directory Read Provider reads Active Directory changes. Because the partition is the unit of replication, the Directory Synchronization control must be invoked on the root of a partition.

Cross-Domain Move (controlType 1.2.840.113556.1.4.521)

This allows an object to be moved from one domain to another. The operation is used in conjunction with the LDAP ModifyDN request. In effect, the object is renamed to exist in a different domain.

Show Deleted Object (controlType 1.2.840.113556.1.4.417)

When an Active Directory object is deleted, it is stored for a configurable period of time to allow the deletion to be replicated. The Show Deleted Object control allows you to view objects that have been deleted but not yet garbage-collected, along with objects that are not marked for deletion. Deleted objects are normally not visible after they are deleted (that is, the isDeleted attribute has a value of TRUE), but you can see them by using Show Deleted Object in conjunction with search commands. To show only objects marked for deletion (also called tombstones), add isDeleted=true to the filter.

Attribute Range Option (controlType 1.2.840.113556.1.4.802)

The LDAP protocol reads a multi-value attribute as a single entity, and this can take a long time or be impossible when there are many values. You can specify the Attribute Range option as part of an attribute description to retrieve the values of a multi-value attribute incrementally. An attribute description includes an attribute type (for example, *member*) and a list of options, one of which can be the *Range* option. When it's presented in a searchRequest message, the Range option specifies a zero-relative range of elements (for example, 0-9) to be retrieved. By specifying the *Range=* option followed by a range *specifier*, you can define the number of values retrieved.

Return Extended Distinguished Names (controlType 1.2.840.113556.1.4.529)

If an application needs to retain a long-term reference to a directory object, such as a user, a computer, or an OU, it can use this control to ensure that the reference does not become obsolete. For example, distinguished names can change after a rename, move, or delete, but the object's GUID never changes. This control returns a special form of the distinguished name that includes the GUID. If an application stores this form instead of the regular distinguished name, the reference stays current.

Windows 2000 Supported Capabilities (controlType 1.2.840.113556.1.4.800)

This is published in the RootDSE under the supportedCapabilites attribute. It indicates that this is a Windows 2000 server and has all the associated capabilities, including Ambiguous Name Resolution (ANR). Consider it a version number for the directory service.

Verify Distinguished Name Server (controlType 1.2.840.113556.1.4.1338)

The DC uses this control to determine which server is needed to verify that a distinguished name exists. For example, when you want to add a reference to an object that belongs to one domain but is stored in another, use this control.

Do Not Generate Referrals (controlType 1.2.840.113556.1.4.1339)

This control tells the DC not to generate LDAP referrals when trying to locate an object. You can use this to improve search performance. For example, if you are not going to be generating referrals, and you want to search only for objects in a particular domain, use this control to minimize server overhead.

Server Search Operations (controlType 1.2.840.113556.1.4.1340)

The client uses this control to pass in flags that control various search behaviors, and it can serve as an all-purpose search control. It passes in flags to turn search operations on and off. For example, the *Do Not Generate Referrals* control is the same as the *Server Search Operations* control with the SERVER SEARCH FLAG DOMAIN SCOPE=0x1 flag, which is one of only two currently implemented flags.

The other flag, SERVER_SEARCH_FLAG_PHANTOM_ROOT=0x2, allows searches to obtain valid results when specifying a base distinguished name that is not actually in the forest of interest. For example, if the distinguished name of a particular root domain is *DC=sales,DC=mydomain,DC=tld*, and a client specifies a base distinguished name of *DC=tld* for a search, the directory returns everything it is aware of below *DC=tld*. In this case, it could return only objects in the *DC=reskit,DC=tld* domain directory partition. Without this flag the server would return an error.

Paging Search Results (controlType 1.2.840.113556.1.4.319)

Paging allows the client to retrieve a result set in small pieces. For example, when an LDAP client is connected to the server across a slow link or if the result set is expected to be very large, the client can request results in pages of a specific size. The new control extension for simple paging has options that allow the client to control the rate at which an LDAP server returns the results of an LDAP search operation.

An LDAP client application can specify a paged results control (*pagedResultsControl*) with a search request (*searchRequest*) that specifies a desired page size (the number of entries to be returned in a single response). Each time the server returns a set of results to the client, the server includes the *pagedResultsControl* control in the *searchResultDone* message. If the server has the ability, it can insert in the message it returns to the client a cookie containing an estimate of the total number of entries in the result set. If the value in the cookie indicates more pages, the client sends another search request, including the cookie and a new message ID, and the process continues until the *searchResultDone* message returns a value of 0 in the cookie.

Sorting Search Results (controlType 1.2.840.113556.1.4.473)

An LDAP client can request when it needs search results to be sorted but cannot perform the sort itself. The client includes the Request control in the *searchRequest* message to the server (*sortKeyRequestControl*) to give the server the information required to sort the result set. The Response control (*sortKeyResponseControl*—included in the searchResultDone message from the server) enables the server to respond to the sort request.

The *sortKeyRequestControl* specifies one or more attribute types and matching rules for the results returned by a search request, as well as a flag indicating forward or reverse order. The server should return all results for the search request in the order specified by the sort keys.

Referrals

A process called Directory Service Agent (DSA) manages the directory hierarchy information (referred to as *knowledge*), which it receives from the database layer. The DSA maintains cross-references of Active Directory domain objects up and down the hierarchy, and also out to other domain hierarchies. When a requested object exists in the directory but is not present on the contacted domain controller, name resolution depends on the given domain controller's knowledge of directory partitioning. In a partitioned directory, by definition, the entire directory is not necessarily available on any one domain controller.

A domain controller uses an LDAP referral to tell a client application that it does not have a copy of a requested object (or, more precisely, that it does not hold the section of the directory tree where that object would be, if in fact it exists) and to give the client a more likely location that the client can use as the basis for a DNS search for a domain controller. Ideally, referrals always reference a domain controller that holds the object, but occasionally a domain controller generates yet another referral, although it should not take long to discover that the object does not exist and to inform the client. Active Directory returns referrals in accordance with RFC 2251.

In its Configuration container, every domain controller has information about the other domains in the forest. When an operation in Active Directory requires action on objects that might exist in the forest but are not located in the particular domain that is stored on a domain controller, that domain controller must generate a message to the client describing where to go to continue this action; that is, the client is "referred" to a domain controller that is presumed to hold the requested object. Without needing to know the name or location of the child domain, clients can query the root domain and reach the appropriate domain controller by being referred there. Two cases generate this type of domain controller response:

- The base distinguished name of the operation is not in this directory, but the domain controller has knowledge of another LDAP directory where it might be found (an *external referral*).

- The base distinguished name of the operation is in this directory, but the operation requires proceeding into portions of the directory tree that are not stored on this domain controller (a *subordinate referral*).

Every domain controller contains information (*knowledge*) about how the directory is partitioned, and this information can be used in combination with DNS to find the correct Active Directory domain. Referrals to other domain controllers can be generated by the DSA according to the Active Directory's information on the existence and location of directory partitions, including the names of the directory partitions, what server is holding read-only copies (partial directory partitions stored on global catalog servers), and what server is holding writable copies (full directory partitions).

There are three kinds of *knowledge* references (explained in more detail below):

- **Subordinate.** Knowledge of a directory partition or partitions directly below a directory partition held by this domain controller.

- **Cross reference.** Knowledge of one directory partition, stored in a cross-reference object. On a given domain controller, the combination of all cross references provides knowledge of all directory partitions in the forest, irrespective of location in the directory tree. The state of cross-reference knowledge at any given time is subject to the effects of replication latency.

- **Superior.** Knowledge about a referral location, used when the domain controller does not know the search base.

Knowledge references form the glue that holds the pieces of the distributed directory together. Because Active Directory is partitioned, either all objects in a directory partition are present on a given domain controller or no objects in the directory partition are present on it. References in effect link the partitions, allowing operations such as searches to span partitions.

In Active Directory, referrals are generated when the directory is asked to locate an object when, based on the position at which the search begins, no copy exists in a local directory partition. When Active Directory can determine that no such object exists in the directory (rather than determining that it might exist but no copy exists here), instead of sending a referral, the directory returns an error that indicates to the client that no such object exists in the forest.

Subordinate References

When a search is requested, the domain controller searches all objects at or below the search base, within the directory partition held by the domain controller. If a subtree search has a search base that includes child partitions, the domain controller uses subordinate references to return referrals (called subordinate referrals) to these partitions. Subordinate referrals are returned as part of the data returned from the base distinguished name partition, and they contain the distinguished name of the subordinate directory partition and the access point to which queries can be referred. An access point consists of a DNS name and a port number, which is the information needed to contact a specific LDAP server. Access points are generated from information on the cross-reference object.

Cross-References

These are stored as directory objects (of the class *crossRef*) that identify the existence and location of all directory partitions, irrespective of location in the directory tree. Cross-references enable every domain controller to be aware of all directory partitions in the forest, not just the partitions that it holds. Because these objects are stored in the Configuration container, the knowledge they store is replicated to every domain controller in the forest. Each cross-reference must have values for these attributes:

- **nCName** is the distinguished name of the directory partition referenced by the *crossRef* object. (NC = naming context, which is a synonym for directory partition.) The combination of all *nCName* properties in the forest defines the entire directory tree, including the subordinate and superior relationships between partitions.

- **dNSRoot** identifies the DNS name of the domain where servers that store the given directory partition can be reached. This value can also be a DNS host name.

Cross-reference objects are used to generate referrals to other directory partitions and to foreign directories. They can be created internally by the system to refer to known locations within the forest, and externally by administrators to refer to locations external to the forest.

An *internal* cross reference object is created by the system. Every directory partition in a forest has an internal cross-reference object in the Partitions container (*cn=Partitions,cn=Configuration,dc=ForestRootDomain*). When you create a new forest, the Active Directory Installation Wizard creates three directory partitions—first Domain, Configuration, and Schema—and automatically creates a cross-reference object for each of them. Thereafter, when a new domain is created in the forest, another directory partition and cross-reference object are created. Because cross-reference objects are located in the Configuration container, they are replicated to every domain controller in the forest, so every domain controller has *knowledge* of the name of every partition in the forest (as well as their superior and subordinate relationships). This means any domain controller can generate referrals to any other domain in the forest, as well as to the Schema and Configuration directory partitions.

You can create an *external* cross-reference object manually to provide the location of an object that is not stored in the forest. If you know that LDAP clients will submit operations for an external portion of the global LDAP namespace against servers in the forest, and you want the forest's servers to refer the client to the correct location, you can create a cross-reference object for that directory in the Partitions container. External cross-references are used:

- To reference foreign directories by their disjoint directory name (a name that *is not* contiguous with the name of this directory tree). In this case, when you create the cross-reference, you create a foreign container that is not a child of any object in the directory.

- To reference foreign directories by a name that is within the Active Directory namespace (a name that *is* contiguous with the name of this directory tree). When you create this cross-reference, you create a virtual container that is a child of a real directory object. In both cases, a non-instantiated, invisible "container" is created in the directory.

Superior References

A superior reference is the distinguished name of a directory partition that is stored in the *superiorDNSRoot* attribute on the *crossRef* object for the forest root domain (the first domain created in the forest). A domain controller uses its superior reference to construct a referral only when a search base does not match any directory partition defined by the cross-reference objects. A superior reference contains no directory tree information; it consists of only an access point to which otherwise unanswerable queries can be referred. By default, superiorDNSRoot does not store a value, but the directory uses the *DC=* components of the search-base distinguished name to construct the equivalent of a superior referral. You can use the value in superiorDNSRoot to define a location to send all queries that cannot be resolved.

Import/Export Methods

You can use LDIFDE, CSVDE, or ADSI scripts to import and export objects in batch mode. These administrative tools allow you to use a single operation to administer large numbers objects such as users, contacts, groups, servers, and printers. They also allow you to export Active Directory data to other applications and services, and to import information from other sources into Active Directory. These tools are installed automatically on all Windows 2000 servers.

The LDAP Data Interchange Format (LDIF) is an Internet standard for a file format to perform batch import and batch export operations for directories that conform to LDAP standards. An LDIF file consists of a series of records that are divided by line separators. A record describes either a single directory entry or a set of modifications to a single directory entry and consists of one or more lines in the file.

LDIF has a command-line utility called LDIF Directory Exchange (LDIFDE) with which you can create, modify, and delete directory objects. You can run it on a Windows 2000–based server or copy it to a Windows 2000–based workstation. Among other things, you can use LDIFDE to extend the schema, export Active

Directory user and group information to other applications or services, and populate Active Directory with data from other directory services.

Here is an example of an LDIF import file format:

```
dn: CN=picturePath,CN=Schema,CN=Configuration,DC=reskit,DC=tld
changetype: add
attributeID: 1.2.840.113556.1.4.7000.125.19
attributeSyntax: 2.5.5.9
cn: picturePath
isSingleValued: TRUE
objectCategory: CN=Attribute-Schema,CN=Schema,CN=Configuration,
DC=reskit,DC=tld
objectClass: attributeSchema
oMSyntax: 2
```

Exporting and Re-Importing Objects

Linked attributes contain information about links to a current object. During a normal export session, a parent object might be exported before its child object; then, during re-import, if the parent object is added before the child object, the operation fails because the child object is not yet in the directory.

However, when you use the *-m* parameter to export objects and re-import them into Active Directory, all entries that contain a linked attribute are appended to the end of the file. Moreover, the link addition is separated from the main object creation call so that the failure in membership addition does not cause the object creation to fail. The linked attribute is appended to the end of the file.

Active Directory has Security Accounts Manager (SAM) properties that are read-only because they are set by the system at the time the object is created. When the *-m* parameter is used to export and re-import objects, all SAM attributes are ignored during the export. The entries can then be successfully re-imported into Active Directory because they do not contain any SAM information. An LDAP call to modify these entries fails.

You can also bulk-import and -export data to and from Active Directory using files that store data in the Microsoft Comma-Separated Value (CSV) file format (called .CSV files). Excel can read and save data in the CSV file format, and Exchange Server administration tools can use the format to import and export data. The CSV format has a command-line utility called CSVDE (CSV Directory Exchange) with which you can add (only) new objects. You can run it on a Windows 2000–based server or copy it to a Windows 2000–based workstation.

The CSV format consists of a simple text file with one or more lines of data values separated by commas. The text file contains entries where the initial entry is a comma-separated list of attribute names. Each subsequent entry in the text file represents a single object in the directory. Attribute values are delimited by commas or some other user-selected character.

When you view data in the .CSV file, the values for multi-value attributes are expressed as a single value that is internally delimited by a second user-definable delimiting character (by default, $). Attribute values are listed left to right in the order in which the attribute names are listed in the initial entry. Values are positional, and every entry must account for each attribute listing in the initial entry. The attribute names must be in the same order as the data in any line that follows the first line, as shown in this example:

```
Cn,Firstname,Surname,Description
1stuserlogonname,1stuserfirstnameJohn,1stusersurname,Manager
2nduserlogonname,2nduserfirstname,2ndusersurname,President
```

Active Directory LDAP Traffic Analysis

This section describes tests that were run against Active Directory to quantify and partially qualify the most common, daily, LDAP operations: binding and authenticating via LDAP against the Active Directory, and accessing and manipulating information by searching, adding, updating, and deleting directory objects.

To compare different access technologies (all based on LDAP but implemented on a different abstraction level) the tests measured straight LDAP API calls against the same functions provided by ADSI scripts, the Microsoft Management Console, and some Windows 2000 GUI tools.

Test Environment

The tests used a sample Active Directory Domain called *rainiersoft.tld*. The domain component in all examples is *dc=rainiersoft,dc=tld*. If you reproduce the tests, the domain component will adapt to your environment and will reflect your implemented naming conventions.

All lab servers were installed with Microsoft Windows 2000 RC2 (Build 2128), Advanced Server; clients ran the Professional version of the same build. All machines were connected by 100 Mbs Ethernet through a hub.

Figure 5.28 shows the layout of the lab environment. Each machine was given a specific task in order to simplify later analysis—especially the network traffic analysis that applied network filters to isolate a pristine cut of packets sent between two nodes by an operation.

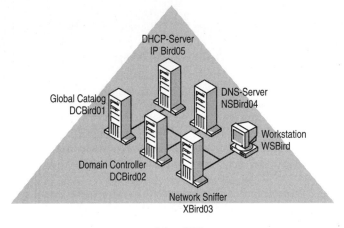

rainiersoft.tld

Figure 5.28   Lab domain *rainiersoft.tld*.

Roles of the Lab Machines

- DCBird01: First domain controller of *rainiersoft.tld* (also a global catalog server).

- DCBird02: Additional domain controller of *rainiersoft.tld*.

- IPBird: DHCP server. (All machines other than Workstation *WSBird* were given static IP Addresses.)

- NSBird: Name server (DNS) of *rainiersoft.tld*.

- Xbird03: Network sniffer station, installed with Windows 2000 Advanced Server, and Microsoft SMS 2.0 SP1 Network Monitor.

- WSBird: Windows 2000 Professional workstation, installed with the *Microsoft Windows 2000 Resource Kit* and the Administration Pack. All operations were run from this machine.

Test Methodology

To quantify network traffic and see how LDAP traffic scales, a logical OU structure was built inside *rainiersoft.tld*. Each OU contained different numbers of objects: most contained *user* objects, but to verify that the LDAP network traffic pattern is independent of the type of object, one OU contained *printer* objects. To verify that an LDAP search is independent of OU structure (flat or deep) the test created one nested OU hierarchy.

OUs and Objects in *rainiersoft.tld*

```
aou1: 1 User Object
bou1: 10 User Objects
cou1: 100 User Objects
```

```
dou1: 1000 User Objects
eou1:  Hierarchy of 10 nested OUs (fou1 to nou1)  each with 100 User
Objects
pou1: 1000 Printer Objects
```

Another important LDAP measurement is the number of attributes set on directory objects. To capture this parameter, each user object had (in addition to its mandatory attributes) 30 additional ones, and each printer object was populated with an additional 15. The tests include string attributes (all set with ten *b* characters) and integer attributes (all set to *1*). For all operations, these attributes were also used.

Additional user attributes.

AdminDescription	AdminDisplayName	comment	Company	department
Description	DesktopProfile	displayName	Division	extensionName
facsimile-TelephoneNumber	GenerationQualifier	givenName	HomePhone	homePostalAddress
Info	MiddleName	mobile	otherFacsimile-TelephoneNumber	otherHomePhone
OtherIpPhone	OtherLogin-Workstations	otherMailbox	otherMobile	otherPager
otherTelephone	Pager	postalCode	title	wWWHomePage

Additional printer attributes.

Description	driverName	location	portName	printBinNames
PrintColor	printEndTime	printKeep-PrintedJobs	printMaxResolution-Supported	printMaxXExtent
printMaxYExtent	printMedia-Supported	printOrientations-Supported	printSpooling	priority

This directory structure was created with the Active Directory population tool DSTool2.exe (included on the CD). It creates OUs, populates them with objects, and sets selected attributes on them. Object naming uses this algorithm:

ObjectPrefix + ObjectType + Loop Number + "-" + Count of Object created

For example, for *aou1*, the Object Prefix is *a*, and the type is *OU*. The *1* indicates that only this OU is created, so the tool *Loops* only once in its internal logic.

Examples of objects created by *dstool2.exe* inside the OUs:

- The user in the *aou1* is created with the name *auser1-1*.
- The users in *eou1* were created as *euser1-1* to *euser1-1000*.
- The printers in *pou1* were created as *pprinter1-1* to *pprinter1-1000*.

How Quantification Was Achieved

To quantify traffic for an "on-the-wire" protocol such as LDAP, you must understand the parameters and how they relate to traffic patterns. Different parameters are specific to different operations, and not limited to the number of objects and number of attributes involved in the operation; also included are the:

- Distinguished Name length of objects
- Length of attributes
- Length of attribute values

For realism and accuracy, all test numbers are based on an average of:

- Distinguished Name length: 10
- Length of attribute: 16
- Length of attribute value (type *string*): 10

Tools Used

- **DSTool2.exe.** Active Directory Population Tool—on the CD that accompanies this book.
- **LDP.exe.** Tool that calls the LDAP APIs directly. Included in the *Microsoft Windows 2000 Resource Kit*. Referred as **LDP**.
- **Windows Scripting Host/ADSI.** To compare the straight LDAP API calls and see how ADSI adds overhead, an ADSI Windows Scripting Host script was written for each LDP test. The scripts are included on the CD that accompanies this book. Scripts are referred as **ADSI script.**
- **Microsoft Management Console.** The MMC is the standard Active Directory administration tool (it comes with Windows 2000). You load it with elements called snap-ins to execute specific administration tasks. The snap-in for administering users (called *Active Directory Users and Computers*) was used in all tests, and this is what is referred to by **MMC**.
- **Windows *Search for People*.** Windows 2000 comes with an address book tool, with which you can query LDAP directories. You can find it in the Windows Explorer shell by selecting **Start->Search->For people**. This is referred to as **WAB** (for Windows Address Book).
- **Windows *Search for Printers*.** Similar to WAB, this searches for printers. You can find it in Windows Explorer Shell by selecting **Start->Search->For printers**.
- **Windows *My Network Places*.** Each Windows 2000 desktop can browse the network and the Active Directory for resources. This feature uses LDAP to query for objects. It is referred as **Browsing AD**.

Isolating LDAP Operations

It is relatively simple to isolate LDAP operations because each API call is exposed in the LDP.exe UI and you can select them separately. To get representative results and to understand how they relate, you need to isolate every tool used in the operations.

Luckily, you can do this easily with ADSI scripts. For example you can isolate an LDAP Bind from the LDAP Unbind operation by inserting a *pause* command before the ADSI script exits. You can also insert simple breaks (for example, message boxes between steps) to separate Search or other LDAP operations from the Bind and Unbind calls.

It is a bit more complex to isolate the other applications involved in the tests. For one thing, you have to avoid creating LDAP traffic with the test itself. To minimize unwanted LDAP traffic, the tests tried to isolate specific operations within the tools. For example, to search with MMC, you have to open the MMC, choose a directory, and start the search dialog. Up to this point, before you begin the search, you have already created LDAP traffic by selecting the Active Directory Domain and displaying the top-level containers that the MMC needs to query. To remove this traffic, the tests started capturing data only after these preliminary steps were complete. When you study the results or set up your own tests, remember that you can't isolate operations such as *bind* or *unbind* within the MMC, the WAB, etc.—the calls are implicit in every action those tools execute.

Analyzing LDAP Port Usage

You also need to know which ports the administrative tools use because it helps you plan how to use the tools and to understand what role global catalog servers play in accessing Active Directory information.

Connecting to Active Directory Using MMC

Because the MMC needs read and write access to directory information, it establishes a connection to a domain controller over LDAP port 389 of the domain to be administered. The client on which you start the MMC queries DNS to find a domain controller in the selected domain.

Searching from the MMC

MMC searches do not require read and write access to an Active Directory domain. You can use the MMC *Find* command to search a domain controller over LDAP port 389 by selecting a specific domain or an OU with a domain. You can also use it to search a global catalog server over LDAP port 3268 by selecting **Entire Directory**.

To search against a domain controller (port 389), select the domain in the **Find** dialog **In** field, or select **Browse** and choose an OU in the Active Directory. See Figure 5.29.

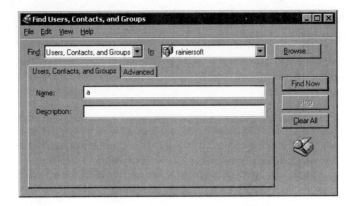

Figure 5.29   Searching against a domain controller.

Figure 5.30 shows how to search against the global catalog (port 3268). Note that you select **Entire Directory** in this case.

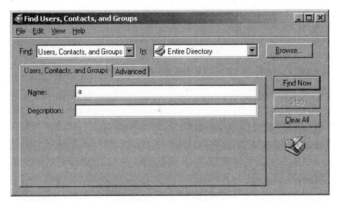

Figure 5.30   Searching against the global catalog.

Searching for Printers

Using the MMC to search for printers is a similar procedure. In the **Search for Printers** dialog shown in Figure 5.31, select a domain or an OU to query the domain controller on LDAP port 389, select **Entire Directory** to query the global catalog server on LDAP port 3268.

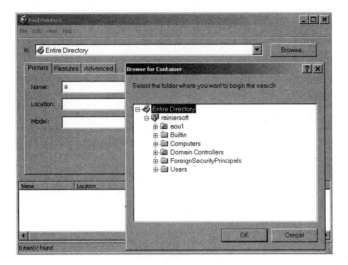

Figure 5.31   Searching for printers.

Windows Address Book

To search for people, use the Windows Address Book (WAB) to run global catalog searches against the Active Directory. You can't change this behavior to run against a domain controller on LDAP port 389, but you wouldn't want to do this anyway: binding a search to a domain controller would not find objects in other domains. To do that you need to use Global Catalog Services to follow these registry settings:

```
HKEY_CURRENT_USER\Software\Microsoft\Internet Account
Manager\Accounts\Active Directory GC

"LDAP Port" change it to use Port 389 (Standard: 3268)
```

One more thing: to function correctly, you have to customize the registry value for *LDAP Search Base* to reflect the proper Active Directory domain component to query (Figure 5.32). In the tests, this is *dc=rainiersoft,dc=tld* for *rainiersoft.tld*" (Standard: Empty).

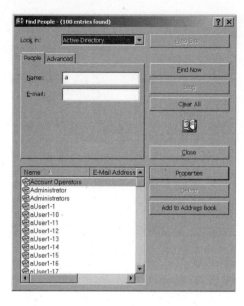

Figure 5.32   Customizing LDAP Search Base registry value.

Browsing the Active Directory

Browsing the directory from **My Network Places** uses LDAP Port 389 to get information about available objects from a domain controller if you select a specific domain (Figure 5.33).

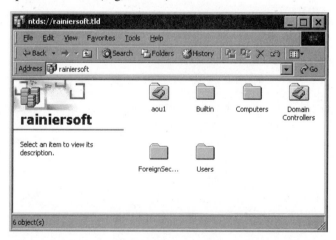

Figure 5.33   Browsing from My Network Places.

If Global Catalog Services Are Not Available

You can't use these tools to execute searches that query a global catalog server if no global catalog services are available on startup: the MMC Snap-in option *Entire Directory* is not available. If services become available after startup, the option is dynamically added to the selection.

Analyzing Authentication with LDP

Use the LDP (part of the Microsoft Windows 2000 Resource Kit) to check straight LDAP operations against the Active Directory. The tests set some configuration options, such as configuring the Auto base distinguished query to *false* to prevent LDP from querying the RootDSE each time. This is configured through the **General** selection on the **Options** menu, as shown in Figure 5.34.

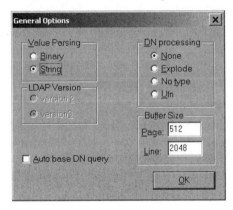

Figure 5.34   Configuring *Auto base distinguished*.

An LDAP client uses Authentication APIs to connect to a Directory Service Agent (DSA), which it does whenever it is searching for a resource, modifying information in the DIT, or running a directory-aware application. Depending on your environment, different authentication mechanisms may be negotiated.

LDAP API

`Ldap_open_s()`

The ldap_open API function creates and initializes a TCP/IP connection block, then opens the connection to an LDAP server.

Note   See the Microsoft Developer Network (MSDN) for a detailed description of the LDAP APIs. Go to http://msdn.microsoft.com/library and find **Platform SDK->Network and Directory Services->LDAP**.

To invoke this API in the LDP, choose **Connections->Connect**, enter the domain name, and press **OK** (Figure 5.35).

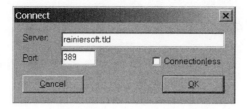

Figure 5.35   Invoking an API through the Connect dialog.

This causes LDP to call this API with the parameters:

```
ldap_open("rainiersoft.tld", 389)
```

and to establish a connection to *rainiersoft.tld*.

There are three ways to bind to an LDAP directory:

- **Server binding:** Specify a specific server in the bind operation
- **Domain binding:** Specify a specific domain (*rainiersoft.tld* in this example)
- **Server-less binding:** Specify neither a server nor a DNS domain in the **Connection** dialog

A network trace shows the connection block established to TCP port 389. For more information about understanding a TCP connection block, see Microsoft Knowledge Base article Q169292, Title: The Basics of Reading TCP/IP Traces.

```
Frame 1
TCP: ....S., len:    0, seq:1171961004-1171961004, ack:        0,
win:16384, src: 1148  dst: 389
Frame 2
TCP: .A..S., len:    0, seq:2701668798-2701668798, ack:1171961005,
win:17520, src: 389 dst: 1148
Frame 3
TCP: .A...., len:    0, seq:1171961005-1171961005, ack:2701668799,
win:17520, src: 1148  dst: 389
```

The operation creates this traffic:

Total	Client->Server	Server->Client
3 frames of 136 bytes	2 frames of 88 bytes	1 frame of 48 bytes

Note   There is no difference between connecting to a Windows 2000 domain controller on port 389 or to a global catalog on port 3268. In either case, a TCP session to a specific port is initiated. When you examine a network trace, look at the destination port to determine whether the connection was opened on the LDAP port or the global catalog port.

The traffic pattern is the same for *domain or server-less binding*. Traffic does change slightly if you specify the server's Full Qualified Domain Name (FQDN) in the LDAP connect (*server binding*). This runs a query against DNS to resolve the FQDN against the IP address, which causes additional DNS-related network traffic, not LDAP TCP traffic.

Total	Client->Server	Server->Client
4 frames of 674 bytes	2 frames of 213 bytes	2 frames of 361 bytes

LDAP API

```
Ldap_bind_s(), ldap_simple_bind_s
```

The ldap_bind_s function authenticates a client to the LDAP server.

To configure the binding options for the LDAP session in LDP, select **Bind Options** from the **Options** menu, as shown in Figure 5.36:

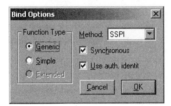

Figure 5.36   Configuring options for the LDAP session in LDP.

The tests used the Microsoft Security Support Provider Interface (SSPI) as authentication provider, so that these results could be compared later with the results for MMC and UI tools, all of which use SSPI.

To bind to the DSA with the LDP client, choose **Bind in LDP** in the **Connections** dialog (Figure 5.37).

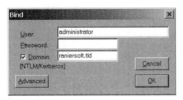

Figure 5.37   Binding to the DSA with the LDP client.

LDP then calls the LDAP Bind API with

```
ldap_bind_s(ld, NULL, &NtAuthIdentity, 1158); // v.3
{NtAuthIdentity: User='administrator'; Pwd= <unavailable>; domain =
'rainiersoft.tld'.}
```

and then authenticates as *dn:'administrator'*.

Note A TCP connection is already established, so the *Bind* request runs against the port used for the *Connect* request. It makes no difference to the Bind which LDAP TCP port is already connected: the traffic pattern is the same for a DC or a GC.

Using the preceding example, using SSPI as authentication provider generates this traffic for the LDAP connection request:

Total

12 frames of 7249 bytes

The traffic is the total for these operations:

- Client Kerberos authentication: 3 frames of 1946 bytes
- Server Kerberos authentication session ticket: 4 frames of 3225 bytes
- Client LDAP bind request: 2 frames of 1626 bytes
- Server LDAP response: 1 frame of 372 bytes
- Two additional acks because of fragmented frames: 2 frames of 80 bytes

Note that SSPI uses Kerberos authentication between two Windows 2000 computers.

If you specify no credentials, the operation uses and authenticates as NULL. Because this sends only the LDAP bind request and response, without any credential information, traffic is significantly reduced:

Total	**Client->Server**	**Server->Client**
2 frames of 124 bytes	1 frame of 62 bytes	1 frame of 62 bytes

Note If you specify NULL for the credentials with ldap_bind_s(), the operation uses the current user's/service's credentials. If you specify a simple bind method (as in ldap_simple_bind_s), it is equivalent to a NULL plain-text password.

LDAP API

`Ldap_unbind_s()`

To close the LDAP session, the client initiates an LDAP_UNBIND_CMD to the DSA. The DSA closes the TCP/IP session but does not return any value to the client.

To close the LDAP session with LDP, select **Unbind** in the **Connections** dialog.

In the network trace, frame 16 shows the client's *Unbind* request to the LDAP server. Frames 17 - 20 show the graceful tear-down of the TCP connection between the client and the server.

```
Frame 16
LDAP: ProtocolOp: UnbindRequest (2)
    LDAP: MessageID // Note the Message ID in the Data = 0x0F
    LDAP: ProtocolOp = UnbindRequest // Value in Data = 0x42

Frame 17
TCP: .A...F, len:    0, seq:2701669131-2701669131, ack:1171962498,
win:17509, src:  389  dst: 1148

Frame 18
TCP: .A...., len:    0, seq:1171962498-1171962498, ack:2701669132,
win:17188, src: 1148  dst:  389

Frame 19
TCP: .A...F, len:    0, seq:1171962498-1171962498, ack:2701669132,
win:17188, src: 1148  dst:  389

Frame 20
TCP: .A...., len:    0, seq:2701669132-2701669132, ack:1171962499,
win:17509, src:  389  dst: 1148
```

Network traffic generated by LDAP *Unbind*:

Total

5 frames of 211 bytes

Traffic pattern:

- LDAP unbind request client: 1 frame of 51 bytes
- TCP/IP session tear down client: 2 frames of 80 bytes
- TCP/IP session tear-down server: 2 frames of 80 bytes

ADSI Scripts

To investigate the ADSI network traffic the test used two Windows Scripting Host Visual Basic scripts (on the CD included with this book).

- **Bind.vbs:** This uses the ADSI *GetObject* API to connect to an LDAP directory, and the credentials of the current logged on user to bind to it.
- **Connect.vbs:** This uses the ADSI *OpenDSObject* API to connect with specific credentials to the directory.

Both methods support all three binding types: server, server-less, and domain. The tests showed no difference between running the operations against a DC or a GC. This is expected because the operation is straight LDAP.

LDAP operation	Total
Binding	14 frames of 4936 bytes
Authenticated binding	21 frames of 10092 bytes
Binding to RootDSE	12 frames of 4628 bytes
Authenticated binding to RootDSE	19 frames of 9938 bytes
Unbind	5 frames of 211 bytes

Note that there is always an implicit TCP connect to the Directory Server in ADSI. The typical traffic pattern for an ADSI *GetObject* call is:

- TCP/IP handshake: 3 frames of 136 bytes
- LDAP search request client: 1 frame of 390 bytes
- LDAP search response server: 2 frames of 1830 bytes
- Bind request client: 2 frames of 1588 bytes
- Bind response server: 1 frame of 372 bytes
- LDAP search request client: 1 frame of 125 bytes
- LDAP search response server: 1 frames of 155 bytes

Note Kerberos authentication happens only when the client establishes the LDAP bind request the first time; later requests use the originally-granted Kerberos ticket. This is why only LDAP traffic (no Kerberos traffic) appears in the results above. Remember, however, that binding to the server creates additional DNS traffic.

Using the MMC

A test started the MMC and measured the traffic. Selecting the snap-in:

Total	Client -> Server	Server -> Client
84 frames of 29 Kbytes	44 frames of 10 Kbytes	40 frames of 19 Kbytes

Selecting the MMC snap-in opened the domain *rainiersoft.tld* to read in the domain-naming context's top containers (see Figure 5.38), but this is already a directory access asking for information and should not create initial startup traffic.

Total	Client -> Server	Server -> Client
88 frames of 36.5 Kbytes	44 frames of 6.5 Kbytes	44 frames of 30 Kbytes

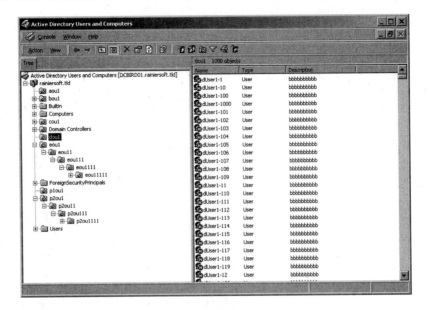

Figure 5.38   Selecting the MMC snap-in.

Note   Microsoft SMS 2.0 Network Monitor doesn't summarize network data after you filter a network trace. The tests used a practical approach to estimate network traffic. Results verified that saving the network trace to a file reduced the file by 10%, at which point it matched the size of the Network Monitor trace. To stay on the safe side, file-size was multiplied by 0.95 to measure larger traces.

Closing the MMC causes the same traffic as the LDAP *Unbind*:

Closing MMC (LDAP Unbind)

5 frames of 211 bytes

Summary of LDAP Binding Traffic

The table below summarizes the LDAP traffic generated by binding or startup operations from the tools used in the tests:

LDAP binding traffic.

	Serverless binding	Domain binding	Server binding	Unbind
LDP	8 frames of 2214 bytes	8 frames of 2214 bytes	8 frames of 2214 bytes	5 frames of 211 bytes
ADSI	14 frames of 4936 bytes	14 frames of 4936 bytes	14 frames of 4936 bytes	5 frames of 211 bytes
MMC	na	na	84 frames of 29696 bytes	5 frames of 211 bytes

The results indicate two relationships, if LDP traffic is defined as the baseline:

- ADSI bind traffic/bytes = LDP x 2
- MMC bind traffic/bytes = LDP x 13

Analyzing Interrogation

The interrogation LDAP APIs query DIT information. You can call these APIs by the UI, an OLE-DB application, or an ADSI application.

LDAP API

```
Ldap_search_s()
```

The ldap_search function searches the LDAP directory and returns a requested set of attributes for each entry matched.

Interrogation with LDP

Tests were conducted to measure traffic caused by LDAP queries against the Active Directory. The tests began with a query returning no attributes, then increased in five steps from 1 to 20, finally querying for all attributes. The *no-attribute* test with LDP bound to the DSA, then selected Search from the **Options** menu, and inserted 1 in the attributes text field. Subsequent steps listed all attributes to be returned by name, separated by a semicolon, in that field. For all attributes, you can use the asterisk (*) as a wildcard.

You can define the base object's DN against which the LDAP query is executed. You can filter the search to find specific objects and set the query scope before you execute the operation. Most of the tests below used the settings shown in the LDP search parameters screen shot (Figure 5.39). Later tests with ADSI scripts showed that an LDAP subtree search does not differ significantly from a plain one-level search against the base object DN container.

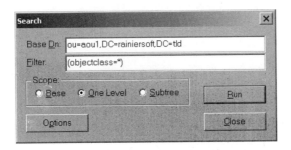

Figure 5.39   Defining base object's distinguished name.

Flat LDP Traffic Search Results

The tables below and Figure 5.40 summarize LDAP search traffic against Active Directory user objects using a domain controller on port 389 and a global catalog server on port 3268.

Frames LDP flat user search.

Objects/ Attributes	1.1 (= No Attributes)	1	5	10	15	20	*
1	3	3	3	3	3	3	5
10	3	3	4	6	7	8	30
100	7	9	23	42	59	77	296
1000	65	102	242	429	601	831	

Bytes LDP flat user search.

Objects/ Attributes	1.1 (= No Attributes)	1	5	10
1	339	384	601	828
10	916	1294	2823	4934
100	6983	10799	26105	46534
1000	69618	108686	262423	465924

Objects/ Attributes	1.1 (= No Attributes)	15	20	*
1	339	1064	1318	3420
10	916	6826	8817	32165
100	6983	65340	85109	321509
1000	69618	653570	850849	

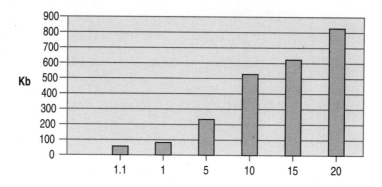

Figure 5.40   LDAP flat-user search scaling.

LDAP searches against the Active Directory scale linearly. This, and the fact that LDAP is an "on-the-wire" protocol, lead to the conclusion that LDAP query traffic depends on the number of objects, and the number and length of the attributes and their values.

For example, you can calculate the traffic caused by adding an attribute (of size 16 bytes with a value of size 10 bytes):

Size of Attribute/LDAP Query = 43 bytes

Because LDAP transports the name of the attribute from the client to the server, and the name and value of the attribute from the server to the client, you can calculate the total amount as (10 + 16 + 16) = 42 bytes.

Caution   To verify this conclusion, you have to take additional measurements with different attribute-value pairs—especially to find the general LDAP query's protocol overhead but also by the continuous TCP/IP packets used by LDAP.

LDP Flat Search for Printers

The *search for printers* test verifies that in general searching for objects is not dependent on object type. Differences are minor and can be explained by the higher number of integer attributes, which are smaller in the tests than when passing back string-values.

Frames LDP flat printer search.

Objects/Attributes	0	1	5	10	15	20	*
1000	66	104	243	423	620	na	na

Bytes LDP flat printer search.

Objects/Attributes	0	1	5	10	15	20	*
1000		70816	109948	260884	446983	655522	na	na

Interrogation with ADSI

To compare LDP with ADSI search network traffic, the test used another WSH VB script (*search.vbs*, on the CD) that uses ADO to execute queries with the different parameters (number of attributes, base container) against the Active Directory. Looking at the following tables and Figure 5.41, you can see that ADSI, unlike straight LDAP calls, adds no overhead to queries.

Frames ADSI flat user search.

Objects/Attributes	0	1	5	10	15	20	*
1	na	19	24	24	24	24	na
10	na	24	26	28	29	30	na
100	na	34	46	63	85	103	na
1000	na	130	268	445	653	842	na

Bytes ADSI flat user search.

Objects/Attributes	0	1	5	10	15	20	*
1	na	6013	6510	6764	7060	7326	na
10	na	7273	8875	10920	13142	15199	na
100	na	17462	32570	52279	74403	94778	na
1000	na	121362	272960	469944	689747	859623	na

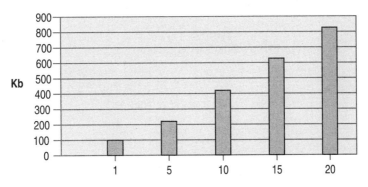

Figure 5.41   Flat user-search scaling.

Comparing Deep Search and Flat Search

Searching user objects in a nested hierarchy of OUs with an ADSI script yields these results:

Bytes ADSI deep user search.

Objects\Attributes	0	1	5	10	15	20	*
1000		na	162	305	484	688	872	na

Bytes ADSI deep user search.

Objects\Attributes	0	1	5	10	15	20	*
1000		na	158474	310656	507665	727320	930757	na

The results show that a deep search is slightly larger than a flat search. This is because LDAP passes a slightly longer DN of each object for a deep search than it does for a flat search (where DNs are more or less constant).

For example if you search *aou1* in a flat search, this user object DN is returned:

```
"cn=auser1-1,ou=aou1,dc=rainiersoft,dc=tld"
```

A deep search through 10 OUs (used in the test) returns this DN:

```
"cn=ouser1-1,ou=nou1,ou=mou1, … ou=gou1,ou=fou1,dc=rainiersoft.tld"
```

Note   There is no significant traffic difference between a flat and a deep LDAP search because only information comes back across the wire. It does not matter what type of object (users or printers) or where the object exists within the DIT, although there may be a small scaling factor for a deep search's extended DNs.

Interrogation with MMC

The interrogation test starts by executing the *Find* dialog. Using the MMC to search for user objects executes an LDAP search that includes the *Name*, *Description*, and *Object Type* attributes in the result set of all the objects.

If you display additional information about an object by selecting properties on the object itself, you initiate an additional LDAP query for that specific object name that returns about 40 attributes in its property pages.

Here is the network traffic generated by selecting the different populated OUs in MMC *Find*, which runs queries against a Windows 2000 domain controller:

Frames MMC search for user objects.

Number of objects	DC initial search, returning 3 attributes	GC initial search, returning 3 attributes	Displaying user object properties, returning about 40 attributes
1	5	5	61
10	6	6	
100	22	22	
1000	205	205	

Bytes MMC search for user objects.

Number of objects	DC (port 389) initial search, returning 3 attributes	GC (port 3268) Initial Search, returning 3 attributes	Displaying user object properties, returning about 40 attributes
1	1205	3404	20686
10	3025	5284	
100	22718	24701	
1000	226700	221984	

The tests ran four queries to compare the MMC DC search network traffic with GC traffic. A name wildcard was specified in the MMC Find **User, Contacts, Group** dialog. Based on the created logical AD structure for the test and its naming conventions, a search with *auser* returns only 1, *buser* returns 10, *cuser* returns 100, and *duser* returns 1000. This matches the results for the DC search, which selected separate OUs and did not specify a wildcard.

Note   Traffic does not vary when you use MMC *Find* to search against a global catalog or a domain controller.

Interrogation with WAB

Searching for people by using the Windows Address Book (WAB) to run global catalog searches against the Active Directory causes network traffic. Because the search is run against a GC, tests to determine the amount of traffic used the same wildcard methodology that was used for the MMC GC search (auser, buser, cuser, duser).

One difference is that the WAB queries the GC to return all user objects with 44 attributes, and after these results are listed in the WAB you do not generate network traffic (or LDAP queries) when you select the details of a user object.

The tests in this section set only five attributes (*info*, *cn*, *givenName*, *homePhone*, and *title*) of the 44 that were returned by the LDAP query.

Bytes WAB "Search for People."

Number of objects	WAB search queries for 44 attributes on objects, 5 returned
1	3792
10	7377
100	41496
1000	240910

In its standard configuration the WAB queries only for 100 objects. To test against 1000 users, this value was changed in the registry key:

```
HKEY_CURRENT_USER\Software\Microsoft\Internet Account
Manager\Accounts\Active Directory GC

"LDAP Search Return"        changed to 1000 (100 standard)
```

Interrogation with "Search Printer"

The **Search Printer** dialog returns a standard attribute set for each printer object: *description*, *driverName*, *location*, *objectClass*, *printerName*, and *serverName*. Selecting properties for a printer object, this method creates an LDAP query (like the MMC and unlike the WAB).

Frames "Search Printer."

Number of Objects	6 attributes queried
1	14
12	15
112	35
1000	237

Bytes "Search Printer."

Number of Objects	6 attributes queried
1	3632
12	5737
112	26865
1000	354404

Note   The test put all printer objects in the same OU and used the wildcard approach again. Printers are named *pprinter1-1* to *pprinter-1000*. Querying against *pprinter1-1* does not query exactly 100 objects, as does querying against pprinter1-10.

Interrogation with "Browse AD"

Browsing the Active Directory via **My Network Places** causes one initial hit when you select the directory to browse. In these tests, this is *rainiersoft.tld*, which has 13 top-level containers.

Traffic "Browse AD" by top level folder hierarchy listing.

13 Top level folders
17 frames of 5103 Bytes

When you select OUs, listing their objects returns the objects and their *Name* and *objectClass* attributes, creating this traffic:

Frames "Browse AD."

Number of objects	2 attributes
1	16
10	18
100	34
1000	203

Bytes "Browse AD."

Number of objects	2 attributes
1	3466
10	5013
100	24056
1000	214590

Interrogation Summary

The captured network traffic, summarized below, shows that comparable searches cause comparable network traffic.

Interrogation summary.

Tool used	LDP search	ADSI search	MMC search	WAB search	Search printer	Browse AD
Attributes queried	5	5	3	44	6	2
Attributes returned	5	5	3	5	6	2
1000 objects	260884 bytes	272960 bytes	226700 bytes	240910 bytes	354404 bytes	214590 bytes

Analyzing Update

Clients use the LDAP Update APIs to create, modify, and delete existing DIT entries.

Creating (Adding) Objects

To test object adds (creation), user objects and group objects were created with only mandatory attributes, then with some additional attributes to see how traffic varies with attributes.

LDAP API

```
ldap_add_s
```

This adds an entry to a DIT. To be successful, four things must be true:

- The parent object must exist as a container
- The new DN must be unique within the DIT
- The new object must conform to the schema

Access controls must permit the creation of the object

Adding Objects with LDP

In LDP, select Add from the **Browse** menu to start the **Add** (objects) dialog, as shown in Figure 5.42.

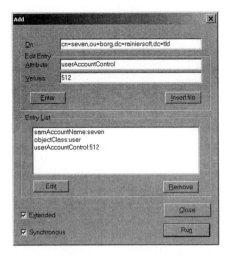

Figure 5.42   Adding users with LDP.

The *objectClass* attribute defines which type of object gets created in the Active Directory. User objects also require the mandatory attribute *samAccountName*.

This test created users with different numbers of attributes: each OU contained different numbers of objects—most contained *user* objects, but to verify that the LDAP network traffic pattern is independent of the type of object, one OU contained *printer* objects. To verify that an LDAP search is independent of OU structure (flat or deep) the test created one nested OU hierarchy.

Network traffic generated is shown below.

Frames adding user and group object with LDP

	Mandatory	"+1" attribute	"+5"	"+10"	"+15"
User	3	3	3	3	3
Group	3	3	3	na	na

Bytes adding user and group object with LDP.

	Mandatory	"+1" attribute	"+5"	"+10"	"+15"
User	354	398	542	715	924
Group	322	359	540	na	na

Note   In LDAP, there is no difference between creating a user or group objects. This should not be, because the *objectClass* attribute determines what kinds of object the DSA creates. But the attribute does not affect the general structure of the LDAP "on-the-wire" transport for creating objects. Network traffic increases only when you add attributes.

Adding Objects with ADSI

A test was designed to measure traffic caused by adding printer objects with ADSI. Printer objects must have four (mandatory) attributes set in the ADSI *create object* call.

Frames adding objects with ADSI.

	Mandatory	"+1" attribute	"+5"	"+10"	"+15"
User	6	6	6	6	6
Group	6	6	6	Na	Na
Printer	6	6	6	Na	Na

Bytes adding objects with ADSI.

	Mandatory	"+1" attribute	"+5"	"+10"	"+15"
User	771	812	956	1145	1353
Group	771	813	959	Na	Na
Printer	912	949	1104	Na	Na

Adding Object with MMC

You cannot use the MMC to create user objects with only mandatory attributes. The first MMC *Add User* dialog requires you to enter the first name and full name, so an MMC LDAP *Add Request* has five attributes: *samAccountName*, *objectClass*, *userPrincipalName*, *displayName*, and *givenName*. At this stage you can also add two other attributes, *initials* and *surname*. The traffic generated is shown below.

The test added no other attributes in this step because it cannot be done with the MMC during object creation. You create the user object, then open the object properties in MMC and finish populating the attributes. This step is covered in the "Modifying Attributes" section, below.

Frames MMC adding a user and group.

Object type	MMC mandatory (5 attributes)	Adding in surname/initials (7 attributes)
User	107	107
Group	9	

Bytes MMC adding a user and group.

Object type	MMC mandatory (5 attributes)	Putting in surname/initials (7 attributes)
User	32288	32816
Group	2798	

Note   The group was created with the *samAccountName*, *groupType*, *objectClass* attributes set.

The MMC generates a high amount of traffic to add a user because it adds LDAP search and modify operations to query on the existence of the object and to set the *userAccountControl* attribute separately. The operation also creates RPC traffic and exchanges Kerberos tickets. The tests had no way to parse for RPC calls or UUID files, so it was not possible to isolate and measure the MMC calls.

Summary Adding Objects

Adding user with five attributes, network traffic summary.

Tool	LDP	ADSI	MMC
Bytes	542	956	32288

Using LDP as the baseline, you can compare the traffic generated by adding users with various tools and arrive at:

ADSI = LDP x 1.75

MMC = LDP x 60

Modifying Objects

Object modification traffic tests were run with LDP, ADSI, and the MMC. Each user object was manipulated with from 1 to 15 additional attributes, and they were added, modified, and deleted again.

LDAP API

```
Ldap_modify_s()
```

The ldap_modify_s function changes an existing entry. Modifying an entry includes adding, modifying, and deleting attributes.

For ldap_modify_s to succeed, four things must be true:

- The object must exist
- All attribute modifications must succeed
- The resulting entry must conform to the schema
- Access controls must permit the modification of the entry

Add, Delete, and Modify Attributes with LDP

In LDP, select Modify from the **Browse** menu to start the **Modify** dialog, as shown in Figure 5.43.

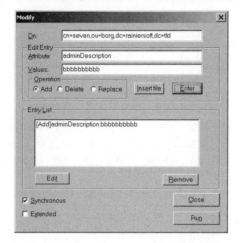

Figure 5.43   Modifying attributes with LDP.

Network Traffic Generated by Manipulating Attributes with LDP

Frames LDP modify attributes of user object.

	1	5	10	15
Add	3	3	3	3
Replace	3	3	3	3
Delete	3	3	3	3

Bytes LDP modify attributes of user object.

	1	5	10	15
Add	302	482	729	951
Replace	298	473	731	951
Delete	290	422	578	771

Adding, Deleting, and Modifying User Attributes with ADSI

Frames, modify user attributes with ADSI.

	1	5	10	15
Add/replace	3	3	3	3
Delete	3	3	3	3

Bytes, modify user attributes with ADSI.

	1	5	10	15
Add/replace	346	526	758	1011
Delete	334	466	638	831

Adding, Deleting, and Modifying User Attributes with MMC

The initial MMC **Show Properties** dialog is already an LDAP request (query) with 63 frames of 20539 bytes each. The test results below show the traffic generated when 20 10-byte attributes are set on the user object. Because the MMC sends a separate LDAP *Modify* request for each changed property page, there is MMC overhead traffic.

Frames, modify user attributes with MMC.

	1	5	10	15
Add	7	7	9	11
Replace	7	7	9	11
Delete	7	9	11	13

Bytes, modify user attributes with MMC.

	1	5	10	15
Add	1373	1570	2039	2478
Replace	1381	1571	2039	2478
Delete	1369	1661	2018	2480

Summary Modifying Objects

The *modify objects* results are summarized below. Note that *Add* and *Replace* caused the same network traffic. In general, *modify* operations don't vary significantly between ADSI and LDP. MMC traffic is about three times the traffic for LDP.

Modifying a user object, network traffic summary.

Tool	LDP	ADSI	MMC
Add/replace	951	1011	2478
Delete	771	831	2480

Analyzing Delete

The last set of the tests analyzed *delete* operations on directory objects and containers. The type of the object does not matter: LDAP sends over the wire only a *Delete* request with the object's distinguished name.

LDAP API

```
Ldap_delete_s()
```

The ldap_delete_s function is a synchronous operation that removes a leaf entry from the directory tree.

For ldap_delete_s to succeed, three things must be true:

- The object must exist
- The object must not have children.
- Access controls must permit the deletion of the entry

Deleting with LDP

In LDP, select **Delete** from the **Browse** menu to start the **Delete** dialog, as shown in Figure 5.44.

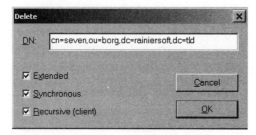

Figure 5.44   LDP Delete object dialog.

Selecting a container (OU) and recursive delete does not use special LDAP controls to execute a server side operation in LDP. Instead, it loops recursively through the container, deleting a single object in each operation.

Deleting with ADSI

The same tests delete a user object with ADSI. No delete was performed on a container.

Deleting with MMC

The tests were repeated with the MMC, plus a run deleting a container. MMC implements the LDAP control to delete a whole container at once, not deleting recursively through the container removing one object at a time. To delete a container, you have to select an OU and delete it. If you select multiple objects the MMC loops the selection and executes single delete calls.

Summary Network Traffic Generated by Deleting an Object through LDAP

Frames deleting a user object.

	LDP	ADSI	MMC
User	5	5	9
Container (MMC)	Na	Na	6

Bytes deleting a user object.

	LDP	ADSI	MMC
User	487	604	1293
Container (MMC)			661

Comparing the results and using LDP as the baseline yields:

ADSI = LDP x 1.5

MMC = LDP x 3

What Is Not Covered

Although these tests give a good picture of LDAP operations and the kind of network traffic they cause, the tests do not address some factors that influence LDAP capacity planning.

First, tests used a fixed set of attributes and object values. To verify linear scaling of the traffic pattern definitively, you should measure with a network monitor and vary the number and length of attributes.

Second, in Windows 2000, LDAP Profiles allow you to customize LDAP settings such as page size and the number of objects returned in a page. The tests above did not vary these settings—using instead the standard out-of-the-box parameters—and they might influence network traffic as well as server performance, resources, and response times.

Third, don't forget that every company has different user behaviors in querying and manipulating directory information. To create a more realistic profile for calculating expected LDAP traffic caused by using the Active Directory, look for numbers in your own organization relevant to similar directory-intensive applications such as address book features in messaging applications.

Conclusion

LDAP is an open protocol standard that provides methods for manipulating data in network directories. Regardless of how it is used (ADSI, the LDAP APIs, or a user searching the Active Directory through the UI) LDAP puts protocol traffic on the wire as the client communicates with the DSA. But because LDAP is a protocol standard, it manifests itself in the same way on the network wire regardless of how the query or modification was generated at the application layer. The tests in this section show that executing LDAP operations with different tools creates the same LDAP queries, but that the tools themselves can create additional traffic, sometimes in the form of additional LDAP calls that add overhead and cannot be avoided.

Because LDP is a straightforward LDAP client, it was used for a baseline against which to measure and evaluate the application design and performance. The tests also show that it should be possible with ADSI, and its LDAP provider, to develop a "thin" client, at least with respect to network usage. Using the MMC as the administrative console creates additional traffic, often in the form of remote procedure calls or queries for object existence.

## PART 2

Migration and Integration Scenarios

Migrating and integrating an existing IT structure with Active Directory can be a daunting task, and this section was designed to alleviate your concerns by outlining scenarios from companies that are moving forward with Windows 2000 implementations—real concepts, fictionalized companies drawn from real-life cases. Chapter 6, "Domain Migration and Consolidation," explains how to migrate from a complex Windows NT 4.0 domain model to a simpler Windows 2000 Active Directory model. Chapter 7, "Integrating Active Directory with a Unix-Based DNS Environment," shows how to implement Active Directory in a pure Unix DNS environment, and discusses the differences between Unix and Windows 2000 DNS implementations. Chapter 8, "Integrating Active Directory with Exchange Server," focuses on issues affecting Exchange interoperability and functionality when you move from a pure Windows NT 4.0 environment to a Windows 2000 native-mode environment. Chapter 9, "Active Directory and Novell NetWare NDS," discusses the Active Directory concepts from a Novell NDS perspective, and explains how to migrate users from NDS to Active Directory.

Active Directory addresses the problems inherent in large networks by enabling you to design and manage your network resources *effectively*. This section discusses a representative range of migration issues to show you how to approach the challenges of your own Active Directory implementation.

CHAPTER 6

Domain Migration and Consolidation

By Jim Gross,
Microsoft
Corporation

Northwind Traders (NWT) is a fictional company that provides investment backing and financial planning services around the world through its network of 120,000 employees in twenty-six countries. NWT deployed Windows NT Server several years ago to provide application services, such as e-mail, to employees, and now more than 70,000 users authenticate on the domain environment worldwide.

Unfortunately, NWT originally deployed a complex domain model, one that became more complex and harder to manage as the network grew, so NWT saw the availability of Windows 2000 and Active Directory as an opportunity to reduce design complexity, sidestep the limitations that drove the original design, and create a new model that was easier to maintain, manage, and enhance. The first section briefly describes the original design and its problems; the rest of the chapter explains how NWT started over with Active Directory.

What You'll Find in This Chapter

- An explanation of how to migrate from a complex Windows NT 4.0 domain model to a simpler Windows 2000 Active Directory model that unifies global directory service, promotes scaling, and simplifies management—and how to do it with minimum impact on the production environment.

- How to perform an in-place upgrade and how to perform a domain consolidation to create a more manageable model.

- Details on migration procedure, with emphasis on concepts, specific tasks, and their order. Useful tools and utilities are discussed and explained.

The Environment

The Windows NT 4.0 Domain Model

Originally, NWT established a very complex Windows NT Server domain model—a centralized three-tier domain strategy in the Americas, where most users are concentrated on two campuses (Figure 6.1). The first tier comprises six regional accounts domains containing the user accounts and global groups for approximately 80,000 employees. The second tier comprises six resource domains, which contain the various computing resources NWT uses to conduct business (workstations, file servers, printers, etc.). The third tier comprises numerous small resource domains that provide services to over 1000 small branch locations.

Outside of the Americas, legal and political issues dictate much of NWT's domain design. For example, all security and management of NWT's resources in a country must take place within that country, so NWT implemented accounts domains and resource domains in each European country where they have an office. To conserve bandwidth, NWT did not implement trusts between European and American domains.

NWT has also been deploying Windows NT Workstations to the development community, recently surpassing 20,000 workstations in the Americas. This has required adding many machine accounts to the existing resource domains, and creating approximately 2,000 global groups within the domain architecture to help manage permissions to shared resources on approximately 2,000 Microsoft Windows NT Servers.

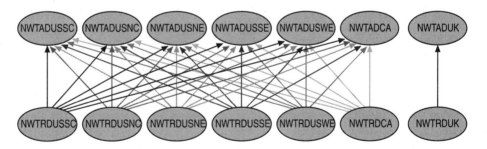

Figure 6.1   Original multi-master domain design at NWT.

Proposed Active Directory Model

Constant additions to the domain environment is increasing the number of domains and trusts, complicating management, and creating problems. Complex domain architecture and the limitations imposed by Windows NT 4.0 Server directory services became so onerous that NWT decided to move to Windows 2000 Servers and Active Directory to unify global directory service, promote scaling, and simplify management.

Active Directory

NWT took advantage of the move to Windows 2000 and Active Directory to clean up the Windows NT 4.0 domain deployment, thus making the environment more global and easier to manage. They discarded the original, technologically-limited domain design and started over. After careful planning they decided that the first step was to flatten the namespace and reduce the number of domains where possible (Figures 6.2 and 6.3).

Note   For clarity, Figures 6.2 and 6.3 show only a representative portion of NWT's Active Directory design.

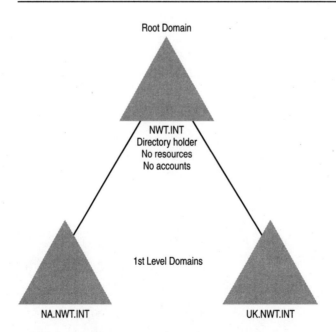

Figure 6.2   Active Directory domains at NWT.

Windows 2000 Domain

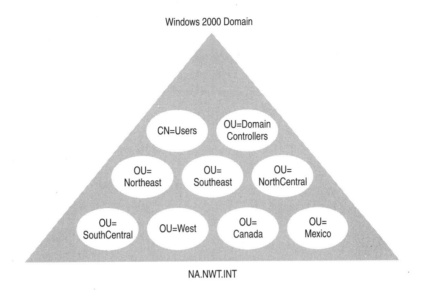

NA.NWT.INT

Figure 6.3   North America domain with first-level OUs.

Migration Goals

NWT wanted the move to Windows 2000 to have the smallest possible impact on the production environment, so that it does not hamper user productivity or access to data, resources, and applications. This relatively simple goal compelled NWT's IT staff to devise migration tactics that would move user accounts and passwords from Windows NT domains to Active Directory automatically, and require minimal changes at the desktop level and to resource permissions.

Determining the Migration Scenario

The first step (before planning the migration) was to complete an Active Directory design that met the two main goals: simpler administration and the creation of a global computing environment. The next step was to define a migration path from the Windows NT 4.0 environment to Windows 2000 and Active Directory.

NWT examined their original domain structure and decided that the European domains, which had to keep their original structure for political and legal reasons, could receive an in-place upgrade. These domains ran under Windows NT 4.0 Server and a mixture of Windows NT 4.0 Workstation and Windows 9x, which fit the supported upgrade path.

NWT decided to restructure the North American domain design because of the number of domains and trusts in place. The goal was to consolidate account domains into one larger domain while maintaining interoperability with the down-level resource domains. To meet these goals, NWT decided to clone users, groups, profiles, and resources from the existing Windows NT source domains to a pristine Windows 2000 domain (*NA*) with a flattened namespace that would allow NWT to consolidate global groups.

Creating the Active Directory Infrastructure

Root-Level NWT.INT Domain

The root-level domain was installed as a place holder in the forest: it was designed to serve as the root and it contains only the user or computer accounts needed for operation (Figure 6.4). The NetBIOS name for this domain is *NWT* and the DNS name for the internal portion of this space is *NWT.INT*, which was registered with the Internic. The external portion of the namespace was registered as *Northwind-Traders.ext* to differentiate between the two so that that clients connecting through a virtual private network (VPN) or point-to-point tunneling protocol (PPTP) would not be confused by a single namespace for both public and private resources.

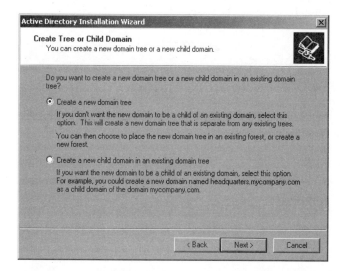

Figure 6.4   Creating a new domain tree in the Active Directory forest.

Second-Level NA.NWT.INT Domain

In this migration scenario, NWT decided to install a pristine Windows 2000 domain for North America (*NA*) with the goal of cloning the user and computer accounts from the old domains to the new pristine domain. All domain controllers for this domain would be Windows 2000 Servers, so the domain would exist in native mode. The Active Directory Migration Tool requires that for the cloning process to run, the target domain must be in native mode. This is because cloning requires the use of SIDHistory, a property of the user object that maintains the security identifier (SID) of the original account, and this is only available when the Windows 2000 domain is in native mode. The first Windows 2000 Server promoted to a domain controller was configured as a child domain for the root-level *NWT.INT* domain (Figure 6.5). The NetBIOS name for this domain would be *NA* and the DNS name *NA.NWT.INT*. This domain did not host WINS or DHCP because those services were handled by the respective resource domains, so the new Windows 2000 Servers were configured to register themselves with an appropriate WINS servers so Windows NT 4.0 and Windows 9*x* clients could resolve them.

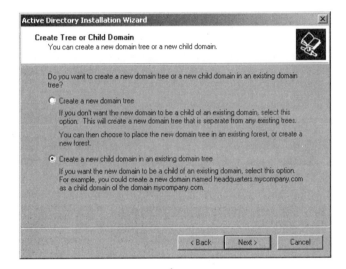

Figure 6.5   Creating a child domain.

Migrating the UK Domain (In-Place Upgrade)

Why In-Place?

NWT decided that an in-place migration best suited the basic criteria for the environment in Europe. First, most European nations have different laws governing data storage and security, and NWT decided that their original domain design granted enough autonomy to each host county to meet requirements. Second, the in-place upgrade is the easiest and safest migration path because it is simply an operating system update that retains most systems settings. Third, as each European domain uses few domain controllers, NWT could upgrade with minimal impact on the production environment because the upgrade maintains trusts to other Windows NT domains and can be transparent to the client.

Order of Upgrade

NWT decided to follow this order to upgrade the United Kingdom environment.

- Preliminary tasks
- "Dry run" upgrade
- Upgrade accounts domain *NWTADUK*
- Migrate resource domain *NWTRDUK* (future)

The Process

Preliminary Tasks

Since there are numerous domain controllers available to service log on requests, it was not expected that there would be a disruption of service during the upgrade process. However, the helpdesk sent out notifications of the upcoming events to inform the users in case there was an unplanned outage during the process.

The Windows NT Engineering team inventoried hardware on all domain controllers slated for upgrade, then checked the existing hardware against the Hardware Compatibility List at ftp://ftp.microsoft.com/services/whql/win2000hcl.txt. Non-compatible hardware, which in some cases was a complete domain controller, was marked for replacement during migration. Domain controllers were upgraded as necessary to meet minimum hardware requirements for Windows 2000 Server.

Support teams, including the helpdesk staff and second- and third-level support, were trained by Microsoft Certified Technical Education Centers (MSCTEC).

"Dry Run" Upgrade

The primary domain controller (PDC) upgrade was verified offline before upgrading the production domain—mostly to determine the state of the SAM database and check for strings inserted into attributes by third-party account management tools that are not allowed by the User Manager or Win32 APIs. The User, Group, and Computer Migration Wizards execute as if the SAM is "clean" and cannot check for all possibilities, so this step was performed to avoid failures. A backup domain controller (BDC) was removed from the production LAN (Figure 6.6), then the team used Server Manager to promote the offline BDC to the PDC for *NWTADUK* (Figure 6.7).

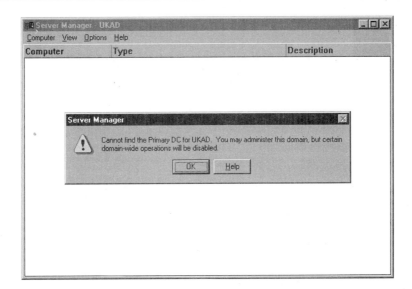

Figure 6.6   **Cannot find the primary DC for UKAD.**

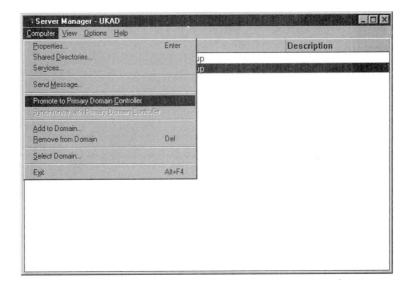

Figure 6.7   **Promoting a BDC to a PDC.**

The testers then added the new PDC to an isolated network segment on which Windows NT Workstations and Windows 9*x* clients logged on and changed the password for a given account. When the testers were convinced this worked correctly, they upgraded the PDC to Windows 2000. The Setup program determined that this server had been a domain controller and started the Active Directory Installation Wizard (DCPROMO) and the team configured the server to create a new forest and new tree because there were no other Active Directory servers on the isolated network. When the Active Directory configuration was complete, the test clients again logged on and changed passwords to make sure the upgrade was successful.

Upgrade the Accounts Domain NWTADUK

Caution   Before starting an upgrade process, create and verify tape backups for all domain controllers and any network services such as file shares, DHCP, or WINS databases.

Verifications complete, the team began the upgrade process. To minimize production environment controller downtime, they synchronized the domain controllers with the PDC then took the PDC offline to allow for disaster recovery and to stop changes from being made to the domain.

Caution   Keep the original PDC available until the upgrade process is complete. You need it *and* the tape backups to recover the domain if there is a failure.

To begin the process, the Windows 2000 Setup was run in upgrade mode. After the operating system upgrade was complete, Setup determined that the server was a domain controller and started the Active Directory Installation Wizard, with which the team configured the Active Directory as a child domain in an existing forest, retaining the NetBIOS name and setting the DNS name as UK.NWT.INT. Since there was no PDC on the production network, the first BDC to be upgraded took the role as the PDC Operations Master during the Active Directory Setup (Figure 6.8).

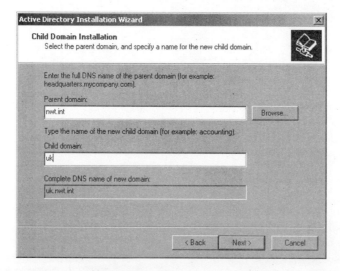

Figure 6.8   Creating the child domain *uk.nwt.int*.

Since UKADBDC1 was already upgraded and the Active Directory configured for an isolated domain, it was necessary to format the drive and re-install it as a Windows 2000 Server in the *NWTADUK* domain on the live network. Then the Active Directory Installation Wizard was run to upgrade the server to a domain controller.

The team used the "Active Directory Users and Computers" snap-in to verify replication with *UKADBDC2*.

From this point, the rest of the upgrade is simply installing software and configuring the Active Directory.

Maintaining Interoperability

NWT devised a testing scenario to determine that interoperability would be maintained during and after the migration. Specifically, this meant maintaining roaming profiles, trusts, permissions, and logon scripts so that users of Windows NT 4.0 Workstation and Windows 9x could log on and gain access to network resources.

Testing Logon Table

Action	Result
Can user NWTADUK\NWTUser1 logon to domain *NWTADUK*?	
Can user NWTADUK\NWTUser1 access resources in *NWTADUK*?	
Can user NWTADUK\NWTUser1 access resources in *NWTRDUK*?	
Can user NWTADUK\NWTUser1 change the password?	

Consolidating the North American Domains

Why Consolidate?

Active Directory scalability impelled NWT to consolidate the numerous North American accounts domains into a single one that was larger and more manageable. This was reflected in namespace planning. Another factor in NWT's decision were the new *transitive trusts*, which simplify trust management between resource domains and accounts domains, especially when compared to management issues in NWT's original multiple-master environment. These changes lowered TCO by reducing administrative overhead.

Having decided to consolidate, NWT next had to decide when in the migration process to do it. Some third party vendors recommended restructuring before upgrading to Windows 2000, but NWT's domains were too large to do this with Windows NT 4.0 Server. It was possible to restructure after upgrade (Microsoft makes tools for doing this) but NWT wanted a clean Windows 2000 environment instead of carrying over their original design, so they decided to restructure during migration.

The Active Directory Migration Tool

The Active Directory Migration Tool (ADMT) is comprised of wizards that perform the tasks of cloning users and groups, creating computer accounts, merging groups, and translating security information when migrating from Windows NT 4.0 domains to Windows 2000 domains. NWT used the ADMT to clone users and groups and to create machine accounts in the Active Directory. The wizards can run from any workstation with appropriate permissions and connectivity, but NWT decided to run it on a Windows 2000 domain controller in the target domain; this was because the wizard stores migration information in a database that, for proper operation, must be secure and recoverable. The domain controller provided physical and logical security, and made it convenient to create regular tape back-ups.

Order of Migrations

Domain migrations can begin as soon as the Active Directory infrastructure is in place. Accounts domains were slated for migration first, to take full advantage of the Active Directory security and management features. Resource domains were migrated after the accounts domains based on some simple criteria.

- **Where applications demand Windows 2000 features.** Some applications, such as Microsoft Exchange 2000, require features available only in Windows 2000 to run, and you should give first consideration to the domains necessary to support those applications.

- **Size of Domain.** Some companies are already facing the limitations imposed by Windows NT 4.0 domains. Windows 2000 and the Active Directory do not limit the number of users or the size of the SAM database, so moving those large domains as soon as possible can solve this problem.

- **Targets for restructuring.** When you collapse domains and restructure the domain environment, it may make sense to upgrade the largest domain first and then collapse the remaining domains into that one.

The Migration Process

Devise and Test a Back-Out Plan

Most of the migration process involves cloning (copying) users, groups, and computer accounts from the Windows NT domain to the Windows 2000 Active Directory. The two environments can run simultaneously, so you can test, run a pilot, and even fall back to the Windows NT domain, without interrupting production. NWT began migration by verifying the migrations without committing them.

Establish and Apply a Duplicate Names Policy

You can have friendly user names, such as **jdoe** or **johnd**, so long as they are unique within their domain. When you consolidate two or more domains into one, you sometimes end up with two user accounts with the same user name. You have to provide a mechanism that guarantees uniqueness. NWT assigns alphanumeric user IDs that are unique across all domains, so name collisions were not a problem during consolidation. There were some group naming issues, though, because some global groups in different domains had the same group name (for example *Sales*, etc.). Consolidation would merge the groups, which often is not acceptable. The ADMT provides for this by renaming accounts when a collision happens by adding a prefix or suffix.

Establish and Apply a Uniqueness Policy

To maintain unique global groups in the target domain, NWT appended to the name a designation based on the source domain. For example, the global group named NWTADUSNE\ExchangeAdmins would become NE-ExchangeAdmins. You can do this before or during migration. If you do it before, you have to create a new global group then reapply permissions to each resource affected. NWT renamed groups during migration because they used the Active Directory Migration Wizard, which allowed them to maintain the original SID history as an attribute (even though a new group was created), so they did not have to re-apply permissions.

Identify and Remove Obsolete Global and Local Groups

You may find some (or many) defined groups that are no longer in use—projects end, reorganizations shift things around, groups become fossils. Every group has an impact on migration and replication, so NWT manually verified the global groups for memberships and deleted any without valid members. They considered using SIDWalker to enumerate the groups associated with resources on the file and applications servers, but decided against it because these groups do not pose a problem or drain resources: if they do not change they are replicated only once in the Active Directory and then again only when a new domain controller is added. It is also possible to write scripts to enumerate group memberships and the SIDWalker utility can report what groups exist in the ACL of a particular resource. The ADMT also has a reporting utility that can report on group ACL memberships and re-apply permissions as necessary.

Establish Necessary Trust Relationships

The Domain Migration Wizard does not require an explicit trust between the source domain and the target domain to verify the migration settings, but it does require trust and administrative privileges on the source and target domains to actually clone the accounts. Also, some level of trust is required to maintain access to resource domains and to administer the source domain from the

Windows 2000 domain. NWT planned to run with both domains active during the pilot phase, so explicit trust relationships were required between the Windows 2000 domain and the source and resource domains (Figure 6.9). The ADMT Trust Migration Wizard helped maintain the necessary trusts by migrating the necessary explicit trusts that existed in the source domain to the target domain to maintain access to resources.

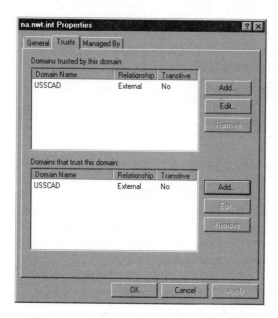

Figure 6.9   Two-way trust between *na.nwt.int* and *USSCAD*.

Clone Global Groups to the Windows 2000 Domain

Typically, you use local groups to set the access control for resources on the local server; you use global groups to maintain user memberships and these are added to the local groups to provide access to resources. This means it makes the most sense to migrate the global groups to the Windows 2000 domain first. There must be an explicit trust between the two domains as well as the global group SIDHistory in the Windows 2000 Active Directory for a user to log on to the Windows 2000 domain and access resources in the Windows NT 4.0 resource domain.

NWT had to clone the global groups to the Windows 2000 domain to retain the groups' original SIDs so that the SIDHistory of the original global group allowed users to continue accessing resources with the old SID. Even though global groups are relevant only within their domain, if the SID is unchanged, users in the Windows 2000 domain can access resources as before and security information does not have to be reapplied. In order to simplify the migration process, NWT decided to migrate the group members during the group migration process (Figure 6.10).

Figure 6.10   ADMT Group Migration Wizard.

When you copy the membership information you must also configure the user migration information (Figure 6.11).

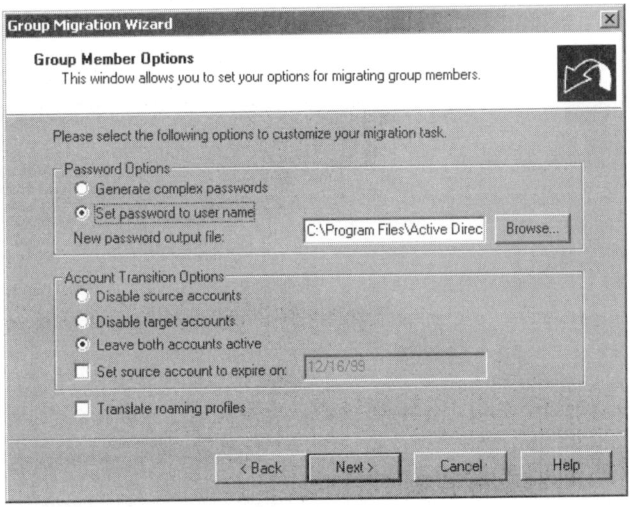

Figure 6.11   Group Member options.

NWT wanted to handle groups in different ways, so they migrated global group in phases. First were groups that had to remain unique when migrated—groups uniquely named globally and groups with names that conflict with groups in other domains. Names for these groups were augmented with a two-digit code denoting their region of origin (Figure 6.12).

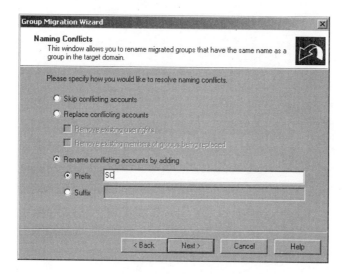

Figure 6.12 Adding a prefix during a migration.

Next were groups that would be merged with other groups. For the first domain migrated, this was a simple group copy, but for subsequent groups the team had to use the ADMT Group Mapping/Merge Wizard to copy the membership of the original Windows NT 4.0 groups to the new Windows 2000 group.

Clone Shared Local Groups to the Windows 2000 Domain

Since the goal of the migration was to decommission the source domain, NWT had to migrate all resources that existed on domain controllers. Some smaller offices used BDCs as application servers and these had to be moved to the target domain because these computers would be offline once the source was decommissioned. NWT used the Group Migration Wizard to copy the shared local groups from the source domain to domain local groups in the Active Directory. Then, NWT had to move its resources to the Windows 2000 domain by upgrading the servers to Windows 2000 member servers in their original domain and using the Active Directory Migration Tool to migrate those computers to the new Windows 2000 domain. It was important to note that during testing, if the BDCs were not migrated to the Windows 2000 domain, any SIDs referenced in any access control list that referred to groups local to those BDCs were not resolved correctly in the Security Editor (Figures 6.13 and 6.14). However, due to SIDHistory, the permissions were still effective. There are three ways to resolve this, use the ADMT Security Translation Wizard to replace those references to the old SID with new ones in the Active Directory, upgrade at least one of the original

BDCs to Windows 2000 Servers in the forest, or administer the Windows NT4
Servers from another Windows 2000 computer in the forest.

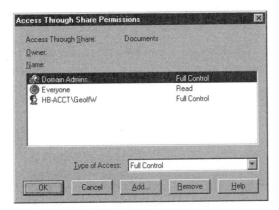

Figure 6.13   Security Editor displaying normal view behavior.

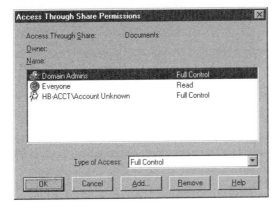

Figure 6.14   Security Editor displaying unexpected view behavior.

NWT used the Translate Security Wizard to read the old ACL and replace
references to the old shared local group with references to the new Windows 2000
domain local group (Figure 6.15). This was not necessary: NWT did it just to be safe.

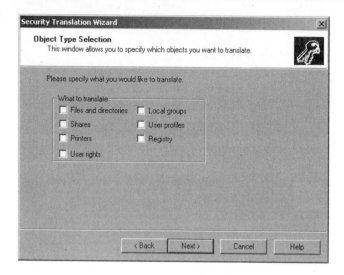

Figure 6.15   Security Translation Wizard.

Clone User Accounts to the Windows 2000 Domain

To be sure that all user accounts were migrated, NWT ran the ADMT User Migration Wizard one last time with it configured to skip any duplicates.

Disabling the Source Accounts

When you migrate users, you can *expire* or *disable* the source account (Figure 6.16).

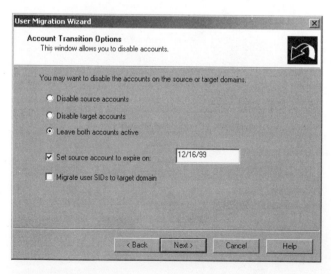

Figure 6.16   Expiring or disabling an account during migration.

Because the NWT environment included Windows NT Workstations and Windows 9*x* desktops, the team had to make sure all domain references on the desktops were updated before any user accounts were expired, otherwise the users would not be able to log on to either domain. This could be accomplished for Windows NT Workstation users during the computer account migration, but some intervention was required for Windows 9*x* users. Because NWT planned to run both domains in parallel during the pilot phase anyhow, they decided not to use the *expire* or *disable* options.

Moving Computer Accounts to the Windows 2000 Domain

Windows NT Workstations and Servers configured as member servers must be migrated to the Windows 2000 domain before you can decommission the Windows NT domains. NWT does not allow computer accounts to exist within the accounts domains, so the only computer accounts in the accounts domains were the Windows 2000 member servers that were previously BDCs. The ADMT Computer Migration Wizard (Figure 6.17) creates a new computer account in the Windows 2000 domain and places an agent on the computer being moved. This agent modifies the necessary domain information in the network configuration and reboots the computer. When the computer boots it is ready to log on to the Windows 2000 domain.

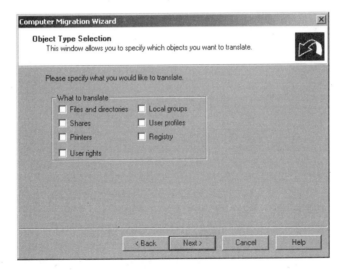

Figure 6.17   Computer Migration Wizard.

Migrate a Pilot Group to the Windows 2000 Domain

To minimize risk, NWT decided not to move users from the Windows NT domain to the new Windows 2000 domain all at once. Instead, they moved 100 users in a pilot phase. User accounts and permissions were already present in the Windows 2000 domain, so all NWT had to do was use a script to change the default logon domain for the pilot users.

If the resource domains did not trust the new Windows 2000 domain, the pilot phase would fail and users logging on to the Windows 2000 domain would not be able to use the resources or to log on from Windows NT Workstations. Users' passwords were reset during the cloning process, and they had to be notified of this before their default logon domain was moved to the Windows 2000 domain. NWT administrators had to apply appropriate password policies (requiring complex passwords) on the Windows 2000 domain to ensure a higher level of security.

Migrate Remaining Domain Members to the Windows 2000 Domain

To minimize helpdesk calls, NWT sent frequent e-mail and inter-office mail to remaining domain users notifying them that their passwords and default logon domains were changed. Of course, they still staffed the helpdesk appropriately during the migration to handle the temporary call increase.

The NA domain ran in parallel with the Windows NT domains, so the team could format and reinstall the domain controllers in the Windows 2000 domain, then clone the user, group, and computer accounts again to make sure that all recent changes were captured. But you don't have to do this if all changes to the Windows NT domain are fully documented—NWT used their documentation to manually apply significant accounts domain changes to the Windows 2000 domain then simply moved the users' default logon domain to that domain.

Interoperability During Migration

Server-Based Profiles

The ADMT User Migration Wizard copies the profile path from the source domain, so during migration the profile is still available from the original location. Many companies store the roaming profiles in the user's home directory on a file server. Because the path to the profile is saved, you can also maintain the profiles by keeping the server as either a Windows NT member server or upgrading it to Windows 2000 member server.

Directory Synchronization

Many NWT domain controllers used the directory replication services to replicate common and highly used files throughout the domain—for instance, to replicate the logon scripts to every domain controller in a domain. Windows 2000 does not support the directory replication service, so these processes had to be moved to the new File Replication Service (FRS). Because it was difficult to tell which scripts might change at any given time, NWT wrote a batch file that copied files from the export directory on the Windows NT 4.0 Server to the SYSVOL on a Windows 2000 Server, then used the Windows NT Schedule Service to schedule the file to run regularly. Here is a sample script that bridges replication services:

```
Xcopy \\usnwtadpdc\Export\scripts \\na.nwt.int\Sysvol\na.nwt.int\scripts
/s /d
```

Permissions

Permissions are maintained to down-level resources because all user and global group security identifiers (SIDs) are copied to the new object's SIDHistory attribute in the Active Directory. The Active Directory SIDHistory attribute provides this functionality. When a user who is logged on to the Active Directory attempts to access a resource, a security token is built that contains the user object's new SID, the user's SIDHistory, the global groups SID, and the global group's SIDHistory. The down-level domains recognize the old SID and allow the user to connect to the resource. The Windows 2000 Security Editor sometimes cannot properly display the user or group because it cannot resolve the SID to a display name. You can fix this by using the Domain Migration Wizard to read the resources' SIDs, then replace the old SIDs with SIDs related to a native Windows 2000 group, usually the copy of the old group.

Decommissioning the Source Domains

Decommissioning a source domain means removing it from the network. This chapter has discussed most of the ramifications of decommissioning; this section discusses some that are pertinent in a simple domain migration.

Service Accounts

In addition to cloning service accounts to the new Windows 2000 domain, you must also change any applications that use the service accounts so that they also reference the new domain. The ADMT's Service Account Migration Wizard can perform the tasks necessary to migrate the service accounts to the new Windows 2000 domain.

Name Resolution

Windows NT and Windows 9x use WINS servers to resolve names in a routed network. WINS resolution must be provided after the migration (either by the new Windows 2000 domain or by another resource domain) or down-level clients will not be able to find other resources on the network. You must also reconfigure the Windows 2000 Servers to register with the WINS servers servicing the down-level clients: Windows 2000 does not require WINS services but down-level clients will not be able to find servers that are not registered in the WINS database.

Printers and Other Services

Many companies use BDCs to provide services such as printing and file serving, and you must either move the services to a member server in the Windows 2000 domain or migrate the BDC. If you move the services, you must also reconfigure the clients so that they can find the appropriate service.

Using ClonePrinciple, Netdom, and MoveTree

ClonePrinciple

ClonePrinciple is a set of Visual Basic scripts that copies Windows NT 4.0 user attributes to Windows 2000 user objects and updates SIDHistory. Using it does not disrupt the source domain in any way, and (a major advantage) it does not require you to re-assign ACL resources to maintain group memberships. Because it is a COM object (unlike the Domain Migration Wizard) you can use it when scripting a migration: it includes Visual Basic scripts to move the global groups, shared local groups, and users.

NetDom

NetDom is a command-line utility you can use to manage Windows domains and trusts. With it you can add a Windows 2000 computer to either a Windows NT or Windows 2000 domain and manage computer accounts for domain member clients and servers. NetDom can establish and manage trusts between Windows NT domains and parent-child Windows 2000 domains. When you are migrating, it can report all trust relationships in a domain. NWT used this functionality to document the domain structure and verify that all required trusts were available after migration.

MoveTree

MoveTree is a command-line tool that can move a sub-tree of objects within an Active Directory forest. It is useful when you have to restructure a domain to fit changing organization needs. MoveTree does support the SIDHistory attribute, so objects moved with it can access resources after the move without reapplying permissions to the resources. Some of its functions are:

- Moving a sub-tree within a domain
- Moving a sub-tree to a new domain
- Moving a domain within a forest
- Moving a domain to a new forest

Although this tool would be useful for scripted domain restructuring, it does not offer a graphical interface and does not provide for rich reporting of migrations, so NWT decided to use the Active Directory Migration Tool instead.

Future Plans

Resource Domain NWTRDUK

Once the upgrade of the accounts domain *NWTADUK* is complete, the resource domain *NWTRDUK* will be migrated to the Active Directory as an OU in *UK.NWT.INT*. This process will be similar to the accounts domains migrations in North America except that the target will be an OU.

North America Resource Domains

The original domain design at NWT was limited by the Windows NT 4.0 SAM. Now that those limitation are removed, NWT plans to migrate the original resource domains in North America to OUs in the *NA.NWT.INT* domain. To do this they will use a process similar to the one they used to migrate resource domain *NWTRDUK*. They have to continue providing down-level services during and after the resource domain migration to Windows 9x clients.

Branch Offices

Currently, branch offices exist as either an independent resource domain trusting a given accounts domain or a completely independent single domain with no trusts to the corporate domains. Branch office resources remain fairly static (computers or printers are only infrequently added or deleted from the network). NWT will migrate the branch office domains as OUs in a single large domain called *BRANCH.NWT.INT*.

Conclusion

New tools make it possible to complete a very complex domain migration with minimal impact to a production environment. With only some basic planning you can upgrade Windows NT domains in place and add them to a tree structure within a forest. For more complex migrations and consolidations, you can use the Domain Migration Wizard, ClonePrinciple, NetDom, and MoveTree.

C H A P T E R   7

Integrating Active Directory with a Unix-Based DNS Environment

*By Ken Durigan,
Microsoft
Consulting
Sevices—
Midwest District*

Name resolution service makes it possible to locate Internet resources without having to know complex IP addresses for network devices. Before today's rapid resolution mechanisms were developed, developers worked around the IP address problem by creating a *hosts* file of common server names and their IP addresses. A *host* was considered to be any device with services or resources accessible by other, *client*, computers. *Clients* looked up a host's address in the hosts file, then used the IP address to initiate communications. Designed for small networks with few computers, this method became cumbersome to maintain and update as networks grew. Clearly, a better way was needed, and that was what Paul Mokapetris was looking for when, in 1984, he developed the concept for today's Domain Name System.

The Domain Name System (DNS) provides a mechanism for associating hierarchical names with DNS data such as IP addresses. The DNS service has been implemented on many platforms, including Windows NT and Unix. Although testing of the mixed environment containing various implementations of the DNS confirms their interoperability, there are some differences between how Unix and Windows 2000 implement DNS. This chapter explains how to implement Active Directory in a pure Unix DNS environment, and discusses the significant differences in the two DNS implementations.

What You'll Find in This Chapter

■ An explanation of the issues involved in implementing the Windows 2000 Active Directory in a pure Unix environment.

■ A discussion of the similarities and differences of the Unix Bind and the Windows 2000 Domain Name System implementations, with detail on unique features and functionality available in Windows 2000.

■ Instructions on configuring clients and the various types of servers needed in this type of implementation.

Note   The fictional examples in this chapter use the extension .TLD (top level domain) in the company domain names rather than .COM to insure that none of the domains are mistaken for those of any actual company or organization.

Before You Begin

The discussion in this chapter is based on the assumption that you understand DNS installation, configuration, and namespace administration.

The information presented here was derived from a real company that is moving forward with a large Windows 2000 implementation. Company and domain names have been changed. The concepts are real, even though ABCD Corp. is fictional.

Infrastructure and DNS Strategy

To get started, Figure 7.1 (on the next page) provides a look at ABCD Corp. infrastructure at ground zero, with its original mix of Unix Bind 4.9.x and 8.1.2 on the DNS servers:

- ABCD.TLD (private network)
  - 72 DNS domains
  - 43 Unix/DNS servers
  - 900 Windows NT servers
  - 10,000 Windows NT workstations
  - 20,000 Windows 9x workstations
  - Multi-master accounts domain
  - Most sites have a DHCP server
  - Most sites have a Unix server

This diagram represents *typical* home office and field locations. Almost all locations have at least one Windows NT server that provides DHCP, authentication, and file services, and at least one Unix server (some large installations have more) that provides application and DNS services. Home office communications are over high-speed LAN connections; remote location link speeds vary up to T1. Each physical location is also its own subdomain with the Unix server authoritative for the zone at that site.

A site's business unit decides whether Windows NT servers at the site hold user accounts for that site. Some units control their user community, some use a centralized service provided by corporate IT. Autonomous business units will retain their autonomy after conversion to Windows 2000. Some Windows NT domains may become organizational units (OUs) under Windows 2000, and this would decrease the number of domains in the organization.

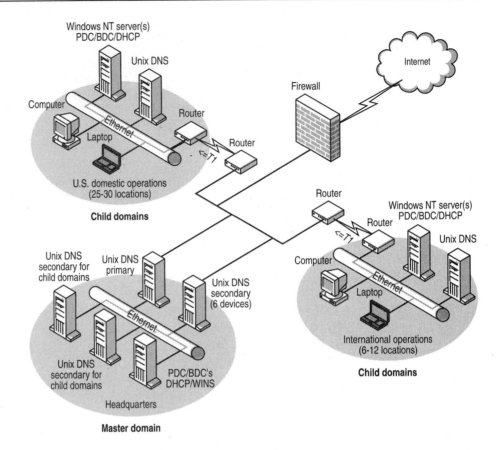

Figure 7.1   **Original ABCD Corp. infrastructure with Unix mix on DNS servers.**

From the Trenches: Which DNS to Use?

There are many planning activities involved in a Windows 2000 project before the lab environment can be set up. One of the early meetings in the ABCD Corp. project was devoted to discussing the DNS strategy. The meeting included several people versed in Unix Bind DNS and some members of the company's internal NT Server team. The DNS decision was important in that it would affect several key aspects of the implementation. A decision to change the corporate DNS to Microsoft's version would involve different people, upgrade strategies, hardware, training and support than would a decision to stay with Unix Bind DNS. The group realized that other technical factors would also differentiate the DNS offerings, and that these would have to be carefully weighed.

Quite often, discussions that involve both Microsoft's version of a product and another, competing solution, get rather emotional. So it was in this case. The Unix team representatives did not like the idea of installing the corporate DNS on a non-Unix platform and although I am not sure, I think that as soon as the meeting ended the Unix team headed to the lab to install Bind so it would be available immediately. As it turned out, ABCD Corp. chose the Unix Bind implementation.

Although the decision was not my preferred solution, good arguments were made on both sides. This chapter is devoted to helping companies that make this decision, and particularly to help Unix Bind advocates, integrate with Windows 2000.

Why a Pure Unix DNS Solution?

ABCD Corp.'s decision to keep DNS under Unix server control had political as well as administrative reasons. They felt that the Unix servers were already in place, that they were proven, and that their management processes and issues were well understood. Staff was already trained, and documentation, training, and change management procedures were established. The development team felt that so long as the Unix Bind servers could meet the minimum requirements for Active Directory, there was no compelling reason to change DNS out from under Unix. The following discussion shows what factors *you* should consider before deciding on a pure Unix DNS solution.

DNS Requirements for Active Directory

You don't need Microsoft's DNS server for Windows 2000 AD deployment, but any DNS server implementation you use must support Service Location Resource Records (SRV RRs) as described by Internet Draft RFC 2052bis, and *should* support Dynamic Update as described by RFC 2136. Bind 8.1.2 (the minimum version for a Windows 2000 environment) includes both of these features, as well as DNS Change Notification described in RFC 1996. DNS Change Notification is desirable, although it is not required for Windows 2000. You should not use a level of Bind earlier than version 8.1.2—these had fewer features and some issues that can crash DNS servers.

Another highly desirable feature for any DNS that supports Windows 2000 clients is Incremental Zone Transfer (IXFR) as described in RFC 1995. Because it transfers only changed records rather than all records in a zone, it reduces network traffic and improves performance—a benefit that grows in importance as dynamic updates and change notification increase change volumes dramatically. This feature was added in Bind 8.2.

Even though Bind release 8.1.2 is sufficient, release 8.2.1 is the recommended release to support Windows 2000 clients. It adds features that reduce traffic, boost performance, and improve security. It includes negative caching as described in RFC 2308 and DNS Security as described in RFC 2535, and it overhauls IXFR code to fix known issues. Companies with a large installed base of Bind 8.1.2 servers can, however, make do with that version, if upgrading is prohibitively expensive or time consuming.

Comparing Bind and Windows 2000 DNS

The Windows 2000 DNS implementation includes all the features described above and some new features (described below) currently unique to Windows 2000.

Active Directory Storage and Replication Integration

In addition to supporting a conventional way of maintaining and replicating DNS zone files, the Windows 2000 DNS server lets you use the Active Directory Services as the data storage and replication engine. This provides several benefits:

- DNS replication is performed by ADS, so you don't have to support a separate replication topology for DNS servers.
- ADS replication provides per-name replication granularity.
- ADS replication is secure.
- A primary DNS server no longer is a single point of failure. Original DNS replication is single-master: it relies on a primary DNS server to update all the secondary servers. Unlike original DNS replication, the ADS replication is multi-master: an update can be made to any domain controller in the Active Directory Service and be propagated to other domain controllers. Integrate DNS into ADS, and the ADS replication engine synchronizes DNS zone information.

ADS integration significantly simplifies DNS namespace administration and supports standard zone transfer to other servers (non MS-DNS Servers and previous versions of the MS-DNS servers).

Secure Dynamic Update

ADS integration also provides Secure Dynamic DNS Updates. The directory service (DS) maintains the Access Control Lists (ACLs) that specify which groups or users are allowed to modify the DS-integrated zones and/or records of a specific name. The Windows 2000 DNS server uses ACLs to support Secure Dynamic Updates for the DS-integrated zones. This allows per-name ACL specification.

Secure dynamic update also avoids a common problem. If during Dynamic Update registration a client discovers that its name is already registered in DNS with another computer's IP address, the client deletes the existing registration (by default) and registers its own resource records (RRs) in its place. This allows you to remove stale records, but is vulnerable to malicious attacks. You can change the default behavior by modifying a registry key that prevents the client from deleting the existing registration and logs an error in the event log. This is impervious to attack but does not let you delete records. Secure Dynamic Updates allows only the owner of the existing record to update it. Bind does not support Secure Dynamic Updates and Unix-only DNS implementations may continue to show this problem.

Caching Resolver

Windows 2000 supports negative as well as positive caching (as described in RFC 2308; this feature was implemented in Bind 8.2). Negative caching stores names and record sets that are known not to exist and prevents lookups for those names. This can eliminate a large proportion of DNS traffic on the Internet. You can turn the caching resolver on or off in Windows 2000 by setting a registry entry; you can also enter the commands *net start dnscache* or *net stop dnscache* at a command prompt or insert them in a batch file.

DNS Snap-In

You can perform administrative tasks in Windows 2000 with the Microsoft Management Console (MMC) snap-in programs, and can customize consoles so that they contain specific tool subsets for users. For example, a DNS administrator may need the DNS and DHCP admin snap-in modules, but not need the server or Active Directory administration modules. MMC snap-in modules have consistent look and feel, making them easier to learn and use.

The DNS Manager snap-in features (unique to Microsoft's DNS) simplify administration. For example, for working with large zones with numerous records, *name filtering* allows you to limit the display to names that start with, or contain specified strings. You can sort the zone records with a single click by name, record type, or IP address.

The DNS Manager's on-line help system explains other DNS manager features not found in most Unix DNS implementations. Just bring up the DNS Management Console, select **Help**, then **Help Topics**.

WINS Integration

NetBIOS name services have been integrated into Microsoft's DNS since Windows NT 4.0. WINS integration makes it possible for non-Windows devices to resolve addresses of legacy Windows systems that are not defined to DNS, or that have dynamic addresses. For example, to access a Windows NT 4.0 server, a Unix or Windows 3.1 workstation must resolve the server name into an IP address.

Without WINS integration, the server must have a static DNS definition—it cannot use a dynamically assigned address and you have to update the DNS manually if you move the server to a different network. WINS integration simplifies client querying. The client sends a DNS query to the DNS server and if the DNS server does not find a record for the Windows NT 4.0 server, it sends a WINS query to the WINS server, then returns the answer to the client.

UTF-8 (Unicode) Character Support

Windows 2000 DNS supports NetBIOS names, and the UTF-8 (Unicode) character set that covers most of the world's written languages. This feature can be important if you are migrating Windows NT 4.0 domain or server names containing characters such as the underscore that are not allowed in standard DNS names. In addition to some international characters, others, such as the underscore, are allowed in Windows 2000's DNS.

Aging/Scavenging Support

Windows 2000 DNS servers support *aging* and *scavenging* features that clean up and remove stale resource records, which can accumulate in zone data over time. With dynamic update, resource records are automatically added to zones when computers start on the network. If those computers are improperly removed from the network, the resource records may not be automatically deleted. If left unmanaged, stale resource records can cause some problems with name resolution. Windows 2000 DNS server features address these problems automatically, so that you don't have to address them manually. A complete description of this feature is provided in the DNS Snap-in online help.

DNSCMD Command Line Utility

Several tools on the Windows 2000 server CD (in the *\support\tools* directory) aid in administration, although they are not automatically installed when the server is installed. One DNS administration tool is *dnscmd*, which allows you to accomplish many DNS-server-related tasks from the command line or in a batch file: add or delete zones, register or delete names, and force zone data refreshes. You can also use it to diagnose problems and set up the Windows 2000 DNS servers. It works only with Windows 2000 DNS servers.

Upgrade Options for a Unix DNS Environment

Bind 8 is the earliest release that fully supports a Windows 2000 Active Directory environment. What options are available to you in environments with 4.x servers? Obviously, the first is to upgrade the Bind servers to 8.2.1, although in some cases (especially large organizations) the number of Bind servers and scheduling issues may mean you don't have time to complete an upgrade.

Here is another issue: even if the Bind servers are running version 8.1.2 or later, you may want to keep the Windows 2000 environment separate from the legacy environment. You can do this by creating a new domain or subdomain with Bind 8 DNS servers or Windows 2000 DNS servers, and use it to support the Windows 2000 Active Directory name space. It is simpler to upgrade the Bind servers in the main domain than to add new subdomains for Windows 2000 servers and workstations. Table 7.1 shows why:

Table 7.1   Upgrade Options for Bind 4.x Environments.

Criteria	Upgrade main domain to Bind 8.x DNS	Keep "legacy" domain and delegate a new subdomain with Bind 8.x DNS	Keep "legacy" domain and delegate a new subdomain with Win2000 DNS
Requires a new domain	No	Yes	Yes
Additional DNS servers required during migration	No	Yes	Yes
Requires changes to DHCP scopes	No	Probable	Probable
Additional traffic to resolve host names in new domain from legacy domain	N/A	Yes (minimal)	Yes (minimal)
Additional traffic to resolve host names in legacy domain from new domain	N/A	Yes (minimal)	Yes (minimal)
Ability to restrict dynamic updates	Worst	Better	Best
Single point of failure	Worst	Better	Best

If you keep the legacy Bind servers and create delegated subdomains, you can leave the existing legacy clients and servers in the legacy domains. As you upgrade clients or servers to Windows 2000 you can add them to the new delegated subdomains defined in the Bind 8.x or Windows 2000 DNS servers. When Windows 2000 and legacy devices coexist, you need both DNS servers so you need additional hardware.

With legacy devices in the old domain and Windows 2000 devices in the new delegated domain, the DHCP server must assign different domain names to the two types of devices. If the devices are on the same physical sub network, the DHCP server must be able to identify the device's operating system and assign the correct domain name for the device. Most DHCP servers cannot do this. If a DHCP cannot make this distinction, you have to configure the DNS and domain name manually in the client's TCP/IP settings rather than using DHCP to assign these values.

When a Windows 2000 client tries to resolve a name in the legacy domain, the process creates additional network traffic because the new DNS cannot resolve the name directly. The new Bind 8.x DNS issues a recursive query to locate devices in the legacy domain and eventually the legacy domain's data ends up in the new DNS server's cache. The process is the same when legacy devices try to resolve names in the new domain.

There are benefits to separating legacy and Windows 2000 domains. For one, you don't have to upgrade all legacy DNS servers before starting the Windows 2000 implementation. You can upgrade DNS and deploy Windows 2000 in parallel. Separating domains can help stabilize the legacy environment by restricting dynamic updates in the legacy domain, while allowing dynamic updates in the new domain. Windows 2000's DNS *secure update* further enhances this ability by restricting DNS updates to the device that created the original *A* record. Finally, fault tolerance is increased by the additional sub domains because addresses are cached in the new DNS servers. Windows 2000 DNS enhances this over Bind servers by allowing dynamic updates on any Active Directory server running the DNS service, not just on the primary DNS.

Configuring a Pure Unix DNS Environment

To support DNS in a Windows 2000 environment you have to configure the components listed below. As a rule you do not have to change Windows 95 and Windows NT 4.0 legacy devices.

- Bind servers
- Windows 2000 servers
- Windows 2000 DHCP servers
- Down-level DHCP servers
- Windows 2000 clients
- Down-level clients

Unix Server Configuration

If your Unix servers are not release 8.2.1 or later, you should get the latest release (go to http://www.isc.org/bind.html) and install it. The installation process is beyond the scope of this chapter, but you can easily find all the information you need on the Internet, or within the documentation that is included with the Bind software.

After you create a functional name server, you must add the appropriate lines to the *named.conf* file to enable dynamic updates. Here is an example, using a very simple *named.conf* for the domain abcd.tld:

```
// BIND Configuration File
options {
    directory "/usr/local/named";
    notify yes;
};
zone "abcd.tld" in {
    type master;
    file "db.abcd";
    check-names ignore;
    allow-transfer { 192.168.0.7; };
    allow-update {192.168.0.5; 192.168.0.6;  192.168.0.100;};
};

zone "0.168.192.in-addr.arpa" in {
    type master;
    file "db.192.168.0";
    allow-transfer { 192.168.0.7; };
    allow-update {192.168.0.5; 192.168.0.6; 192.168.0.100;};
};

zone "0.0.127.in-addr.arpa" in {
    type master;
    file "db.127.0.0";
};

zone "." in {
    type hint;
    file "db.cache";
};
```

This file is considered simple because it has only a few statements that are important to Windows 2000 or that are new to a dynamic DNS environment. The *notify yes* statement in the options section informs the master DNS to send change notification to the secondary servers whenever changes are made to the zone files. Without notification, the zone is not transferred until the refresh interval expires.

Once the secondary DNS servers receive change notification, they respond to the notify message, comparing the serial number of the zone sent by the master and the copy on the secondary. If the serial number on the master is greater than on the secondary, each of the out of date secondary DNS servers requests an incremental zone transfer (only records that require updating, not the entire zone). For large zones with frequent dynamic updates, incremental zone transfers greatly reduce network load.

Active Directory servers add many unusual names to DNS that do not conform to traditional DNS names. The *check-names ignore* statement makes sure that some *A* records required by Windows 2000 domain controllers register properly.

You should also specify which network devices are allowed to initiate zone transfers. Use the most restrictive set of IP addresses possible to prevent unauthorized zone transfers. This requirement is not new to the Windows 2000 environment. In the preceding example file, only address 192.168.0.7 can transfer zone files.

The *allow-update* statement in the zone sections allows the IP addresses specified to update zone records dynamically. It takes an address list as an argument, or you can use *{any;}* if you want any IP addresses to be able to make updates or *{none;}* if you want to disallow dynamic updates on a specific zone. To enhance security and administration you should restrict the list of IP addresses as tightly as possible.

To update addresses on the DNS, yet keep them somewhat restrictive, you have a couple options. To allow all devices on a specific subnet (for instance, 192.168.0) to directly update the server, you can specify *allow-update {192.168.0/24;}*. To be more restrictive, you can disallow client workstations from directly updating the DNS and relegate the task to the DHCP servers. In the preceding example zone file, only the DHCP servers or domain controllers on 192.168.0.5, 192.168.0.6 and 192.168.0.100 can directly update the DNS. ABCD Corp. decided to allow only domain controllers and DHCP servers to make dynamic updates.

It is important to note that restricting the list of devices that can make dynamic updates does not dramatically improve security. One client's *A* and *PTR* records can be overwritten by another client when the DHCP server performs updates on behalf of the clients. Unlike Bind servers, Windows 2000 DNS servers implement secure dynamic updates, which use authentication to decide if an update is allowed. This feature is one of the significant differences between Bind and Windows 2000 DNS servers.

Other security and performance options that you can configure in the *named.conf* file are neither unique to Windows 2000 implementations nor required, but you should consider them carefully: they can prevent denial of service attacks, and they maximize performance and security.

Windows 2000 domain controllers automatically add some service locator (SRV) records to the zones to enable clients to locate domain controllers, global catalog servers, and KDCs for specific domains and sites. The following zone file shows the records for the *mis.abcd.tld* zone. The SRV records shown in the zone are registered by the NETLOGON service running on the DC's in the *mis.abcd.tld* Active Directory domain.

```
;  Database file mis.abcd.tld.dns for mis.abcd.tld zone.

@                         IN  SOA pdc1root.mis.abcd.tld.  administrator. (
                          368        ; serial number
                          900        ; refresh
                          600        ; retry
                          86400      ; expire
                          3600     ) ; minimum TTL
@                NS   pdc1root.mis.abcd.tld.
@                     600    A   10.10.10.17
@                     600    A   10.20.10.17
client-nt4            900    A   10.10.10.51
client-w2k            1200   A   10.10.10.52
pdc1root             1200   A   10.10.10.17
pdc1child1           1200   A   10.10.10.15
srv1                 1200   A   10.10.10.56
pdc1child2           1200   A   10.20.10.17
```

(Note! The following lines were split as a result of the limitations of this book's page width. The real zone file would have the complete SRV record on one line.)

```
76b0ab48-f761-11d2-b19f-0008c79f5236._msdcs          600 CNAME
    pdc1root.mis.abcd.tld.
e1af4ded-f768-11d2-b1a0-0008c79f5236._msdcs          600 CNAME
    pdc1child2.mis.abcd.tld.
eb9f02f1-f8b6-11d2-b1a1-0008c79f5236._msdcs          600 CNAME
    pdc1child1.corp.mis.abcd.tld.
f35fdfbb-f8c2-11d2-ace2-0008c78c8134._msdcs          600 CNAME
    n1dom13.corp.mis.abcd.tld.
gc._msdcs                                            600 A  10.20.10.17
                                                     600 A  10.10.10.17
_kerberos._tcp.default-first-site-name._sites.dc._msdcs 600 SRV 0 100 88
    pdc1root.mis.abcd.tld.
                                                     600 SRV 0 100 88
    pdc1child2.mis.abcd.tld.
_ldap._tcp.default-first-site-name._sites.dc._msdcs    600 SRV 0 100 389
    pdc1root.mis.abcd.tld.
                              600 SRV 0 100 389 pdc1child2.mis.abcd.tld.
_kerberos._tcp.dc._msdcs                             600 SRV 0 100 88
    pdc1root.mis.abcd.tld.
                         600 SRV 0 100 88 pdc1child2.mis.abcd.tld.
_ldap._tcp.dc._msdcs                                 600 SRV 0 100 389
    pdc1root.mis.abcd.tld.
                         600 SRV 0 100 389 pdc1child2.mis.abcd.tld.
```

(continued)

```
_ldap._tcp.default-first-site-name._sites.gc._msdcs      600 SRV 0 100 3268
    pdc1root.mis.abcd.tld.
                                     600 SRV 0 100 3268 pdc1child2.mis.abcd.tld.
_ldap._tcp.gc._msdcs                                     600 SRV 0 100 3268
    pdc1child2.mis.abcd.tld.
                                     600 SRV 0 100 3268 pdc1root.mis.abcd.tld.
_ldap._tcp.pdc._msdcs                                    600 SRV 0 100 389
    pdc1root.mis.abcd.tld.
_gc._tcp.default-first-site-name._sites                  600 SRV 0 100 3268
    pdc1root.mis.abcd.tld.
                                     600 SRV 0 100 3268 pdc1child2.mis.abcd.tld.
_kerberos._tcp.default-first-site-name._sites            600 SRV 0 100 88
    pdc1root.mis.abcd.tld.
                                     600 SRV 0 100 88 pdc1child2.mis.abcd.tld.
_ldap._tcp.default-first-site-name._sites                600 SRV 0 100 389
    pdc1root.mis.abcd.tld.
                                     600 SRV 0 100 389 pdc1child2.mis.abcd.tld.
_gc._tcp                                                 600 SRV 0 100 3268
    pdc1child2.mis.abcd.tld.
                                     600 SRV 0 100 3268 pdc1root.mis.abcd.tld.
_kerberos._tcp                                           600 SRV 0 100 88
    pdc1root.mis.abcd.tld.
                                     600 SRV 0 100 88 pdc1child2.mis.abcd.tld.
_kpasswd._tcp                                            600 SRV 0 100 464
    pdc1root.mis.abcd.tld.
                                     600 SRV 0 100 464 pdc1child2.mis.abcd.tld.
_ldap._tcp                                               600 SRV 0 100 389
    pdc1root.mis.abcd.tld.
                                     600 SRV 0 100 389 pdc1child2.mis.abcd.tld.
_kerberos._udp                                           600 SRV 0 100 88
    pdc1root.mis.abcd.tld.
                                     600 SRV 0 100 88 pdc1child2.mis.abcd.tld.
_kpasswd._udp                                            600 SRV 0 100 464
    pdc1root.mis.abcd.tld.
                                     600 SRV 0 100 464 pdc1child2.mis.abcd.tld.
_ldap._tcp.76b0ab49-f761-11d2-b19f-0008c79f5236.domains._msdcs
                                     600 SRV 0 100 389 pdc1root.mis.abcd.tld.
                                     600 SRV 0 100 389 pdc1child2.mis.abcd.tld.
_ldap._tcp.eb9f02f0-f8b6-11d2-b1a1-0008c79f5236.domains._msdcs
                               600 SRV 0 100 389 pdc1child1.corp.mis.abcd.tld.
                               600 SRV 0 100 389 n1dom13.corp.mis.abcd.tld.
```

Service locator records have a unique format. The name includes the service, as well as the protocol that is to be looked up. In the preceding example, the SRV record *_ldap.tcp* represents the SRV records that you should retrieve if you are trying to find the *mis.abcd.tld ldap* servers in order to access LDAP in the *mis.abcd.tld* domain.

SRV records have four resource-record-specific fields: priority, weight, port, and target. *Priority* and *weight* are used for load balancing among servers as described in Internet Draft RFC 2052bis. *Port* can specify non-standard ports that clients should use to access a given service. *Target* specifies the domain name of the hosts where the service is running.

The SRV records in the above example were automatically registered to the DNS by the Windows 2000 domain controller Netlogon service. To force a re-registration of SRV records, simply stop and restart the Netlogon service on the Windows 2000 server. Windows 2000 servers create a text file in *%systemroot% \system32\config\netlogon.dns* that shows all SRV records that need to be registered with the DNS. You can add these records manually to Bind servers that do not support dynamic update.

Make sure that DNS is functioning properly and accepting dynamic updates *before* you install Windows 2000 Active Directory servers. To ensure that updates are restricted properly, try to add and delete records from the DNS by using the Unix *Nsupdate* command from authorized and non-authorized IP addresses. To verify that zone transfers are taking place as well, use the Unix *Nslookup* command.

Any Unix Bind servers participating in a Windows 2000 environment should be at version 8.1.2 or greater *before* you install Windows 2000 servers with Active Directory, because these versions support dynamic update. Zone transfers to Bind server versions earlier than 4.9.6 will fail because these versions do not support SRV records. Due to the additional features in Bind 8.2.1 such as incremental zone transfers, it is recommended that you upgrade to 8.2.1 or greater before you implement Windows 2000 servers running Active Directory.

Windows 2000 Server Configuration

When Windows 2000 servers use a Unix Bind server for DNS, you have to perform additional configuration only when the Windows 2000 server is also a DNS server. This chapter is intended for companies configuring a pure Unix DNS, so it does not discuss configuring the Windows 2000 DNS.

Many large companies use multiple DNS servers to provide fault tolerance, to balance loads, and to lower WAN utilization. ABCD Corp. uses a distributed DNS hierarchy, with a DNS authoritative server in each large site. In this kind of case, you have to configure the two closest DNS servers as preferred and alternate DNS servers by specifying the DNS servers' IP addresses in the Windows 2000 server's Internet Protocol (TCP/IP) Properties dialog box.

If the preferred DNS server specified in the TCP/IP configuration is not the primary authoritative DNS, additional traffic will be generated whenever dynamic updates are performed. On Unix Bind DNS servers, all updates are made at the master server, and dynamic updates sent to non-authoritative DNS servers are forwarded up the replication topology until they reach the primary authoritative server. In contrast, with Windows 2000's DNS server, an update for a record can be sent to any DNS server running on a domain controller if the updated zone is AD integrated.

Before sending a dynamic update, the client sends an SOA query to the preferred DNS server. In the case where the preferred DNS server is authoritative for the client's name, it resolves the original SOA query without recursion. The dynamic update process described above is common for any Windows 2000 client, including DHCP servers and domain controllers.

To configure DNS preferred and alternate DNS servers, right-click on My Network **Places**, select **Properties**, then right-click **Local Area Connection**. Select **Properties**, open the properties for **Internet Protocol (TCP/IP)**, then specify the primary and alternate DNS servers addresses at the bottom of the dialog box.

Windows 2000 DHCP Server Configuration

In a Windows 2000 Active Directory environment, the Windows 2000 DHCP server is crucial to name registration for down-level clients. You can configure the Windows 2000 DHCP server to register DNS records on behalf of down-level clients such as Windows NT 4.0 and Windows 9x. You can also configure Windows 2000 clients so that updates are made by the DHCP server, instead of the clients. There are several advantages to this approach when using Bind DNS servers.

It is desirable to limit the number of devices that can make dynamic updates to DNS records in a Bind environment. An easy way to do this is to disallow all workstations from making updates. You can use the *allow-updates* statement of the */etc/named.conf* file on the Bind server to authorize specific devices such as the DHCP servers and disallow all other devices.

Network efficiency is best served by locating the DHCP server and the DNS server on the same physical network when the DHCP server is configured to make updates on behalf of the clients. If you have a central DHCP server and distributed DNS servers, the client's dynamic DNS registration may generate additional WAN traffic even if the client and the DNS server are on the same physical network. Also, consider that if the client, DNS server, and DHCP server are on different physical networks, the client may obtain an address from the DHCP server, yet the DNS server may be unreachable from the DHCP server due to a network failure. This could cause name resolution to return the wrong address for a client until the DHCP server is able to send updates to the DNS server. You should put the DHCP and DNS servers on the same subnet whenever possible.

You can configure the DHCP server to remove records when the DHCP lease expires—a good idea in that it automatically deletes from DNS computers that no longer exist regardless of whether the client ever rejoins the network. This is more important in Bind environments than in Windows 2000 DNS server environments, which have record aging and scavenging capabilities.

To configure DHCP options applicable to Dynamic DNS, select **Administrative Tools** from the **Start**, **Programs** menu, then select **DHCP**. Right-click on the DHCP server that you want to modify and select the **Properties** option. You can configure these options for individual scopes by right-clicking on the scope and selecting the **Properties** option. Click on the **DNS** tab and this screen (Figure 7.2) appears:

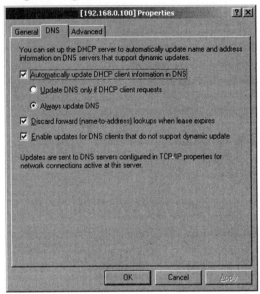

Figure 7.2   Properties screen for configuring DHCP options for Dynamic DNS.

This shows that DHCP server 192.168.0.100 has been configured to register names automatically for Windows 2000, Windows NT, and Windows 9x clients. If you select **Always Update DNS**, the DHCP server will make the update on the client's behalf even for Windows 2000 clients that are capable of updating the Bind DNS server. In most cases, clients do not have direct update ability because it is restricted on the Bind server via the *allow-update* statement in the *named.conf* file. In the configuration shown above, the option has been set to cause the DHCP server to remove records automatically when the client's lease expires.

Down-Level DHCP Servers

If the DHCP server cannot perform dynamic DNS registration on behalf of clients, you have only a few options:

- Allow Windows 2000 clients to register their records in DNS and do not register non-Windows 2000 clients in DNS

- Do not register any clients in DNS

- Manually register records for the statically defined clients in DNS

- Move Windows 2000 clients to subnets serviced by Windows 2000 DHCP servers

- Upgrade down-level DHCP servers to Windows 2000 DHCP servers

 Of these, the recommended option is to upgrade the down-level DHCP servers to Windows 2000, which now has enhancements such as rogue DHCP server detection, easier administration, and fault tolerance. DNS registration for down-level clients allows other legacy devices to locate the legacy resources without requiring you to register them manually in DNS.

Windows 2000 Clients

Windows 2000 client computers have an updated DHCP client service that is capable of dynamic updates. You can direct the client to register its own DNS records, or define it so that the DHCP server registers them. To limit the number of devices that could directly update DNS records, ABCD Corp. configured the Bind server to disallow updates submitted directly by clients. Selecting the option **Always Update DNS** in the DHCP server's DNS properties causes all clients records to be registered by the DHCP server even if the client is a Windows 2000 client that is capable of registering its own DNS records. The **Advanced DNS** configuration of the client computer's TCP/IP properties should have the option **Register this connection's addresses in DNS** checked. This is the default setting.

In the **Advanced DNS** configuration section of the client computer's TCP/IP properties, there is a checkbox to **Use this connection's DNS suffix in DNS registration.** You can use the option to register adapter-specific domain names. For example, suppose your computer is member of the Windows 2000 domain *seattle-branch.abcd.tld* and by default it is also the computer's primary DNS Suffix. Also, suppose the computer is getting IP addresses from DHCP with a DHCP-assigned Domain Name of *research-lab1.abcd.tld*. In this case you should register the computer in DNS with both domains, so it can be reached by the short name from all the research lab machines, and the *Seattle* branch (as well as from the *abcd*, due to name devolution). This option will only work if the computer itself registers its names within DNS. If this option is checked, name registration will be made by the client, not the DHCP server, without regard to the **Always Update DNS** setting on the DHCP server. For name registration to succeed, the client must be listed in the *allow-update* statement in the Bind *named.conf* file.

To force a Windows 2000 client to refresh its DHCP lease and re-register its DNS names, enter *ipconfig /registerdns* at a command prompt. This command is useful when name registrations do not match what is currently configured on the client.

Down-Level Clients

Down level clients (Windows 9*x*, Windows NT 3.51/4.0, etc.) cannot perform dynamic DNS registration without the help of a DHCP server that can make dynamic updates. If you are using a Windows 2000 DHCP server and have checked the option **Enable updates for DNS clients that do not support dynamic update**, it will perform dynamic DNS registration on behalf of the down-level clients.

Any statically defined clients that do not use DHCP should be reserved in the DHCP scope, and you should manually register them in DNS. Note that when you add a DHCP reservation for a statically defined device, the DHCP server does not automatically update the DNS.

Additional Considerations

This section discusses a few other issues you may encounter in a Unix-only DNS environment.

Bind 4.x and 8.1.2 Servers

Bind 4.x servers do not support dynamic updates or incremental zone transfers. Bind 8.2.1 corrects problems that Bind 8.1.2 has with incremental zone transfers. Active Directory adds SRV records with names that may not be understood by earlier name servers (Bind 4.9.6 and later are aware of SRV records). In a Windows 2000 Active directory environment you should upgrade all Bind servers to release 8.2.1.

If you use an older version of Bind on any zone that does not support incremental zone transfers, you should disable *notify* on that zone to avoid sending useless *notify* messages. You can add the *notify no;* statement to a specific zone or to the options section in the *named.conf* file.

All updates for a zone are made to its primary DNS server, so it becomes a single point of failure; if it fails, records on the secondary server can become stale until the master server becomes available. When the master server does come back up, the DHCP server applies all queued updates, which initiates a zone transfer on the secondary servers for the zone. DNS servers integrated with Windows 2000 Active Directory avoid this by allowing multiple primary DNS servers to be updated, not just the master. If a Windows 2000 Active Directory Integrated DNS server is down, others can process the dynamic updates.

Any Bind servers that are earlier than version 4.9.6 do not support SRV records. If the Active Directory namespace overlaps with the existing DNS namespace and the authoritative name server does not support SRV records, you must delegate the zones that contain records specific to the Windows 2000 domain controller to a

Windows 2000 DNS server, or to an upgraded Bind server that does support SRV records. These are zones you must delegate: _msdcs.*yourdomain*, _tcp.*yourdomain*, _udp.*yourdomain* and _sites.*yourdomain*. The Windows 2000 domain controller servers will still periodically attempt to register their *A* records with the authoritative name server, which will generate errors in the event log. When the domain controllers attempt to register their SRV records, the DNS server that is authoritative for the delegated zones will be updated. To avoid delegation and errors in the event logs it is recommended that you update to Bind 8.2.1.

Windows 2000 Domain Controllers and DHCP Servers

Before you install Active Directory servers, make sure the master Bind DNS is successfully performing dynamic updates. After you install the first Windows 2000 Active directory server, allow some time for zones to transfer to the secondary DNS before you install any more domain controllers.

When a domain controller with Active Directory starts, it generates at least 40-50 Kb of traffic as it contacts its preferred DNS to register its SRV records and to gather information about where services are located within the domain. Servers re-register records when they are restarted, when the Netlogon service is restarted, or when the server's IP configuration changes. Initially, the Netlogon service updates the DNS with SRV records very frequently, but eventually settles on once per hour. Each re-registration for all of the standard SRV records puts about 12 Kb of data on the LAN.

You can put Windows 2000 DHCP servers anywhere on the network and in addition to standard DHCP leasing traffic they will often perform dynamic updates on behalf of clients. This generates traffic proportional to the number of clients and the frequency of dynamic updates, so whenever possible you should put the DHCP server on the same subnetwork as the zone's primary DNS server (or close to it, from a networking perspective). If your network is stable and does not change frequently, you should also increase DHCP client lease duration.

Conclusion

In a Windows 2000 Active Directory environment you can implement DNS with a pure Unix Bind architecture, a pure Windows 2000 architecture, or a combination. This chapter has discussed issues encountered when using Unix Bind DNS servers exclusively. Windows 2000 DNS offers some features not available even in Bind 8.2.1, but you still may prefer or require a pure Unix DNS architecture. Configuring one requires some special steps; this chapter has also identified some optional steps that can help create a name space that performs better and is more stable.

CHAPTER 8

Integrating Active Directory with Exchange Server

**By
Rick Varvel,
MCS—PacWest
and David A.
Clark, MCS—
Central Region**

Other chapters in this book discuss moving from flat Windows NT 4.0 NetBIOS domains to Microsoft's hierarchical Active Directory. But if you have already implemented the foundation for Active Directory with Microsoft Exchange Server (when you created sites, containers, and a global address list), you face a different challenge in building an enterprise directory: when you upgrade to Active Directory you must consider how this will affect the existing Exchange environment and how upgrading to Exchange 2000 will influence directory structure and implementation.

This chapter focuses on issues affecting Exchange interoperability and functionality when you move from a pure Windows NT 4.0 environment to a Windows 2000 native-mode environment. It looks at how integrating Exchange Server 5.5 environments and planning for Exchange 2000 affect namespace design, message flow, administration, and directory replication. It does not detail the Windows 2000 upgrade process. Rather, it helps you devise a Windows 2000 upgrade strategy that minimally affects resource access, directory availability, and message delivery.

For a baseline, it uses an operational Windows NT 4.0/Exchange 5.5 model based on a fictitious company called All-Terrain Trucking. The model is small enough to understand easily but large enough to present most of the real-world issues you'll encounter. The process moves first to Windows 2000 (mixed mode)/Exchange 5.5 and then to Windows 2000 (native mode)/Exchange 5.5. Each stage reviews the impact to the messaging environment, documents necessary issues and workarounds, and highlights any Exchange 2000 factors that might influence an upgrade plan.

What You'll Find in This Chapter

- A summary of the Windows NT 4.0 to Windows 2000 upgrade process, based on real-world experience.

- An overview of the Active Directory Connector.

- Best practices for maintaining messaging connectivity during each stage of an upgrade.

- Active Directory Connector configuration and troubleshooting tips.

- A summary of real-world lessons learned, including recommendations on what to do and what to avoid.

Caution   To maintain message flow with minimal impact on the user community, you must carefully plan and implement modifications to the existing Windows NT 4.0 and Exchange environments. Out-of-sequence changes can cause severe message routing problems. Test all proposed changes in a lab environment before implementing them.

Upgrade Strategy Overview

The major upgrade phases are covered in this chapter in three sections: "Upgrading Windows NT 4.0 Domains to Windows 2000," "Directory Replication and Synchronization," and "Planning for Exchange 2000." The basic upgrade stages are:

Stage 1. Upgrade the account domain (ACCOUNTS) and the Exchange resource domain (EXCHANGE) to Windows 2000 mixed mode domains and leave the business unit resource domain (RETAIL) as Windows NT 4.0 with a down-level trust.

Stage 2. Convert the ACCOUNTS domain to native mode after all Windows NT 4.0 servers have been upgraded to Windows 2000. (You do not have to use native mode to use the ADC. In some cases, you may have to implement the ADC before you move to native mode, in order to facilitate migrating directory-enabled applications such as Exchange 2000.)

Stage 3. Collapse the EXCHANGE domain into an organizational unit (OU) in the ACCOUNTS domain.

Stage 4. Install the Active Directory Connector (ADC) between the ACCOUNTS and RETAIL domains.

Stage 5. Upgrade the Exchange servers running on Windows 2000 to Exchange 2000.

Stage 6. Upgrade the RETAIL resource domain to a Windows 2000 child domain.

Stage 7. Upgrade the RETAIL domain Exchange 5.5 servers to Exchange 2000 and remove the ADC.

The first four stages present the greatest technical challenge, and this discussion focuses on them. It discusses briefly some issues likely to arise in the last three.

Profile of All-Terrain Trucking

All-Terrain Trucking, based in Portland, Oregon, supports operations in four west coast branch offices. A recent merger added a large office in Seattle, which is still being absorbed. All-Terrain's network is a mix of approximately 8,500 desktop computers and 100 servers spread across a central location and 4 branch offices. It's a hub and spoke network connected over T1/T3. The challenge facing All-Terrain is to maintain seamless messaging while upgrading Windows NT 4.0 domain controllers and member servers to Windows 2000 and Exchange 5.5 servers to Exchange 2000 servers. Their solution is to develop a seven-stage migration plan that focuses on minimizing impact to the user community.

Project Background

All-Terrain Trucking has decided that upgrading to Windows 2000 will advantageously reduce the number of domains, tighten administrative control, and simplify basic software distribution. The network consists of two primary geographic locations (**Home Office** and **Retail**) connected by T3 links, and three remote offices connected to the Home Office location by T1s. One remote location (Canby) does not have its own Exchange server and relies on the Portland office for messaging. See Figure 8.1.

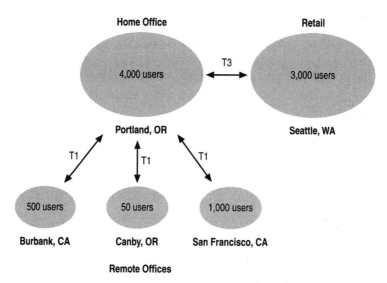

Figure 8.1   All-Terrain Trucking network physical layout.

The original domain architecture consisted of the ACCOUNTS and EXCHANGE domains but a recent merger added the RETAIL domain (see Figure 8.2). The acquisition is run as a separate business with its own user accounts and Exchange servers. Exchange was installed after the merger, so there are no issues with multiple Exchange organizations—all Exchange servers are part of the Exchange organization—*Allterrain*. The long-term plan is for the RETAIL domain to become a child domain of the ACCOUNTS (root) domain.

The desktop environment includes over 8,500 PCs with approximately 60% Windows 9x and 40% Windows NT 4.0 Workstation. Windows NT user and machine accounts are split between the ACCOUNTS and RETAIL domains and there is a one-way trust between the two domains with RETAIL trusting ACCOUNTS.

There are two Exchange service accounts: one in the ACCOUNTS domain (used for the Exchange servers in the RETAIL domain) and one in the EXCHANGE domain (used for servers in the EXCHANGE domain only). To avoid future problems, the Exchange servers in the RETAIL domain use a service account from the ACCOUNTS domain. (For detailed information on the issues with service accounts and Exchange, refer to the section "Collapsing Resource Domains," later in this chapter.) All Exchange servers run Exchange 5.5 Service Pack 3; all Windows NT 4.0 servers run Service Pack 4.

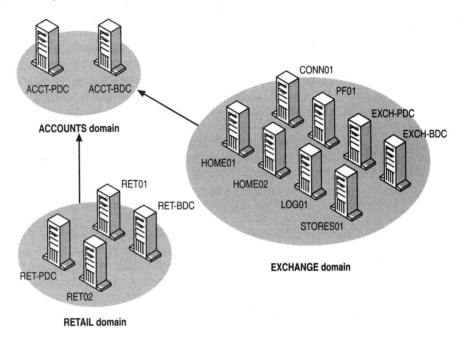

Figure 8.2   Windows NT 4.0 domain architecture before the Windows 2000 upgrade.

The objective is to upgrade all existing Windows NT 4.0 domains to Windows 2000 and all Exchange 5.5 servers to Exchange 2000 with minimal impact to message delivery and Outlook client functionality. During the course of the upgrade the Exchange resource domain will be collapsed into an organizational unit (OU) and the RETAIL domain will become a child domain.

The Domain Naming System (DNS) root zone for All-Terrain Trucking is **allterrain.tld**. When upgrading to Windows 2000, the first domain in the forest will be called **corp.allterrain.tld** so that internal proxy servers can distinguish between internal and external domain names. External customers will still access the company using **allterrain.tld**, but internal applications such as Exchange and Internet Explorer will use **corp.allterrain.tld** as root.

In addition to DNS, the ACCOUNTS domain also hosts WINS and DHCP services for All-Terrain Trucking. Two WINS servers (primary and secondary) and two DHCP servers are located in Portland. The primary DNS server is in Portland but the secondary is in Seattle.

Besides Exchange's normal directory replication and message delivery functions, Canby users are using OWA extensively and a few users in Seattle are using IMAP4. The upgrade must not disrupt these services.

At each step of the way some or all of these questions will be considered:

- What effect does this change have on message routing?
- Can users still access their mailboxes? If not, what needs to be modified?
- What is the effect on network traffic?
- Can the product be administered from both Windows NT 4.0 and Windows 2000?
- How is performance affected?
- What new features are available?
- Are there alternatives? If so, what are their pros and cons?

Each of the four Exchange sites corresponds to a geographic location (see Figures 8.3 and 8.4). The corporate offices in Portland have the messaging hub for the other sites. The two smaller sites connect to Portland with T1s and the larger site in Seattle with a T3.

With the exception of the LOGISTICS server, each Exchange server is configured to support up to 2,000 users, each with a 50-MB mailbox limit.

Note For clarity, only DNS and a subset of Exchange servers are represented in this view.

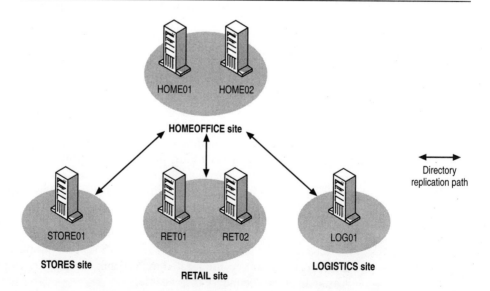

Figure 8.3   Exchange Site layout before the Windows 2000 upgrade.

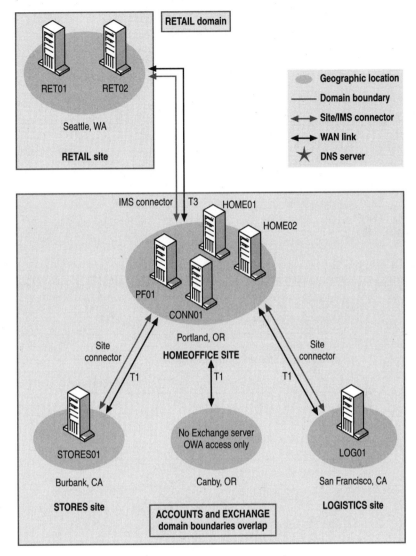

Figure 8.4   All-Terrain Trucking network—combined view.

The servers are configured as follows:

Hardware

Quad processor Pentium Pro Xeon (450 MHz)

- 512 MB RAM (error correcting)
- Array A = Raid 1 (9 GB)
- Array B = Raid 1 (9 GB)
- Array C = Raid 5 (150 GB)

- (All arrays configured in hardware)
- Single Ethernet NIC (100BaseT) with IP protocols.

Software

- Windows NT 4.0 with SP4
- Exchange 5.5 with SP3

Physical memory requirements.

Item	Requirement
Exchange Administrator	5 MB
Windows NT O/S	16 MB
MTA	5 MB
Store	14 MB
DSA	7 MB minimum
Additional services	10 MB
Exchange process space	943 MB
Total physical memory	**1 GB**

Physical disk space requirements.

Item	Requirement
Exchange log files	20% of Message store (rounded up to nearest MB)
Exchange root directory	120 MB
Windows NT operating system physical disk requirements	124 MB
Store requirements	150 GB (approx. 2,000 users x 50MB per mailbox + allowance for repair utilities)
Total Physical Disk Requirements	**150.25 GB**

Configuration.

Drives	Drive letter	Size	Contents
	N/A	~36 MB	Hardware manufacturer system files
Array A (0 & 1) mirrored	C: (partition 1)	2 GB	Operating system and swap file
Array A (0 & 1) mirrored	D: (partition 2)	7 GB	Exchange system files
Array B (2 & 3) mirrored	E:	9 GB	DSAdata and MDBdata log files (on separate controller from message store)
Internal in RAID 5	F:	150 GB	Priv.edb and/or Pub.edb

> **Note**   All-Terrain has configured an Exchange server with 200 GB of disk storage and set it aside to be used as a disaster recovery server. If your company cannot afford an extra server, it's a good idea to configure your production Exchange servers with disk drives double the size of your largest messaging database. Exchange will need most of this space in the event of a disaster recovery.

Upgrading Windows NT 4.0 Domains to Windows 2000

The first step in the upgrade process is to establish the forest root, which is always the first Windows 2000 Active Directory domain controller that you set up. You must plan this carefully because once you establish it you cannot change the name of the forest or the forest root role.

Since there is only a single Windows NT 4.0 account domain, All-Terrain Trucking decided to perform an in-place upgrade—upgrading the existing PDC then the remaining BDCs. The alternative is to establish a parallel Windows 2000 domain structure and then move users from the old domain to the new one. They did not choose the parallel domain approach primarily because it requires cloning user accounts and re-assigning passwords.

Basic upgrade steps:

1. Set up a BDC in the Windows NT 4.0 ACCOUNTS domain and synchronize it with the domain.

2. When synchronization is complete, promote the BDC that you just added to the role of PDC, then disconnect it from the LAN, clearly mark it as a critical backup server, and place it in a safe, secure location for contingency use (to restore the domain if DCPROMO fails, for instance). Access to the PDC can constitute a security risk so be sure to keep it locked away until you can decommission it.

3. Now promote the original PDC back to its former status. You now have two machines capable of performing the LMREPL master role, the original PDC and the one you created in step 1. This allows you to restore Windows NT 4.0-style file system replication if necessary (it maintains support for logon script replication when multiple servers are involved).

4. Create a zone file in DNS for the new Windows 2000 domain you're creating and set it to "Allow Updates" so that Active Directory SRV records can be created.

5. Upgrade the PDC to Windows 2000 and run DCPROMO.

6. Verify AD functionality and domain access.

7. If this has been successful, you can now format and reuse the backup BDC for something else.

8. If this is not successful, remove the Windows 2000 machine from the network, put the secured BDC back online, and promote it to the PDC. You will lose any changes made between the time the original PDC was upgraded to Windows 2000 and the time the backup BDC is promoted to a PDC.

Summary of ACCOUNTS Domain Upgrade

After Upgrading the ACCOUNTS Domain PDC to Windows 2000

At All-Terrain, the domain upgrade went without a hitch from the perspective of the down-level clients and Exchange. Messages continued to flow between all the sites, new mailboxes could be created, and directory replication occurred on schedule.

When designing their Windows NT 4.0 domain, All-Terrain had installed DNS on the ACCOUNTS domain PDC. They created a new zone (**corp.allterrain.tld**) on the existing Windows NT 4.0 DNS, but they converted it to Windows 2000 DNS during the in-place upgrade because Windows NT 4.0 DNS does not support dynamic updates. Dynamic update support is not required for DCPROMO, but it is highly recommended because without it you have to maintain all Windows 2000-related DNS entries manually. For example, when DCPROMO is run to create a new Windows 2000 domain, _MSDCS, _SITES, _TCP, _UDP and multiple SRV records are added to DNS. Without dynamic update support you have to copy these entries from Netlogon.dns into the appropriate zone file in DNS after DCPROMO runs. From then on, you will have to reflect in DNS any changes made to the location of DCs in your domain.

After a reboot, All-Terrain configured the DNS zone **corp.allterrain.tld** to "Allow Updates" and then stopped and restarted the NetLogon service to dynamically enter the appropriate SRV records into DNS. (To make sure the Host and Pointer records are entered correctly, you can also run *ipconfig /registerdns*.)

WINS: There were no apparent changes to WINS at this point.

DNS: Configuration issues aside, DNS continued to work fine after the upgrade. However, Exchange servers and existing clients could not resolve IP addresses for machines in the new zone (**corp.allterrain.tld**) and computers in the new zone could not resolve IP addresses for machines in the old zone (**allterrain.tld**). A ping returned only the NetBIOS name, not the expected FQDN, indicating that WINS was doing the resolution, not DNS. To fix the problem, they added both DNS zone names (**allterrain.tld** and **corp.allterrain.tld**) to the Domain Suffix Search list on each of the Exchange servers and to the Windows 2000 DC (with **corp.allterrain.tld** as primary).

When prompted for the down level NetBIOS name during the DCPROMO process, they retained the name ACCOUNTS so that existing service accounts that rely on a domain prefix (such as ACCOUNTS\EXservice for the Exchange servers in the RETAIL domain) would continue to work. If you change the down-level NetBIOS name it is hard to predict which functionality will break. *Do so at your own risk.*

Running NSLOOKUP still returned **acct-bdc.allterrain.tld** as the default server, which is what was needed to maintain the correct MX record for Exchange.

Note   If DNS is on a member server, it is much simpler to upgrade the PDC in-place. Just upgrade the member server containing Windows NT 4.0 DNS to Windows 2000—this upgrades the existing DNS in the process—then create a new zone (in the case of All-Terrain Trucking the zone was called **corp.allterrain.tld**), set it to "Allow Updates," and you're all set.

DHCP: No changes were made to DHCP at this stage and client leases were still issued correctly. The upgrade team decided that any new Windows 2000 clients added to the domain would point to **corp.allterrain.tld** and that after they collapsed the Exchange resource domain into an organizational unit (OU) they would use DHCP to change the remaining clients' domain name to **corp.allterrain.tld**.

EXCHANGE: After upgrading to Windows 2000, you cannot use the Active Directory Users and Computers tool to create mailboxes when you add users unless the ADC is installed. The Exchange Admin tool still allows you to assign Windows NT user accounts to mailboxes, but it uses the down-level NetBIOS name, and all authentication uses NTLM.

After Upgrading the Remaining BDCs in the ACCOUNTS Domain to Windows 2000

No major problems at this stage.

WINS: Only one of the upgraded BDCs had WINS installed. After the first reboot, setup displayed a message stating that the WINS service would not start because the WINS database had not been upgraded. When prompted by the Windows 2000 setup routine, the team initiated a process called JETCONV to perform the conversion as part of the upgrade.

DNS: No new issues. Name resolution and dynamic machine registration continued to work for Windows 2000 servers and workstations through records in the DNS zone **corp.allterrain.tld**. When the upgrade was complete, the team modified the ACCOUNTS PDC Domain Suffix Search list. Later, when the domain was completely upgraded to Windows 2000, the team configured all the remaining down-level clients and new Windows 2000 clients and servers: they added both DNS zone names (**allterrain.tld** and **corp.allterrain.tld**) to the Domain Suffix Search list on each Exchange server, and did the same for the Windows 2000 DC (setting **corp.allterrain.tld** as primary). DHCP does not support changes to the Domain Suffix Search list, so the team used a resource kit tool (*SetTCPIPParams.exe* by Georg Zanzen) from a login script.

DHCP: After the first reboot, setup displayed a message (similar to the one it returned for WINS) stating that the DHCP server would now terminate because the DHCP database had not been upgraded. Again, when Windows 2000 setup, at the beginning of the JETCONV process, asked if it should convert the Windows NT 4.0 DHCP database to a version compatible with Windows 2000, the team answered yes. After that, DHCP appeared to be operating correctly (clients with existing leases could still access the network) but after approximately two hours some users reported problems with browsing. The team checked the event log and found this error: "The DHCP server is not authorized in the directory. Until the server is authorized, you can change the configuration, but it will not respond to client requests."

Note   To authorize the DHCP server, open the DHCP administration program, click on **DHCP**, select **Browse Authorized Servers**, click the **Add** button and put in the server's name or IP address.

After Converting the ACCOUNTS Domain to Native Mode

No issues at all, but this made available some new features such as universal security groups and nesting of global groups. For a complete list of native-mode features, see the *Microsoft Windows 2000 Server Deployment and Planning Guide* "Migration" chapter.

IMAP4, OWA, organizational forms and public folder access functions were all unaffected by the upgrade and conversion. Message flow and replication were unaffected. The Exchange administration tools worked equally well from either Windows 2000 or Windows NT 4.0.

Note   The Windows 2000 Active Directory Users and Computers tool still cannot be used to create mailboxes when adding users. To manage Exchange users from Active Directory you have to install the ADC and its management console, and define at least one connection agreement.

Now that the ACCOUNTS domain is in native mode, Windows 2000 clients and down-level clients that have the upgraded client for Microsoft network software can log on using DNS. The basic process is:

1. If DHCP is enabled, a DHCP lease is returned to the workstation, otherwise the static IP address is used.
2. The workstation's registry contains a value that defines what site it is in. Using this site information, the workstation queries for a DC at random from its site and establishes a connection with the DC that replies the quickest.
3. The name of the quickest responding DC in the site is cached to speed up subsequent logons.
4. The workstation requests a ticket-granting ticket from the DC and if approved receives one in return.
5. The ticket granting ticket is used to obtain a workstation session ticket.
6. Any workstation-related group policy objects are downloaded.
7. The client connects to the local DC in its site, requests a ticket-granting ticket from the DC and if approved receives one in return.
8. The ticket-granting ticket is used to obtain a client session ticket.
9. The local DC authenticates the user and builds access token.

10. The local DC contacts the global catalog to get the user's universal group membership.
11. The local DC adds universal group SIDs to the access token and returns it to the client.
12. User and group-related group policy objects are downloaded and the logon process is complete.

Summary of EXCHANGE Resource Domain Upgrade

After upgrading the ACCOUNTS domain to Windows 2000, the team used the same basic steps to upgrade the EXCHANGE resource domain (Figure 8.5). The upgrade went very smoothly but some issues related to service accounts and permissions to connectors, public folders, and the Exchange administrator program required special consideration. They are detailed in the next section, "Collapsing Resource Domains."

The team did not convert the EXCHANGE resource domain to native mode; this meant they could roll it back to a Windows NT 4.0 domain if conditions required.

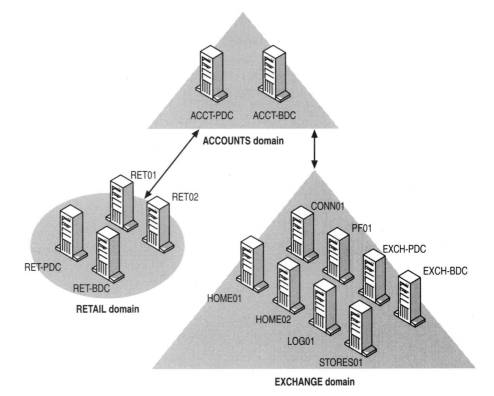

Figure 8.5   Domain Architecture after upgrading the ACCOUNTS and EXCHANGE domains to Windows 2000.

Note   For clarity, Figure 8.5 does not show all servers. DHCP and WINS reside on separate servers and were upgraded after the PDC. DNS was on the ACCOUNTS domain PDC and upgraded with it.

Collapsing Resource Domains

Most current Exchange messaging designs place Exchange on member servers. To save money, All-Terrain decided to create a dedicated messaging resource domain and put Exchange servers on BDCs and even the PDC. They also put the Exchange service account (**EXservice**) in the EXCHANGE resource domain instead of in ACCOUNTS (Figure 8.6). This last step makes the upgrade to Windows 2000 more challenging because as soon as the resource domain containing the Exchange service account is collapsed, all Exchange servers residing in the ACCOUNTS domain will have services that reference an account (EXCHANGE\Exservice) that no longer exists.

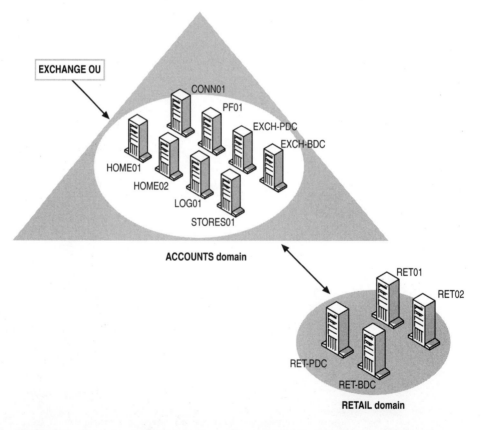

Figure 8.6   Domain architecture after collapse of the Exchange resource domain.

You have two options for maintaining Exchange functionality while upgrading:

- Keep the EXCHANGE resource domain intact and just upgrade it to Windows 2000. Then when you upgrade the Exchange servers to Exchange 2000, the service account will default to the local system account instead of a domain account and you can move the servers freely among any Windows 2000 domain in the forest. When you have them where you want them, you can collapse the EXCHANGE resource domain. *This is the safest approach.*

- Change permissions on the Exchange Org, Site, Configuration and Schema containers and all the Exchange services from EXCHANGE\EXservice to ACCOUNTS\EXservice. This is a good solution for small companies with one Exchange server per site. Large Exchange installations can also use it, but Microsoft does not support it unless the Exchange databases are backed up, the Exchange server software is reinstalled with the new service account and the Exchange databases are restored. *This is a less-safe approach:* it requires careful planning and good backups.

All-Terrain used a hybrid approach that appears to work (read about it in the From the Trenches section below) but option 1 is highly recommended unless your Exchange servers were installed using a service account from a domain other than the domain they are running in.

Note   If you decide to use option 2 and you have Exchange installed on the PDC in your resource domain, you should add another BDC to the domain and promote it to the PDC role for contingency purposes. Before you can collapse Exchange servers into an OU you must first demote them to member servers; once you do that, any accounts that were in the SAM database of the domain being collapsed are gone unless the PDC role has been assigned to a non-Exchange server. You should keep the PDC on-line until all Exchange servers have been relocated.

From the Trenches: Collapsing an Exchange Resource Domain

Many companies upgrade to Windows 2000 to simplify domain administration and reduce hardware costs by reducing the number of servers required. At All-Terrain recently we collapsed the messaging resource domain, eliminating a PDC and a BDC in the process. That's a good deal, but this is not an operation to be taken lightly—if you don't do it correctly Exchange services may not start and you will be prevented from performing Exchange Administration until you rebuild your Exchange server(s).

Still willing to give it a try? I've outlined the procedure I used. You will have to adapt it to your situation but the principles are the same.

What We Started With

We started with a Windows 2000 root domain (**accounts.allterrain.tld**) and a Windows NT 4.0 resource domain (**EXCHANGE**). The Windows 2000 domain retained ACCOUNTS as the NetBIOS name and I established a one-way trust between the two domains (EXCHANGE trusts ACCOUNTS). The EXCHANGE domain contained a PDC and 7 BDCs, 6 of which had Exchange installed.

The Exchange servers represent three Exchange sites (HOMEOFFICE, STORES, and LOGISTICS). All Exchange servers were originally installed using a service account from the Exchange resource domain and not the ACCOUNTS domain. This is significant: if they had been installed with an account from the ACCOUNTS domain we would not have had any problems collapsing the domain.

Our Objective

We wanted to reclaim two servers and simplify domain administration by collapsing the EXCHANGE resource domain into an Exchange OU inside of ACCOUNTS, while maintaining e-mail connectivity, administrative access to Exchange, and changing the Exchange service account and password.

The Problem

To collapse the Exchange resource domain we had to convert all the Exchange servers from BDCs to Windows 2000 member servers, join them to the ACCOUNTS domain, and then turn off the PDC and BDC for the EXCHANGE domain. The problem is that once the PDC in the EXCHANGE resource domain is turned off, Exchange Administrator permissions and Exchange services both reference an account from a domain that no longer exists so you cannot administer the site or start the services. If you edit the services so that they start with an account from ACCOUNTS, Exchange services start but you no longer have access to the Exchange Admin program as administrator, the Exchange service account or any other account—to get back in, you have to reinstall Exchange.

How We Did It

I used the steps that follow to collapse the domain while maintaining message delivery during preparation. We added the Exchange Administrator accounts and modified the Exchange services during weeknights, and collapsed the domain over a weekend because it required shutting the Exchange system down for about eight hours.

Please keep in mind that we walked through the entire process in a lab before ever touching a production Exchange server. This is a *high-risk* procedure and you must have a proven backup of all Exchange servers in your resource domain before you start in on it.

That being said, here are the steps we followed:

1. Created an Exchange service account in the ACCOUNTS domain (ACCOUNTS\ex2000). **Note:** The target domain service account name does not match the source domain service account name.

2. Opened the Exchange Administrator program on each Exchange server and assigned ACCOUNTS\Administrator and ACCOUNTS\ex2000 Service Account Admin permissions at the Org, Site, and Configuration container levels. **Note:** I did not do this in RAW mode.

3. Opened the Exchange Administrator program on each Exchange server in RAW mode (**\exchsrvr\bin\admin.exe /r**) and used this procedure to add ACCOUNTS\ex2000 to the schema object:

    1. To view the raw directory, select the **View** menu, then select **Raw Directory**. (The **Schema** object is added in the left-hand pane of the **Exchange Administrator** window.)

    2. Open the **Schema Properties** dialog box.

    3. Select the **Schema** object.

    4. From the **File** menu, select **Raw Properties...** to display the **Schema Properties** dialog box.

    5. Add the new Service Account to the **NT-Security-Descriptor** object.

    6. From the **Object attributes** list box, select the **NT-Security-Descriptor** object.

    7. Click **Editor...** to display the **Attribute Editor Selection** dialog box.

    8. From the **Editor type** list box, select **NT security descriptor** and click **OK** to display the **NT-Security-Descriptor Properties** dialog box.

    9. Click **Add...** to display the **Add Users and Groups** dialog box.

    10. From the **List Names From** drop-down list box, select the domain where you created the new Service Account.

    11. From the **Names** list box, select the new Service Account and click **Add**. (The new Service Account appears in the **Add Names** box.)

    12. Click **OK**.

13. From the **Windows NT accounts with permissions** list box, select the new Service Account.

14. From the **Roles** drop-down list box, select **Service Account Admin**.

15. Click **OK**.

16. Click **OK** to close the **Schema Properties** dialog box.

17. Close Exchange Administrator.

4. Edited each Exchange service on each Exchange server so that they started up with ACCOUNTS\ex2000 instead of EXCHANGE\exservice.

5. Rebooted to make sure all the services still worked. They did.

6. Created a zone on **corp.allterrain.tld** called **exchange.corp.allterrain.tld** and enabled updates.

7. Upgraded the EXCHANGE domain PDC (EXCH-PDC) to a Windows 2000 child domain DC, keeping the down-level domain name of EXCHANGE. Now I have a child domain called **exchange.corp.allterrain.tld**, which is running in mixed mode. The PDC is Windows 2000 RC2 and the BDCs are still Windows NT 4.0. **Note:** All Exchange services still start at this point and I can still send messages in both directions.

8. Upgraded EXCH-BDC to a Windows 2000 member server in the EXCHANGE domain. **Note:** I tried to join the member server directly into the ACCOUNTS domain, but when you cancel out of DCPROMO the option to join a different domain is grayed out. I got around this by running DCPROMO, selecting **Leave as a member server**.

9. Joined EXCH-BDC to a workgroup and rebooted. **Note:** I don't think this is necessary but I did it anyway just in case.

10. Joined EXCH-BDC to the ACCOUNTS domain.

11. Added ACCOUNTS\Administrator and ACCOUNTS\ex2000 to the Administrators local group on EXCH-BDC.

12. Gave ACCOUNTS\ex2000 "Logon Locally, Logon as a Service, Act as part of the Operating System and Restore Files and Directories" permissions to EXCH-BDC.

13. Ran SECEDIT /refreshpolicy MACHINE_POLICY and SECEDIT /refreshpolicy USER_POLICY to force the application of the additional rights. Exchange still worked and I could modify permissions on EXCH-BDC when logged in as ACCOUNTS\Administrator. **Note:** During this entire process the Exchange services on EXCH-BDC were not available.

14. Started Exchange services on EXCH-BDC (STORES site) and it came right up. I could send and receive mail with (HOMEOFFICE) site, which at this point was still on a Windows 2000 DC in the EXCHANGE domain. We had to recreate the MAPI profile on EXCH-BDC after the move because the account associated with it remained in the EXCHANGE resource domain and could no longer be resolved to a valid account name in the ACCOUNTS domain. As long as the alias name associated with a particular MAPI profile can still be resolved, upgrading the server that Exchange 5.5 is installed on and moving it to a different domain should not affect existing MAPI profiles.

15. Repeated steps 8 through 14 on the remaining BDCs and member servers in the EXCHANGE resource domain.

16. Ran DCPROMO on the PDC (EXCH-PDC) to demote it to a member server. Since it was the last DC in the domain, it automatically became a member of "workgroup." I changed the domain to "ACCOUNTS" and rebooted. **Note:** I *did not stop* EXCH-BDC Exchange services while EXCH-PDC was being upgraded (contrary to some Knowledge Base articles) because I didn't see why it would be necessary. It turns out it's not.

17. Added ACCOUNTS\Administrator and ACCOUNTS\ex2000 to the Administrators local group on EXCH-PDC.

18. Gave ACCOUNTS\ex2000 "Logon Locally, Logon as a Service, Act as part of the Operating System and Restore Files and Directories" permissions to EXCH-BDC.

19. Ran SECEDIT /refreshpolicy MACHINE_POLICY and SECEDIT /refreshpolicy USER_POLICY. Exchange services would not start. I checked the event log and it said that SA couldn't start because a dependent service didn't start. It turns out that the RPC Locator service was somehow disabled during the demotion and move to ACCOUNTS. We enabled the RPC service and then all the Exchange services started.

20. Last step: moved all the EXCHANGE resource domain servers (EXCH-PDC, EXCH-BDC, CONN01, etc.) from the Computers container into an OU called Exchange in the ACCOUNTS domain.

Summary—Collapsing an Exchange Resource Domain

So far, everything appears to be working, but I still recommend avoiding this altogether and waiting for Exchange 2000, which does not rely on domain-based service accounts, as does Exchange 5.5. In theory, we could have just upgraded the EXCHANGE domain to Windows 2000, upgraded the Exchange servers to the Active-Directory-aware version and moved them into the ACCOUNTS domain. Once they were all relocated it would just be a matter of running DCPROMO on the EXCHANGE DC to demote it to a member server and reassigning it to a different domain, effectively eliminating the EXCHANGE child domain. This was not tested but is an alternative to consider, based on early Exchange 2000 release notes.

Collapsing resource domains to reclaim servers is a lot of work and involves great risk. Rule of thumb: to justify the effort, you should get back one server for every five Exchange servers you move. If I haven't scared you away yet, here are the highlights from our upgrade:

- Back up all Exchange servers before beginning and make sure you can restore them.

- If the PDC and all the BDCs in the Exchange Resource domain are also Exchange servers, add another BDC to the domain, promote it to the PDC, and leave it around after the last Exchange server is removed so you can roll back in case of emergency. Once that PDC is gone you will have to reinstall Exchange if you get locked out of the Exchange Administrator program.

- Make sure Exchange services are starting with the account you expect them to start with. When you change 10 service accounts and passwords per Exchange server, it's easy to make a mistake.

- If you use override accounts on X.400 or site connectors, be sure that you also modify the connection account.

- Make sure that the Exchange service account has all the rights it needs to the member servers running Exchange. By default only "Logon as a Service" is assigned when changing the account name. You also need "Act as part of the operating system" and "Restore files and directories" rights and local Administrator group membership.

- If you have any mailboxes with a Primary Windows NT account from the resource domain, you will have to change them to a valid account after moving the Exchange server into the new domain.

- If you have OWA configured, be sure to add the *IUSR_ServerName* account to the Configuration container and assign it Admin permissions.

Directory Replication and Synchronization

To take advantage of Windows 2000, All-Terrain Trucking wanted to consolidate as many resources as possible, using existing IT staff and hardware. They decided to collapse the existing Exchange resource domain into a Windows 2000 organizational unit (OU) but leave the RETAIL domain in Windows NT 4.0 and set up an Active Directory Connector (ADC) between the RETAIL Exchange site and the ACCOUNTS domain. They decided not to upgrade the RETAIL domain to Windows 2000 immediately because of namespace differences and a lack of support personnel. They plan to use the PDC and BDC left over from the EXCHANGE resource domain as Exchange 2000 migration servers later.

So their immediate goal was to use the ADC to assimilate the recently purchased trucking company (the RETAIL Exchange site) into the All-Terrain network and clean up the namespace at the same time. The long-term goal was to upgrade RETAIL to a Windows 2000 child domain of ACCOUNTS: they did not want to collapse it into the OU structure within ACCOUNTS because the two locations have separate business functions, IT staff, and security requirements.

When all servers in the ACCOUNTS and EXCHANGE domains are upgraded to Windows 2000 and the ACCOUNTS domain has been switched to native mode, the next step is to establish communication between the Active Directory in the ACCOUNTS domain and the Exchange directory service in the RETAIL and HOMEOFFICE sites.

Here is some background information on the Active Directory Connector.

The Active Directory Connector

The Windows 2000 Server Active Directory Connector (ADC) enables synchronization and management between Windows 2000 Active Directory and the Exchange Server 5.5 directory service. At the least, the Exchange server targeted to communicate with Active Directory must be running Exchange 5.5 because it is the first version to support LDAP writes, which the ADC requires.

The ADC can decrease migration time. If you have a lot of information in the Exchange Directory, you can 'bulk upload' much of it to the Active Directory and the ADC will synchronize it with Exchange 5.5. Without the ADC, you would have to re-enter data and updates manually in both directory services. The ADC also allows the Active Directory administrator to manage (on a basic level) the Exchange 5.5 users.

ADC functionality includes:

- **Active Directory Schema Extensions.** Installs Exchange schema extensions to map between Exchange Server 5.5 and Active Directory. This requires that you run Setup from an account that belongs to the Schema Administrators group.

- **Bi-directional synchronization.** Changes initiated on the Active Directory are automatically communicated to the Exchange Server directory, and vice versa. This allows you to manage changes from Active Directory, Exchange Server, or both.

- **Selective attribute synchronization.** You can select or exclude Active Directory and Exchange Server attributes for synchronization.

- **Replicate Attribute-level changes.** When synchronizing objects to Active Directory, the ADC compares attribute values and synchronizes only changed attributes from Exchange Server. For example, if the phone number on an

Exchange Server mailbox is modified, the ADC compares the attributes of the mailbox with the corresponding user object in the Active Directory and synchronizes only the phone number.

■ **Multiple Connections.** Only one instance of the ADC service can be active on a single computer running Windows 2000 Server, but you can establish multiple *connection agreements* (CAs) and configure each to perform specific synchronization tasks. For example, you can configure one CA to continuously update the Windows 2000 Server Active Directory from three distinct Exchange sites, and another to update the Windows 2000 Server contacts to the Exchange Server directory at a specified time daily.

■ **Full fidelity of recipient objects.** Objects (such as Mailbox, Distribution List, and Custom Recipient) are replicated to the Active Directory. All address book information is transmitted—none of it is lost in the replication process.

■ **Customizable attribute mappings.** The replication agent allows administrators to define mapping between the Exchange attributes and Active Directory attributes, including the 15 Exchange custom attributes.

Using Connection Agreements to Establish Relationships

Installing the ADC on a Windows 2000 Server adds a service (MSADC), modifies the Active Directory schema with Exchange attributes, and installs tools that allow you to administer Exchange mailboxes from Active Directory. But, to establish a relationship between an existing Exchange Server site and Active Directory, you have to configure a connection agreement (CA). CAs hold information such as the server names to contact for synchronization, object classes to synchronize, target containers, and the synchronization schedule. You can define multiple CAs on a single ADC. For example, an ADC in one Windows 2000 domain could have three CAs, each one going to a different Exchange site.

Specifically, a connection agreement defines:

■ Directory or directories to be synchronized
■ Windows 2000 Server synchronization objects
■ Exchange Server 5.5 synchronization objects
■ The direction in which synchronization takes place
■ Synchronization schedule
■ Method for deleting objects
■ Details surrounding some of the advanced options, such as:
  ■ Mapping attributes
  ■ Creating new objects
  ■ Authenticating each of the directories
  ■ Specifying which OUs or containers you want to synchronize

Replication

The new Windows 2000 site model manages Active Directory inter-site replication. Active Directory is efficient in that it replicates only changed attributes for an object. This presents a challenge during co-existence because modifying 1 attribute of 10,000 objects within Active Directory replicates only 10,000 attributes (about 1 MB) but when the ADC passes the modifications to Exchange, Exchange replicates 10,000 objects (almost 40 MB).

As the ADC replicates objects from the Exchange Directory to the Active Directory, it must write various attributes into each Exchange object that it touches. Each Exchange object in the Site must be re-replicated within the native Exchange environment (a one-time hit) but because Exchange supports only object-based replication, the directory objects must re-replicate to the rest of the Exchange organization. Rule of thumb: for each Exchange directory object changed on a server, about 5 Kb of data is sent to all of the other servers within the site. For inter-site replication, each object is compressed to about 1 Kb. In very large Exchange systems this can flood directories and the network. You can mitigate this risk by staggering CA deployments.

Synchronization

There are two ways to set up synchronization between Exchange Server containers and Active Directory OUs. The first method is to create multiple separate CAs that map each Exchange Server container to corresponding Active Directory OUs. For example, you can map cn=**Custom Recipients** in Exchange Server to ou=**Contacts** in Active Directory, and so on.

A second method is to create a single CA between the parent container of all the sub containers in Exchange Server and the parent container of all the sub containers in Active Directory. When you synchronize directories for the first time, the ADC automatically creates containers below the parent container in Windows 2000 Server to mirror those in Exchange Server. Therefore, if *Mailboxes*, *Custom Recipients*, and *Distribution Lists* were Exchange containers, they would be replicated along with the objects contained in them to similar containers maintaining the directory hierarchy.

If you use an Exchange one-way CA, the second method is the better way to populate the Active Directory because you create fewer CAs and the system does most of the work for you. However, most enterprises need control over Exchange replication and object creation, and this requires multiple CAs. As you can tell, there are several combinations for which you can set up connection agreements to synchronize Exchange Server directory services with Active Directory.

Note   Multiple domains or sites do not always require creating a CA between every Windows 2000 Server domain and every Exchange Server site. When all Exchange mailboxes have their primary owner account in one domain, one CA can synchronize all Exchange sites into Active Directory.

If the ADC can match a mailbox to a Windows 2000 Server account in any domain it connects to, it will synchronize the two objects. Network resources are consumed by synchronization of directory objects between directories and by replication within the Active Directory and Exchange Server directory replication environments.

The ADC bridgehead server should be on the same LAN segment as a global catalog server, because the ADC searches a global catalog when it performs target-matching searches to avoid accidentally creating a corresponding Active Directory object in a domain. If the Exchange Server environment employs connector servers that do not host mailboxes, consider configuring these servers as ADC bridgehead servers, or creating a special Windows 2000 Server with Exchange 5.5 installed to act as the DSA bridgehead between Exchange and Active Directory.

Note   It is recommended that you install the Windows 2000 ADC before you upgrade to Exchange 2000. If no ADC exists, the configuration CA is automatically created, but because no other CAs are in place, Exchange 5.5 users would not appear in the global catalog and Exchange 2000 users cannot send them mail.

Installing and Configuring the Active Directory Connector

So much for the ABCs of ADC. This section outlines the basic steps to install the ADC at any company, using as an example the process used at All-Terrain Trucking.

If you've worked on multiple Windows NT domain and Exchange Server implementations, some of these steps may look familiar. However, many things have changed from Exchange Server 5.5 on Windows NT 4.0. These steps were used to implement the ADC at All-Terrain trucking:

1. Examine Windows NT domain structure and Exchange Server site topology.
2. Determine which directory service will manage object identity.
3. Perform Active Directory schema modifications.
4. Define objects for directory synchronization.
5. Map Exchange Server sites/containers to Active Directory domains/OUs.
6. Determine the attribute map between Active Directory and Exchange Server.
7. Set up the Active Directory Connectors.
8. Create connection agreements to populate Active Directory from Exchange.

9. Determine a schedule for directory replication and synchronization.

10. Create connection agreements for maintaining directory synchronization.

11. Secure directory services to prevent collisions and maintain identity.

Step 1: Examine Windows NT Domain Structure and Exchange Server Site Topology

To begin gathering information for the ADC connection agreements, you need to understand the Exchange 5.5 sites, Windows NT Server domains, and Windows 2000 Server Active Directory structures in your organization. You need to know how many Exchange Server sites you have, how they are managed, and whether they are candidates for synchronization. To synchronize those Exchange Server sites you need detailed information on their recipient containers and the objects to be synchronized.

For each Active Directory domain that will participate in directory synchronization, you need to install the ADC on a Windows 2000 Server global catalog server, member server, or domain controller. It is important to identify where mailboxes reside for users in each domain. Exchange Server sites may contain mailboxes that are associated with Windows NT Server accounts from multiple domains. In the ideal environment, you should upgrade each of these master account domains to Windows 2000 and the Active Directory before you deploy the ADC—to avoid creating duplicate AD accounts. For Exchange Server Custom Recipients, Distribution Lists, and Mailboxes that do not have a corresponding Active Directory user object, the ADC will create new objects in an Active Directory domain: you'll need to decide which domain that will be.

You may need to configure additional CAs as part of the ADC planning process so that all existing Exchange objects—including those mapped to Windows NT4.0 domains—are represented somehow in the Active Directory. For example, suppose an existing Exchange Site has Mailboxes for which the Primary Windows NT Account is mapped to a pure Windows NT4.0 domain. To make these accounts visible to Exchange 2000 mail recipients, you can configure a CA so that NT 4.0 accounts are duplicated in a Windows 2000 domain. These accounts can be configured as a Contact, User, or disabled User account. If they are not replicated to the Active Directory they will not be part of the global catalog that Exchange 2000 uses for locating recipients.

To facilitate upgrades and create an authoritative directory, All-Terrain Trucking chose to use the ADC to synchronize accounts from the entire Exchange organization (including the Windows NT 4.0 RETAIL domain) into Active Directory. For Mailboxes owned by users in the legacy RETAIL domain, the ADC will create disabled User accounts in the **corp.allterrain.tld** domain under OU=retail.

Step 2: Determine Which Directory Service Will Manage Object Identity

To deploy the Active Directory with the ADC you have to re-examine how you manage users and common directory information. The directory administration model currently used by most Exchange Server customers generally focuses on the Windows NT User Manager for Domains and Exchange Administrator tools. Now, the ADC provides a single method for managing information on security accounts, directory identity, and messaging from within Active Directory. You can administer mail recipient objects from Exchange Server, Active Directory, or from both directory services, and that means one of the first steps in your planning is to determine which directory service you want to administer which objects from.

At All-Terrain, the initial impulse was to continue managing objects through the Exchange Directory Service and Exchange Administrator interface. If you continue to manage objects from the Exchange Administrator, you should configure unidirectional CAs to populate and update Active Directory. Or you can deploy a single, one-way connection agreement to only one Exchange Server site and use it to synchronize the entire Exchange Server directory with Active Directory, eliminating the need to create and manage multiple CAs between every Exchange site. As long as the connection agreement is configured only to pull from Exchange into the Active Directory, you can select any Exchange Server site as a source container. By selecting all sites as source containers, you can synchronize the entire set of recipients in the Exchange Server directory.

All-Terrain's goal was to manage objects from the Active Directory, which mean that each CA had to be deployed to each existing Exchange Site (which assumes LDAP and RPC connectivity) and configured so that they can write to the Exchange Directory. Using the Active Directory for administration allows you to delegate administrative tasks to the attribute level, provides for richer user identification, and supplies better tools and scripts. And Exchange eventually will rely completely on the Active Directory. All-Terrain created a two-way connection agreement to administer users and be "move-safe" within Exchange. If the same object is modified in both directories, the most recent modification prevails, although it may take two synchronization cycles for this object to synchronize, depending upon whether it was modified before or during the first ADC synchronization cycle.

Another important fact is that the ADC handles the synchronization of deleted objects between the two directories differently than it handles other revised objects. By default, it will not synchronize the deletion of any object from the source directory to the target directory. Instead, it writes an import file to a disk containing the item to be deleted. An administrator can review the deleted objects in this file, and then import it, thereby deleting the set of target objects. You can directly synchronize object deletions between the two directories by selecting an option on the **Deletion** tab in **Properties** of the connection agreement property pages.

Step 3: Perform Active Directory Schema Modifications

To minimize potential issues and validate the schema modifications required for the Active Directory Connector, All-Terrain used the ADC Setup application to prime the directory with the **/schemaonly** switch. Priming the directory prior to setting up CAs and turning on replication avoids the chance that you might flood your network with excess traffic. Afterwards, they added custom **May Contain** attributes to the User class-schema for job code, store number, and sales boundaries.

Step 4: Define Objects for Directory Synchronization

You do not have to replicate objects within Exchange Server into the Active Directory. Some organizations use the ADC CAs to mask objects from an Exchange Site Global Address List (GAL). All-Terrain Trucking created some guidelines and objectives for the directory synchronization process between Exchange Server and Active Directory:

- Allow Active Directory as the primary replica of directory data
- Provide corporate LDAP directory services through Active Directory
- Allow all user identity administration through Active Directory
- Provide only necessary objects of interest to distinct Exchange environments
- Allow users, administrators, and developers accessibility to objects of interest
- Clean-up unnecessary containers and extinct foreign custom recipients

Having agreed on these guidelines, they had to decide how objects from Exchange Server would be represented in Active Directory. By default, an Exchange Server Mailbox mapped to a Windows NT 4.0 account will appear in the Exchange Directory as a mailbox, but will map across to the Active Directory as a mail-enabled Contact.

You can change this to either a User or a disabled User in the CA configuration. An Exchange Server Mailbox mapped to an Active Directory account appears as a Mailbox in the Exchange Directory and maps across to the Active Directory as a mailbox-enabled User (which means the attribute msExchHomeServerName is set). The Exchange Mailbox's Object-GUID attribute is set to the GUID of the Active Directory object, and the Active Directory object's *legacyExchangeDN* attribute is set to the Distinguished Name of the corresponding object in the Exchange Directory.

A Distribution List in the Exchange Directory will appear in the Active Directory as a mail-enabled Group (type: Distribution, scope: Universal), and a Custom Recipient (of any address type) in the Exchange Directory will appear as a mail-enabled Contact. The AD entry will have only an SMTP address; this is the primary SMTP proxy for non-SMTP Custom Recipients (that is, CCMAIL, MSMAIL, NOTES). For objects sourced from the Exchange Directory replicating to the Active Directory, All-Terrain modified the object fidelity class table this way:

Exchange Directory Object	Active Directory Object Class Mapping
Mailbox with Primary Active Directory Account	Mailbox-enabled User
Mailbox with Primary Windows NT Account	Mail-enabled disabled User in the target OU
Custom Recipient	Mail-enabled Contact in the target OU
Distribution List	Mail-enabled Group (type: Distribution, scope: Universal) in the target OU

Note Universal Groups are used because Distribution Lists may contain Users (Mailboxes) and contacts (Custom Recipients) synchronized to disparate domains. Since universal groups are replicated throughout the forest, using them can have a negative impact on global catalog replication in some environments. You may need to consider using the Active Directory Migration Tool to consolidate users into fewer domains, allowing the use of global groups instead of universal groups.

For objects sourced from the Active Directory replicating to the Exchange Directory, you can use this object fidelity class table:

Active Directory Object	Exchange Object Class Mapping
Mailbox-enabled User	Mailbox
Mail-enabled User	Custom Recipient in the target container
Non-mail-enabled User	*Not replicated*
Mail-enabled Contact	Custom Recipient in the target container
Non-mail-enabled Contact	*Not replicated*
Mail-enabled Group (type: Distribution)	Distribution List in the target container
Mail-enabled Group (type: Security)	Distribution List in the target container
Non-mail-enabled Group (type: Distribution)	*Not replicated*
Non-mail-enabled Group (type: Security)	*Not replicated*

Step 5: Map Exchange Server Sites/Containers to Active Directory Domains/OUs

This is one of the most important steps for any organization deploying the ADC. The objective is to couple the Exchange Directory Namespace and Container hierarchy with the Active Directory Namespace and OU hierarchy to create a logical path over which objects can travel between Exchange and Active Directory. CAs are based on these paths.

If you have a clean and simple Exchange container hierarchy, you can map entire Exchange Server sites directly to Active Directory OUs.

Note It is not recommended to use the Active Directory **Users** built-in container as a target because it does not support group policy objects and delegated security. If you have a complex Exchange Directory, then you may have to work with multiple maps to get things right.

Most enterprises need a complex map that accommodates LDAP structure, administration, and synchronization. All-Terrain used the container map below to map the Exchange container hierarchy to the Windows 2000 OU hierarchy. You can use it as a template for mapping your container to OU relationships.

AD domain = corp.allterrain.tld	Exchange site	Exchange container	NetBIOS domain
Ou=admin	N/A	N/A	N/A
Ou=home	HOMEOFFICE	Recipients	ACCOUNTS
Ou=logistics	LOGISTICS	Recipients	ACCOUNTS
Ou=stores	STORES	Recipients	ACCOUNTS
Ou=partners	HOMEOFFICE	Corp Friends	ACCOUNTS
Ou=remote	HOMEOFFICE	Recipients	ACCOUNTS
Ou=retail	RETAIL	Recipients	RETAIL

Note   An Exchange container can map to multiple Active Directory OUs and an Active Directory OU can map to multiple Exchange containers. You can control new account creation in either direction. For example, if the CA Attribute *msExchIsBridgeheadSite* = **True**, new accounts are read from Active Directory and created in Exchange if they don't already exist at replication time. If *msExchServerIIs Bridgehead* = **True**, new accounts are read from Exchange and created in the Active Directory if they don't already exist. These attributes are set using the "Is Primary" checkbox on the Advanced tab of the CA.

Step 6: Determine the Attribute Map Between Active Directory and Exchange Server

You can map attributes within Exchange Server directly to attributes within Active Directory or you can re-map them to new custom attributes within Active Directory. Each CA uses a table-based schema map for the majority of attributes on objects synchronized between the two directories. The default map is located on the ADC policy object in Active Directory. By modifying the policy, you can control the set of attributes synchronized from either directory as well as the set of rules used by the ADC to match objects in either directory. If an attribute value for an attribute to be mapped does not exist in the source directory, that mapping is ignored.

It is important to note that some object attributes *will not* synchronize, including Exchange Advanced Security settings and Access Control Lists (ACLs) in both Active Directory and Exchange.

If for business or technical reasons you do not want all attributes to be replicated on objects between the Exchange and Active Directory, you can adjust the property sheets of the ADC to hide the attributes from replication. Also, the ADC by default tries to match objects between the two directories based on the *NT-security-descriptor* field. In most cases this is fine, but if you want to change the attribute mappings (for example, match the Exchange alias name to the Active Directory user name) you can specify the attribute mapping rules or define a drop-through list containing many rules.

All-Terrain Trucking used all of the extended attributes in Exchange to hold rich identity information (such as job code, store number, and sales boundaries) on which they wanted to be able to perform Address Book lookups and LDAP queries. The attribute matching rules are held on the ADC's **Default ADC Policy** object (which is not CA-specific) in a binary large object (blob) attribute called *msExchServerXSchemaMap* (where X equals 1 for Active Directory to Exchange mapping and 2 for Exchange to Active Directory mapping). To facilitate automatic synchronization of these custom attributes to the new schema attributes within Active Directory, they made these changes to the object map:

Windows 2000 Attribute (LDAP Name) All Object Classes	Exchange Attribute (LDAP Name) All Object Classes
StoreNumber	Extension-Attribute-1
JobCode	Extension-Attribute-2
RemoteUser	Extension-Attribute-3
SalesDivision	Extension-Attribute-4
SalesRegion	Extension-Attribute-5
SalesDistrict	Extension-Attribute-6
extensionAttribute7	Extension-Attribute-7
extensionAttribute8	Extension-Attribute-8
extensionAttribute9	Extension-Attribute-9
extensionAttribute10	Extension-Attribute-10
extensionAttribute11	Extension-Attribute-11
extensionAttribute12	Extension-Attribute-12
extensionAttribute13	Extension-Attribute-13
extensionAttribute14	Extension-Attribute-14
extensionAttribute15	Extension-Attribute-15

How to Modify the msExchServerXSchemaMap

1. Modify the schema mapping files in the MSADC directory. LOCAL.MAP for *msExchServer2SchemaMap* or REMOTE.MAP for *msExchServer1SchemaMap*.

2. Save as Unicode or UTF-8.

3. Run LDAPMOD.EXE (from the *Microsoft Windows 2000 Resource Kit*) to import the mapping file into the binary attribute.

   a. Domain controller fqdn

   b. Simple Ldap bind for the administrator

   c. Administrator password

   d. Container path (i.e. CN=Default ADC Policy,CN=Active Directory Connections,CN=Microsoft Exchange,CN=Services,CN=Configuration, DC=Domain,DC=com)

   e. Attribute name (msExchServer2SchemaMap)

   f. Mapping file

4. Verify replication of attribute.

5. Verify replication of attribute.

Step 7: Set Up the Active Directory Connectors

To install the ADC, you need at least one Windows 2000 server, one Active Directory domain, and, at each connected site, at least one Exchange Server 5.5 with Service Pack 3. To deploy the ADC you also must consider how many ADC servers are required to replicate the data. An ADC can have CAs for multiple Active Directory domains, but each Active Directory domain in a separate site that will host synchronized mailbox objects should have a separate Active Directory Connector server configured to avoid ADC traffic across the WAN. Because the ADC server uses LDAP and RPC requests (the latter is used when writing to the Exchange Directory), it requires direct-IP connectivity. There are eight server configurations to choose from when you set up an Active Directory Connector within a domain. You can set up ADC on:

1. AD domain controller

2. AD domain controller with Exchange Server

3. AD global catalog

4. AD global catalog with Exchange Server

5. AD member server

6. AD member server with Exchange Server

7. AD member server with Exchange Server on AD domain controller

8. AD member server with Exchange Server on AD global catalog

Of these eight configurations, only 1, 3, 5, and 6 are truly scalable within an enterprise. For the best overall performance, configure the ADC as a member server with a high-speed connection to a global catalog for each domain the ADC will synchronize and Exchange Server installed to act as an ExDS bridgehead.

Putting the ADC on a domain controller can be a good idea for a single domain forest with medium intra-domain replication traffic; putting it on a global catalog can be a good idea for a multi-domain forest with medium intra-domain replication and light catalog replication.

To localize traffic and get the best performance out of the server, use bridgehead servers, which (like gateways) receive and forward traffic at each end of a connection agreement. All-Terrain created an ADC-ExDS bridgehead server to host all of the CAs by acting as a member of the corp.allterrain.tld domain and installing Exchange Server as a member of the HOMEOFFICE site. Since the Seattle location is very well connected and the majority of users are in the HOMEOFFICE site, the same ADC server will host CAs for the RETAIL Exchange site.

Step 8: Create Connection Agreements To Populate Active Directory from Exchange

Since All-Terrain upgraded a domain to Active Directory, they used the ADC to backfill directory data from the Exchange Server directory to the pre-existing Active Directory accounts. This allows them to map Exchange directory objects to security objects in Active Directory.

For this initial one-way agreement, All-Terrain synchronized all Mailboxes from the entire Exchange Server organization instead of synchronizing individual recipient containers. This CA was not configured to create new objects in Active Directory because the new OU hierarchy could not be maintained. To allow synchronization but prevent creation of new objects, clear the Primary Connection Agreement checkboxes on the **Advanced** tab of the CA.

Any time after the initial synchronization, you can change the OU hierarchy or the location of individual objects in the Active Directory. If you move objects to a new OU or new domain, the next time the ADC synchronizes, it will find the new locations and synchronize with the existing recipients—*if* it is within the search scope of defined import and export containers. After All-Terrain had created an OU-Container map and the ADC server, they created the following one-way connection agreement to populate Active Directory with Exchange information:

Attribute/CA	CA1 to HOMEOFFICE (corp.allterrain.tld)
Type	One-way
Source AD containers	N/A
Objects from AD	N/A
Custom Search Filter	N/A
Target Exchange container	N/A
Source Exchange containers	/o=All-Terrain /ou=HOMEOFFICE /o=All-Terrain /ou=LOGISTICS /o=All-Terrain /ou=STORES /o=All-Terrain /ou=RETAIL
Objects from Exchange	Mailboxes, Custom Recipients
Custom Search Filter	None
Target AD container	dc=corp, dc=allterrain, dc=tld
Exchange Primary CA	N/A
Windows Primary CA	NO

This was a good way to begin the ADC deployment because it pushed the established Exchange Server directory data into Active Directory without changing the production Exchange Server system. Once they had adequately populated the Active Directory, they were ready for new CAs to pull from Active Directory into Exchange. After the ADC completed one cycle, they moved the users into the new OU structure created in step 5.

Step 9: Determine a Schedule for Directory Replication and Synchronization

A single distributed directory repository (such as all Exchange 5.5 servers in the same organization) uses directory replication to keep all copies of the directory up-to-date. Directory synchronization can also make two disparate directory repositories appear as one. For example, two different Exchange organizations do not have knowledge of each other's recipients, but you can establish Inter-Org Dirsync with VIA, or the Inter-Org connector.

Of course, when the CA is synchronizing data between the two environments, the objects replicated will also change, thus causing replication in the native directory. You have to take this into account before configuring each CA.

When using Active Directory as the update master, you should reexamine the Exchange Directory replication schedule and set it for non-peak hours to allow for the initial replication of every object within the Exchange Directory. Once Active Directory becomes the update master, Exchange Server replicates only object changes.

Remember that when bulk updates or modifications are performed on the Active Directory, an attribute mapped to Exchange Server may trigger another mass replication event within Exchange. Remember too that intra-site replication cannot be scheduled or compressed: be mindful of how many objects are modified at any one time. The new site model manages Active Directory inter-site replication. Active Directory is efficient in that it replicates only changed attributes for an object. For example, before creating a two-way connection agreement, you could set all directory replication connector (DRC) schedules on the site to **Never** until intra-site replication completed the ADC updates, then enable one DRC at a time to throttle the directory inter-site traffic.

Each CA has its own schedule and you can set up individual CAs to schedule synchronization advantageously. If you synchronize more than 10,000 users or mailboxes, you can improve performance by setting up multiple CAs to synchronize different objects at different times.

Note   Groups and Distribution Lists require multiple queries (one per member) to synchronize successfully. Any sizeable CA that synchronizes Distribution Lists should be separate of and scheduled after CAs responsible for the member objects. This facilitates complete membership and faster synchronization.

If you make daily changes to either directory and do not need the changes to appear in the other directory until the next day, you can schedule synchronization for lower-use night hours. If you understand the internal replication schedules for both Active Directory and the Exchange Server directory, you can ensure timely and efficient use of resources by staggering ADC synchronization with respect to internal directory replication. If directory manipulation is commonly done at a specific time, customize synchronization to occur soon after (and only after) the changes are made.

Because All-Terrain uses Active Directory as the directory master, they created the serialized schedule below to complete all updates within 12 hours:

Time	Event
00:00	
01:00	
02:00	Batch updates to Active Directory at home site
03:00	ADC synchronization event (Exchange to AD)
04:00	Active Directory replication
05:00	ADC synchronization event (AD to Exchange)
06:00	Exchange Directory replication
07:00	
08:00	

Time	Event
09:00	
10:00	
11:00	
12:00	ADC synchronization event (Exchange to AD)
13:00	Active Directory replication
14:00	ADC synchronization event (AD to Exchange)
15:00	Exchange Directory replication
16:00	
17:00	
18:00	
19:00	Batch updates to Active Directory at home site
20:00	ADC synchronization event (Exchange to AD)
21:00	Active Directory replication
22:00	ADC synchronization event (AD to Exchange)
23:00	Exchange Directory replication

This schedule doesn't list each CA to be completed at each event. An ADC server on a dual processor Xeon 450 MHz with 512 MB RAM can process a two-way synchronization event at about 12,000 objects per hour. The same ADC server can process a one-way synchronization event at about 20,000 objects per hour. Distribution List membership is so varied and requires so many queries to complete that you should plan on these CAs processing about 5,000 objects per hour. Of course, the best way to create a schedule is to take a snapshot of your directories and then run tests in a lab environment.

Step 10: Create Connection Agreements for Maintaining Directory Synchronization

To maintain the OU hierarchy and facilitate the use of the Active Directory as the directory master, All-Terrain had to create multiple CAs from Exchange to Active Directory and from Active Directory to Exchange with special filters. The custom filters used require editing a CA attribute called *msExchServerXSearchFilter*, where *X* equals 1 for the Active Directory and 2 for the Exchange Directory. This string represents an RFC2254 rule (LDAP search filter).

Note   If you edit the CA after the filter is inserted, you may overwrite the filter. To avoid disrupting service, All-Terrain created the CAs during the batch process windows.

Attribute/CA	CA2 to HOMEOFFICE (corp.allterrain.tld)
Type	Two-way
Source AD containers	Ou=home, dc=corp, dc=allterrain, dc=tld
Objects from AD	Users, Contacts
Custom Search Filter	(!(RemoteUser=1))
Target Exchange container	/o=All-Terrain /ou=HOMEOFFICE /cn=Recipients
Source Exchange containers	/o=All-Terrain /ou=HOMEOFFICE /cn=Recipients
Objects from Exchange	Mailboxes, Custom Recipients
Custom Search Filter	(!(extension-attribute-3=1))
Target AD container	Ou=home, dc=corp, dc=allterrain, dc=tld
Exchange Primary CA	YES
Windows Primary CA	YES

Attribute/CA	CA3 to HOMEOFFICE (corp.allterrain.tld)
Type	Two-way
Source AD containers	Ou=home, dc=corp, dc=allterrain, dc=tld
Objects from AD	Groups
Custom Search Filter	None
Target Exchange container	/o=All-Terrain /ou=HOMEOFFICE /cn=Recipients
Source Exchange containers	/o=All-Terrain /ou=HOMEOFFICE /cn=Recipients
Objects from Exchange	Distribution Lists
Custom Search Filter	None
Target AD container	Ou=home, dc=corp, dc=allterrain, dc=tld
Exchange Primary CA	YES
Windows Primary CA	YES

Attribute/CA	CA5 to STORES (corp.allterrain.tld)
Type	Two-way
Source AD containers	Ou=stores, dc=corp, dc=allterrain, dc=tld
Objects from AD	Users, Contacts, Groups
Custom Search Filter	None
Target Exchange container	/o=All-Terrain /ou=STORES /cn=Recipients
Source Exchange containers	/o=All-Terrain /ou=STORES /cn=Recipients
Objects from Exchange	Mailboxes, Custom Recipients, Distribution Lists
Custom Search Filter	None
Target AD container	Ou=stores, dc=corp, dc=allterrain, dc=tld
Exchange Primary CA	YES
Windows Primary CA	YES

Attribute/CA	CA6 to HOMEOFFICE (corp.allterrain.tld)
Type	Two-way
Source AD containers	Ou=partners, dc=corp, dc=allterrain, dc=tld
Objects from AD	Users, Contacts, Groups
Custom Search Filter	None
Target Exchange container	/o=All-Terrain /ou=HOMEOFFICE /cn=Corp Friends
Source Exchange containers	/o=All-Terrain /ou=HOMEOFFICE /cn=Corp Friends
Objects from Exchange	Mailboxes, Custom Recipients, Distribution Lists
Custom Search Filter	None
Target AD container	Ou=partners, dc=corp, dc=allterrain, dc=tld
Exchange Primary CA	YES
Windows Primary CA	YES

Attribute/CA	CA7 to HOMEOFFICE (corp.allterrain.tld)
Type	Two-way
Source AD containers	Ou=remote, dc=corp, dc=allterrain, dc=tld
Objects from AD	Users, Contacts, Groups
Custom Search Filter	(&(RemoteUser=1))
Target Exchange container	/o=All-Terrain /ou=HOMEOFFICE /cn=Recipients
Source Exchange containers	/o=All-Terrain /ou=HOMEOFFICE /cn=Recipients
Objects from Exchange	Mailboxes, Custom Recipients, Distribution Lists
Custom Search Filter	(&(extension-attribute-3=1))
Target AD container	Ou=remote, dc=corp, dc=allterrain, dc=tld
Exchange Primary CA	YES
Windows Primary CA	YES

Attribute/CA	CA8 to RETAIL (corp.allterrain.tld)
Type	Two-way
Source AD containers	Ou=retail, dc=corp, dc=allterrain, dc=tld
Objects from AD	Users, Contacts, Groups
Custom Search Filter	None
Target Exchange container	/o=All-Terrain /ou=RETAIL /cn=Recipients
Source Exchange containers	/o=All-Terrain /ou=RETAIL /cn=Recipients
Objects from Exchange	Mailboxes, Custom Recipients, Distribution Lists
Custom Search Filter	None
Target AD container	Ou=retail, dc=corp, dc=allterrain, dc=tld
Exchange Primary CA	YES
Windows Primary CA	YES

Even though All-Terrain synchronizes a container to two Exchange Sites, which in turn are replicated to each other, they can set the *This is the primary connection to the connected Exchange Organization* flag to **true** on all of the CAs because they use filters to mask objects. Without the filters, setting more than one primary connection flag would cause the ADC to replicate the same Contact and Group objects to each Exchange Site, which would result in duplicate entries in the Exchange GAL.

Note   This is a highly controlling CA configuration. You may not require anything this drastic in your organization. All-Terrain implemented these to maintain a strict structure that could be used by other directory-enabled applications.

Step 11: Secure Directory Services To Prevent Collisions and Maintain Identity

The last step is to secure the Exchange directories so that only the Exchange administrator, the Exchange service account, and the ADC service account can make updates to the Exchange Directory. Verify administrator permissions on the Exchange ORG, SITE, and Configuration containers. As with any security policy, change the Exchange service account password and Exchange admin password. The objective of Exchange security is to minimize the possibility of unknown or unscheduled changes being made to the now "down-level" directory. Active Directory security can be tricky with the ADC, because the administrator bit must be set and delegation is required to each domain.

From the Trenches: Using the Active Directory Connector

I always recommend using the */schemaonly* switch before you install any schema modifying application. It separates setup into two stages and allows the Active Directory (NTDS) to replicate the schema changes before the application services are installed. To use it you must have Schema Admin security privileges.

The ADC setup uses some older NetBios domain APIs and requires NetBios name resolution. During our production rollout, WINS had a corrupt record that prevented the ADC from completing setup successfully and returned the error message "Server is not operational." We used LMHOSTS files to preload the PDC server IP address and domain name to work around the WINS error.

The ADC service account requires domain admin rights in the domain where the ADC server is a member, local admin rights to the ADC server, and admin rights to the configuration container in the forest (Enterprise Admin by default). The ADC stores all CAs in the configuration container and creates an LDAP trigger that notifies the MSADC service of any changes to the ADC settings. These security privileges are a little heavier than normally required by a service, so keep the account and password secure.

When configuring the ADC with a two-way CA, directory updates may appear to stop working. Keep in mind that the ADC was originally designed and optimized to synchronize from Exchange Server 5.5 (ExDS) into NTDS. One-way CAs are more efficient at processing replication simply because they have only one mapping to complete. Two-way agreements take much longer to complete, and begin by synchronizing from ExDS into NTDS, then finish by pulling from NTDS into ExDS. This means that changes made from Exchange will always replicate into Active Directory on a two-way CA and could overwrite changes made in Active Directory.

Multiple CAs may synchronize the same objects if they draw from the same source container in NTDS or ExDS. We created multiple two-way connection agreements that have different NTDS source and targets pointing to the same ExDS source and targets. After the first run, each CA synchronizes the same data from ExDS into NTDS. This is because the CA starts from Exchange, ignores the signature, and replicates all objects that match the filter within the container.

We configured a CA to bring mailboxes into Active Directory as users, but some of the mailboxes had Windows NT 4 accounts as owners. When the ADC found a mailbox, it created a user account within the Active Directory (regardless of ownership) based on the Primary CA to Windows Domain setting. Windows NT 4.0 doesn't have a method to distinguish between disabled users and normal users. This causes problems when the ADC is used to populate Active Directory by creating disabled users (as recommended), since a Windows NT4 Server administrator can't tell if the account is valid. These users also have two SIDs; one in the Windows NT 4.0 domain and a new one in Active Directory created as a result of ADC replication. The passwords between the two accounts are not synced, and only one SID is allowed access to the mailbox (the primary owner from Windows NT 4.0). These issues will remain until the users are ready to be migrated and then you can use ADClean.exe (included on the Exchange 2000 CD under the support directory) to merge the two accounts and assign one of them as the "Primary NT" account for each corresponding Exchange mailbox. By default the original Windows NT 4.0 account will be assigned as primary.

Each connection agreement allows you to set the LDAP page size for each direction. We used 60 for both page sizes (NTDS and ExDS) to maximize memory utilization and minimize the effect of network-related errors. We could have used 100 against NTDS due to the quality of the domain controller's connectivity and hardware. The LDAP page size is directly proportional to the amount of available RAM on each system (as the page size increases more buffers are used).

The Active Directory Connector has two important tuning parameters that prevent it from burying the NTDS with LDAP additions and searches. You should change these parameters only during a known bulk update period or when the global catalog hardware is oversized for the forest. The settings are located under HKLM\System\CurrentControlSet\Services\MSADC and are not created by default.

- REG_DWORD   Sync Sleep Delay (secs)
- REG_DWORD   Max Continuous Sync (secs)

Sync Sleep Delay (secs) says how long the ADC is going to pause between replication period, and Max Continuous Sync (secs) says how long each replication period is going to be. Both default to 300 seconds. This creates a 5-minute-on/5-minute-off replication cycle that allows the NTDS to process searches and maintain responsiveness as a domain controller. Since we scheduled the initial bulk synchronization event to take place after hours, when the domain controllers wouldn't have much to do, we changed the sync sleep delay to 60 seconds to allow the ADC to work harder and complete faster. We then changed the registry entries back and stop/start-ed the MSADC service before the outage was over.

For large containers, you always want to separate User synchronization from Group synchronization. Since Groups depend on User membership, Users should always replicate before Groups. Group membership is maintained with back-linked attributes, the *Members* attribute on the Group and the *MemberOf* attribute on the member object (User or Group). If a User object is replicated before the Group object is created, the *MemberOf* attribute is kept in a special attribute called *UnmergedAtts* (unmerged attributes). Once the Group object is created, the Group CA populates the *Members* attribute of the Group and the *MemberOf* attribute of the member object. If the Group contains members that don't yet exist, they are placed in the *UnmergedAtts* attribute of the Group. If these attributes are somehow deleted or corrupted, group membership will not be completely synchronized until a forced re-replication of the entire directory is completed.

With diagnostic logging set to anything but none, an event is logged for every object to be synchronized. If an object doesn't exist in the target directory, or the target DS time out, there is an 8033 event (no such object or object not found) in the application log. Once the object is created or modified successfully, the log shows an 8035 event (successfully added or successfully modified) in the application log. Note: the ADC has immensely detailed logging that can fill up 20 MB of application logs really fast. I suggest that you use minimal logging on all components initially, but change to none after the initial synchronization is complete.

Summary of Active Directory Connector

All-Terrain's implementation of Active Directory with the Active Directory Connector caused no loss of service. They used the ADC to populate the Active Directory with Exchange attributes. They established an OU hierarchy and masked uninteresting objects from containers that were not maintained properly. Active Directory is now the master replica and is primed as the corporate LDAP server. All user identity administration should now be completed through Active Directory. (See Figure 8.7 on page 351.)

Best practices:

- Create a dedicated ADC-ExDS bridgehead for large domains or Exchange sites.

- On anything over 5,000 always synchronize users before groups with different CAs.

- Increase the LDAP page size to 60 or higher. The setting you use is directly proportional to the amount of RAM available on your domain controllers and Exchange servers. As page size increases, more buffers are used.

Under heavy use the ADC performed exceptionally well. Almost every issue that came up was due to stressing the NTDS with prolonged LDAP queries and thousands of additions. The All-Terrain team was worried initially because of apparent pauses in replication, but later learned that this is tunable and that pausing helps the NTDS "catch its breath."

For detailed instructions on how to install and configure the ADC in your environment, see Paul Bowden's white paper "PT101 – Windows 2000 & Exchange 2000—Deploying the Active Directory Connector."

Planning for Exchange 2000

Exchange 2000 is more than just an upgrade. Its changes, some of which are architectural, can affect an upgrade depending on the type of connectors in use, how long you need to coexist with the current Exchange system, extent of public folder and distribution list use, in-place security features, etc.

For example if you currently use IMS as a connector between two Exchange sites and upgrade the bridgehead servers to Exchange 2000, the IMS will automatically be converted to an Exchange 2000 SMTP connector and users will be unaware of any changes. A site connector would be converted to a routing group connector. X.400 connectors that use TP4 however, will not work. Neither will most third party connectors unless the manufacturer provides an upgrade to support Exchange 2000.

Exchange 2000 Uses the Active Directory

Exchange 2000 does not include a directory service of its own, relying instead on the Windows 2000 Server Active Directory for object browsing, security, and name resolution. If you have already deployed Exchange Server 5.5, co-existence between the Exchange 5.5 directory and the new Active Directory will be a vital prerequisite for the Exchange 2000 upgrade process.

Along with the Active Directory, Exchange 2000 relies heavily upon the global catalog for locating recipients.

Exchange 2000 ADC Update

The Windows 2000 Server ADC synchronizes objects in the Exchange Site naming context (recipients containers, etc.) to the Active Directory. Exchange 2000 Server installs an updated ADC that also synchronizes data from the Configuration naming context, providing support for mixed-version Exchange sites and downstream routing.

Before Upgrading to Exchange 2000

First you have to decide which upgrade method to use: in-place, move mailbox, or swing. The current recommendation is to upgrade mailbox and PF servers first, then IMS connector/site connector boxes, then the server running the ADC.

If you have multiple forests, you will need to provide some sort of external directory synchronization between Exchange 2000 organizations, because Exchange 2000 uses global catalogs (which have forest-wide scope) instead of the Global Address List to look up users.

Exchange 2000 converts address book views to address lists, but address lists created in Exchange 2000 are not converted back into address book views. Exchange 5.5 and Exchange 2000 maintain their own offline address books.

Exchange 2000 public folder permissions are more granular than Exchange 5.5 permissions and can cause security problems when replicated back to Exchange if you assign permissions that are available on both platforms. The current recommendation is to create permissions only on Exchange 2000 servers.

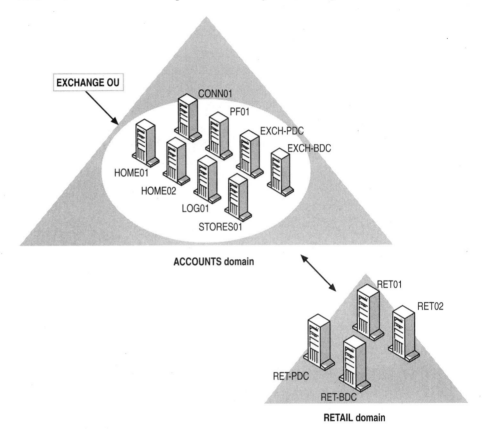

Figure 8.7   Final domain design after upgrade and restructure.

Conclusion

All-Terrain's upgrade to Windows 2000 and collapse of the Exchange messaging domain went smoothly. Users experienced only a short downtime, which was restricted to non-peak late-night weekend hours. This was acceptable at All-Terrain Trucking, but you need to consider how downtime will affect your environment.

Lessons Learned

- Careful planning and thorough lab testing were crucial. They are *always* crucial.

- If you have an Exchange messaging resource domain to which the Exchange service account is local (rather than in a trusted master account domain) you should *not* collapse it into a Windows 2000 domain. Instead, consider upgrading the Exchange messaging resource domain to Windows 2000, upgrading all the Exchange servers to Windows 2000 member servers, upgrading all Exchange servers to Exchange 2000, and *then* moving them to a different domain to consolidate resources. Because Exchange 2000 uses local system accounts as service accounts, you should be able to move Exchange 2000 servers between domains at will and still start services and administer servers. Keep in mind that this was not tested and that you need to verify it in your environment.

- Back up and restore any Exchange servers you can't afford to lose. Verify the backups.

- Test your upgrade plan in a lab first, using the servers restored from production as your test environment.

- Keep the Exchange resource domain PDC around until you are sure you have no account-related problems with mailbox accounts, Exchange administrator permissions, PF permissions, Exchange service accounts, site connector and X.400 over-ride accounts, and organizational forms.

- If you decide to change the name of the Active Directory DNS root to something other than the name of your existing DNS root zone, existing clients will not be able to locate new Windows 2000 resources, and new Windows 2000 clients will not be able to locate existing clients and servers via DNS. You can work around this by modifying all client and server DNS suffix search order lists to include both DNS zone names: at All-Terrain, this was **corp.allterrain.tld** and **allterrain.tld**. You could also delete the DNS root zone and set up the Windows 2000 DNS zone to forward unresolvable requests to the existing DNS server.

- If you have to troubleshoot Exchange issues after upgrading your messaging resource domain to Windows 2000, make sure that services are starting up with a valid account. In testing, All-Terrain encountered situations where only SA would start up using a valid domain service account. They fixed this by starting the Exchange services with the domain Administrator account—which always seemed to work, but for reasons unknown.

- Any mailboxes that had accounts in the Exchange resource domain configured as the Primary Windows NT account no longer worked after the resource domain was collapsed. Assigning a valid account from the new domain restored access.

- Although it's not necessary, All-Terrain got good results by creating a DNS zone and enabling it to Allow Updates *before* they ran DCPROMO. When they let DCPROMO create the zone, it sometimes created a DNS *domain*. This problem should disappear in production versions of Windows 2000.

- The Active Directory Connector allows you to migrate Exchange directory recipients, distribution lists and custom recipient objects to Active Directory quickly while maintaining identity information from Exchange.

- The ADC is required when upgrading to Exchange 2000 and is used to replicate Exchange configuration settings.

- Early testing with the Active Directory Migration Tool indicate that it may resolve the issues with Exchange service accounts and avoid all the steps outlined in the *From the Trenches* section on collapsing resource domains. The tool is available on www.microsoft.com.

- When installing the Windows 2000 ADC, security is the biggest issue. You need to have Administrator privileges on the local machine and to all three naming contexts: Configuration, Schema, and Domain.

- The ADC has a very light memory footprint (maxed at about 20 MB) and uses processor more than RAM or disk. Currently, the ADC implements USNChanged queries with an LDAP sort order control to retrieve updates in the same order of change. This requires the NTDS to server-side sort the response, which takes much more processor time. Microsoft is considering removing the sort order control from ADC queries to improve DS response times. This could mean that certain changes will be not be implemented in ExDS in the same order from NTDS.

- The ADC uses LDAP directly against Active Directory and Exchange. Compression is not supported.

- When the ADC is installed and a CA is created for a down-level domain that contains user accounts configured as "Primary NT" accounts on Exchange mailboxes, upgrading the down-level domain to Windows 2000 creates duplicate accounts. You can avoid duplicate objects in the Active Directory by upgrading the down-level domain to Windows 2000 before installing the ADC. If you can't avoid duplicate accounts, use **ADClean.exe**—located on the Exchange 2000 CD—to reconcile the duplicate accounts and merge them into a single account in what was the original down-level domain. This is necessary to avoid breaking the "Primary NT" account status on the Exchange mailboxes.

C H A P T E R   9

Active Directory and Novell NetWare NDS

*By David Skinner
and Sean Gordon,
Microsoft
Consulting
Services—
Scotland, U.K.*

A mere decade ago, when PC-based server technology was in its infancy, PC network operating systems provided simple file and print services: users stored data files on centrally managed servers, and printed documents on printers that were either connected to the file servers, or directly to the network. Access to these server-based resources was controlled through use of user IDs with associated access control lists (ACLs). Although IDs and ACLs are still used today, the early systems stored individual copies of the user database and access control lists on each server. When additional servers were added to the infrastructure, an administrator had to manually recreate user IDs on each new server and assign the appropriate access control rights.

When Microsoft introduced Windows NT, it caused a sea of change in the role of the PC-based server for the following reasons:

- Windows NT was both an application and file/print server in the form of a preemptive, multi-tasking, network-integrated operating system that hosted network applications—in addition to the traditional file and print services.

- Windows NT enhanced the domain model (originally introduced by LAN Manager 2.0). The domain eliminated the need to provide a user accounts database on every server. Instead, a single copy of the database was hosted on one or more domain controllers, and accessed by the resource servers and desktop PCs. With the inclusion of trusts (enabling cross-domain authentication), Windows NT provided the administrator with a single point of account creation, and the users with a single ID and password that provided access to all appropriate resources throughout the enterprise.

What You'll Find in This Chapter

- Overview of the network directory

- Building blocks of directory design

- Comparison of Active Directory and NDS technology

- Comparison of Active Directory and NDS directory design

In its day the concept of a domain was revolutionary, but since then software, hardware, infrastructure, and enterprise demands have moved on. From an information technology perspective, today's enterprises are far larger, with thousands of users and associated desktop PCs, all requiring access to the corporate network. Instead of merely sending and retrieving files from file/print servers, desktops now interoperate with databases, e-mail servers, Web servers, fax systems, application servers, and more.

As enterprise networks continue to expand, administrators require a modular and scalable mechanism to manage the environment. A network directory can provide this service by representing desktops, servers, users, and peripherals as a cohesive unit that mirrors the logical structure of the enterprise. Aside from the administrative benefits, the network directory aids the user by providing a quick and efficient mechanism to locate data or resources within the enterprise.

Windows 2000 delivers a Microsoft network directory solution in the form of Active Directory. Based on the assumption that you already understand Novell's NDS, this chapter discusses the Active Directory concepts from an NDS perspective. It explains Active Directory terminology, discusses the NDS/Active Directory design differences, and explains how to migrate users from NDS into Active Directory.

Network Directory Overview

In simple terms, a network directory is a database containing information about all entities that interact with a corporate network. In addition to user information (such as UserID, email address, job description, address, etc.)—application configuration and infrastructure details are also represented. Unlike NT domains (which have a fixed schema), a network directory is extensible, meaning that the database schema can be extended and grow with the demands of the enterprise.

A network directory aims to consolidate the management of the information technology infrastructure into a single cohesive unit. Figure 9.1 illustrates a typical scenario, in which the directory manages details of applications, servers, network devices, external directories, and user information. For administrators, the directory provides a central point from which to manage and control access to all network resources. For users, the directory provides a central point from which to locate information such as another user's e-mail address, a network printer location, a file, etc.

Prior to the release of Windows 2000, Windows NT user details were stored and managed in the domain-based security accounts manager (SAM). SAM was designed with one aim—the storage and retrieval of Windows NT user account data. For this reason, it did not provide a mechanism of extending its schema to include additional (enterprise specific) user detail. The key distinction between NT4 domains and Active directory is that Active Directory is concerned with extensible end-to-end enterprise management of all resources (including Windows NT), whereas legacy domains are focused purely on Windows NT user management.

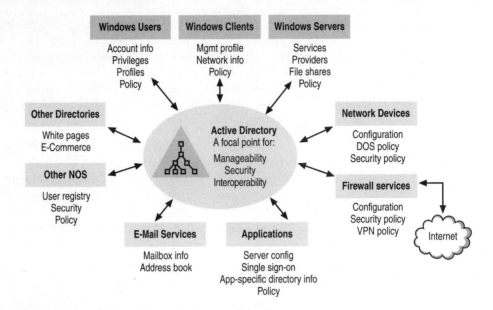

Figure 9.1   Typical Network Directory Implementation.

Analysis of enterprise organizational structures reveals that no two companies are organized in exactly the same way. For example, reporting lines, geographical layout, business function, and customer requirements differ on an enterprise-by-enterprise basis. Despite this, a network directory aims to logically represent each enterprise it will manage, requiring that the directory service architecture be sufficiently modular to enable its integration in all environments—without placing artificial constraints on the directory design.

Active Directory and NDS achieve this modularity through adoption of concepts defined in the X.500 recommendations. The X.500 recommendations are a series of ISO/ITU documents, providing a framework for development of a scalable directory service. Some concepts brought forward from the X.500 recommendations are as follows:

The Schema: Objects, Classes, and Attributes

Directories aim to store information about many different types of real world entities. Typical examples include users, computers, printers, etc. Entities are represented within the directory as objects.

Objects (or instances) are derived from object-classes, and there is a different class for each different type of entity. The object-class can be thought of as a template for the object since attributes are associated with it that defines specific properties of the real-world entity. Figure 9.2 shows a simplified view of attributes associated with the "user" object.

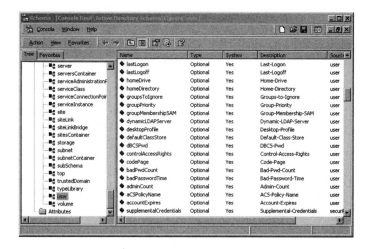

Figure 9.2   User object and associated attributes.

The schema formally defines the relationship between classes and attributes. The schema can be extended to include new relationships.

In order to ensure a globally interoperable directory implementation that can interact with other (non-Microsoft) directories, each object-class or attribute is assigned an OID. OIDs are globally unique object identifiers (issued by the International Standards Organization) that ensure each new object-class or attribute is assigned a code that guarantees to be unique throughout the world. When an organization wishes to extend the directory schema, they should apply to the ISO for appropriate OIDs.

Hierarchy and Containers

All large-scale enterprises organize themselves around some form of hierarchy to increase the efficiency of management from a business unit, geographical, or task-based perspective. Network directories are often based upon a hierarchical model, to enable logical grouping of resources, and delegation of administrative control. Figure 9.3 illustrates an example directory structure.

The X.500 directory recommendations define several types of container objects such as Country, Organization, Location, and Organizational Unit. In the above example, organizational unit (OU) containers represent the real-world business hierarchy within the directory. The OUs may contain additional OUs, or subordinate objects such as users, computer, servers, printers, etc.

Aside from the formation of hierarchy, OUs can be used to assign configuration data to subordinate objects. The benefit of using OUs to assign configuration data is that users automatically inherit the configuration simply by being a member of the container.

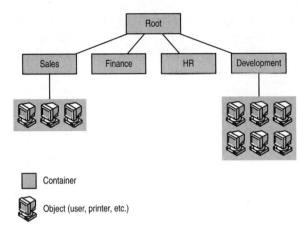

Figure 9.3   Example directory structure.

By using OUs to define hierarchy, directory-based entities mirror their real-life counterparts from a management perspective. For example, if John Smith changes jobs and moves from **Human Resources** to **Marketing**, the network administrator can simply move John from the **Human Resource** container into the **Marketing** container. If configuration data has been associated with the containers, John will automatically inherit the appropriate configuration set.

Security and Delegation

The network directory can provide an integrated security mechanism, allowing administrators to place restrictions on directory objects or attributes to achieve granular control over the dataset. Attribute-level security means that all attributes relating to a single entity can be stored in the same object without compromising security, since only appropriate personnel can view private attributes such as salary, etc.

Through a combination of granular security and hierarchy, Windows 2000 can delegate a (definable) subset of administrative rights to OUs. For example, you could delegate the "change password" right to the team leaders of the Human Resource department, enabling them to reset passwords for users within their teams. Since only the "change password" right would be delegated, and the scope of this delegation only applies to the Human Resource department, overall system security is not compromised.

Replication and Synchronization

Since the network directory represents all entities that interact with the corporate network, it becomes a focal point for management, authentication, configuration, and data location. Given the criticality of its role, the directory must be available at all times—especially in large-scale or geographically separated environments where availability, performance, and reliability are prime concerns.

High performance and reliability are achieved by replicating (or shadowing) the directory onto multiple directory servers throughout the enterprise. Placing local copies (replicas) of the directory close to its user population increases performance by optimizing use of the LAN/WAN infrastructure. Reliability is automatically achieved through the presence of the additional replicas. If a single directory server fails, the remaining servers will provide continued directory access.

Active Directory and NDS support multi-master updates, meaning that the directory can be updated on any directory server holding a writable replica. Replication ensures that the modified object (or attribute) is propagated to all remaining replicas. In the unlikely event that different users on different directory servers modify the same object at the same time, the replication engine must resolve this conflict and propagate only one update.

Partitioning

As use of the network directory expands to include a large number of objects over many geographical regions, it becomes impractical (and undesirable) to place complete replicas on all directory servers throughout the enterprise.

Consider the scenario in Figure 9.4. Users in Germany probably don't need information on a printer located in the UK finance department. Assuming a non-partitioned directory design, one or more complete directory replicas would be placed at each location throughout the world; all directory updates (regardless of relevance) would be forwarded to all geographic locations. This ensures consistency, but it incurs needless WAN traffic, server loading, and administrative overhead.

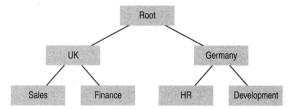

Figure 9.4   Replication scenario.

Partitioning overcomes this problem by dividing the global directory structure into sub-trees. Each sub-tree (partition) contains a geographically relevant portion of the directory, which can be hosted on local directory servers. In the example above, each geographical location is a partition. Partitioning does not reduce the quantity of information available from a global perspective; it merely hosts the locally relevant information at optimal locations, providing a balance between availability, management, and communication requirements. If a user requires information from a remote partition (for example, a user in Germany requiring information about a UK printer), the directory service retrieves it seamlessly. Although this action will incur network activity to retrieve the information, it is more network-efficient than global replication.

Comparing NDS and Active Directory

Using the basic building blocks discussed above, Microsoft and Novell have developed competing network directory products—Active Directory and NDS. Both are scalable and fault-tolerant, robust directory services that are integrated into the network operating system. This section examines how these building blocks have been implemented in Active Directory and NDS.

Container Objects

Container objects enable the formation of tree structures, providing hierarchy and structure to the directory. Subordinate objects such as users, computers, printers, etc. can be placed at appropriate levels within the tree, representing the object's real-life hierarchical position. Active Directory and NDS both support container objects. NDS supports four variants, whereas Active Directory supports one—the organizational unit. As you will see from the sub-sections below, Active Directory loses no functionality over NDS.

Country (NDS Only)

Multinational companies can use the NDS *country* object to represent separate geographical regions within a unified global directory tree. The country object is optional, but if implemented one or more countries can reside directly beneath the NDS root.

The country object is based on the ISO3166 naming standard, which identifies each country using a two-letter identifier. NDS does not enforce adherence to the standard, it merely checks for the presence of two characters. The country object can complicate directory design because it:

- Increases the depth of the directory tree
- Imposes a geographical design
- Can increase design complexity
- Cannot easily represent cross-geographical activity. For instance, if a company has UK and US marketing departments and the UK reports to the US, the model could not easily represent this.

Locality (NDS Only)

The *locality* object represents geographical regions within the directory structure. For example, if you define the UK as a *country* object, you can define sub-locations (London, Edinburgh, Manchester, etc.) as locality objects. You can place locality objects directly beneath root, country, organization, and organizational unit objects. They are optional and are not generally recommended for use in NDS because the Novell administration utilities do not fully support their use.

Organization Objects (NDS) and Domains (Active Directory)

Every NDS tree must contain at least one *organization* object. Placed beneath the root or country object, it defines the namespace of the enterprise. Generally, only one organizational object is used, but if multiple namespaces are required then multiple organization objects can be implemented.

Rather than implement an organization object, Active Directory defines namespace through creation of a root domain. The root domain is the first domain in the domain tree, and defines the namespace and schema for all subordinate domains. If multiple namespaces are required, then multiple root domains can be created—forming a forest.

Figure 9.5 shows that a forest is a set of domain trees, each with different root domains. Since each root domain defines the namespace for its subordinates, the namespace for each forest is unique—enabling you to represent multiple companies within one directory system. Although the namespace is unique, the schema is shared throughout the forest enabling consistent use of directory-enabled applications.

northwind.tld   microsoft.tld   expedia.tld

Figure 9.5   Forest.

Organizational Units (Active Directory and NDS)

Organizational units are the most frequently used container objects in Active Directory and NDS, and perform the same management task in both. In NDS, you can place an organizational unit beneath locality, organization, and other organizational unit objects. In Active Directory, organizational units are contained within a domain and can be nested beneath other organizational units.

Organizational units provide several important benefits to the network administrator:

- Configuration data can be assigned with the OU. Subordinate objects such as users or computers will automatically inherit this configuration through association with the container. Windows 2000 provides this facility through group policy objects, enabling detailed configuration of desktop or application environments. Group policies follow the inheritance model meaning that the child objects can inherit policy associated with parent objects.

- Organizational units can provide administrative boundaries. In Windows 2000, a rich set of permissions can be associated with each organizational unit. Permissions can be delegated to appropriate users providing them with a subset of administrative control for an organizational unit. For example, the "change password" right could be assigned to the team leaders of the Human Resource department, enabling them to reset password for people within their team.

Partitioning

Partitioning divides the directory into sub-trees enabling them to be hosted on separate servers, increasing access efficiency and reducing network traffic. Active Directory and NDS both implement partitioning, although each does so in a different manner.

In Active Directory, the basic unit of partitioning is the domain. To illustrate this, suppose a fictitious company (Northwind) has facilities in London, Edinburgh, and Manchester, and subsidiary offices in America and Asia. The WAN facilities are already overused, so Northwind wants to create a network directory solution that minimizes WAN requirements.

Figure 9.6 shows how this objective is achieved by geographically partitioning the directory. A root domain (NORTHWIND.TLD) has been created which defines the namespace and schema. Child domains have been created for each geographical location, and are hosted on separate domain controllers. Each child domain represents a geographical partition.

Note   The fictional examples in this chapter use the extension .TLD (top level domain) in the company domain names rather than .COM to insure that none of the domains are mistaken for those of any actual company or organization.

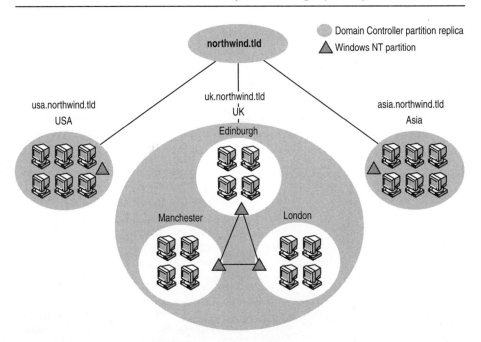

Figure 9.6   Northwind solution.

In NDS, the first partition (the [ROOT] partition) is automatically created when the first server is installed. All subsequent partitions must be created manually.

Using the NDS Manager tool, NDS partitions are created by selecting a subordinate container object (generally an Organizational Unit) and performing a split operation. The split creates a child partition (separate database) that assumes the name of the selected object. The selected object becomes a partition root, and all subordinate objects become members of the new partition.

The flexibility of this approach means that the complete directory hierarchy can be modeled within the root partition. Once complete, partitions can be created and delegated to specific directory servers.

Figure 9.7 shows how this can be done. Northwind is represented by the organizational object NORTHWIND, which defines the namespace for all subordinates within the tree. Beneath NORTHWIND, organizational units define the logical (geographical) hierarchy (UK, USA, Asia). Each geographical region has been partitioned to avoid unnecessary WAN traffic, and at least three replicas are located around the network to provide resilience.

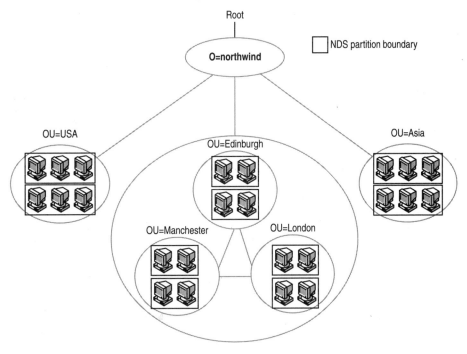

Figure 9.7   Process.

Key Points

- Active Directory partitioning is based on the *domain*. Domains implement an efficient indexing mechanism enabling storage and retrieval of millions of objects per partition. NDS (prior to version 8) stores object data in flat (non-indexed) files, imposing a performance limitation of about 5000 objects per partition. In a large-scale directory implementation, it is likely that NDS will require more partitions than Active Directory.

- In NDS, creation or merging of partitions is achieved via the NDS Manager utility. The utility provides a simple GUI interface enabling easy modification of the partition structure while the directory is operational. The simplicity of the interface belies the complexity of the action, and such modifications must be implemented with extreme care in a live environment.

  In Active Directory, creating partitions requires the addition of new domains. Domains require the configuration of dedicated domain controllers imposing a larger deployment overhead, but providing longer-term benefits in terms of scalability.

- In NDS, each directory server can host multiple partitions; Active Directory domain controllers can only host a single partition (domain). Since Active Directory can optimally support larger partitions than NDS, it is unlikely that an administrator will need to partition Active Directory purely based on the number of objects it contains. This means that an Active Directory-based design is likely to require fewer partitions than NDS.

- Design recommendations limit the number of objects in an NDS partition, and do not allow the contents of a container to span partitions. Administrators must design organizational unit hierarchies carefully to fit within partitions, or they may later have to restructure and rebalance the partitions manually as objects are added and partitions fill up. This limitation raises the specter of the administrator having to modify the logical design of the directory to compensate for limitations on the underlying directory service.

Catalogs

Partitioning places data at the most appropriate location within the enterprise, providing a balance between data availability and network usage. Even with the best partitioning strategy, there is likely to be a subset of partitioned data that will be of interest to the entire company—for example, user contact details. Catalogs provide a mechanism of delivering this data to each partition, eliminating the need to traverse the network for commonly used (cross-partition) data.

In Active Directory, each domain has a global catalog—a read-only replica of key attributes from all other domains in the forest. For example, in Figure 9.8 the global catalog in UK.NORTHWIND.TLD contains a read-only replica of objects from ASIA.NORTHWIND.TLD, USA.NORTHWIND.TLD, and the NORTHWIND.TLD root domain. Global Catalogs replicate an administrator-defined subset of objects from remote partitions into local partitions, allowing tree-wide queries to be resolved from the local catalog. Administrators can specify which domain controllers hold global catalog information, and the Schema Manager tool can specify which attributes will be replicated to the catalog. When an object is added or updated in the tree or forest, the update is automatically propagated via the standard replication process.

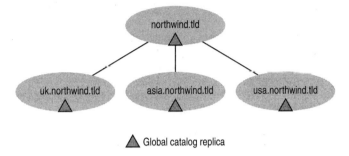

Figure 9.8   Active Directory global catalog replica.

As shown in Figure 9.9, NDS also provides catalogs but the implementation is significantly different. Unlike Active Directory, catalogs are generated by a scheduled "dredging" process, which collates objects from remote partitions and copies them into a local catalog. Catalogs do not participate in the NDS replication cycle, meaning that attribute updates are not automatically propagated. Moreover, the contents of the catalog cannot be incrementally updated; it must be completely rebuilt at the next dredging cycle.

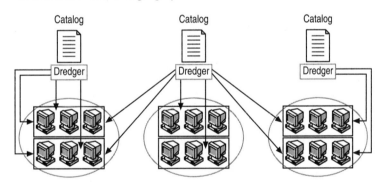

Figure 9.9   NDS catalogs.

Key Points

- The global catalog is stored as part of the Active Directory and is updated and replicated with the directory, ensuring data consistency.

- Storing the global catalog as part of the Active Directory ensures that there is a single method of accessing all directory objects.

- In Active Directory, objects and attributes in the global catalog retain their original access control lists, preventing catalog operations from compromising security. In NDS, however, dredged objects lose their original access control properties because access control rights are applied to the entire catalog. So users with access to a catalog also have access to all its objects and attributes—even objects to which they may not originally have had access.

- NDS catalogs are not based on incremental updates. When the Dredger is executed, it begins with an empty file, queries each partition individually, then replaces the old version of the file with the updated version.

- Dredging requires significant processing and network traffic, so NDS catalogs should be rebuilt in 24-hour cycles, with the dredge performed at off-peak times. This solves resource issues, but increases the probability that the NDS catalog will be out-of-synch with the directory.

- In NDS, efficiency and security may require the use of multiple catalogs, each representing a different view (and security settings) of the objects.

Replication Overview

Active Directory and NDS provide a multi-master directory service, meaning that objects or attributes can be modified on any writable replica and the directory service will propagate that modification to the remaining replicas. In this environment, there is the potential that different users on different directory servers could update the same object. When replication occurs, there will be a collision between the two updated objects which must be resolved to ensure only one change is propagated.

Active Directory uses update sequence numbers to ensure data consistency. USNs can be thought of as change counters, and represent the number of changes (since last replication) to each domain controller. Each domain controller stores the USNs of its replication partners. When a directory attribute if modified, the USN of the updating domain controller is incremented. At the time of replication, controllers exchange USNs, and if the newly exchanged USNs are of higher value than the stored USNs, then directory changes are replicated. In the event that two domain controllers have the same USN for attribute modifications, then time stamps are used to determine the most recent update.

In contrast, NDS uses time stamps and relative time to ensure data consistency. This requires implementation of a reliable time server, and all directory servers must be synchronized with it. Timing inconsistencies between directory servers can lead to replication anomalies.

Multi-Master Updates

In multi-master environments like NDS and Active Directory, it is necessary to establish a central point of control for system-critical directory operations. NDS and Active Directory implement this control in different ways:

In NDS, you can create three types of replica:

- **Read/Write Master.** This is the primary (master) controller for all replicas of a specific partition. System-critical functions are forwarded to this controller for action and as such, the Read/Write master must be available to allow critical changes such as schema modifications to take place. The first server within a partition automatically becomes the R/W master; you can change this designation later using the administration tools.

- **Read/Write replica.** These are standard replicas of the partition, providing full read and write capabilities to the partition, and performing tasks such as password changes, etc.

- **Read-only replica.** Read-only replicas have limited uses other than for system recovery and some custom applications.

Active Directory implements Flexible Single Master Operation (FSMO) roles to establish configuration authority in the multi-master environment. Five FSMO roles are defined per domain, and automatically assigned to domain controllers:

- **Schema Master.** Only the DC holding this role for the forest can update the schema. (Forest-level.)

- **Domain Naming Master.** Only the DC holding this role can add or remove domains from the Active Directory forest. (Forest-level.)

- **RID Master.** User (or group, or computer) objects can be created on any DC within a domain. When a security principal object is created, it is assigned a unique security identifier (SID) that is composed of the domain SID, plus a relative identifier (RID). The RID master is responsible for delivering pools of RIDs to domain controllers, and after 512 User objects have been created, a DC must communicate with the RID Master DC before creating any more. (Domain-level.)

- **PDC Emulator.** In a mixed-mode environment, the DC holding the PDC emulator role appears as the PDC to Windows NT 3.51 and Windows NT 4.0 systems. In both mixed and native modes, the PDC emulator still serves as a PDC to down-level clients that need a PDC for specific operations (such as password changes) or that query WINS for a <Domain> entry. (Domain-level.)

- **Infrastructure Master.** The Infrastructure Master tracks objects that were moved from one domain to another. If these objects are still referenced in the old domain (in group memberships, for example), the DCs need to know where to find them. (Domain-level.)

Authentication

In addition to hierarchical management of resources, the network directory represents an opportunity to consolidate security protocols within the enterprise. Strong security is required—especially in cases where directory services can be accessed from the Internet—but the challenge is to protect resources without placing unnecessary design restrictions on networks or increasing management complexity.

Active Directory facilitates extranet development through the support of multiple extensible security authentication protocols such as Kerberos, X.509 certificates, and Smart Cards. Additional protocols can be added, if required. Once a user has authenticated to Active Directory, authorization is performed in a consistent fashion across files, applications, and other resources.

NDS supports X.509 certificates but does not support Kerberos or Smart Cards for authentication. It also computes access control rights differently when accessed through LDAP instead of directly through NDS due to the fact that NDS Access attributes do not map exactly onto the LDAP rights. Also, those operations that require NDS Supervisor rights are not available through LDAP.

Security and Inheritance

Inheritance simplifies directory administration by enabling child objects to inherit access control behaviors from the parent object. Any subsequent changes to the parent object will be automatically propagated to the child. There are two methods of implementing security inheritance:

- *Dynamic* inheritance computes the access control behavior of each object (by examining all parent objects) each time the child object is accessed.
- *Static* inheritance computes the access control behaviors of child objects at time of creation, or subsequent modification of parent/child rights. Recalculation is performed automatically, and the associated rights are attached directly to the child object.

NDS implements dynamic inheritance, which calculates access permissions at run time. For example, to calculate permissions for an object located at depth **N** in a tree, NDS walks the tree from the target object to the root and computes the effective access rights. In a distributed environment, this can result in unnecessary network traffic and delays to the user—especially in cases where remote partitions must be accessed.

Active Directory implements static inheritance because directories should be optimized for read behavior. Since the access rights are pre-calculated and attached to the child, there is no computational overhead required to calculate effective security rights.

Internet Standards

In today's Internet-based environments, it is essential that all network services can interoperate with each other. From the perspectives of network directories, two Internet standards are of particular importance:

- The Lightweight Directory Access Protocol Version 3 (LDAP V3) for querying, accessing, and managing objects stored in directory services.

- The Domain Naming Service (DNS) for locating computers and services over the Internet using a standardized naming format.

LDAP

The lightweight directory access protocol provides a standardized mechanism for accessing data in network directories. LDAP is not defined in the X.500 documentation, but was first developed by the University of Michigan (and later refined via the RFC/IETF process) to overcome some of the perceived limitations of the native X.500 mechanism—DAP (Directory Access Protocol):

- LDAP is designed to run over TCP/IP. DAP requires implementation of OSI which its not practical in today's desktop environment. LDAP can be easily implemented on today's desktop environment.

- LDAP clients communicate with an LDAP service on the directory servers. The LDAP service takes responsibility for processing the LDAP requests. This means that directory vendors can implement LDAP services to convert the requests into the native format of the directory.

- LDAP moves the responsibility for resolving referrals to the LDAP server. Only the errors/results are returned to the client. Contrast this with DAP— which requires the client to resolve referrals.

Active Directory and LDAP V3

Several years ago, Microsoft recognized that application vendors and enterprise customers would require a high level of LDAP V3 compliance from their directory services. For this reason, Active Directory was designed as a native LDAP server. In other words, it can process LDAP-based requests directly without having to translate them against the Active Directory data store (Figure 9.10). Active Directory also exposes all of its functionality via LDAP interfaces. For example, Active Directory provides LDAP-based support for schema management, change history, and query scoping.

LDAP-compliant applications

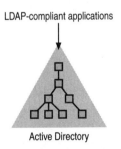

Active Directory

Figure 9.10   LDAP and Active Directory.

NDS and LDAP

As illustrated in Figure 9.11, NDS can support the use of LDAP via the LDAP Service for NDS add-on. Unlike Active Directory, LDAP is not completely integrated into NDS since it translates LDAP requests into the native NDS format—NDAP. Although better integrated in the latest release (for Netware 5), the key differences of implementation are as follows:

Figure 9.11   LDAP and NDS.

- LDAP is built into Active Directory as the primary client access protocol used by all user interfaces of Windows 2000 Professional workstation. With NDS, you have to install LDAP Services on every NDS server that will provide LDAP access.

- LDAP and NDS use different naming syntaxes.

- NDS's support for LDAP comes from LDAP Services for NDS. This service acts as a translator between LDAP requests and the native way that NDS accesses data out of partitions. Using this "middleman" approach between applications and NDS to process LDAP requests adds overhead to processing.

- NDS does not expose *all* of its functionality via LDAP. Schema management, for instance, is not exposed through LDAP extended controls, and this forces applications to access NDS using several methods to get to certain features.

- Enabling access to NDS namespaces containing more than 1,000 objects through LDAP requires companies to either expose applications to the performance limitations of tree walking (needed to search multiple partitions) or use catalogs that may be out-of-date with the underlying objects in their partitions.

DNS

Active Directory and DNS

Companies implementing directory services want to simplify information retrieval and management by moving toward a *global root* that connects all name spaces.

With Windows 2000, Microsoft's approach was to base Active Directory domain names on the Domain Naming System (DNS)—the mechanism that the world already uses to find services on the Internet. Because domains have a one-to-one relationship with Active Directory partitions, you can locate Active Directory name spaces directly through DNS: an Active Directory object's fully distinguished name contains the DNS name of its partition, is globally unique, and completely describes how to find the object on an intranet or across the Internet. This approach adheres to the details of RFC2247.

NDS and DNS

In contrast, NDS object naming does not incorporate DNS names. To locate an object in NDS, users must first know how to find the appropriate NDS server. And because NDS and LDAP use different naming syntaxes, intranet applications written to directly access NDS use different object names from Internet applications that access NDS through LDAP; this lack of DNS integration further complicates the use of LDAP in an NDS environment, making object naming and location more complex.

Designing Solutions in Active Directory and NDS

Active Directory and NDS implement network directory solutions differently. This section discusses how these differences affect the development of a system design.

Rules for Designing a Directory

When designing a network directory there are many variables to consider, and some of them are moving targets. For example, each enterprise will have unique directory requirements with different organizational structures and network infrastructures. Over time, the enterprise will probably restructure or expand to meet market demands. The network directory design must be sufficiently flexible to grow with the company—without requiring extensive modification. A good quality directory design usually is a compromise between two competing objectives: logical representation of the business hierarchy and efficient use of infrastructure.

To aid the design process, you can apply rules to both Active Directory and NDS, which provide a framework for the design process by ensuring critical tasks, are undertaken in the correct order. To show how to use these rules, this section examines the design of a sample directory for the fictional company Northwind.

About Northwind

Northwind is a fictitious company that is used as an example of an organization that provides technical support, manufacturing, and telesales for its clients. It integrates seamlessly into each client's business and provides all outbound customer-focused services (technical support, telesales, distribution, etc.), leaving the clients free to concentrate on the core business of developing software.

According to our fictitious example, Northwind is headquartered in Edinburgh. Their fictitious site contains a call center, and centers for sales, customer technical support, outbound telesales, and human resources. Northwind also has a software localization unit in Glasgow (which converts commercial applications into European languages), a manufacturing plant in Liverpool (which provides printing and disk duplication facilities), a small sales office in Florida, and another call center in Asia.

The Design Process

Step1—Identify Network Directory Requirements

In our example, Northwind wants to implement a network directory to meet the following requirements:

- **Single point of logon.** Northwind currently supports a mixture of network technologies. Users store information on a range of legacy file and print servers and e-mail systems, each with different passwords. A directory can provide a central point of authentication.

- **User management consolidation.** With many servers, staff turnover, and internal restructures, it is time consuming to create new user accounts and assign permissions across multiple servers. A directory can provide a single point of administration for all user accounts.

- **Location of data.** There is no obvious data storage structure within the current environment. Before users can find data, they have to know pretty much where it is. A directory (with appropriate searching software) can provide a more usable structure, allowing users to find data wherever it is.

- **Administrative delegation.** The helpdesk currently spends a lot of time servicing requests for password resets. The IT department would like to speed things up by delegating this task to local team leaders.

- **WhitePages.** Northwind would like to create an employee information store (phone number, e-mail address, manager, etc.) that users can search from the desktop.

- **High availability.** The directory service must be available at all times, even if a server fails.

- **Low WAN impact.** The global directory service cannot impose excessive WAN activity.

These are common requirements for a directory; designers have to implement all of the basic directory building blocks to achieve them.

Step 2—Physical Layout

A company's geographic layout has a large impact on a directory's performance and usability. An inefficient directory design can cause excessive WAN traffic, affecting the performance of the directory and directory-based applications.

The second step in a directory design is to gather detailed information about the company's geographical layout and its network infrastructure: usage statistics, bandwidth utilization, and reliability metrics. You need to research and specify these sorts of characteristics:

- **WAN diagram.** Illustrate the layout, topology, and interconnectivity of all WAN components. Include performance and reliability details, because they directly affect the distributed aspects of directory design.
- **Map of locations.** Show the physical location of all interconnected buildings on the network. Compare (overlay) the map's detail with the network diagram. Use the map when you consider optimal server locations.
- **Resources.** Each location has a set of company resources, computer-based and human. To determine a location's role and placement within the directory structure, you need complete resource lists. You also have to track resources that "float" between geographical locations.

Figure 9.12 shows Northwind's geographical layout. LAN topologies are based on Ethernet 10Mb/s; larger offices have more efficient switched LANs. Presently NetBEUI, IPX, and TCP/IP are used on LANs, but only TCP/IP is forwarded over the WAN.

Each location has local file, print, and applications servers. HQ and the Asia call center use several large UNIX databases to handle calls.

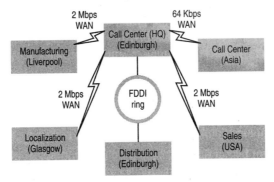

Figure 9.12   Northwind's geographical layout.

Step 3—Organizational Structure

To ensure efficient physical operation of a geographically dispersed company, the organizational structure must provide a management framework that is both flexible and extensible. As a result, companies are generally organized by geographical or business function. To ensure an integrated network directory solution, the directory should (where possible) mirror the structure of the real-world organization.

This step gathers enterprise hierarchy information so that it can be accurately represented within the directory. There are two levels of this information:

- **Management.** How the company is structured, possibly by geographical region, product line, or other specialty.
- **Task.** The working arrangement for resources within a given sector, product line, business sector, etc.

Use organizational charts to sketch out and understand the hierarchy. If sections of the hierarchy transcend the geographical boundaries outlined in step 2, highlight them for later analysis. Figure 9.13 shows Northwind's organizational structure.

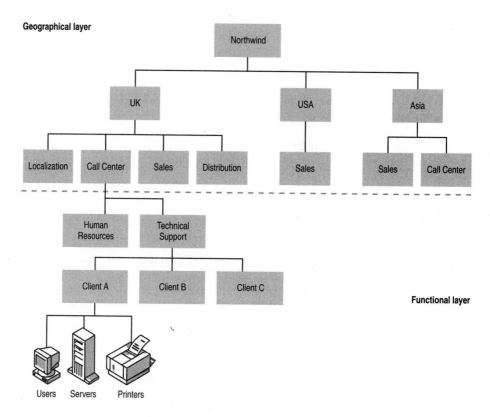

Figure 9.13   Northwind's organizational structure.

The top layer, representing the company mission or direction, should not change very often. The bottom layer is more likely to change as it reflects staff turnover, altered working practices, new network components, etc.

Step 4—Designing the Tree

Using the information you have gathered, in this step you begin designing the network directory. Some things to consider first:

- In a large enterprise, the design will necessarily represent a compromise between global (ideal) structure and infrastructure practicality. Study the information you have collected on the enterprise so you can make efficient and effective compromises.

- You probably won't get it right the first time, and that is one reason why you should plan carefully and fully before you start to build. There are always several workable solutions, and the most efficient may not be the most apparent. Design and refine several times to increase the reliability of your choices.

- Plan for change. A good directory design can adapt easily and efficiently to the changing demands of the enterprise. Make sure you identify enterprise areas that change frequently and model them correctly in the directory.

- Keep the design simple. Rule of thumb: if you increase design complexity you usually increase administrative labor and management effort, whilst decreasing extensibility and performance.

Begin all designs by modeling the enterprise within a single Active Directory domain or NDS partition. You may reach a point, especially in a large-scale environment, where it is obvious that a single partition is impractical, but *start simple*.

Top Layer

To design the top layer of the directory tree, combine the management structure (Figure 9.13) with the topology of the networking environment (Figure 9.12). Figure 9.14 shows how to implement this in Active Directory. A single domain is created to represent the Northwind company, and organizational units are defined within it to represent geographical aspects of the management hierarchy. Because Northwind conducts all its business under the same company name there is no need to maintain multiple namespaces and thus no need to implement a multi-tree forest.

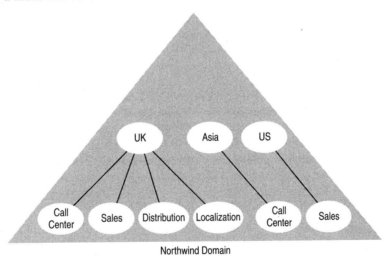

Northwind Domain

Figure 9.14   Preliminary Active Directory top-layer configuration for Northwind.

Figure 9.15 shows how to implement the top layer in NDS. Beneath the root object, an organization object defines the company name. Because Northwind conducts all its business under the same company name there is no need to maintain multiple namespaces and thus a single organization object is used.

Beneath the organization object, organizational units represent the management hierarchy.

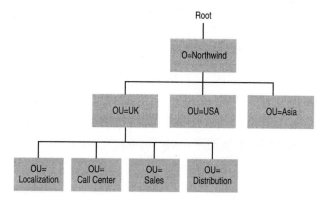

Figure 9.15   Preliminary NDS top-layer configuration for Northwind.

Although NDS supports the use of a Country object, it is more efficient to use organization units to represent geographical hierarchy because:

- The Country objects reside directly beneath the root, requiring that an organizational unit be defined for each country. This increases tree complexity by adding a layer, and increasing path length.

> **Note**   NDS imposes a 256-character limit on distinguished names. This means that if names associated with containers are too long then the number of layers will be reduced. Keep container names short.

- The Country object identifies each country by a two-character mnemonic and these may not be intuitive to users.

Bottom Layer

Using the top layer as a solid foundation, a functional (bottom) layer is added to contain all business units and resources (users, computers, etc.) that interact with the directory. The advantages of the two-layer approach are:

- The top layer helps define a partitioning strategy by highlighting the geographical boundaries.

- The bottom layer represents business services within each geographical location. For example in Figure 9.13, the UK Call Center provides human resources and technical support services, representing Northwind's day-to-day operation.

- The bottom layer provides containers for business resources, grouped by function. This allows administrators to configure user desktop environments (applications, desktop colors, etc.) by associating configuration data with the container. Users placed within a container object automatically inherit the container's properties.

- In a two-layer model, staff turnover, promotions, etc., do not affect the overall directory design. Instead, administrators can simply move users between bottom layer containers on the basis of job function. If a new business service is offered, it can be added to the model as another organizational unit.

You define the bottom layer by transposing the organizational structure (department by department) from the organizational charts into the network directory. This sounds simple enough, but it can become complicated because real-life organizational structures often have multiple reporting lines and other characteristics that do not correlate to operations at the task level. In these cases, you have to identify the services provided by each department and figure how best to implement them within the directory.

To increase the design's longevity, ensure that each element represented in the directory is relevant to the overall business structure and has a clearly defined role and purpose. Figure 9.16 shows the logical hierarchy within Northwind's Human Resources department. Based in Edinburgh, HR deals with all European employees. It is headed by a Human Resource Executive, beneath whom are two teams (each with a team leader) responsible for different sections of the company.

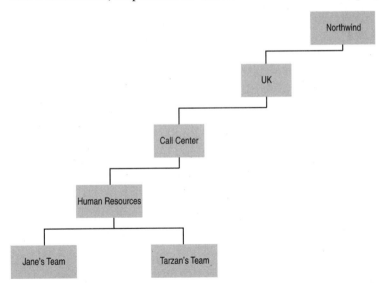

Figure 9.16   Logical hierarchy for Northwind Human Resources department.

You want to create a design that does not require frequent modification, so you have to make sure that the hierarchy represented is not overly granular and complex. In this example, the simplest and most flexible solution is to model HR as a single organizational unit beneath the UK Call Center, and to delegate security privileges to Tarzan and Jane so they can reset passwords for their teams. It would be inadvisable to increase the granularity and model *Tarzan's team* and *Jane's team* because:

- Both teams provide the same classification service to the company, and have the same desktop/user configuration requirements. Modeling the individual workgroups provides no management advantage.

- Virtual team leaders may change, requiring a change to the organizational unit structure, if it were (inadvisably) based on team-leader name.

- Such workgroup names would be meaningless to a system administrator.

- If teams require different access rights to network resources, use *groups*.

In any moderately large environment, bottom-layer design is an iterative process requiring many revisions to represent the business structure accurately enough to enable centralized resource management, yet not so granularly that the directory requires constant modification. Here are some questions to ask before transposing each item from an organizational chart into the directory:

- What is the container's purpose? Each should have a clearly defined purpose that adds business value.

- How long will it remain in the directory? If the object is short-lived, consider representing it in the directory through some other method or not at all.

- Who will manage the container? Each container must be managed and you should define responsibilities within the tree. In large environments, it is impractical for one person to manage each container.

- What will the container contain? Create containers only if there are objects for them to hold. If there are no objects to represent, do not create the container.

Once you have identified the containers you can represent them as organizational units within the directory tree.

Figure 9.17 shows an example Active Directory implementation based on a single domain (partition). The business functions of the UK Call Center are represented in a hierarchical tree. Notice that each technical support client has a separate container: this allows administrators to delegate resource control for each client to appropriate team leaders.

In addition to benefiting administrators, this structure benefits users by making it easy to identify resources within the company. For example, users can search the directory for *members of the 'Client A' technical support team*, or for all of that team's associated printers.

Figure 9.18 shows the same directory design in a single partition of NDS.

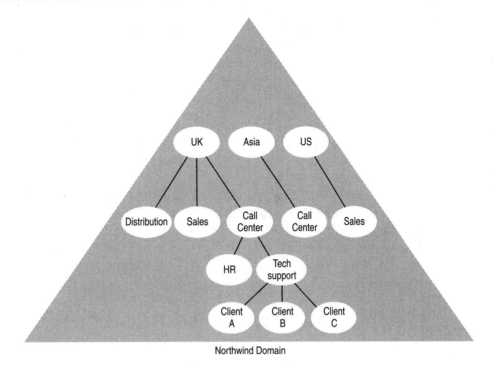

Figure 9.17   Single-domain Active Directory implementation.

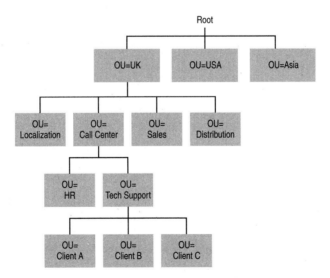

Figure 9.18   Single-partition NDS implementation.

Step 5—Partitioning

Once the basic business structure is translated into corresponding organizational units, you can consider partitioning the database to optimize network and server performance and to prevent replicating data unnecessarily around the enterprise. Both Active Directory and NDS support partitioning, but significant differences in their implementations can affect the design.

Partitioning in NDS

Partitioning recommendations for NDS suggest representing each geographical region or WAN segment as a separate partition, and implementing another partition if there are more than 3,500 objects. This reduces WAN activity by eliminating needless replication, and increases server performance by reducing the quantity of data managed on each server. It also means that any large-scale or geographically dispersed enterprise must incorporate geography as a principal factor of the directory design, even when this is contrary to the company's logical hierarchy. (Active Directory does not require this in geographically dispersed environments because it allows you to control replication traffic between servers.)

Because NDS requires that you model each of an enterprise's geographical areas in a separate partition, the number of partitions can become quite large in any moderately large enterprise. Partitioning within NDS, however, is simple: the unit of partitioning is the organizational unit, and the NDS Manager utility provides a simple GUI interface for creating and re-joining partitions. You can also create partitions at any time during the tree's life cycle.

Figure 9.19 shows the NDS partitions for Northwind. The tree partitions defined for the UK operation are required by the low speed network links in Liverpool and Glasgow, and the high number of people in the Edinburgh Call Center.

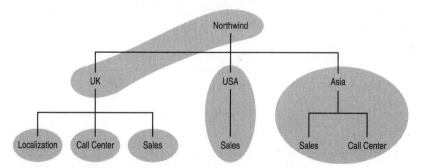

Figure 9.19   NDS partition configuration for Northwind.

Partitioning in Active Directory

In Active Directory, the unit of partitioning is the domain. Domains use the ESE database engine, which is an enhanced version of the directory service engine supplied with Microsoft Exchange. Its indexing system enables each partition to cope with millions of objects. (Independent testing has confirmed performance and reliability when scaled to about 40 million objects.)

This capability can remove geography as a design factor when you combine it with site implementation. Sites define a collection of interconnected servers that share high-speed network connectivity. Site-links are logical connectors between sites using lower-speed (WAN) connections. You can configure site-link properties so that Active Directory replicates more efficiently over these links by using compression and allowing the administrator to schedule replication based on network environment.

By using sites in a directory service, you can focus partitioning decisions on logically modeling the business requirements, rather than on WAN structure. The WAN infrastructure still plays an important role, but not as important as its role in NDS.

In addition to the performance-based reasons for partitioning, certain types of configuration can only be applied at the domain level. If one or more of the following scenarios apply, then the Active Directory design will require multiple domains:

- Security policy is applied at domain level. If password length, account lockout, certificate authorities, IP security, etc. differ by location, then you need multiple domains.

- Domains provide administrative boundaries, meaning that in a distributed environment, you can assign separate administrators to each domain. This is ideal for companies that do not wish to centralize administrative control completely.

- In an environment where Active Directory must be backwardly compatible with Windows NT 4 domains, you can define a mixed-mode domain containing only the legacy Windows NT 4 systems. Mixed-mode is relevant only for BDCs, not for any member servers or workstations running applications. All functionality for these down-level machines is provided by a native-mode domain. This provides a stable migration platform because once the upgrade procedures are in place you can integrate the Windows NT 4 domains into the native Active Directory domain.

- There are more than one million objects in a domain.

Figure 9.20 shows the implementation of domains for Northwind. Notice that the Active Directory design requires fewer domains than NDS. For example, Northwind's UK operation is modeled in a single partition. Sites and site-links have been defined for each geographical region within the UK domain (Edinburgh, Glasgow, and Liverpool).

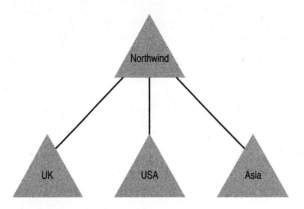

Figure 9.20   Active Directory domain configuration for Northwind.

This approach provides administrative and business benefits, but initial implementation of this environment incurs a higher investment because:

- Each domain (partition) is hosted by a dedicated domain controller, requiring a minimum of one controller per domain. For the purposes of resilience and performance, multiple controllers should be deployed.

- Domain creation and removal requires that you configure dedicated hardware, which requires proper planning and support procedures.

Synchronization Between Active Directory and NDS

If you already have a directory service that contains valuable business data, upgrading to a Windows 2000 system may require you to run Active Directory in parallel with the legacy system until all users are migrated. For administrators, the ideal solution would be automatic synchronization of both directory systems during this transition period, so users are unaffected by the change.

The Need for Synchronization

Northwind is in the process of migrating users from their NDS environment into Active Directory. This process will take considerable time because there are many users, and the business units are causing delays as they get into line. During migration, users must be able to access both NDS and Active Directory, and they need a single point of logon for both systems. To ensure a smooth transition, directory data will be migrated on a business-unit-by-business-unit basis. The newly migrated users will use Active Directory as their principal directory service, but still access data on legacy (non-Windows 2000) file servers.

In this scenario, it is desirable to synchronize Active Directory with NDS so that if a migrated user changes a directory attribute (on Active Directory), that change will be automatically propagated to NDS. Windows 2000 provides this functionality in the form of MSDSS (Microsoft Directory Synchronization Services), a synchronization engine that enables directory-specific providers to exchange data between Active Directory and external directory systems.

MSDSS is part of the Windows 2000 Services For NetWare, and it must be installed on an Active Directory domain controller. MSDSS ensures compatibility with the NDS environment by using the Novell IntraNetWare client for all NDS communication. Any changes to objects in Active Directory environment are "pushed" (via the IntraNetWare client) to NDS. This service is configured through the Directory Synchronization MMC snap-in.

Publishers, Subscribers, and Sessions

In order to synchronize data between disjoint directories (that may not share the same logical design), MSDSS provides mechanisms to define the objects that will be synchronized, and mechanisms to translate data between directories:

- MSDSS introduces the concept of publishers and subscribers. A publisher is an administrator-defined set of objects (or directory sub-tree) that are mapped into the subordinate (subscribing) directory service. In an AD/NDS environment, Active Directory is always the publishing directory, and NDS the subscriber. Publisher/Subscriber relationships enable definition of which objects will be synchronized between directories.

- Attribute mapping – Attribute names in disjoint directory services can be different. For example, the "display name" attribute in Active Directory is analogous to the "full name" attribute in NDS. Attribute mapping provides a mechanism of translating this data during the synchronization process.

The relationship between publishers and subscribers is defined by a *directory synchronization session*. The session formalizes this relationship by defining publishing/subscribing directories; objects or attributes that will be synchronized; synchronization type (one or two way); and synchronization schedule. Sessions are defined using the MMC snap-in for MSDSS, and many sessions can be defined to reflect the different mappings between directories.

Configuring MSDSS

The first step is to use the session wizard to define the publishing/subscribing relationship and the type of synchronization to be performed. MSDSS supports both one-way and two-way synchronization, as Figure 9.21 illustrates.

Next, you have to specify a publishing organizational unit. In the Northwind example, this is the *Human Resource* container, based in the Edinburgh Call Center. You must also specify the name of the Windows 2000 domain controller that hosts the MSDSS service (Figure 9.22).

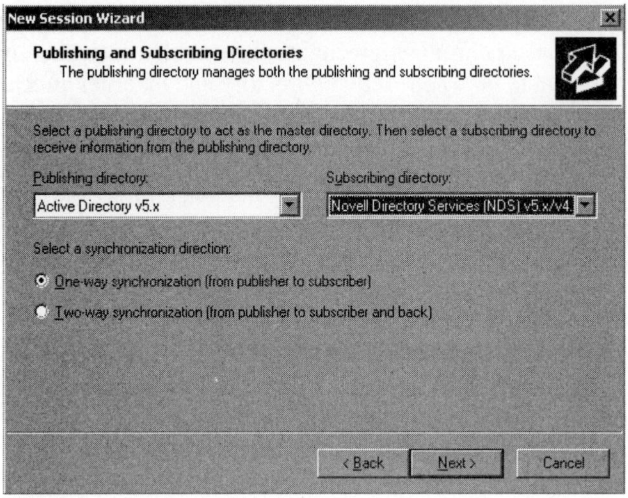

Figure 9.21   Session Wizard.

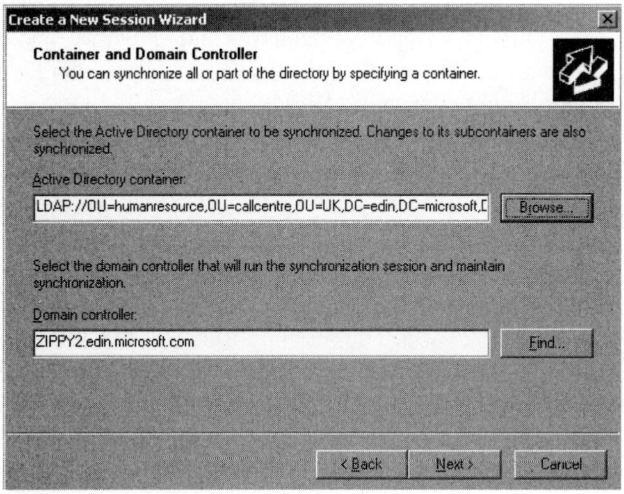

Figure 9.22   Specifying the host MSDSS DC.

Next, you have to configure the subscription component. Specify the complete path to the NDS *Human Resource* container, along with an appropriate NDS user account and password. MSDSS uses these credentials to access the NDS environment using the Novell IntraNetware client, so the naming syntax on the user ID must meet NDS requirements. Using the Novell client for all NDS communication ensures compatibility with the Novell environment (Figure 9.23).

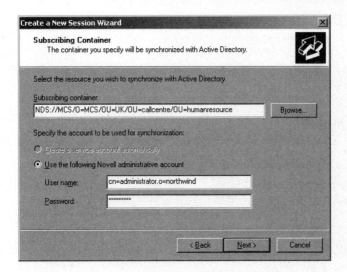

Figure 9.23   Specifying the subscription container.

When publisher and subscriber are configured, MSDSS (by default) reads the contents of the subscriber directory and populates the publisher. This is known as *reverse synchronization,* and shown in Figure 9.24.

Note   MSDSS cannot extract raw passwords from NDS, but it can write them. In order to synchronize passwords, newly populated Active Directory accounts are assigned passwords based upon administrator-definable rules (username, random, blank, etc.). The newly created Active Directory password is synchronized with NDS—overwriting the NDS original password.

If a newly migrated user changes their password, the update is propagated to all Windows 2000 domain controllers, but also pushed (via MSDSS) to NDS during the next session synchronization. MSDSS uses the Novell client to update the NDS password (stored in Novell's native format). Until NDS is decommissioned, there are two accounts for each migrated user (one in Active Directory and one in NDS)—but by using MSDSS, there is only one point of management, which is Active Directory.

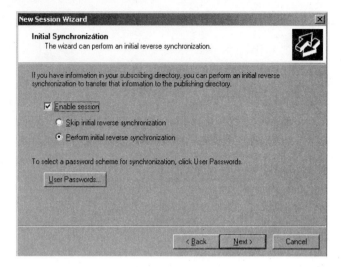

Figure 9.24   Initial reverse synchronization screen.

When you have configured the initial session properties, you assign a "friendly" name to the session, which will be displayed in the Directory Synchronization snap-in. You can edit the session properties later to alter the replication schedule, NDS login credentials, event logging (detail), and attribute mapping.

You can map an attribute (with a different name) to a corresponding entity in Active Directory. Figure 9.25 shows the attributes of the (subscriber) NDS and (publisher) Active Directory *user* objects. Attribute mapping is extensible, so you can include custom attributes for synchronization.

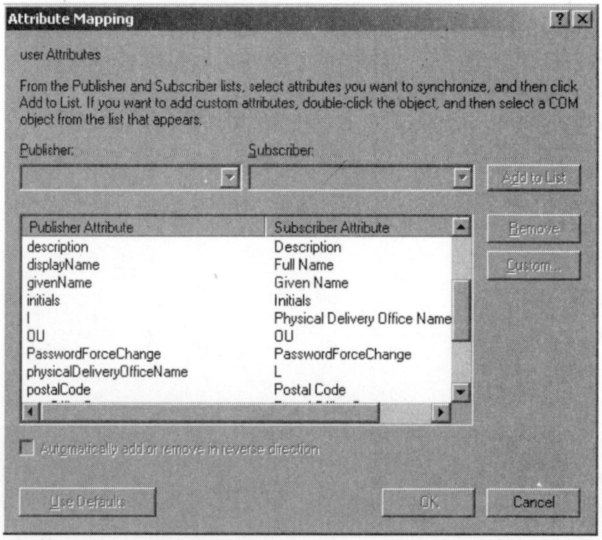

Figure 9.25   Attribute mapping screen.

Synchronization Types

In the previous example, "location level" synchronization has been used to ensure that the contents of the *Human Resource* department OUs are kept consistent on the publishing and the subscribing systems. If an object (user) within the scope of the session is moved between OUs on the publishing system, this change is reflected on the subscriber system. This approach keeps the tree designs consistent: if a new OU is created beneath the published container, it is automatically created on the subscriber.

This approach works well when there is a clear functional mapping between containers on disparate directories. When the mappings are not obvious (in a flat namespace, for example), you may have to use another method such as *object-level* synchronization, which maps individual objects between directories and synchronizes only attribute changes—object location is irrelevant.

Management

Once directory synchronization is in place, Active Directory provides a central point of administration for all migrated users. Any attribute changes in Active Directory will be reflected in the subscribing directory. This allows new and legacy systems to run in parallel, until the migration is complete.

Conclusion

Active Directory and NDS both provide robust and scalable directory services. However, the key differentiators are as follows:

- Active Directory aims to abstract directory hierarchy from physical network design to achieve a pure representation of the enterprise. This aids management of resources, and location of information since the logical entities mirror their physical counterparts.

- Active Directory provides a consistent programming interface and development platform for the authoring of directory-enabled applications. When combined with adherence to Internet standards such as LDAP, DNS, and Kerberos, the directory could be used by non-Microsoft operating systems to store or retrieve data.

- Active Directory is based on an enhanced version of the Exchange directory service. It has been independently tested with ~40million objects per partition, illustrating scalability of the platform.

- Active Directory provides full backwards compatibility with down-level clients, enabling staged migrations from legacy Microsoft environments, in addition to interoperability with other vendors.

- Windows 2000 Professional workstations are fully directory aware, enabling granular management and configuration. Users can take advantage of Active Directory immediately from the desktop, and begin using it to search for resources and information within the organization.

Administration and Security

Windows 2000 Active Directory provides many new tools and capabilities that assist in managing and securing a directory. This section provides information on three Active Directory technologies. Chapter 10, "Scripting the Active Directory," provides information on how to use graphical tools to administer the Active Directory if you are looking for an easy way to generate reports or summarize information to track configuration changes, rollout progress, etc. Scripting provides these capabilities. Chapter 11, "Delegating Tree/Forest Operations," talks about how Active Directory provides a mechanism for delegating the administration of domains, organizational units, sites, site links, and subnets. With the appropriate access controls, Active Directory allows you to delegate some of the tasks initially assigned to the Administrators group: schema, child domain, sites, and management of RIS and DHCP. Chapter 12, "Building a Windows 2000 Public Key Infrastructure," focuses on PKI, a crucial technology for distributed and heterogeneous computer environments, which require a security system to provide authentication, confidentiality, and nonrepudiation services.

Active Directory enables centralized management of distributed networks. With an abundance of tools and capabilities to make the management of a network more efficient and secure, Active Directory ensures the network you build today supports your directory and infrastructure needs of tomorrow.

CHAPTER 10

Scripting the Active Directory

By David Trulli,
Microsoft
Corporation

Many administrators and infrastructure designers don't take advantage of the power of currently available scripting languages—sometimes because they think scripting is too hard to learn or master, sometimes because they think scripting requires a developer's expertise, sometimes because they simply are not aware of the possibilities that scripting can open up to them. This chapter focuses on using scripting to extract information from the Active Directory. It explains how to take advantage of scripting resources, and provides scripting examples you can easily adapt to access the management information you need.

What You'll Find in This Chapter

- A discussion of basic scripting concepts and methods.

- An introduction to basic Active Directory Services Interface (ADSI) concepts and methods, including sample scripts for performing basic tasks such as reading/updating an object, searching, etc.

- Explanations of how to use scripts to manage domain and enterprise configuration information—down to the level of specific tasks such as creating groups or user accounts, listing or creating sites, and so on.

- A discussion of Windows Management Instrumentation (WMI), a Windows 2000 component that allows applications and scripts to view and change properties, execute methods, and receive events about modeled objects. This final section explains how to use WMI and includes example scripts.

Basics

When you are using graphical tools to administer the Active Directory you may find yourself looking for an easy way to generate reports or summarize information that you can use to track configuration changes, rollout progress, etc. Scripting provides this capability. This section discusses basic components and methods.

What Is ADSI?

Active Directory Services Interface (ADSI) is a set of Common Object Model (COM) programming interfaces. Like ODBC, ADSI provides common access to directories by adding a provider for each directory protocol type (Figure 10.1). Windows 2000 contains providers for:

Name	Provides access to
WinNT	Windows NT 3.51/4.0
LDAP	LDAP directories including Windows 2000 Active Directory, Site Server 3.0, Microsoft Exchange 5.5, and third-party LDAP servers
NDS	Novell NDS

This chapter focuses on the LDAP ADSI provider which provides access to the Active Directory as well as other LDAP servers. For more information on specific ADSI providers see *Microsoft Windows 2000 Active Directory Programmer's Guide.*

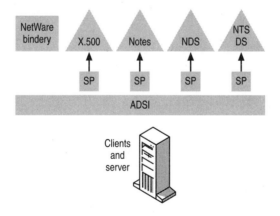

Figure 10.1   ADSI Provider Model.

Accessing directories with ADSI offers these features and benefits:

■ **Open Architecture.** Any directory provider can implement an ADSI provider; users gain freedom of choice in directory services without sacrificing manageability.

- **DS-independent.** Administrative applications are not tightly bound to a vendor's directory service. The same application can work on multiple directories using a single API. This reduces development time and support costs.

- **Security.** ADSI supports authentication and authorization programming models.

- **Simple programming model.** You don't have to understand vendor-specific directory APIs to develop administrative and other directory-enabled applications.

- **OLE Automation Server.** You can use any OLE automation controller (Visual Basic, Perl, Rexx, C/C++, and others) to develop directory service applications. Using tools you already know reduces development time and support costs.

- **Functionally rich.** ISVs and sophisticated users can develop complex scripted administrative applications, using the same ADSI models used for simple applications.

- **Extensible.** Directory providers, ISVs, and users can extend ADSI with new objects or functions to add value or meet unique needs.

Windows Scripting Host

The Windows Scripting Host (WSH) is a language-independent scripting host for 32-bit Microsoft Windows operating system platforms. Microsoft provides both Visual Basic Script and Java Script scripting engines with WSH; other software companies are working on ActiveX scripting engines for other languages, such as Perl, TCL, REXX, and Python.

You can run WSH from either the Windows-based host (Wscript.exe) or the command line based texts host (Cscript.exe).

Cscript.exe uses this syntax:

cscript *[host options...] [script name] [script options]*

- *Host options* (always preceded by two slashes—//) enable or disable WSH options.

- *Script name* is the name for the script file; for example, CHART.VBS.

- *Script options* (parameters, always preceded by one slash—/) are passed to the script.

Cscript.exe host options:

Option	Description
//R	Reregister script extensions (.vbs, .js, .tcl) by searching for registered script engines. NOTE You do not need to provide a script file name when using the //R switch.
//I	Interactive mode (default—opposite of //B).

Option	Description
//B	Batch mode. Suppress all non-command-line console UI requested from script.
//T:nn	Time-out, in seconds. Maximum time the script can run (default = no limit). Use this option to set a timer to prevent excessive script execution.
//logo	Display an execution banner at execution time (default—opposite of //NoLogo).
//nologo	Prevent display of execution banner at execution time.
//C	Make Cscript.exe the default application for running scripts.
//S	Save current command-line options for this user (per user).
//?	Show command usage (same as execution with no options).

Active Server Pages

Active Server Pages (ASP) is an open, compile-free application environment in which you can combine HTML, scripts, and reusable ActiveX server components to create Web-based business solutions. ASP enables server side scripting for IIS with native support for both VBScript and Jscript. ASP files can activate a Web site using any combination of HTML, scripting—such as JavaScript or Visual Basic Scripting Edition (VBScript)—and components written in any language. Basically, an ASP file is simply a file that can contain any combination of HTML, scripting, and calls to components. The examples below use VBScript.

ASP allows developers to use scripting and COM objects to generate highly interactive Web sites.

```
<%@SCRIPT LANGUAGE="VBSCRIPT"%>
<HTML>
<HEAD>
<META NAME="GENERATOR" Content="Microsoft Developer Studio">
<META HTTP-EQUIV="Content-Type" content="text/html; charset=iso-8859-1">
<TITLE>ASP Example</TITLE>
</HEAD>

<BODY BGCOLOR="WHITE">

<%For x = 1 to 6%>
    <FONT FACE="ARIAL" SIZE=<%=x%>>
    Hello World
    </FONT>
    <P>
<%Next%>

</BODY>
</HTML>
```

HTML Applications

HTML applications (introduced with Internet Explorer 5) allow you to write real Windows applications using only HTML, DHTML, and scripting. They use scripting and are run as local secure applications so they have full access to the operating system. Normal Web pages cannot contain controls that are not marked "safe" for scripting, so by default you cannot access the ADSI from a normal HTML page.

```
<HTML>
<HEAD>
<TITLE>Simple HTML Application</TITLE>
  <HTA:APPLICATION ID="hta"
    APPLICATIONNAME="sample hta"
    WINDOWSTATE="normal">
</HEAD>
<BODY>
This is a simple HTML Application.
<BR>
<BUTTON onclick="self.close()">Exit</BUTTON>

</BODY>
</HTML>
```

Using Visual Basic for Applications in Office 2000

Microsoft Office 2000 applications contain Visual Basic for Applications (VBA) which allows you to write programs that can access the Active Directory. Excel and Access are of particular interest here, because they can be targets for, or sources of, data to be added to the Active Directory.

ADSI Basics

Before examining scripts and ASP pages, here is a short introduction to some basic ADSI operations. For a complete overview of ADSI see the ADSI SDK available at http://msdn.microsoft.com.

Architecture

ADSI objects are COM objects which represent objects in an underlying directory service. Objects can be *container* objects (which hold other objects) or *leaf* objects (which do not). Each has a unique ADSI path—a provider name followed by an object path. ADSI provides an abstract schema which describes the type of objects and attributes supported by each provider. Objects are read into a cache when *getinfo* or *getobject* are called. Changes reside in cached memory on the client until a *setinfo* is issued to write data back to the underlying directory store.

Connecting to the Active Directory

Using the LDAP Provider

> **Note**   The examples below assume that the user's current credentials are used to access the directory. If other credentials are needed, they can be supplied using the *openDSobject* method.

Serverless Binding

The preferred method for connecting to an object is to use serverless binding, which lets the default domain controller be the source of the LDAP requests. If the requested operations cannot be honored in the local domain, a referral to the correct server is generated when possible, allowing the system to pick the closest server.

A serverless path is of the form **LDAP://object**.

To bind to the domainDNS object which is the root container of the domain naming context:

```
Set Odse = GetObject("LDAP//DC=corp,DC=Microsoft,DC=com")
```

RootDdse

```
Set Odse = GetObject("LDAP//RootDse")
```

RootDse is a special LDAP object that exists on all LDAP V3 servers. With it you can write scripts that are independent of the domain or enterprise on which they are run.

For example, to reference an object in the current domain you can read the value for DefaultNamingContext to determine the current domain:

```
Get Path to the configuration naming context.
Set RootDse = GetObject("LDAP//RootDse")
Path =  "LDAP://" & RootDse.get("DefaultNamingContext").
```

Domain-based information such as users, groups, and computers resides in the *domain* naming context. Enterprise configuration information such as sites and subnets can be found in the Configuration naming context. You can learn the path to naming contexts by examining ConfigurationNamingContext and SchemaNamingContext.

Non-Windows 2000 Clients Using ADSI

ADSI serverless binding is not available on Windows NT 4 or Windows 9*x*, so on these platforms you must always supply the name of an LDAP server for the connections:

```
Set Odse = GetObject("LDAP//servername/RootDse")
```

> **Note**   You must supply a server name when connecting to the Microsoft Exchange LDAP Server.

Using the Global Catalog

A global catalog (GC) server is a domain controller that contains a partial read-only replica of every object in every naming context. The replica is used to quickly search the enterprise for an object. The GC contains all objects from all naming contexts, but it is partial in that it contains only attributes designated for replication to the GC. The GC is accessed using port 3268 or by the **GC** provider alias. In ADSI any reference to the GC is mapped to the LDAP provider on port 3268.

Some of the common uses for searching the GC are:

- Finding users' address book information.
- Looking up members of a universal group.
- Mapping the User Principal Name to a specific user account.

Reading an Object

To read an object you must first use *Getobject* to bind to it:

```
Set objuser = Getobject("LDAP://CN=dtrulli,CN=Users,DC=jdp,DC=com")
```

This fills the object cache in the client's memory with the object's attributes. You can access each attribute by its name:

```
Wscript.echo objuser.givenName & " " & objuser.sn & " " & objuser.mail
Set objuser = nothing
```

Updating an Object

To update attributes on an existing object you have to first bind to the object with *Getobject*, set each attribute's value (to update the values in the local object cache on the client), then issue a *setinfo* to write the changes back to the directory. This example sets the mail address and the user's last name on user account:

```
Set objuser = Getobject("LDAP://CN=dtrulli,CN=Users,DC=jdp,DC=com")
Objuser.mail = "dtrulli@microsoft.com"
Objuser.sn = "trulli"
Objuser.setinfo
Set objuser = nothing
```

Enumerating a Container

To enumerate a container such as on OU, first bind to the OU and then use a loop to enumerate the container's objects. To list all objects in the Users container:

```
Set ou = GetObject("LDAP://CN=Users,DC=jdp,DC=com")
For each obj in ou
   Wscript.echo obj.name
Next
```

Searching

OLE DB provides a common way to query for information in a database-like way. The ADSI OLE DB provider allows you use ActiveX Data Objects (ADOs) to search the Active Directory. The provider is read-only, so if you need to modify an object after you search for it, use *GetObject* with the *AdsPath*.

To search the Active directory you must first create the ADO connection and command objects:

```
' list all objects in the domain naming context
Dim con , rs, Com

Set con = wscript.CreateObject("ADODB.Connection")
Set com =  wscript.CreateObject("ADODB.Command")
```

Next, open the ADO provider:

```
'Open a Connection object
con.Provider = "ADsDSOObject"
con.Open "Active Directory Provider"
```

Then set the command object to use the current connection object, and build the query using either a simple SQL format or the LDAP search filter format (used in the example below). The query specifies the search's starting path and a filter for matching (the example below looks for any type of object). Then list the attributes you want the query to return. Finally, specify the depth of the search: *subtree* for a deep search, *base* for a single object, or *one-level* for searching a container.

```
Set Com.ActiveConnection = con
Com.CommandText =
"<GC://DC=hq,DC=jdp,DC=com>;(objectClass=*);adspath;subtree"

'
'Set the preferences for Search
'
Com.Properties("Page Size") = 512
Com.Properties("Timeout") = 30 'seconds
```

When you execute the query, the results are returned in a recordset. Loop through the recordset and print out the value, then move on to the next record.

```
Set rs = Com.Execute

While Not rs.EOF
   Wscript.echo rs.Fields("Adspath").Value
   rs.MoveNext
Wend
```

Managing Domain Information

Extracting Computer Information

Network administrators have always wanted an easy way to get a list of network workstations along with operating system and service pack information. You can now do this by using new attributes on Windows 2000 computer accounts to identify the computer's current status. The *computer* object is now automatically updated with information (from the netlogon service during secure channel setup) about the client's operating system, operating system version, and service pack level.

You can identify unused or possibly inactive computer accounts: accounts that have never been used do not have the operating system and version attributes set. If the *whenChanged* attribute is more than a month old, the computer probably is not active on a network making periodic password changes. The *whenChanged* attribute is a non-replicated attribute which means it is calculated on each DC. The *lastLogon* attribute is not replicated between DCs; to determine the last logon time you have to examine it on all DCs.

Attributes of interest:

Attribute	Function
Name	Computer name
dNSHostname	Full DNS hostname of the machine
UserAccountControl	Type of account: ADS_UF_WORKSTATION_TRUST_ACCOUNT ADS_UF_SERVER_TRUST_ACCOUNT
operatingSystem	Windows NT, Windows 2000 Server, or Windows 2000 Professional
operatingSystemVersion	Operating system version and build: 4.0, 5.0 (2128)
operatingSystemServicePack	Operating system service pack number
operatingSystemHotfix	List of hotfixes
whenCreated	When the object was created
whenChanged	When the object was modified

The listing below queries for computer object and displays operating system information.

```
strADOQueryString = "<" & path &
">;(objectCategory=computer);name,DnsHostname,UserAccountControl,operati
ngSystem,OperatingSystemVersion,whenCreated,whenChanged;subtree"

Set objADOconn = Server.CreateObject("ADODB.Connection")
    objADOconn.Provider = "ADSDSOObject"
    objADOconn.Open "ADs Provider"
Set objADOcom =   Server.CreateObject("ADODB.Command")
Set objADOCom.ActiveConnection = objADOconn

    objADOCom.Properties("Page Size") = 250
    objADOCom.Properties("Cache Results") = False

    objADOcom.commandtext = strADOQueryString
    Set objRS = objADOcom.execute

    nmachines = 0
    response.write "<table border=1>"
    response.write "<thead><tr><td>Computer</td><td>DNS
Name</td><td>Role</td><td>OS</td><td>Version</td><td>Created</td><td>Mod
fied</td></tr></thead>"
    While Not objRS.EOF and nmachines < MAXENTRY
        response.write "<tr><td>"
        response.Write objRS.Fields(0)& " "
        response.write "</td><td>"
        Response.Write objRS.Fields(1) & " "
        Response.Write "</td><td>"
        if (objRS.Fields(2) and ADS_UF_WORKSTATION_TRUST_ACCOUNT ) then
            s = "Workstation or Server"
        elseif (objRS.Fields(2) and ADS_UF_SERVER_TRUST_ACCOUNT ) then
            s = "Domain Controller"
        else
            s = ""
        end if
        Response.Write s & " "
        Response.Write "</td><td>"
        Response.Write objRS.Fields(3) & " "
        Response.Write "</td><td>"
        Response.Write objRS.Fields(4) & " "
        Response.Write "</td><td>"
        Response.Write objRS.Fields(5) & " "
        Response.Write "</td><td>"
        Response.Write objRS.Fields(6) & " "
        Response.Write "</td>"
        Response.Write "</tr>" & vbNewline
        nmachines = nmachines + 1
        objRS.MoveNext
    Wend
    response.write "</table>"
    objRS.Close
    response.write "<p>Total = " & nmachines
    if nmachines = MAXENTRY then response.write " MAX Query Limit Hit"
```

Trust Relationships

When you want to document your configuration, it is useful to have a list of all domain trust relationships, especially during migrations, when you usually have a mix of trusts between Windows 2000 domains, Windows NT account domains, and Windows NT 4.0 resource domains. Each trust relationship in a domain has a trusted domain object that resides in the System container in the Domain naming context:

Object	Contents
flatName	The NetBIOS name of the domain for this trust.
trustDirection	The direction of the established trust relationship: 0 = disabled 1 = inbound (trusting domain) 2 = outbound (trusted domain) 3 = both (trusted and trusting)
trustPartner	A string representing the DNS-style name of Windows 2000 domains or the NetBIOS name of down-level trust domains.
trustType	The type of trust relationship established to the domain: 1 = downlevel trust 2 = Windows 2000 trust 3 = MIT 4 = DCE

```
Set objADOconn = Server.CreateObject("ADODB.Connection")
Set objADOcom =   server.CreateObject("ADODB.Command")

objADOconn.Provider = "ADSDSOObject"
objADOconn.Open "ADs Provider"

Set objADOCom.ActiveConnection = objADOconn
objADOCom.Properties("Sort On") = "trustPartner"


strADOQueryString = "<" & path &
">:(objectCategory=trustedDomain);trustPartner,flatName,trusttype,
trustdirection;onelevel"

objADOcom.commandtext = strADOQueryString
Set objRS = objADOcom.execute

    response.write "<Table border=1>"
    response.write "<thead><tr><td colspan=4 align=center>" &
dc2dns(domain) & "</td></tr><tr><td>Domain</td><td>NetBios
Name</td><td>Type</td><td>Direction</td></tr></thead>"
```

```
While Not objRS.EOF
  response.write   "<tr>"
  response.write   "<td>" & objRS.Fields(0) &  "</td>"
  response.write   "<td>" & objRS.Fields(1) &  "</td>"

  select case objRS.Fields(2)
     case 1  s = "Downlevel Trust"
     case 2  s = "Windows 2000 Trust"
     case 3  s = "MIT"
     case 4  s = "DCS"
  end select
  response.write   "<td>" & s & "</td>"

  select case objRS.Fields(3)
     case 1  s = "Inbound"
     case 2  s = "Outbound"
     case 3  s = "Bidirectional"
  end select
  response.write   "<td>" & s &  "</td>"

  response.write "</tr>"
  objRS.MoveNext
Wend

response.write "</Table>"

objRS.Close
```

Creating User Accounts

When creating a new user account, you must set the *CN* (unique in the account's OU) and *Samaccountname* (unique in the domain) attributes. The *userPrincipalName* attribute (unique in the enterprise) is optional. To create a user object:

```
Dim Container
Dim NewUser
Dim Odse
Dim strUser

strUser = "test123"

Set Odse = GetObject("LDAP://RootDSE")
Set Container = GetObject("LDAP://CN=Users," &
Odse.get("DefaultNamingContext"))
```

First, create a reference to the container that will hold the user account:

```
Set NewUser = Container.Create("User", "CN=" & strUser)
```

Next, set the mandatory attributes and save the settings to create the account. New accounts are disabled by default, so the next steps are to set the password, enable the account, and require the user to change the password on first use:

```
NewUser.Samaccountname = struser
NewUser.SetInfo
NewUser.SetPassword "abc123"
' enable the account
Newuser.UserAccountControl = NewUserAccountControl and not &H2
NewUser.SetInfo
```

Creating Groups

There are three scopes for groups:

Scope	Members	Grant Permissions	Member of Other Groups
Universal	From any Windows NT or Windows 2000 domain in the forest: Universal Groups, Global Groups, and users (including contacts).	On any domain in the forest	Can be a member of Local Groups and Universal Groups in the forest.
Global	Only from the domain containing the group: Global Groups and users (including contacts).	On any domain in the forest	Can be a member of any group in the forest: Global Groups, Local Groups, and Universal Groups.
Domain Local	From any domain in the forest: Global Groups, Universal Groups, and users (including contacts). Domain local groups from the domain containing the group	Only on the domain containing the group	Can be a member only of Local Groups in the domain containing the group.

Groups are of these types:

- **Security.** Use security groups to control access to resources. You can also use them as e-mail distribution lists.
- **Distribution.** Use distribution groups if the group is used only for e-mail distribution lists or for grouping purposes. These are primarily used to combine related objects—you cannot use them for access control. You can explicitly

disable security on these groups to avoid unnecessary evaluation of these groups during a user's logon process. This makes log on more efficient by not examining these groups when the log on process creates the user's security token, and makes evaluation of access rights more efficient by reducing security token size.

Group type is required. Specify an integer that contains the flags that specify the group type and scope using these combinations:

Group	Flags
Global security	ADS_GROUP_TYPE_GLOBAL_GROUP | ADS_GROUP_TYPE_SECURITY_ENABLED
Domain local Security	ADS_GROUP_TYPE_DOMAIN_LOCAL_GROUP | ADS_GROUP_TYPE_SECURITY_ENABLED
Universal security	ADS_GROUP_TYPE_UNIVERSAL_GROUP | ADS_GROUP_TYPE_SECURITY_ENABLED
Global distribution	ADS_GROUP_TYPE_GLOBAL_GROUP
Domain local distribution	ADS_GROUP_TYPE_DOMAIN_LOCAL_GROUP
Universal distribution	ADS_GROUP_TYPE_UNIVERSAL_GROUP

The process of creating a group is similar to other objects. First bind to the OU which will contain the group. Next create the group object. Then set the group type, and *samAccountname* for down-level clients.

```
Set ou = GetObject("LDAP://OU=DSys,DC=Northwind,DC=tld")
Set grp = ou.Create("group", "CN=Distributed System Admin")

'----Creating a domain local group----
grp.Put "groupType", ADS_GROUP_TYPE_LOCAL_GROUP Or
ADS_GROUP_TYPE_SECURITY_ENABLED
grp.Put "samAccountName", "DSysAdmin"
grp.SetInfo
```

Use the **add** method to add members to a group using the path to the user's object.

```
'----Adding a user to a group----
grp.Add ("LDAP://CN=James
Smith,OU=Marketing,OU=DSys,DC=Northwind,DC=tld")
```

From the Trenches: Using the Active Directory To Track a Pilot

During a Windows 2000 Pilot, Microsoft Consulting Services wanted a self documenting method that would track the configuration of the organizations in which they delegated administrative management for a subset of users, groups, and computers. By using an ADSI Web page it was possible to trace the list of delegated groups and provide a list of the administrative contacts for each group.

When there is a well known OU structure for the pilot groups, this is easy to do, so for each pilot group, they created an OU structure based on site name, and a global group for the groups administrators (Figure 10.2).

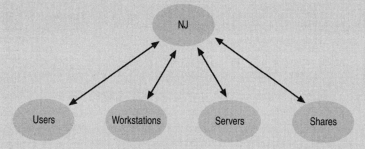

Figure 10.2   OU structure for MCS pilot.

For a pilot group named NJ, they created an OU called NJ and a global group called NJ-Admins.

On each site OU they set these attributes for tracking:

Attribute	LDAP Name
Description	description
Street	street
City	l
State/Province	st
Country	c

They then set each administrator's account to contain a phone number and e-mail address.

At this point, they could write ASP pages that used this structure to create a dynamic table of all the delegated sites; by drilling down in this table they could find each administrator's contact information as well as information on the number of servers, workstations, and users at each site. (See the samples on the CD that accompanies this book).

Managing Enterprise Configuration Information

Configuration information is global information shared among all domains in the enterprise and usually managed by the enterprise administrator. This section examines some of the configuration information you need to look at frequently.

Partitions

The partitions container's **crossRef** objects list the enterprise naming contexts— one for Configuration, one for Schema, and one for each Domain. You can add objects to point to partitions on other LDAP servers that are not part of the enterprise, in which case you generate an LDAP referral to the proper partition when requesting an object from that portion of the namespace.

Listing all domains from the partition information is easy: simply enumerate the objects in the partition container.

```
Set domain = GetObject( ldapprefix() & "CN=Partitions," & configpath ))

domain.filter = array( "CrossRef")

response.write "<table border=1 cellspacing=0>"
response.write "<thead><tr><td>Enterprise Domains</td></tr></thead>"
For each obj in domain
    if (obj.systemflags and 3) = 3 then
        response.write  "<tr><td><A HREF=domain-menu.asp?domain=" &
obj.dnsroot & ">" & obj.dnsroot & "</A></td></tr>"
    end if
Next

response.write "</Table
```

Examine the *systemflags* attribute of the CrossRef object to determine if the object refers to an enterprise, domain, or external partition. These are:

Bit	Meaning
1	If set partition is in this forest.
2	If set naming context represents a domain.

To list all domains in the enterprise, enumerate the partitions container examining the *systemflags* of each entry

```
If  (obj.systemflags and 3) = 3 then wscript.echo obj.name
```

Listing Sites

Sites in the active directory model contain groups of computers that share a high-speed connection and thus are considered "close" to each other. To identify membership in a site, examine the computer's IP address and match it with a list of IP subnets. Each site contains one or more IP subnets.

The site objects reside in the site containers in the configuration naming context. So for the enterprise with a root domain called **corp.Microsoft.com** the path to the sites container would be:

```
CN=Sites,CN=Configuration,DC=corp,DC=Microsoft,DC=com
```

The example below generates a Web page listing for each site in the enterprise along with some key site attributes. There are two items of particular interest: the InterSite topology generator (a DC in the site responsible for generating all inter-site connections for the site) and the site option attributes (which contain advanced site settings that have to be set with LDAP and can't be set with normal administration tools). The CD contains an example page for setting the site options attribute; its bit fields are:

Bit	Function
1	Disables automatic intra-site topology generation by the Knowledge Consistency Checker (KCC).
2	Disables the cleanup of outdated replication connections.
3	Disables the generation of extra optimizing connections in a site. These connections keep the maximum-hop counts to 3 or fewer.
4	Disables detection of failed replication links and the rerouting of replication traffic.
5	Disables automatic inter-site topology generation by the KCC.

```
<%@ LANGUAGE = VBScript %>
<% Option Explicit    %>
<HTML>
<HEAD>
<LINK REL="STYLESHEET" HREF="STYLE.CSS">
<SCRIPT LANGUAGE=vbscript RUNAT=Server SRC=ds.inc></SCRIPT>
</HEAD>
<BODY>
<%

dim Objdse
dim ObjSite
dim Objsites
dim Site
dim obj
dim options
dim soptions
```

```
Set ObjSites = GetObject( "LDAP://CN=Sites," & configpath)

objSites.filter = array("Site")
%>
<TABLE border=1>
<thead>
   <tr>
   <td>Site</td>
   <td>Topology Generator</td>
   <td>Location</td>
   <td>Options</td>
   <td>Description</td>
</tr>
</THEAD>
<%
For each obj in ObjSites
  set objsite = obj.getobject("nTDSSiteSettings", "CN=NTDS Site Settings")
  options = objsite.options
  soptions = ""
  if options and 1 then
     soptions = soptions & "Disable IntraSite Topology Generation<br>"
  end if
  if options and 2 then
     soptions = soptions & "Disable Cleanup<br>"
  end if
  if options and 4 then
     soptions = soptions & "Disable Optimizing Edges<br>"
  end if
  if options and 8 then
     soptions = soptions & "Disable Stale Link Detection<br>"
  end if
  if options and 16 then
     soptions = soptions & "Disable InterSite Topology Generation<br>"
  end if
  site = mid(obj.Name,4)
%>
   <tr>
   <td><A HREF=siteinfo.asp?site=<%=site%>><%=site%></td>

<td><%=getldapcomponent(objsite.interSiteTopologyGenerator,1)%> </td>
   <td><%=obj.location%> </td>
   <td><%=soptions%> </td>
   <td><%=obj.description%> </td>
   </tr>
 <% Next %>

</TABLE>

</BODY>
</HTML>
```

Creating Sites

To create a new site you have to create four objects:

- A *Site* container object
- A *NTDSSiteSettings* object
- A *LicensingSiteSettings* object
- A *Servers* container

```
Option Explicit

' Create a new Site in Container
sub mksite(strsite,osites)

Dim Ontds
Dim Ontlic
Dim osite
Dim OServers

Set Osite = Osites.create("site", "CN=" & strSite )
Osite.setinfo
Set Ontds = Osite.create("NTDSSiteSettings", "CN=NTDS Site Settings")
Ontds.setinfo
Set Ontlic = Osite.create("LicensingSiteSettings", "CN=Licensing Site
Settings")
Ontlic.setinfo
Set OServers = Osite.create("ServersContainer", "CN=Servers")
OServers.setinfo

end sub

Dim Odse
Dim Osites
Dim strSite

if wscript.arguments.count = 0 then
    wscript.echo "Usage: mksite.vbs Sitename"
    wscript.quit
end if

strSite = wscript.arguments(0)

set Odse = GetObject("LDAP://RootDSE")
Set Osites = GetObject( "LDAP://CN=Sites,"
&_Odse.get("ConfigurationNamingContext"))
mksite strSite, Osites
```

> **Note**   To ensure all sites are reachable in the replication topology, each site must be in at least one site link. Each site link must contain two or more sites and there must be path to each site link to prevent orphaned sites.

Listing Subnets

Subnet objects are contained in the subnets container in the configuration naming context. The path to the subnets container in enterprise **corp.Microsoft.com** would be:

```
CN=Subnets,CN=Sites,CN=Configuration,DC=corp,DC=Microsoft,DC=com
```

You can list the subnet objects by enumerating the Subnets container. Subnet names use the network address and number of bits in the network portion of the subnet. For example a class C subnet 192.168.1.0 with netmask 255.255.255.0 would have the name CN=192.168.1.0/24 (there are 24 bits in the network portion of the netmask).

The listing below contains a wscript to list subnets as well as an ASP page which lists subnets in a table. The *siteobject* attribute contains the distinguished name of the subnet's site. Use the *location* attribute to search for nearby printers.

```
cscript to list subnets.
set dse = GetObject("LDAP://RootDSE")
Set domain = GetObject( "LDAP://CN=Subnets,CN=Sites," &
dse.get("ConfigurationNamingContext"))

domain.filter = array( "Subnet")
'Enumerate objects in the domain container
For each obj in domain
  wscript.echo  "  Subnet: " & obj.Name & " Site: " & obj.siteobject
Next
```

> **Note**   The CD accompanying this book has an ASP version of Subnet List.

Creating Subnets

Creating a subnet is straightforward: create a subnet object with a name derived from the network address and netmask as shown above. Each subnet needs to reside in a site, so set the *siteobject* attribute to the distinguished name of the site object containing this subnet. Subnets also have a *location* attribute you can populate; it is used by clients to search for nearby.printers.

```
Cscript to create a subnet
Option Explicit

Dim Odse
Dim Osubnets
Dim Osubnet
Dim strSubnet
Dim strSite
Dim strSites
Dim count

count = wscript.arguments.count

if count = 0 then
   wscript.echo "Usage: mksubnet.vbs subnet [site]"
   wscript.quit
end if

strsubnet = wscript.arguments(0)

if count > 1 then strSite = wscript.arguments(1)

set Odse = GetObject("LDAP://RootDSE")
strSites = "CN=Sites," & Odse.get("ConfigurationNamingContext")

Set Osubnets = GetObject("LDAP://CN=Subnets," & strSites)

Set Osubnet = Osubnets.create("subnet", "CN=" & strSubnet)
if strsite <> "" then
   osubnet.siteobject = "CN=" & strsite & "," & strsites
end if
Osubnet.setinfo
```

Note   Each subnet can reside in only one site but each site can contain many subnets. If you do not assign a site to a subnet, the client will not locate the closest domain controller.

Listing Domain Controllers

Each domain controller in the enterprise is represented by several objects:

- A *computer* object residing in the Domain naming context (the computer account for the machine).

- An *nTDSDSA* object (*NTDS Settings*) residing in the Configuration naming context. *NTDS Settings* is a container that represents an instance of the directory service; it holds the DC's inbound replication connections. If you accidentally remove a NTDS Setting, the DC owning the object will resurrect the deleted object.

■ A *Servers* object residing under the *Serverscontainer* object in the DC's site.

To get a list of all enterprise DCs, issue a query with a base path of the site's container that searches for object category *nTDSDSA*. Some attributes of interest:

■ **Adspath.** Use the full path to the object to find the parent object, which contains the DNS hostname of the DCs.

■ **HasMasterNCs.** A multi-valued list of all the writeable naming contexts. For this release of Windows 2000, these are Schema, Configuration, and Domain.

■ **HasPartialReplicaNCs.** A multi-valued attribute; on global catalog servers this contains the names of the GC's partial naming contexts.

■ **Options.** Bit 1 indicates if this DC is also GC.

```
<HTML>
<HEAD>
<META NAME="GENERATOR" Content="Microsoft Visual Studio 6.0">
<LINK REL="STYLESHEET" HREF="STYLE.CSS">
<TITLE></TITLE>
</HEAD>
<SCRIPT LANGUAGE=vbscript RUNAT=Server SRC=ds.inc>
</SCRIPT>
<BODY>

<%

dim myarray
dim objdse     ' root ds object
dim config     ' name of configuration
dim base       ' path to start search
dim isGCs      ' if Dc is a GC
dim dc         ' DC server name
dim objcurr

config = getconfig() ' my helper function to lookup config name

site = request("Site")

Base = "LDAP://"

if len(site) > 0 then
   base = base & "CN=" & site & ","
end if

base = base & "CN=Sites," & config
```

(continued)

```
Set objADOconn = Server.CreateObject("ADODB.Connection")
objADOconn.Provider = "ADSDSOObject"
objADOconn.Open "ADs Provider"

    '-- Perform an LDAP query =
    strADOQueryString = "<" & Base &
">;(objectCategory=nTDSdsa);adspath,hasMasterNCs,hasPartialReplicaNCs,op
tions;subtree"


Set objRS = objADOconn.Execute(strADOQueryString)

If err <> 0 then
    response.write "Site does not exist:<br>" & base
    response.end
end if


    response.write "<table border=1>"
    response.write "<thead><tr><td>Server</td><td>Options</td><td>Naming
Contexts</td></tr></thead>"
    While Not objRS.EOF
      response.write "<tr>"
      set objcurr = getobject(objRS.Fields(0))
      set objserver = getobject(objcurr.parent)
      dc = objserver.DNShostname
      if dc = "" then dc = objserver.cn
      response.write "<td><a href=" & chr(34) & "repmon.asp?dc=" &  dc &
chr(34) & ">" & dc & "</a></td>" & vbNewline
      isGC = objRS.Fields(3) and 1
      if isGC then options = "GC" else options = "" end if
          response.write "<td> " & options & "</td>"
          response.write "<td>"
          NCList = objRS.Fields(1)
          for each n in NCList
              response.write  n & "<br>"
      Next
      if isGC then
        response.write "<b><u>Partial Naming Contexts(GC)</u></b><br>"
        NCList = objRS.Fields(2)
            if Vartype(NCList) <> 1  then
            for each n in NCList
                      response.write  n & "<br>"
          Next
          end if
      end if
          response.write "</td>"
            response.write "</tr>"
          objRS.MoveNext
          set objcurr = nothing
```

```
      set objserver = nothing
   Wend
   response.write "</table>"
   objRS.Close

%>
</BODY>
</HTML>
```

Site Links

Site links define the network connection between sites. A site link contains two or more sites that can replicate together with a common cost and schedule. (See Chapter 2 for more information on replication topology.) By default they are transitive, thus the Knowledge Consistency Checker (KCC) can connect them to form a replication path. A set of site links apply to an inter-site replication transport such as IP or SMTP. The site links for the IP transport reside in the container's Configuration naming context: CN = IP, CN = inter-site transports. They are represented by site link objects, each of which has a replication cost, a multi-valued list of sites, options settings, and a schedule. You have to use LDAP or ADSI operations (not the Sites and Services MMC snap-in) to set these advanced options:

- **Notification.** Bit 1 defines notification on a site link, which causes inter-site replication to be triggered based on changes to the directory rather than on the replication polling interval. This is useful when two or more sites are connected by high-speed connections and you want very low inter-site latency: it is not appropriate for low-speed WAN connections and it is not the default.

- **Two-way sync.** Defined by bit 2, you should use this for dial on demand connection, where replication should occur in both directions during the same dial-up session.

```
Set objdse = GetObject(  ldapprefix() & "CN=IP" & ",CN=Inter-Site
Transports,CN=Sites," & getconfig())

objdse.filter = array("SiteLink")
response.write "<Table border=1>"
response.write "<thead><tr><td colspan=""6""><p align=""center"">" &
Transport & " Transport Site Links</td></tr>"
response.write "<tr><td>Site
Link</td><td>Cost</td><td>Interval</td><td>Sites</td><td>Options</td><td
>Description</td></tr></thead>"
For each obj in objdse

   response.write  "<tr><td>" & mid(obj.Name,4) & "</td><td>" & obj.cost
& "</td><td>" & obj.replInterval  & "</td><td>"

   sites = obj.getex("sitelist")
```

(continued)

```
for each s in sites
  response.write getldapcomponent ( s , 0 ) + "<br>"
  next
response.write "</td><td> "
if (obj.options and 1 ) then
  response.write "USE_NOTIFY<br>"
end if
if (obj.options and 2 ) then
  response.write "TWOWAY_SYNC<br>"
end if
response.write "</td><td> " & obj.description & "</td></tr>"
Next

response.write "</Table>"
```

This example uses *getex* to obtain the value of a multi-valued attribute (an attribute—such as a list—that can contain one or more values). The *sitelist* attribute contains a list of sites.

Replication Connections

When documenting or analyzing the current replication topology, it helps to have a complete list of all the replication connections in the enterprise and in the site. It is difficult to gather this information in the MMC because not all of it resides on a single node in the Sites and Services MMC snap-in. To get a list of replication connections, issue a query for *NTDSConnection* objects. You can adjust the scope of the search by varying its search base.

For all replications connections in the enterprise:

```
CN=Sites, CN=configuration,DC=…
```

For all replication connections in a site:

```
CN=Sitename,CN=Sites,CN=configuration,DC=…
```

For replications connections for a particular DC:

```
CN=Servername,CN=Servers,CN=Sitename,CN=Sites,CN=configuration,DC=…
```

Attributes of interest:

Attribute	Function
DistinguishedName	Used to determine the server
FromServer	The source server for this connection
TransportType	The transport used (IP, RPC SMTP)
Options	Options for this connection (admin generated, two-way, notification based)

```
Set objADOconn = Server.CreateObject("ADODB.Connection")
    objADOconn.Provider = "ADSDSOObject"
    objADOconn.Open "ADs Provider"

  strADOQueryString = "<" & path &
">;(objectCategory=nTDSConnection);distinguishedName,FromServer,transpor
ttype,options;subtree"
    Set objRS = objADOconn.Execute(strADOQueryString)

    response.write "<table border=1>"
    response.write "<thead><tr><td>Dest Server</td><td>Dest
Site</td><td>From Server</td><td>From
Site</td><td>Transport</td><td>Type</td></tr></thead>"
    While Not objRS.EOF
      response.write "<tr><td>"
    myarray = split (objRS.Fields(0), ",", -1, 1)
      Response.Write mid(myarray(2),4)
      response.write "</td><td>"
      Response.Write mid(myarray(4), 4)
      Response.Write "</td><td>"
    myarray = split (objRS.Fields(1), ",", -1, 1)
      Response.Write mid(myarray(1),4)
      response.write "</td><td>"
      Response.Write mid(myarray(3), 4)
      response.write "</td><td> "
      if objRS.Fields(2) <> "" then
              myarray = split (objRS.Fields(2), ",", -1, 1)
                  Response.Write mid(myarray(0), 4)

    else
            Response.write "RPC"
    end if
        Response.Write "</td><td>"
    if (objRS.Fields(3) and 1) = 0 then
        Response.write "Admin"
    else
        Response.write "Auto"
    end if
        objRS.MoveNext
        response.write "</td></tr>"

    Wend
    response.write "</table>"
    objRS.Close
```

FSMO

Chapter 2 introduced *Flexible Single-Master Operations* (FSMO), which implement operations (there are only a few) that must be handled in a single-master replication model. There are five FSMO roles, two per enterprise and three per domain, and you can use scripting to find out which DCs hold which FSMO roles.

Schema Master

The Schema Master is unique in the entire enterprise; it alone can create new classes or attributes, after which it replicates updates to all domains in the forest. To identify it, read the value of the *fsmoRoleOwner* attribute on the Schema container found under the Configuration container. Schema and Configuration naming contexts are enterprise-wide and reside on all domain controllers.

```
Set objRootDse = Getobject("LDAP://RootDse")
Set objSchema = getobject("LDAP://"
&objRootDse.get("SchemaNamingContext"))
wscript.echo objSchema.fsmoRoleOwner
```

Domain Naming Master

The Domain Naming Master is unique in the enterprise; it manages the addition and removal of domains into the forest. To identify it, read the *partitions* container object and examine its *fsmoRoleOwner* attribute:

```
Set objRootDse = Getobject("LDAP://RootDse")
set objDomains = getobject( "LDAP://CN=Partitions," & _
ObjRootdse.get("ConfigurationNamingContext"))
wscript.echo objDomains.fsmoRoleOwner
```

PDC Emulator

The PDC Emulator is a per-domain role. To identify it, read the value of the *fsmoRoleOwner* attribute on the DomainDNS object:

```
Set objRootDse = Getobject("LDAP://RootDse")
set objPDC = getobject("LDAP://" &
ObjRootdse.get("DefaultNamingContext"))
wscript.echo objPDC.fsmoRoleOwner
```

RID Master

The RID Master is a per-domain role. It allocates RID blocks for all DCs in a domain that are used for SIDs in security principals such as users and groups. To identify it, read the value of the *fsmoRoleOwner* attribute on the rIDManager object of name CN="Rid Manager$" found in the domain's System container:

```
Set objRootDse = Getobject("LDAP://RootDse")
set objRID = getobject("LDAP://CN=Rid Manager$,CN=System," & _
ObjRootdse.get("DefaultNamingContext"))
wscript.echo objRID.fsmoRoleOwner
```

Infrastructure Master

The Infrastructure Master is a per-domain role. To identify it, read the value of the *fsmoRoleOwner* attribute on the InfrastructureUpdate object for the domain:

```
Set objRootDse = Getobject("LDAP://RootDse")
set objInfra = getobject("LDAP://CN=Infrastructure," &
Objdse.get("DefaultNamingContext"))
wscript.echo objInfra.fsmoRoleOwner
```

IADSTools Examples

IADSTools is a scriptable interface to many common Windows 2000 directory operations. It is supplied with the other support tools on the operating system CD. Replmon uses IADS tools extensively; you can use them in applications.

List All Global Catalog Servers

This script gets the list of enterprise Global Catalog servers from "server1":

```
Set DLL=CreateObject("IADsTools.DCFunctions")
Result=DLL.GetGCList("server1")
if result=-1 Then
    Wscript.echo "The error returned was: " + DLL.LastErrorText
else
    Wscript.echo "The number of Global Catalog servers returned is: " +
cstr(result)
    wscript.echo "----------------------------------------------------"
    for i=1 to Result
        'print out the name of each GC server
        wscript.echo DLL.GCName(i)
    next
end if
```

Trigger Replication

This script demonstrates how you can use a script to initiate replication between two servers:

```
Dim TargetServer
Dim SourceServer
Dim NamingContext
```

(continued)

```
TargetServer="server1"
SourceServer="server2"
NamingContext="cn=configuration,dc=mydomain,dc=com"

Set DLL=CreateObject("IADsTools.DCFunctions")
Result=DLL.ReplicaSync(Cstr(TargetServer),Cstr(NamingContext),Cstr(Sourc
eServer))
if result=-1 Then
    Wscript.Echo "The error returned was: " + DLL.LastErrorText
else
    Wscript.Echo "The command completed successfully."
end if
```

Replication Status

You can use IADStools to query the replication status of each DC. With functions such as *GetdirectPartnersEx* you can obtain the same type of replication information you get with the *repadmin* tool.

This script combines functions that lists all DCs, lists their directory partitions, and checks each partition's replication status:

```
Set DLL=CreateObject("IADsTools.DCFunctions")
'read the list of domain controllers
Result=DLL.DsGetDCList("server1","mydomain.com",1)
if result=-1 Then
    Wscript.echo "The error returned was: " + DLL.LastErrorText
else
    Wscript.echo "The number of Domain Controllers returned is: " +
cstr(result)
    wscript.echo "-------------------------------------------------"
    for i=1 to Result

        'for each domain controller, get the number of Directory
Partitions (non-partial) it hosts
        wscript.echo "Checking domain controller: " +
DLL.DCListEntryNetBiosName(i)

PartitionResult=DLL.GetNamingContexts(DLL.DCListEntryNetBiosName(i))

        'if we couldn't reach the server, skip it
        if PartitionResult=-1 then
            wscript.echo "Could not reach the server: " +
DLL.DCListEntryNetBiosName(i)
        else
            wscript.echo "Found " + CStr(PartitionResult) + " Directory
Partitions (non-partial) on (" + DLL.DCListEntryNetBiosName(i) + ")."

            'query the status of each directory partition
            for j=1 to PartitionResult
```

```
ReplResult=DLL.GetDirectPartnersEx(DLL.DCListEntryNetBiosName(i),DLL.Nam
ingContextName(j))

                'see if there's a failure code other than zero for any
of the replication partners
                for k=1 to ReplResult
                    if DLL.DirectPartnerFailReason(k) > 0 then
                        wscript.echo "Failure detected replicating
partition (" + DLL.NamingContextName(j) + ") from (" +
DLL.DirectPartnerName(k) + ")."
                    else
                        'if you wanted to enable the following line, you
could see the ones that are OK as well
                        'wscript.echo "OK --- Replicating partition (" +
DLL.NamingContextName(j) + ") from (" + DLL.DirectPartnerName(k) + ")."
                    end if
                next
            next
        end if
    next
end if
```

WMI

Windows Management Instrumentation (WMI) is a scaleable, extensible management infrastructure, included as part of Windows 2000. An implementation of the Web-based Enterprise Management (WBEM), and based on the Common Information Model (CIM) adopted by the Distributed Management Task Force (DMTF), it includes a rich set of management data about computer systems, the operating system, and applications on a given managed system. Through a set of object classes derived from the CIM model, applications and scripts can view and change properties, execute methods, and receive events about modeled objects. For example, WMI exposes a wealth of information about the operating system (how many processes are running, the operational state of a particular service, current processor usage, etc.) and publishes it in a common schema that is accessible locally and remotely though standard script languages. Other benefits of WMI include:

- **Uniform Scripting API.** All managed objects are defined under a common object framework based on the CIM object model. Scripts can use one API (WMI) to access information for disparate sources such as the Win32 API, Windows NT Event Log, the registry, performance counters, device drivers, SNMP and, of course, the Active Directory. You can also write scripts for ASP and HTML pages in Windows Scripting Host (WSH) languages.

- **Remote Administration.** Objects managed within WMI are by definition locally and remotely available to applications and scripts. No additional work is needed to manage remote objects.

- **Discoverability and Navigation.** Applications and scripts can discover what information is available about a system by enumerating available classes. You can detect relationships between related objects and traverse them to see how one managed entity affects another.

- **Query Capability.** WMI manages data much like a relational database so you can submit SQL queries that filter and focus data of interest.

- **Powerful Event Publication and Subscription.** You can request events for virtually any change in the managed objects in the system—even those that do not support an internal event capability. Event subscribers can request notification of very specific events rather than receiving a set of events that were predefined by the original developers. The architecture allows virtually any user-defined action to be taken upon the receipt of a given event.

WMI is complementary to Active Directory, bringing detailed information about an individual system together with the Active Directory's distributed, enterprise-level view. Since there are many occasions where a script or application writer might be interested in collecting information or performing configuration based on both the Active Directory and WMI, it is extremely convenient to have both available in a common format. This integration is supplied by the WMI's Active Directory provider, which automatically discovers and maps the information stored in the Active Directory to a set of equivalent WMI classes that you can view and manipulate the contents as if they were any other WMI class.

Before looking at how to work with Active Directory data in a WMI script, here is some information on how to access WMI data: reading and writing a property, executing a method, and registering for an event.

To read and write a property, you need to select a class of interest. The example below reads the current delay setting to be used before booting the default operating system, displays the value, then writes the value back, incremented by ten seconds. The *Win32_ComputerSystem* class contains the correct property for this (*SystemStartupDelay*).

```
Set CompSysSet =
GetObject("winmgmts:").InstancesOf("Win32_ComputerSystem")
for each CompSys in CompSysSet
    Wscript.Echo "Previous boot delay was "&  _
CompSys.SystemStartupDelay & " seconds."
    CompSys.SystemStartupDelay = CompSys.SystemStartupDelay + 10
    CompSys.Put_()
WScript.Echo "Boot up delay time set to " & CompSys.SystemStartupDelay &
" seconds."
next
```

Using moniker support, the first statement requests all instances of the *Win32_ComputerSystem* class from the WMI service (winmgnts). Next, the script iterates through the returned instances (there is really only one instance in this case, because each computer can be only one computer system). Within the loop, the current delay value is first displayed. It is then incremented by ten seconds in the local script variable, and the *Put_()* method is called against this instance; it writes the modified instance back to WMI and it is displayed. You can verify the actual change to the system by either rerunning the script (the beginning delay value will be 10 seconds larger) or looking at this value in the Control Panel. Note that the *SystemStartupDelay* property is being treated as an automation property of the object, making the script much more readable and intuitive.

In the next example, the *PauseService()* method of the *Win32_Service* class is used to pause the Windows Scheduler service. To demonstrate the query ability of WMI, rather than ask for all instances of the *Win32_Service* class, an SQL query is submitted requesting the particular service that has its *Name* property set to "Schedule".

```
Set ServiceSet = GetObject("winmgmts:").ExecQuery("select * from
Win32_Service where Name='Schedule'")
for each Service in ServiceSet
        RetVal = Service.PauseService()
        if RetVal = 0 then
            WScript.Echo "Service paused"
        else
            if RetVal = 1 then
                WScript.Echo "Pause not supported"
            else WScript.Echo "An error occurred:" & RetVal
            End If
        End If
next
```

After retrieving the instance that matches the query criteria, the script again iterates through the returned information. This time, however, the *PauseService()* is invoked against the returned object, pausing the Windows Scheduler service. The return value of the method is then checked to see if the operation was successful. If you run this script twice in a row, it will succeed the first time and return an error result the second time. This is correct behavior: the error in the second instance indicates that the service is already paused if it has not already been restarted manually or with the *ResumeService()* method.

WMI also supports events based on events generated by the underlying managed system and those based on changes in the instance data it reports. An example of the first type is an SNMP (Simple Network Management Protocol) trap, an event generated by an SNMP agent that can be mapped into an equivalent WMI event using the WMI SNMP provider. WMI can also monitor for events about instances including creation, modification, and deletion, which means you can have WMI watch for a change of interest in an instance property, then generate an event when the criteria are met. For example, you can request an event when processor utilization on a critical server reaches a threshold. The script on the following page requests an event be generated when the CPU utilization exceeds 70% and then reports those events as they occur.

```
set events = GetObject("winmgmts:").ExecNotificationQuery _
    ("select * from __instancemodificationevent within 5 where
targetinstance isa 'Win32_Processor' and targetinstance.LoadPercentage >
70")
if err <> 0 then
    WScript.Echo Err.Description, Err.Number, Err.Source
end if
' Note this next call will wait indefinitely - a timeout can be
specified
WScript.Echo "Waiting for CPU load events..."
WScript.Echo ""
do
    set NTEvent = events.nextevent
    if err <> 0 then
        WScript.Echo Err.Number, Err.Description, Err.Source
        Exit Do
    else
WScript.Echo NTEvent.TargetInstance.DeviceID                 WScript.Echo
NTEvent.TargetInstance.LoadPercentage
end if
loop
WScript.Echo "finished"
```

Virtually all of the work is done in the very first line of this script. First, using the *ExecNotificationQuery()* call, the script registers using a query for instance modification events where the modified class is *Win32_Processor*. To refine the request, the query specifies that in order to be a modification of interest, the *LoadPercentage* property (CPU utilization) must be greater than 70%. The only other item is that the query specifies a *WITHIN 5* clause, requesting WMI to check only every five seconds for this condition (that is, the script expects no input for five seconds at a time). The rest of the script simply waits for the events and then displays them as they arrive.

Finally, to bring both Active Directory and WMI scripting together, a script is built that first retrieves a list of all computers running Windows 2000 Server listed in the Active Directory. This is done by directing the initial *GetObject()* call to the *//./root/directory/LDAP* namespace, where the WMI Active Directory provider publishes its information. When no namespace is specified (as in the previous examples) the call uses the default, *root/cimv2*, where most WMI classes are located. The period (.) at the beginning of *//./root/directory/LDAP* simply indicates the query is directed at the local machine. WMI uses namespaces to logically partition information rather just placing all information for the computer, operating system, directory, applications, and so on in a single large area.

```
On error resume next
Set ADServers = GetObject("winmgmts://./root/directory/LDAP").ExecQuery
("select ds_name from ds_computer where ds_operatingsystem='Windows 2000
Server'")
for each Server in ADServers
```

```
        WScript.Echo Server.ds_name

        ConnectString = "winmgmts://"+ Server.ds_name + "/root/cimv2"

        Set TargetServer =
GetObject(ConnectString).InstancesOf("Win32_ComputerSystem")
        if Err <> 0 Then
            WScript.Echo Err.Description
            Err.Clear
        End if
        for each CompSys in TargetServer
            WScript.Echo "Previous boot delay was "&
CompSys.SystemStartupDelay & " seconds."
            CompSys.SystemStartupDelay = 30
            CompSys.Put_()
            WScript.Echo "Boot up delay time set to " &
CompSys.SystemStartupDelay & " seconds on " & Server.ds_name
        next
next
```

The script again uses a query to request a specific property, *ds_name*, for all computers listed in the Active Directory that are known to be Windows 2000 Server installations. This uses the WMI class, *ds_computer*, discovered automatically in the Active Directory by the WMI Active Directory provider. Next, the script iterates through all the returned server names and directs a new WMI request at each server for instances of the *Win32_ComputerSystem* class.

Just as in the first WMI script example, this script is retrieving the *SystemStartupDelay* property. Note, however, that the *GetObject()* call specifies a concatenated URL string that contains the name of the machine retrieved from the Active Directory and specifies the *root/cimv2* namespace as the place to find the *Win32_ComputerSystem* class. The script also adds some error-checking code. By default, a user must be part of the Administrators group on the machine receiving a request for data. Because this script is going out to many machines where the user may not be considered an Administrator, the request for *Win32_ComputerSystem* class information may return an access denied message. The code has been inserted to handle this situation gracefully.

As in the first example, above, once the script gets the *Win32_ComputerSystem* instance back from the remote machine, it reads the current setting for *SystemStartupDelay*. Next, it sets the local value of the variable to 30 and then writes it back to the remote system. As stated before, if the user of the script does not have the appropriate access to do this, the WMI disallows any attempt to read or modify the property value. Remember: this script can change the value of the *SystemStartupDelay* on every Windows 2000 Server system in your domain, so think carefully about what you want to do before using it.

As you can see even from these simple examples, WMI effectively complements the Active Directory. The WMI Active Directory provider allows you to create scripts that combine an d manipulate enterprise-view data and specific information or settings on a particular machine. For information on more sophisticated tasks that you can script using both WMI and Active Directory, and on the full set of information available through WMI, see the WMI Software Development Kit (SDK) available at http://msdn.microsoft.com/developer/sdk/wmisdk/default.asp. You can also download WMI components for Windows 95, Windows 98 and Windows NT 4.0 from this site.

Conclusion

Using the information in this chapter you will be able to integrate scripting into your daily Windows 2000 work. ADSI and WMI provide you with powerful tools to access directory and management information from any programming language. Use the examples in this chapter, as well as the full sample on the CD, to build new scripts to solve you enterprise management tasks.

CHAPTER 11

Delegating Tree/Forest Operations

By Zev Yanovich,
Scott Lengel,
Todd Briley,
Jeff Wagner, and
Michael Wirth,
Microsoft
Consulting
Services;
and Samuel
Devasahayam,
Microsoft
Corporation

Organizations vary widely in size, revenue, number of employees, geographical extension, etc., and while IT departments tend to reflect these characteristics they generally follow one of four models:

- **Single IT organization with centralized management.** This model typically provides end-to-end IT services for users. Simple administrative tasks such as the assignment of group memberships still can be delegated.

- **Centralized control with decentralized management.** This model creates a core team that handles base infrastructure services and delegates most day-to-day operations to distributed management groups that provide local user support.

- **Outsourced IT.** Organizations can outsource all or part of the IT organization. If all of it is outsourced, the group will be organized as one of the two previous models; if only part is outsourced, you have to create a delegation model that allows your IT group to control your environment without compromising service level agreements with the outsourced company.

- **Federated IT organization.** This model allows business units to select the IT model that meets their needs. The organization ends up with IT groups that have varying methods and objectives, so to implement company-wide initiatives, the various IT groups meet, express their business unit interests, and work together.

For the first three types, organization and delegation are straightforward. The federated model, however, requires some complex arrangement and planning. This chapter examines how to delegate needs within this model.

What You'll Find in This Chapter

- The reasons for delegating administrative activities, how to decide on a model for delegation, and the consequences.

- How to set up a central group that manages Active Directory core components and allows you to implement a workable design across a decentralized organization.

- How to handle management (site, schema, site link, etc.) and security.

- Complete delegation procedures, with explanations.

Delegating: Reasons and Consequences

Some reasons for delegating tree/forest administrative activities are based on company politics, some are based on technical merits. Active Directory provides a mechanism for delegating the administration of domains, organizational units, sites, site links, and subnets. Before working out any details, however, you need to decide if you want to implement a single domain with delegated administration at the organizational unit level, or a tree/forest structure with delegation at domain level.

To delegate at the organizational unit level, a domain administrator grants some rights to other users within a container. The various Microsoft management console (MMC) snap-ins provide wizards to help you do this. For example, you can allow the help desk to reset passwords for user accounts within a specified container, or can allow the network group to operate infrastructure components such as DHCP and DNS.

If delegation at the organizational unit does not fit your business requirements, you have to create a more complex Active Directory design. Some possible reasons:

- A business unit—perhaps feeling that corporate counterparts aren't meeting users' needs—may outsource IT operations to a service provider.

- Some companies may have independent business units, each with IT groups that may not trust other groups or that simply wish to operate independently.

- IT groups may need to keep some directory information out of the reach of external entities participating in the environment.

- A group may think a subset of information, rather than all domain content, is all that needs to be replicated to remote locations.

- A location may typically be disconnected from the corporate WAN, requiring an SMTP connector, in which case another domain is needed.

In previous versions of Windows NT a domain represents an autonomous unit of administration; this changes in Windows 2000, where components such as the Schema and Configuration naming contexts are shared across the tree/forest. Windows 2000 Active Directory allows you, with the appropriate access controls, to delegate some of the tasks initially assigned to the Administrators group: schema, child domain, sites, and management of RIS and DHCP. For example, an understaffed IT group in a distributed organization can delegate the creation of child domains to some other group, and this requires giving *domain administrator* rights on the root Active Directory domain to the child domain administrator (internal or outsourced). Easy enough, but not quite simple: assigning these rights is also a security issue, because they allow the recipient to perform lots of other tasks as well.

Background

To get the most out of Active Directory plans, many federated IT organizations deploy a tree/forest across the company. This can create a lot of interaction between child domain administrators and the forest root administrator—the IT group can reduce it by delegating some root administrator tasks. Figure 11.1, based on an actual scenario, can help you understand the steps for delegating responsibilities to the child administrators within a federated IT organization.

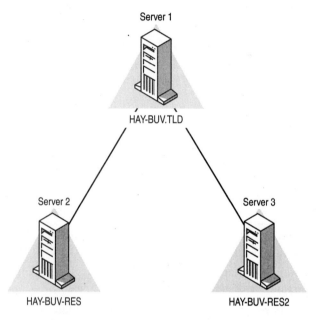

Figure 11.1   Sample domain structure.

Central Office

To implement a workable Active Directory design across a decentralized organization, you have to create a central office. This manages Active Directory core components and guarantees all business units participating in the tree/forest that it will handle tasks such as root domain management, schema management, pre-creation of subordinate domains, DNS root management, and site link management. Basically, this is a core IT group that controls important Active Directory management issues centrally, so that regardless of the amount of delegation there is focused and consistent control over operating characteristics.

Root Domain Management

The core IT group's first step in building a tree/forest is to create the root domain. It is a good idea to build this as a placeholder—using it only to host key components such as the tree/forest wide Flexible Single-Master Operation

(FSMO) roles and not user accounts or groups. Most WAN infrastructures are based on a hub and spoke model, where the company's headquarters or regional centers are major network hubs and other remote facilities are spokes, connecting directly to the nearest hub. Under these circumstances, you should consider locating tree/forest root domain controllers in key points of presence within the network to facilitate connectivity to the child domains. These servers will act as replication hubs to the overall network, so they must be configured as global catalogs.

Schema Management

The central group is also responsible for managing the schema—the hierarchy of Active Directory objects, which defines the types of objects stored in the directory (classes, and attributes). The schema is extensible, so you can modify it to meet needs unique to your circumstances.

After the design is built and in place, schema management tasks are performed only infrequently, so the privileges are restricted to a group in the root forest called *Schema Administrators*.

You can extend the schema, but the changes must be replicated to every domain controller in the forest, so it is a complex task. When you consider extension, think the situation through carefully to make sure an extension is *necessary*. Follow these guidelines:

- Extend the schema only if no existing object class meets your needs.

- Do not add elements you may want to delete at a future date—you can only mark them as defunct, not delete them.

- Limit the use of *must-contain* attributes—it may force others across the forest to adhere to the same rules.

- Test the schema extension first on a lab environment before implementing it in a production environment.

- If you are extending the schema for an in-house application, contact an Object Identifier (OID) issuing authority for the proper classification:

  - IANA hands out OIDs for free under the "Private Enterprises" branch.

  - ANSI hands out OIDs under the "US Organizations" branch for USD 1000.

  - BSI hands out OIDs under the "UK Organizations" branch.

  - Or visit http://www.iso.ch for information on your country's National Registration Authority.

You can modify the schema with the Schema Management MMC or an ADSI script.

Child Domain Pre-Creation Procedures

The central IT group (the root administrator, specifically) also is responsible for pre-creating subordinate domains across the tree/forest. By performing this preparatory work, the group can control domain naming conventions, the purpose of the domain, and who will administer the domains. The central group has several options. It can build and configure the child domain controllers at a staging location managed by the central office and then ship them to their destinations. It can install Terminal Services on the server and allow a group within the central office to connect over the network and execute the DCPROMO process. These alternatives do not require any changes to the Active Directory default configuration. They also provide a way to maintain a high level of control over the Administrator's accounts in the various child domains, while delegating the day-to-day tasks to other user accounts; this is an advantage but these methods may not meet the needs of many decentralized IT organizations.

The group has a third alternative: it can pre-create a cross-reference for the child domain in the root forest, then set the appropriate ACLs on the Schema, Configuration, and Domain naming contexts to allow a non-administrative account to execute DCPROMO. This requires an Enterprise Administrator in the root domain to create a cross-reference object to the child domain. This object ties together LDAP referrals that span the forest. The child administrator then must use the credentials of a user in a special group in the root to execute DCPROMO. This approach, which requires changing the Active Directory ACL structure, granting a non-Domain Administrator account privileges to complete the process, allows you to delegate the DCPROMO process but requires the procedure below to prepare the root domain.

 Warning   The processes below require you to edit Active Directory internals. Before you change anything, make sure you understand how to restore it if a problem occurs.

Root Domain Preparation for Delegation of Child Domain Creation

To delegate the DCPROMO process for the creation of child domains, you have to:

1. Create a group for the sole purpose of running DCPROMO (to create the first domain controller in the new child domain).

2. Use this group to create appropriate privileges (on an ACL) for the appropriate Active Directory objects. These steps, which you perform only once, are discussed in the remainder of this section. (Four steps are required to create a child domain. They are discussed in the next section.)

The first step in delegating any task is to identify which user or set of users will be given permissions to perform it. You can simplify long-term administration by identifying a group then adding users to it as needed. This method allows you to apply all ACL changes to objects using the group instead of to individual users. For example, create a *Domain Creators Group* in the root domain and add the account Dcreator1. The account will later be used to run DCPROMO. To allow a child administrator to join the tree/forest without any administrative rights on the root, the root administrator must make changes to the Schema, Configuration, and Domain naming contexts.

A number of the ACL changes rely on the use of a Well-Known SID group, *Creator Owner*, that allows you to transfer object permissions to groups when they create new objects. For example, a user account has *create* privileges on an object and the *Creator Owner Group* is given *full* rights to that object. When the object is created, *Creator Owner Group*'s *full* rights are transferred to the user account that created the object. One of the side effects of using this approach is that you may not want the user account that created the object to be its owner. Once the object is created, you can remove all rights from the account that created the object and allow some other account to take ownership of it.

The Schema and Configuration naming contexts are shared across the Active Directory tree/forest, so the *Domain Creators Group* must have the rights to read and replicate their contents. Grant the following permissions to the *Domain Creators Group* on both the Configuration (cn=Configuration, dc=hay-buv, dc=tld) and Schema (cn=Schema, dc=hay-buv, dc=tld) containers:

- Read
- Manage Replication Topology
- Replicating Directory Changes
- Replication Synchronization

The Default-First-Site is the first site in the tree/forest. New servers are assigned to it whenever their TCP/IP subnet is not assigned to an existing site. The *Domain Creators* group must have permission to create a new server in the Default-First-Site. These permissions are applied to the Default-First-Site container:

- Add the *Domain Creators* Group and give it rights to *Read* and *Create* child objects for THIS OBJECT AND ALL CHILD OBJECTS.
- Add the *Creator Owner* Group and give it *Full Control* for THIS OBJECT AND ALL CHILD OBJECTS.

If the root administrator also wants to control the site creation process, you have to create a new site where the child domain server will reside. To register the server in the proper location, you would also have to add the server's subnet and associate it with the new site (the site has no meaning without a subnet). Then the root administrator needs to grant the two permissions above to the new site.

This gives the Domain Creators group permission to replicate the Configuration and Schema information and to create a new server in the appropriate site.

Child Domain Creation

Now that the root domain is prepared, perform these steps to create each child domain:

1. Create a cross-reference object for the new domain.
2. Set the Access Control List (ACL) on the appropriate objects.
3. Perform the DCPROMO process.
4. Grant full control of the new DC to the Domain Administrators of the new child domain.

To create a cross-reference object for the child domain, use the command line utility NTDSUTIL. You have to be logged on to the root domain with an account that has Enterprise Administrative rights, and when you specify the cross-reference to the child domain you must use the NetBIOS name of the child domain in UPPER CASE. Here are the steps required to pre-create the child domain cross-reference, HB-RES where server2.HB-RES.HAY-BUV.TLD is the first server in that domain.

1. NTDSUTIL
2. Type **Domain Management**
3. Type **Connections**
4. Type **Connect to Server SERVER1.HAY-BUV.TLD**
5. Type **quit**
6. Type **precreate dc=HB-RES,dc=hay-buv,dc=tld server2.hb-res.hay-buv.tld**

After you create the cross-reference you have to give the *Domain Creators Group* permission to access the information. Locate the new cross-reference in the Partitions container within the Configuration-naming context, then set the permissions. Add the *Domain Creators* Group and give it *Full Control* on the object.

Active Directory uses Kerberos transitive trusts between the domains within the tree/forest. The trust objects reside in the *system* container within the Domain naming context of the parent domain, so you have to allow the *Domain Creators Group* to create a trust object for the child domain that is being promoted.

1. Add the *Domain Creators* Group to the System container under the Domain naming context and give the group the rights to *Read* and *Create* child objects privileges.
2. Add the *Creator Owner* Group and give it *Full Control* privileges.

The last preparatory step is to make sure the server where DCPROMO will be executed from is properly registered with DNS. Under the properties of *'My Computer'* you will find a dialog box for the primary DNS suffix. Verify that it contains the Fully Qualified Domain Name (FQDN) of the new child domain. In addition, you can use the DNS NSLOOKUP command to verify that the server host record (A) exists.

Now the local administrator on the member server can start DCPROMO. The DCPROMO wizard prompts for credentials under which it should execute and these should be an account that is a member of the *Domain Creators Group* (for example, *dcreator1*). After completing DCPROMO, the root administrator must grant full control permissions to the child domain administrators group on the new domain controller; this allows the child domain administrator to take ownership of the server and install additional domain controllers or other resources without having to involve the root forest administrator.

By default the Enterprise Administrator group will have permissions to the child domain. To control the level of access the members of the root administrators have over the child domain's naming context, the child domain administrator can remove the Enterprise Administrator group from having any permissions over the dc=hb-res, dc=hay-buv, dc=tld object.

At this stage, the child domain administrators cannot create sites, subnets, site links, or other associated objects: the root administrator has to perform these tasks, or delegate them to a separate group or to the individual child domain administrators (discussed in the "Site Management" section, below).

Create Replica Domain Controllers

It often is necessary to delegate the creation of additional domain controllers to another group or a third party, in which case you normally give them a user account without administrative rights on the domain, so they can complete the process without affecting any of the other servers.

As with delegating child domain creation, the recommended procedure is to create a group for this process, then add members to it as necessary. The server will hold a copy of the Domain naming context, so you have to allow this group the right to replicate it as well as the Configuration and Schema naming contexts (dc=hb-res, dc=hay-buv, dc=tld):

- Read
- Add/Remove Replica in Domain (Domain Naming context only)
- Manage Replication Topology
- Replicating Directory Changes
- Replication Synchronization

Since the process for promoting a domain controller requires an authenticated domain account, the server must join the domain before it is promoted. This allows you to use an authenticated domain account and to use group policies, which make delegation easier.

The group you delegate the DCPROMO process to must be able to log on locally to the server to start it, so make this group a member of the Machine Local Administrators group. Also, use the Group Policy object in the Domain Controllers container to give the group the right to *log on locally* and to *enable computer and user accounts to be trusted for delegation*.

Because DCPROMO changes the properties of the server object in the Domain naming context, you have to give this group permissions to *Read* and *Write* to the server object. One step in the promotion process is to move the server object from the Computers container to the Domain Controllers container. This requires administrative rights, so you need to move the object before it is promoted.

The final step is to allow the group to create the server object in the configuration container, so the domain controller is advertised across the tree/forest and link topology generator can create the appropriate number of replication links. Give the group the permission to create a new server in the site where it is located:

- Give the group rights to *Read* and *Create* child objects for THIS OBJECT AND ALL CHILD OBJECTS.
- Add the *Creator Owner* Group and give it *Full Control* for THIS OBJECT AND ALL CHILD OBJECTS.

Grandchild Domain Creation

The process of delegating grandchild domain creation is similar to the process for child domains, but it requires coordinated efforts between the administrators of the root forest and the child domain. At the root domain, you must create the cross-reference object and give *Full Control* to the Domain Creators Group, just as you do when you pre-create a child domain. The Domain Creators Group already has proper permissions for the various objects in the schema and configuration naming contexts.

Because the Kerberos trust is established between a child and its parent domain, you have to give the Domain Creators Group permission to create the trust object in its parent's domain naming context. When you create a child domain, you give permission in the root Domain naming context because the root is the child domain's parent. Now you have to grant permission in the system container in the child Domain naming context because it is the grandchild's parent.

Site Management

An Active Directory site is a collection of highly connected IP subnets. A single site can host multiple Active Directory domains or a single Active Directory domain can span multiple sites. Because objects such as Group Policies have site-wide reach, it is not easy to separate *site* and *domain* administration. If a site includes one or more Active Directory domains within the same forest, you have to identify the child domain administrators' rules of engagement for managing site-wide policies. Otherwise, you should ensure that a site and all its domains are managed by the same entity. If you have truly federated IT groups, you should assume that domains do not always span sites when you consider delegating site creation and management.

If you delegate site creation and management within the tree/forest, you have to give domain administrators permissions to control their own sites. For simplicity, the examples below give permissions only to the domain administrators in child domain HB-RES. On the Sites container in the Configuration naming context, change these ACLs:

- Give the *HB-RES\Domain Admin Group* the rights to *Read* and *Create* child objects for THIS OBJECT ONLY.
- Add the *Creator Owner* Group and give it *Full Control* for THIS OBJECT AND ALL CHILD OBJECTS.
- Deny the *HB-RES\Domain Admin Group* the right to *Create Inter-Site Transport container objects* for THIS OBJECT ONLY.

Because Active Directory Sites are a collection of subnets, you must also allow child administrators to create and assign subnets to the site(s) they manage. On the Subnets container in the Configuration naming context change these ACLs:

- Give the *HB-RES\Domain Admin Group* the rights to *Read* and *Create* child objects for THIS OBJECT ONLY.
- Add the *Creator Owner* Group and give it *Full Control* for THIS OBJECT AND ALL CHILD OBJECTS.

The *deny* ACL entry on the creation of inter-site transport objects allows the child administrator to administer sites and subnets but not to create or manipulate site links. This is important because you do not necessarily want child domain administrators to be able to change how the replication topology is generated. When a child domain administrator creates a site, an error message indicates that the site cannot be associated with any site links. The root administrator can make the association or can grant the child domain administrator write permission on the appropriate site link(s). Even though this right can be delegated, remember that site link management has wide-reaching effects and is best handled by a central group.

Site Link Management

In a distributed Active Directory, site link management plays a crucial role in streamlining how the various naming contexts are replicated across the tree/forest. A company with a federated IT organization typically places firewalls between business units and the rest of the company, so replication planning has to include opening ports on the firewall, selecting SMTP as the replication protocol, or setting up a Virtual Private Network (VPN) between the child domain bridgehead and the root forest domain.

Note Even when you delegate site link management to child domain administrators you should continue to control it from a central location.

To grant site link creation privileges to a child administrator, you have to identify the link type (IP or SMTP) and grant the appropriate access at the appropriate container in the Configuration naming context under Inter-Site Transports:

- Give the child *Domain Admin Group* the rights to *Read* and *Create* child objects for THIS OBJECT ONLY.
- Add the *Creator Owner* Group and give it *Full Control* for THIS OBJECT AND ALL CHILD OBJECTS.

To simplify administration, it is recommended that you switch the domains to *native* mode. This simplifies assigning ACL permissions to the Sites container by allowing the root administrator to create a universal group that includes the administrator accounts from various child domains.

DNS Root Management

The central office also manages the root forest DNS domain, which includes routine handling of DNS domain delegation and server GUID registrations. The central office can either create new DNS domains for each Active Directory child in the tree or delegate a zone to the organization operating the Active Directory child domain.

Active Directory registers a number of entries with DNS. While most of these are registered within the Active Directory domain DNS zone, you must register an alias record under the root's DNS domain *_msdcs.<domain name>* within the root forest DNS domain. This entry represents a GUID for each domain controller in the tree/forest and is used for replication. The *_msdcs.hay-buv.tld* domain is so important that you should delegate it to a new zone and make sure that all child DNS servers replicate it within its name space. (If you don't do this you should at least make this zone available on all of the points of presence where the root domain has domain controller replicas.)

If you integrate the *_msdcs.<domain name>* zone in Active Directory, then its information will be replicated as part of the overall replication, which makes it simpler to ensure the zone information is available throughout the forest. As long as a server that supports dynamic registration hosts the domain *_msdcs<domain name>*, the registration management is minimal. Otherwise each child domain administrator has to notify the root DNS administrator of a server addition or deletion.

Other Windows 2000 Services

You can also delegate to child domain administrators Windows 2000 services such as DHCP and RIS configuration and management.

DHCP Authorization

To prevent rogue DHCP servers from assigning TCP/IP addresses to clients across the domain, you must register them before they are allowed to operate. By default, only the *Domain Administrators Group* in the root domain is authorized to do this, but in a decentralized environment it is not practical for child domain administrators to contact the root administrator every time a DHCP server needs to be authorized. To allow the child domain *DHCP Administrators Group* to authorize DHCP servers, set these ACLs on the NetServices container (CN=NetServices,CN=Services,CN=Configuration,DC=hay-buv,DC=net):

- Give the child *Domain DHCP Admin Group* the rights to *Read*, *Write*, and *Create* child objects for THIS OBJECT ONLY.

- Add the *Creator Owner* Group and give it *Full Control* for THIS OBJECT ONLY.

RIS Authorization

RIS server management is similar to DHCP. To allow the child domain *RIS Administrators Group* to authorize RIS servers, set these ACLs on the NetServices container (CN=NetServices,CN=Services,CN=Configuration,DC=haybuv, DC=net):

- Give the child *Domain RIS Admin Group* the rights to *Read*, *Write*, and *Create* child objects for THIS OBJECT ONLY.

- Add the *Creator Owner* Group and give it *Full Control* for THIS OBJECT ONLY.

Security

There are challenges inherent in securing a distributed system such as Active Directory wherein certain components are shared across all domain controllers in the tree/forest. It is impossible to anticipate every possible attack, and it is beyond the scope of this chapter to document every known Windows 2000 security setting (see the *Microsoft Windows 2000 Server Deployment and Planning Guide*). Here are some basic steps you can take to protect domain controllers from unauthorized access.

First, provide for physical security of all network components such as domain controllers. This protects against threats ranging from disgruntled employees damaging the equipment to someone removing the server from the network and starting some sort of brute force attack against it.

Second, use the System Key (SYSKEY) utility that comes with Windows 2000. It uses a 128-bit cryptographically random password encryption key to boost the protection for user account passwords stored in Active Directory, passwords stored in the local SAM registry, and the password used for system recovery.

Third, control the administrator account carefully. By default only the Domain Administrators group has permissions to install services on a domain controller or schedule tasks with the Task Scheduler service. Control the Administrator account and restrict membership to the Domain and Enterprise Administrator groups. As root administrator, you can promote the child domain servers on behalf of those administrators—that is, without giving them access to the administrator account—but delegate the administrative functions to another account. Make sure all non-system services are executed within the context of an authenticated service account.

Fourth, protect objects that are shared across the system. You can use ACLs to protect them from being modified by an authenticated user, but this does not protect against a malicious service using the system context to execute changes against the Configuration or Schema containers.

The Active Directory security system can require that object modifications or deletions take place on domain controllers in the domain where the object was created before being subject to ACL evaluation. You do this by using the DNPROTECT.EXE utility (included on the CD that comes with this book) to set or remove a bit from any object on the system. The bit must be manually set on any object that needs to be protected, and it cannot be inherited, so you have to set it on every child object that needs to be protected. Once this bit is set on an object, the operating system will not even evaluate the ACLs on it if you are making the change from a domain controller that isn't in the domain in which the object was originally created.

When using this utility, you have to be careful not to prevent certain Active Directory operations from completing successfully. For example, if you set the bit on the schema FSMO at the root domain, you won't be able to transfer the FSMO object to a child domain because that object was originally created in the root domain and the domain SID portion won't match the object owner's SID.

DNPROTECT has a number of available switches. For a complete list, use the DNPROTECT.EXE command with the "/?" command line switch. For example, if you want to set the protection bit on *server5* object in the *hay-buv.tld* domain, you would log on with administrator rights on the server in the root domain. Then from the command prompt, you would execute the following command:

```
DNPROTECT -s:server1.hay-buv.tld -dn:cn=server5,cn=servers,cn=default-
first-site-name,cn=sites,cn=configuration,dc=hay-buv,dc=tld -scope:base
-op:set
```

From the Trenches:
Active Directory in a Decentralized Environment

Many companies with decentralized IT environments have a variety of directories deployed across their enterprise to address their various business needs. The directories range from custom-built systems, to Novell, to Exchange, to Windows NT, to HR systems like PeopleSoft, and many others. This obviously creates a very complex environment for users and for network administrators.

Customer Background

MCS started a planning project with a multinational organization that has offices in over 160 countries and that grows constantly through expanded markets, increased product sales, and mergers/acquisitions. In the past, decisions made at a corporate level were often not implemented by field offices. It was anticipated that the correct Active Directory design could help propagate changes more consistently throughout the organization.

Active Directory Design

The IT group evaluated multiple forests, a single tree, and a forest, finally (after considerable discussion and testing) selecting a single forest for the entire company. To take into account frequent acquisitions, the architecture can accommodate additional forests while an acquired company is assimilated into the enterprise forest. The idea is to use the ClonePrincipal tool to move the user objects between domains.

The company also has some software development groups, and they likely will give these groups their own "test" forests within which they can test Windows 2000 schema extensions without affecting the network infrastructure.

Permissions

While Windows 2000 Active Directory has a good delegation model for objects within the Domain naming context, the company wanted to go beyond its capability and delegate tasks of objects (DHCP servers, subnets, and sites) that reside in the configuration container.

If you look at what makes up the Configuration container, you can see that some of the containers do not reflect the actual forest hierarchy, and this means you have to grant multiple child domain administrators permissions to the various containers. For example, to delegate the authorization of DHCP servers in the enterprise you need to look under:

```
CN=NetServices,CN=Configuration,dc=hay-buv,dc=tld.
```

> The best way to delegate who can authorize DHCP servers is to create a security-enabled group, give it the ability to *Read* and *Create* a child object in the container, then give the CREATOR OWNER group *Full Control* over the container. This gives the group that created the object *Full Control* over *only* the objects they create.

Conclusion

Windows 2000 Active Directory has built-in wizards with which you can delegate many day-to-day tasks to various groups across your organization. For instance, you can delegate authority for password resets to the help desk, DHCP administration to the network group, application assignment to the workstation deployment team, and so on. Most organizations can use Windows 2000 out of the box to delegate within their environments, but if you have a more complex environment, with needs or conditions that are not addressed by the default product settings, you can customize most areas of the directory. If you choose to do this, make sure you test any proposed changes in a lab environment before you implement them in a production environment.

CHAPTER 12

Building a Windows 2000 Public Key Infrastructure

By Jan DeClerqc, Compaq Computer Corporation

This chapter focuses on public key infrastructure (PKI)—a crucial technology for distributed and heterogeneous computer environments, which require a security system to provide authentication, confidentiality, and non-repudiation services. The discussion provides background information on PKI, what you can use it for, how you can implement it as a part of a Windows 2000 Active Directory, and what components make up the Windows 2000 PKI. It also shows how you can plan and design a Windows 2000 PKI, and, at the end of the chapter, illustrates the process with an example drawn from the real world.

What You'll Find in This Chapter

- An explanation of encryption basics, leading to a discussion of public key infrastructure, the Windows 2000 PKI and its components and functionality.

- How to plan a PKI, beginning with analysis of business requirements and progressing through topology design considerations, intended application use, and seven stages for specifying certification Authorities.

- References to a fictitious company that clarify specific situations, tradeoffs, and choices.

- How to create important documentation—a Security Policy, Certificate Policies, and the Certificate Practice Statement—that carry through planning considerations for your organization.

Introduction to Public Key Infrastructure

A public key infrastructure (PKI) is a set of services that allow applications to use public key cryptography to provide strong security services. It's an infrastructure that many applications can use to provide strong asymmetric-cryptography-based security. The infrastructure can also provide security between companies, not just within a single company, through the use of *trusts* (covered below).

Encryption

Encryption allows you to transmit sensitive information securely by turning *plaintext* (information you want to transmit) into *ciphertext* (which is unreadable to anyone except the intended recipient). *Symmetric key encryption* uses one *key* (a password or number) to encode *and* decode the information.

Public key encryption (also called *private/public key or asymmetric key encryption*) uses two different keys: a public key to encrypt the information, and a private key to decrypt it (Figure 12.1). The private key cannot be derived from the public key or the encrypted data, which means you can safely distribute the public key to users. There is a one-to-one mathematical relationship between the private and the public key. Only one person knows the private key; it is stored securely in an encrypted area on the user's hard disk or on a smart card. Public key encryption was created so that a key (in this case the public key) did not have to be transferred between sender and receiver along with every encrypted message. It should be transferred only once over an "authentic" channel to assure the receiver that the public key does indeed belong to the sender with the corresponding private key.

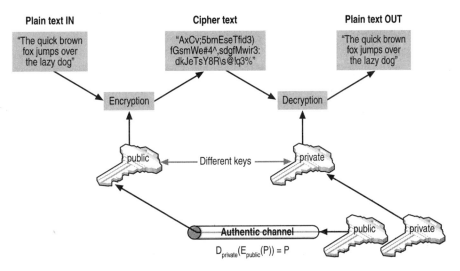

Figure 12.1   Asymmetric cipher.

Public key encryption tends to be slower than symmetric key because its required calculations take computer time. For this and other reasons real-world systems usually combine methods. A common tactic is to use a symmetric key and algorithm to encrypt the plaintext, then use the recipient's public key to encrypt the symmetric key (into what is called a *lockbox*) that is attached to the message along with the encrypted information being sent to the recipient. The recipient uses the private key to decode the lockbox and retrieve the symmetric key with which the message can be decrypted. This method uses fast symmetric key encryption on the bulk of the message and retains the benefits of more secure public key encryption. By using the recipient's public key to encrypt the lockbox you ensure that only the intended recipient (who has his private key) can get the symmetric key.

Digital Signatures

Security is important, but so is reliability: in addition to ensuring that a message can be read only by the people who are supposed to read it (confidentiality), you also need to ensure that the message is not altered in transit (integrity) and that it really originates from the sender you think it comes from (data origin authentication). This can be guaranteed by creating a *digital signature*. Using a hash function, a unique *hash* value is computed from the original (unencrypted) message which is then encrypted using the sender's private key and is added to the end of the message (the *message digest*). Along with the message, the recipient opens the digital signature and uses the sender's public key to decrypt the hash value. The same hash function is used to recompute the value, which will differ from the original if the message contents are off by even one bit. If they are not the same, the recipient is notified that the contents of the message may have changed. If the recipient can decrypt the message digest, it proves that the sender sent the message. This feature is called *non-repudiation* because only the user possesses the private key needed to sign the message digitally.

Digital Certificates

A digital certificate is used as a guarantee of authenticity of the public key contained in the certificate. Besides the public key it also includes the user or computer name and the purposes the certificate can be used for. An issuing authority digitally signs a digital certificate. To verify the binding between the public key and the identity, the recipient has to validate the digital signature and this requires the issuer's public key (certificate).

Certificates have a limited lifetime, after which they expire or are revoked. This safeguard helps cope with advances in cryptography and computer science: cryptographic ciphers that were secure 10 years ago can now be hacked in a couple of days.

If the private key linked to a certificate is compromised, the certificate must be revoked. In practice the certificate is added to a blacklist (called the certificate revocation list—CRL) that must be checked every time the certificate is used.

Certificates can be used in different applications: to log on to a workstation with a smart card, to encrypt files, to digitally sign e-mail, and to encrypt e-mail.

Trust and Certificate Authorities

Digital certificates are issued by a certificate authority (*CA*). Using its own private and public key pair, the CA takes the information provided to it, creates a digital certificate, digitally signs it using its private key, and then returns the certificate to the user.

The CA also has its own certificate (which includes its public key). It is signed by the CA itself or by another CA. A *root CA* can sign its own certificate; CAs that carry certificates signed by other CAs are called *subordinate CAs*. Subordination creates a hierarchy, with the root CA at the top, signing certificates for subordinate CAs, which in turn sign certificates for other subordinate CAs, which eventually sign certificates for users (Figure 12.2). Windows 2000 PKI can be used to create a hierarchical CA "trust" model.

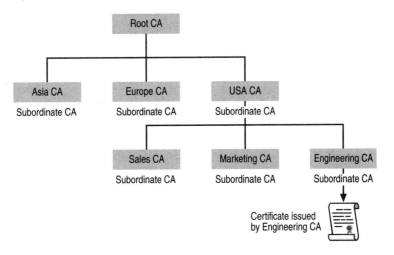

Figure 12.2   Certificate authority hierarchy.

If you know the public key of the root CA, you can validate any subordinate CA's certificate by verifying their associated signatures. The certificates of some popular root CAs are included in Windows and Internet Explorer.

CAs also issue certificate revocation lists (CRLs) to inform recipients of certificates that were originally issued by the CA but have since been revoked because the private key was compromised or the user's information changed. You can check any certificate issued by this CA against the list to ensure that it is still valid.

You can trust certificates and CAs at three levels. You can trust the certificate's root CA (an issuer on the Internet, or another company's CA), you can trust the subordinate CA that issued it (which implicitly trusts the root CA that created the subordinate), or you can trust just the certificate (not the issuing authority, but simply this single certificate).

Core Components of the Microsoft PKI

The Microsoft PKI uses the Certificate Server and the Active Directory. This section describes these two "core" components.

Certificate Server

You can install the core of the Microsoft PKI—the Certificate Server—as either a root or a subordinate CA. The Microsoft Certificate Server issues X.509 version 3 certificates. It has two configurable modules: *policy* and *exit*. The *policy* module tells the engine if the certificate needs any additional settings, if any settings must be modified, and if a certificate request should be issued, denied, or left pending. When a certificate has been created, the *exit* module tells the server what to do with it (publish it to the directory, write it to a file, etc.).

When you install Certificate Server, you are prompted to specify what type of server you are creating: *standalone* or *enterprise*. The standalone policy module creates certificates independently of the Active Directory (much as Certificate Server does in Windows NT 4.0). The enterprise policy module ties in directly with the Active Directory (which must be present before Certificate Server is installed). It publishes the certificates it issues to the directory, publishes CRL information to the directory, uses certificate templates, and can issue certificates with appropriate permissions and extensions for use with smart card logons. Once installed, an Enterprise Certificate Server automatically deploys its root certificate to all the users and computers in the domain.

Once you install the Certificate Server, you should not change its name or its role in the domain. The CA's digital certificate, which is created on installation, includes this information, so *before you install* Certificate Server you should set up the server with its permanent domain role and name. If it isn't finalized when you install Certificate Server, you will have to uninstall Certificate Server, change the server's role or name, then re-install.

Active Directory

Certificates issued by the Certificate Server can be stored in the Active Directory, generally in distinguished encoding rules (DER) encoded binary X.509 format. As a secure repository for user and computer certificates, the Active Directory is a single reference location for certificate information. Its replication model ensures that certificate information is distributed securely.

You can use group policy objects to distribute trusted CA information to Windows 2000 Professional workstations. Group policy objects are explained more fully below in the section "Defining Public Key Policy Settings (GPO)."

The Active Directory also can store CRL information in the CA configuration.

If you want to use the Active Directory to store certificates and CRLs, you need an Enterprise CA—the standalone CA does not write to the Active Directory. The integration of a CA with Active Directory offers the additional advantage of publishing the CA's location in the Directory.

Protected Store

Each workstation has to have a secure place to store the trusted root CA certificates, as well as the private encryption keys. Windows workstations use the protected store—where applications and users can store and retrieve information securely regardless of how it is stored in the system (in the registry, on a smart card, etc.). Windows 98 and Windows 2000 install the protected store as a part of the operating system (in earlier versions it was installed with Internet Explorer 4) and distribute the root CAs for several popular security providers (providing a baseline of root CAs with which to get started).

Why Use the Microsoft PKI?

The Microsoft PKI is flexible, standards-based, and extensible. As a part of Windows 2000 Server, it can scale to millions of certificates and can handle large amounts of certificate generation. It can be used to enhance security for applications such as the Encrypting File System, Web connections, and e-mail.

Microsoft PKI is highly flexible. As is explained later in this chapter the Windows 2000 CA can be customized to meet different security needs. You can also simplify administration of user-related PKI settings by using group policy objects and applying them on different levels in the Windows 2000 organization.

To help provide interoperability, Microsoft PKI supports the open standards ITU-T X.509, and IETF PKIX and PKCS. A white paper on Windows 2000 PKI interoperability is available from the Microsoft Windows 2000 Web site.

Planning and Designing a Public Key Infrastructure

Case Study: Trey Research

To illustrate how to plan and design an enterprise PKI, this section uses a scenario based on the fictional Trey Research.

A multinational company with customers in North America, Europe, and Asia, Trey Research is a market leader in IT services and IT hardware ranging from desktops to mainframe systems. Last year's strong growth in e-commerce services has strengthened Trey Research's market position by allowing it to buy one major competitor in Europe and one in Japan.

Analyzing Business Requirements

The rollout of a Public Key Infrastructure in a corporate environment is driven by core business needs and by security requirements for information and network communication.

Rule of thumb: some security issues don't need a certificate-based security solution and can be resolved with simpler arrangements. Another one: not every certificate-based solution requires rolling out an enterprise PKI, so companies often decide to outsource the job or simply buy a limited set of certificates from a commercial certification authority. If you are laying the initial plans for a PKI, remember that it is an *infrastructure* that many other applications can take advantage of. Consider what kinds of applications you want to build on top of it.

This section examines the *insourcing-outsourcing* and *application* topics you need to evaluate as you analyze business requirements. You also need to consider:

- **Cost.** How much will the PKI solution cost? What resources will be required to administer and maintain it?

- **Ease of use.** How difficult is it to enroll for a certificate? How long does it take? How long does it take to renew a certificate? How complex is PKI environment administration?

- **Time to market.** How long will it take to get the PKI into operation? How soon can you get an application running on top of it?

- **Availability.** What sort of availability does the PKI need within the organization? This affects the CAs, the CA databases, and the directories used in the PKI solution.

- **Scalability.** Does the PKI have to be scalable? Will it have to cope with rapid or enormous growth of the number of required certificates? Does planning have to take into account possible future mergers? Will a lot more PKI-based applications be deployed in the near future?

- **Performance.** Public key cryptography operations place load and performance demands on client-server systems. Is it acceptable? Should hardware be upgraded? Should you buy and install hardware that will speed up PKI functions?

- **Support for open standards.** Is the PKI solution based on open standards? They are key to interoperability. The major ones are: X.509, PKCS, and PKIX. The ITU-T X.509 standard defines certificate format. PKCS (Public Key Cryptography Standards) defines the format of public key-related messages. PKIX defines Public Key Infrastructures that use X.509 certificates.

Insource or Outsource?

You have three choices to implement an enterprise PKI: insource, outsource, or a hybrid approach.

Insourced solutions you install, implement, administer, and maintain all by yourself. Your IT department must take the lead in implementing all related PKI technologies: CA hardware, CA database, PKI directories, and the communication links between all participating entities. Naturally, this path offers you complete independence. You can create your own liability rules and security policies, and can decide how to implement, administer, and maintain the PKI. You also have complete control over who gets a certificate.

Outsourced solutions turn most of this over to another company. The degree of outsourcing can range from a little (generating some server certificates) to a lot (outsourcing multiple CA services that are dedicated to your company). You have to trust the company you hire, but this is often the best solution for smaller companies or for those without the funds and resources required to install and maintain a PKI.

Hybrid solutions combine insourcing and outsourcing: your company maintains part of the CAs in the hierarchy, another company maintains others.

Which Applications Will Be Built on Top of the PKI?

A PKI is an *infrastructure* and many Windows 2000 applications (built-in and otherwise) can take advantage of it to provide strong security: networking systems, VPN systems, ERP software, document signing, and smart-card-based applications. The types of certificates that will be needed and the entities to which certificates will be issued (machines or users) depend on the applications you want to support in your corporate environment.

You can build these types of Windows 2000 applications on top of a Windows 2000 PKI:

- **Secure Web.** In a corporate intranet or extranet environment, you can use certificates for *strong authentication*, which uses Secure Sockets Layer (SSL) to provide client authentication, server authentication, and data confidentiality. Each authenticated entity requires a certificate.

  If you host Web sites and directories on Microsoft Internet Information Server (IIS), you can map a certificate-based account to a Windows NT account so that users who authenticate via certificate are treated just like any other user in post-authentication processes such as access control. On the IIS-level, you can define one-to-one mapping or a many-to-one mapping, which maps certificates of the same *type* (for example, issued by the same CA) to the same Windows NT account. Mapping definitions are contained in the IIS-metabase or in the Active Directory. A new feature of IIS5.0 running on top of Windows 2000 is the possibility to point a Web server to the Active Directory database to check for certificate mappings.

- **Secure mail.** Signing and sealing electronic mail messages using S/MIME (Secure Multi-Purpose Internet Mail Extensions) is also based on public-key cryptography and certificates. *Signing* uses the sender's private key, while *sealing* uses the receiver's public key. Microsoft Exchange, Outlook, and Outlook Express all can provide secure mail. Most secure mail applications use a dual-key pair system to provide non-repudiation of signed mail messages and recovery of encrypted mail messages.

- **File system encryption.** Windows 2000 comes with the Encryption File System (EFS) extension to the NTFS version 5 file system. It provides file-system-level encryption. A built-in feature provides recovery of encrypted data by another person than the one that originally encrypted it. Because it performs encryption and decryption transparently, it is also easy to use. Windows 2000 allows you to encrypt files or folders through a GUI or a command-prompt interface.

- **Code signing.** This helps protect against downloads of altered (hacker) code from Web sites. Using a private key, the original code-developer signs the code, and the user downloading a piece of it can use the developer's public key to verify the code's origin. The Microsoft code-signing technology is known as Authenticode.

- **Smart card logon.** This provides strong two-factor authentication (based on knowledge and possession) in a Windows 2000 domain environment. Classic Windows NT 4 logon using a userID/password provided one-factor authentication (based on knowledge only). Smart card logon in Windows 2000 is implemented as an extension to the Kerberos protocol; it is called PKINIT because it uses public key cryptography only for initial authentication. The smart-card logon process replaces all occurrences of the user's password with the user's public key credentials. The Active Directory contains a mapping between a user's certificate and a Windows 2000 account.

- **Secure Web and secure mail using Fortezza crypto cards (US only).** The Fortezza crypto card standard is a smart-card standard developed by the US National Security Agency (NSA). They can be used like any other smart card for secure storage of public key credentials. Fortezza also enables secure Web and secure mail applications that use public key technology.

- **Virtual private networking.** Windows 2000 supports the IPsec tunneling protocol, which can use certificates to authenticate between two IPsec tunnel-endpoints. This is an ideal solution for strong authentication between two tunnel-endpoints that are part of different domains that don't have a trust relationship set up. Untrusted domains cannot rely on the standard Windows 2000 authentication protocols such as Kerberos and NTLM.

- **Remote access authentication.** The Windows 2000 Remote Access Service (RAS) supports the Extensible Authentication Protocol (EAP) authentication protocol, which uses (among other methods) Transport Layer Security authentication. The IETF-successor to SSL, TLS uses certificates for client and server authentication.

- **Authentication of SMTP site connections.** You can connect Windows 2000 sites with asynchronous SMTP connections, in which case the bridgehead domain controllers at both ends authenticate one another using certificates.

Not all of these applications require the presence of a corporate PKI or CA infrastructure. You can use EFS, for example, on laptops even if no CA is present.

Case Study: Trey Research's Business Requirements Analysis

One of Trey Research's key business requirements is to get new technology implemented as soon as possible within the internal IT infrastructure.

Trey Research has deployed new workstations worldwide: Pentium III systems with 256 MB RAM. They currently run Windows NT 4 Workstation, but Trey Research is planning to deploy Windows 2000 and migrate all systems before mid-2001.

Recently there was a serious security breach. An employee intercepted an e-mail message from one of the key technology managers and passed it through to a competitor. Not surprisingly, the CIO now wants to implement a system to encrypt and authenticate mail messages as soon as possible.

Trey Research also plans to deploy PKI worldwide, but to keep control completely under its own IT department. They plan to roll out the PKI first in three regional headquarters, and to complete the deployment by the end of 2000. The head of IT created a PKI-based application priority list:

- Secure e-mail
- Encryption of laptop data

- Secure Web access to intra- and extranet Web sites with both client and server authentication
- Smart card logon to servers
- Secure Internet connection of some smaller locations to the headquarter locations

The secure e-mail and Web access application should be interoperable with similar systems implemented by Trey Research's partners.

After weak financial results this quarter, the CIO cut back a project to provide each employee with a home PC. Minimizing educational costs for technology deployed over the next year is also a priority.

Defining a PKI Topology

You define a PKI topology by creating trust relationships between multiple CAs—trusted third parties that establish and vouch for the authenticity of an entity's public key.

Registration authorities (RAs) perform all PKI-related administrative tasks except certificate generation: they identify users, generate certificate requests, publish certificates and CRLs. The current version of Windows 2000 PKI does not support RAs, but they are supported for the issuance of Exchange S/MIME certificates if you implement Exchange advanced mail security in combination with Microsoft Certificate Server. This case uses the Exchange Key Management Server as the RA, but can deal only with Exchange S/MIME certificates.

You may require multiple CAs for sizing, administrative, and practical reasons (if your organization generates too many certificates to be maintained on one CA). Setting up multiple CAs can also provide flexibility:

- You can support applications that require different security policies. Suppose, for example, you have one certificate-based application dealing with large financial transactions and another dealing with the distribution of corporate information. Both use certificates for client authentication, but the first obviously needs a much higher level of user identification than the second. CA servers in such cases also require different degrees of physical and logical security.

- You can map the PKI structure to the organizational structure more effectively. Organizations often have units that require different security policies. Members of the human resources department should have to satisfy higher security requirements to get a certificate than should members of the logistics department, which usually do not deal with confidential information.

- You can map the PKI structure to the organization's geographical structure more effectively. Some locations may require different security policies, or some foreign subsidiaries may not want any external involvement in certificate issuance for their users.

- You can cope with political requirements. A part of your organization might require its own CA because it cannot tolerate any external involvement in security-related topics such as PKI.

To design the PKI topology, you should choose the best trust model then map it to the Windows 2000 domain and site model.

Trust Models

Trust models are very important from a certificate validation point-of-view. To validate the signature on a certificate you need the public key of a CA that you *trust*. In CA terminology *trust* means that you consider every certificate issued by a CA as trustworthy.

In the world of PKI 3 different trust models can be defined: the hierarchical, the networked, and the hybrid trust model.

The primary CA trust model of Windows 2000 is a hierarchical trust model. Windows also supports a special kind of "networked trust model" through the use of Certificate Trust Lists.

In PKI projects of limited scope, you might choose a standalone CA solution. Given the growing interest in PKI however, this is a bad idea. You should *always* consider the possibility of linking your CA trust model with others.

A *hierarchical trust model* consists of a tree of CAs. The top of the hierarchy is a root CA—the authorizing principal for the hierarchy and, as such, the only entity authorized to sign its own certificate. The self-signed root certificate makes it impossible for just anyone to pretend to be the root CA: only the root CA knows and possesses its private key.

The root CA certifies the tier-1 CAs (one tier below) which in turn certify the tier-2 CAs, and so on. The non-root CAs are called subordinate CAs. The hierarchical trust model provides delegation, so a CA can delegate part of its certificate-issuing responsibilities to a lower-level CA. Organizations with a clear hierarchical structure can easily be mapped to the hierarchical CA trust model.

A hierarchy can contain two types of subordinate CAs: intermediate CAs and issuing CAs. In theory, intermediate CAs should issue only *subordinate CA* certificates. This allows you to take intermediate CAs offline, which can provide another level of security and can lower PKI hardware costs by eliminating the need for fault-tolerant hardware. To take an intermediate CA offline you can shut down the entire machine or just stop the CA service when it is not performing any certificate-related task.

From the point of view of security, it's best to keep every non-issuing CA (root CAs and intermediate CAs) offline—installed on a machine that is not a part of your Windows 2000 domain, that is not connected to any network, and that is shut down most of the time.

Key advantages of a hierarchical trust model are its scalability and administrative flexibility.

- As your organization or its certificate usage grows you can create new subordinate CAs without affecting the existing trust infrastructure. Linking CAs in a hierarchy allows you to define different policies for each CA, which might be required for different applications, geographical locations, or organizational units.

- A hierarchy can provide an efficient "certificate validation" system in a large organization containing multiple CAs. Every certificate issued by a Windows 2000 CA contains its certificate chain. A certificate chain contains the certificates of every CA that is located on the shortest path (from a hierarchy point-of-view) between the certificate and the hierarchy's root CA. To be able to validate a certificate it is sufficient to trust the root CA of the hierarchy.

- In a hierarchy each CA has exactly 1 role: it is a root or a subordinate CA. Each CA also has its own set of responsibilities: who to issue certificates to, when to revoke certificates, how to deal with CRL publication, etc.

In a *networked trust model* CAs issue certificates to one another. This process is also known as *cross-certification*. In a networked trust model every CA can be root and subordinate CA at the same time.

Cross-certification is typically used to allow client systems using CA hierarchy A to communicate securely with client systems using CA hierarchy B. If a client's trusted CA A cross-certifies with another CA B, the client will also trust certificates issued by CA B. Cross-certification does not affect previously issued certificates or subsequently issued ones. Because of this feature cross-certification is very important. Without it you would have to provide every PKI client with a certificate issued by your own CA. Some clients could end up with a whole set of certificates, one for each CA-hierarchy that didn't cross-certify with their own CA-hierarchy.

A major disadvantage of the networked trust model is its need for a directory containing the certificate of every CA. A networked trust model doesn't have the hierarchical notion of "certificate chain." The certificate validation process needs to get the CA certificate from somewhere. If the CA certificate is not available on the client it needs to be downloadable from a directory.

Windows 2000 PKI provides a special kind of networked trust through the use of Certificate Trust Lists (CTLs)—signed lists containing certificates of trusted CAs that are distributed using Group Policy Object (GPO) settings. You can put an expiration date on a CTL, and can limit it to a subset of certificate types. Just like regular cross-certification, CTLs can provide uni- or bi-directional trust.

The Windows 2000 CTL model serves the same goal as cross-certification but is fundamentally different from this model in three ways:

- Policy enforcement in the CTL model is very limited (expiration date and certificate type specifications).

- Using CTLs, CAs don't issue certificates for one another. There is just an exchange of CA certificates between two organizations.

- CTLs are defined on the Active Directory level (using GPOs). Real cross-certification happens on the CA level.

A *hybrid trust model* combines the hierarchical and networked trust models.

To choose a PKI trust model you have to decide:

- How many hierarchies do you need? Will you have to create multiple hierarchies for political or administrative reasons?

- Which CA certificates will be contained in the Certificate Trust Lists? Will the trust be uni-or bi-directional? What will be the limitations on the CTLs (certificate types, lifetime of the cross-certification)?

PKI Topology and Windows 2000 Domains and Sites

Because the trust model established between CAs is totally independent of the trust model existing between Windows 2000 domains, one CA can span multiple domains and a domain can contain multiple CAs.

A good practice in Windows 2000 is to increase availability by installing one Windows 2000 domain controller or global catalog (GC) server in each site. In a PKI environment, the availability of the CA services is much less important than the availability of the directory that holds the certificates and the certificate revocation lists (CRLs). If you integrate the certificate server with the Active Directory, the certificates and CRLs are automatically published to the directory and replicated throughout the forest as part of the global catalog.

Case Study: Trey Research's PKI Topology

Trey Research decided to create their own PKI topology, primarily to retain complete control over the issuance of certificates that are used in their corporate environment. They decided to implement two PKI hierarchies: one overall hierarchy for the whole company and one for the recently-purchased Europe-based Service Company (Figure 12.3). The decision to go with two hierarchies was primarily political: the Service Company wants to administer its own CA hierarchy and wants to have complete control over its PKI trust decisions.

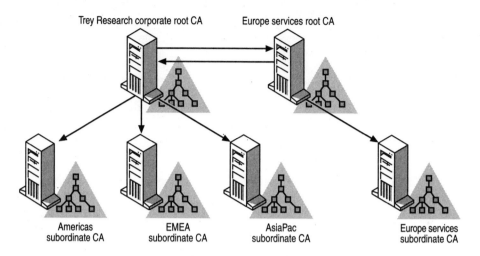

Figure 12.3   Trey Research's PKI topology.

Trey Research wants to set up a networked trust between the two hierarchies for secure e-mail and Web authentication. The Service Company has agreed to make the trust two-way. Trey Research also wants to set up trust links with its main partners for secure e-mail (S/MIME) and extranet access (SSL). Partners that don't have their own CA can enroll for a SSL or S/MIME certificate from the Trey Research standalone CA, which is accessible on a secured Web page on Trey Research's Web site and will be subordinate to the Trey Research corporate root CA.

The corporate PKI hierarchy will consist of a root CA (in Europe), and a subordinate CA for the Americas, one for Europe, Middle East, and Africa (EMEA), and one for Asia-Pacific (AsiaPac). All these are issuing CAs, as shown in Figure 12.4.

The Europe Services PKI hierarchy will consist of a root CA and a subordinate CA (the last one is an issuing CA).

For security reasons, both root CAs will be installed as offline CAs—disconnected from the network and not part of any Windows 2000 domain.

Trey Research's Windows 2000 domain structure consists of two forests: a corporate Windows 2000 forest and a single-domain forest in the Trey Research DeMilitarized Zone (called DEF). The corporate forest consists of one parent domain (*TreyResearch.tld*) and one child domain (*Europe.TreyResearch.tld*). The Trey Research corporate subordinate CAs are installed on Windows 2000 domain controllers belonging to the Trey Research parent domain. The European Services Company's subordinate CA is installed on a Windows 2000 controller belonging to the Europe.Trey Research child domain. Remember that the two root CAs are

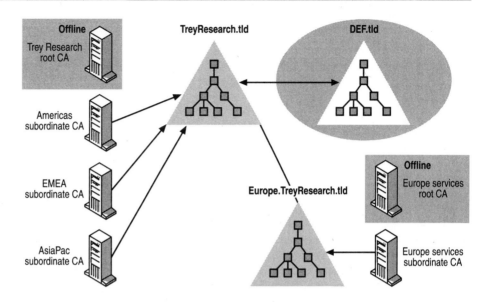

Figure 12.4   Trey Research's Domain topology and CA locations.

installed as offline CAs. The DEF domain contains Trey Research's standalone CA (not integrated with the Active Directory). It also contains a Web server that hosts a secured Web site through which external partners can:

- Download Trey Research's CA certificates and CRLs.

- Access the standalone CA to request new certificates.

- Query the Active Directory of DEF.tld to download certificates of Trey Research users.

The certificates of the users in the Trey Research domain are replicated to the Active Directory in the DEF domain. Users' queries coming from the Web site are sent as LDAP calls to the Active Directory. To handle certificate replication between *TreyResearch.tld* and *DEF.tld*, Trey Research runs Microsoft's Active Directory Connector (ADC) between the two Active Directories. (Another product such as Compaq's LDSU would also work.)

Specifications of the Individual CAs

The certification authorities are key PKI components, so you need to spend enough time and effort to create detailed designs of the individual CAs. You need to consider:

- CA architecture

- CA keys and certificates

- Active Directory integration

- CRL generation and distribution
- User identification and certificate requests
- Supported certificate types
- "Hardening" the CA server

CA Architecture

The Microsoft CA architecture includes two important customizable modules: *policy* and *exit*:

- The *policy* module receives certificate requests, identifies the requestor and evaluates the requests. It also determines the state of a request—issuing a certificate or tagging the request as *pending*—and can add certificate properties to the request. To check out the policy module that has been installed on a CA, look at its properties on the level of the MMC snap-in GUI or use the command prompt tool *certsvr.exe* with the *-z* switch.
- The *exit* module publishes issued certificates and CRLs in a location such as the Active Directory.

You can develop new policy modules to cope with special user-identification procedures, and can develop exit modules to publish certificates and CRLs in directories from other vendors. These sorts of customizations are explained in the *Windows 2000 Software Development Kit* (SDK).

CA Keys and Certificate

When you set up a CA, you have to choose the length of its key pair. When you do this, remember that the CA is the heart of your security system, and if its private key is compromised, so is the entire PKI. Protect against attacks by choosing the longest key possible—at least 1,024-bits. Also assure that the disk or the smart card on which you store the CA's private key is physically secured. Don't let just anyone get to the server, disk or smart card containing the private key: put the server in a highly-secured area of your company's computer room, lock the hard disk or smart card in a safe.

A smart card is by far the safest way to store the CA's private key: to get access to the CA's private key someone must possess the card and know the card's PIN. Windows 2000 supports two types of smart-card readers: Gemplus and Schlumberger. When you install the CA you'll have to specify which of these is used to store the CA's private key (see Figure 12.5). Other specialized hardware devices (RACAL cryptocards, etc.) can provide high-security CA key storage, but these are not yet supported by Microsoft.

If you do not plan to use smart cards on the root CAs and intermediate CAs, remember that it is a best practice to keep these servers offline. Keeping the offline CA servers in a secured area also offers private key protection.

To validate certificates, all entities using certificates must have access to the issuing CA's certificate (the public key). Making this available should not be a problem in a Windows 2000 forest, tree, or domain environment. You can use a Web site to make it available to external entities.

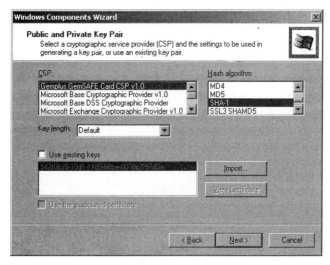

Figure 12.5   Specifying CSP, hash, and key length settings for the CA public-private key pair.

Active Directory Integration

When you install Certificate Server on a server hosting the Active Directory, you can choose *standalone* mode or *enterprise* mode (which integrates Certificate Server with the Active Directory). These install different CA policy modules.

If you install the CA in standalone mode you can issue only SSL and S/MIME certificates, and every certificate request is set to *pending* (by default) meaning that the CA administrator has to approve every request manually. This mode is clearly targeted towards the issuance of certificates to external users. Standalone mode can also be an interesting solution to take advantage of the new features of the Windows 2000 CA in an existing Windows NT 4 environment, without having to install the Active Directory and other Windows 2000 features such as dynamic DNS.

Installing the certificate server in Enterprise mode provides full integration with the Active Directory, offering these advantages:

- The Certificate Server uses the Active Directory to store and publish certificates and certificate revocation lists (CRLs). Each certificate published in the AD is automatically mapped to the Windows 2000 account of its requestor (you can also map certificates manually to Windows 2000 accounts).

- The Active Directory contains the location of the Certificate Servers. When a system requests a certificate, it can query the global catalog to find a CA.

- Any internal PKI client can launch LDAP-queries on the Active Directory to look up and retrieve certificates.

- The ability to provide smart-card logon to your Windows 2000 domain. Smart card certificates are automatically mapped to Windows 2000 accounts during the smart-card enrollment process. During the logon process the Kerberos KDC queries the Active Directory for a mapping between the user's certificate and a Windows 2000 account. The same process validates the user's identity using the public credentials, not the password.

- Your CA can issue all the different types of certificates that come with Windows 2000. You can set the types of certificates that are issued by your CA by loading the appropriate templates in your CA's policy module.

- You can take advantage of the integration of the certificate templates with the Active Directory. You can set ACLs on certificate templates just as you can on any other Active Directory object. This enables you to control who can get which type of certificates based on, for instance, group membership.

To illustrate the last two features, consider the example of root CAs or subordinate CAs that issue certificates only for other subordinate CAs. In this case you can load just one template in the CA and set ACLs on the subordinate CA template so that only a limited set of machine accounts can enroll for it.

Generating and Distributing CRLs

In the PKI planning stages, you should carefully consider how certificate revocation lists (CRLs) will be generated, distributed, and checked. CRLs list certificates that have been revoked because their associated private key has been compromised, deleted, or lost. Before being used, each certificate should be checked against the CRL, and this process obviously should be automated. The Windows 2000 PKI support for CRL distribution points (CRLDPs) greatly simplifies automation (Figure 12.6). CRLDPs are an extension to the X.509v3 standard. Here is how it works:

- Each certificate generated by a Windows 2000 Certificate Server includes one or more pointers to a CRLDP, which can be an Internet URL, LDAP URL, FTP URL, or a file system share address.

- Before a certificate is used, its CRLDPs are checked for an up-to-date CRL. If a new CRL is available, it is downloaded and cached for its lifetime on the client.

Besides automated revocation checking, CRLDPs also offer a way to limit the CRL size and to increase CRL availability. Each certificate can contain different CRLDPs: if one CRLDP is unavailable, the CRL can be found at another one. In big organizations, dealing with many certificates, CRLs may become pretty large. By using CRLDPs the PKI administrator can:

- Define different CAs, each one having different CRLs and different CRLDPs.

- Change the CRLDPs' settings on the level of the CA policy settings at regular intervals. You can change the location of the CRLDP and the name of the CRL. Certificates issued after the change will point to the new CRL at the new CRLDP. Certificates issued before the change can continue to use the old CRL and CRLDP.

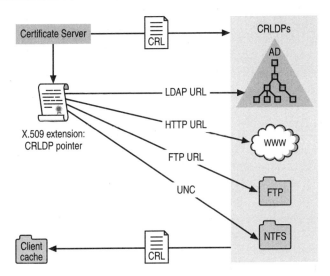

Figure 12.6   CRLDPs and Certificate Server.

When you design a PKI-architecture, consider these CRL-related parameters:

- **CRL lifetime.** The shorter the CRL lifetime the faster the user is apprised of a revoked certificate. Setting CRL lifetimes too short can burden the network traffic with CRL downloads; you can't set CRL lifetime to less than one hour.

- **CRLDPs.** For CRL downloads within your Windows 2000 organization the Active Directory is an obvious storage location for CRLs. If you also communicate with entities outside your organization using certificates, you'll need to consider alternative locations such as FTP sites or Web pages.

- **CRLDP and CRL naming**. As explained above, big organizations can consider using different CRLDPs and different CRL names, and changing these parameters at regular intervals.

User Identification and Certificate Requests

Before a certificate can be issued, the requestor must be identified and must have the private key linked to the requested certificate's public key. Depending on the interface used for the request, these authentication methods are available:

- MMC snap-in: Kerberos authentication.
- Web interface: anonymous, plaintext, digest, NTLM, or Kerberos authentication (in other words: all authentication methods available on the level of IIS).

You can create a custom Web page for certificate requests made via a Web interface. If you allow Web requests, you should set the properties of the corresponding **Certsrv** Web directory to *at least* Digest or Kerberos authentication.

Note that a Web interface is not very useful for root or intermediate CAs that issue certificates only to other CAs.

Supported Certificates

On the level of the *user* or *machine* certificates issued by your CAs, you need to consider these certificate characteristics:

- **Certificate type.** The certificate *type* is defined in the **usage** field, which is defined as an X.509v3 extension. A certificate's intended usage affects which applications it can be used for.

  You can load certificate templates to enable a Windows 2000 Certificate Server to issue different types of certificates. Certificate Server comes with numerous templates, each one defining a certificate type and containing different **usage** fields.

  These certificate templates are supported in Windows 2000:

Certificate template name	Certificate purposes	Issued to	Availability (Enterprise, Standalone, or both)
Administrator	Code signing, Microsoft trust list signing, EFS, secure e-mail, client authentication	People	E/S
Authenticated session	Client authentication	People	E
Basic EFS	Encrypting File System	People	E
Certification authority	Certificate signing, CRL signing	Computers	E/S
Code Signing	Code signing	People	E
Computer	Client authentication, server authentication	Computers	E
CTL Signing	Microsoft trust list signing	People	E
CEP Encryption	Certificate request agent	Computers	E
Domain Controller	Client authentication, server authentication	Computers	E
EFS Recovery Agent	File recovery	People	E
Enrollment Agent	Certificate request agent	People	E
Enrollment Agent (Computer)	Certificate request agent	Computers	E
Exchange Enrollment Agent (Offline Request)	Certificate request agent	People	E
Exchange User	Secure e-mail, client authentication	People	E
Exchange User Signature	Secure e-mail, client authentication	People	E
IPSEC Tunnel	IP security	Computers	E
Router (Offline Request)	Client authentication	Computers	E
Smartcard Logon	Smart-card logon, client authentication	People	E
Smartcard User	Smart-card logon, client authentication, secure e-mail	People	E
Subordinate CA	Certificate signing, CRL signing	Computers	E/S

Certificate template name	Certificate purposes	Issued to	Availability (Enterprise, Standalone, or both)
Trust List Signing	Microsoft Trust List signing	People	E
User	Encrypting File System, secure e-mail, client authentication	People	E/S
User Signature Only	Secure e-mail, client authentication	People	E/S
Web Server	Server authentication	Computers	E

- **Certificate and private key lifetime.** Certificate and private key lifetimes both impact the number of renewal requests that are send to CAs. Remember that a certificate renewal is not necessarily linked to a key renewal, but from a security point of view it is strongly recommended to limit the lifetime of user-certificates and to renew the keys at every certificate renewal. Shorter key lifetimes are also advisable when they provide security for highly confidential information or critical applications.

- **Cryptographic algorithms.** Each certificate contains fields that describe the asymmetric cipher that was used to sign the certificate and the hash that was used to protect the certificate integrity. Stronger ciphers (longer key lengths) increase certificate validation processing time but offer stronger security.

- **Certificate Storage.** Certificates can be stored on hard disk or on a smart card (preferred). If you store certificates on a hard disk, mark them as *non-exportable* at enrollment time.

Hardening the CA Server

A CA's private key is the most critical element of PKI security. If a root or intermediate CA's private key is compromised, all or part of your PKI-trust infrastructure falls to earth. This is why it is so important to store the CA's private key securely, to keep root and intermediate CAs offline, and to "harden" your CA server by boosting its physical, logical, and communications security. Remember that the most secure way to store the CA's private key in a Windows 2000 environment is on a smart card.

- **Physical security.** Install Certificate Servers on computers in *secure* areas where physical access is controlled and there is protection against fire, power loss, and other disasters.

- **Logical security.** Implement software access control systems on the computer to prevent unauthorized access to computer systems. In a Windows 2000 environment, logical security depends on the quality of the operating system's authentication and access control system.
  - You can provide high quality authentication by equipping all servers with smart-card readers, which provide two-factor authentication.
  - You can provide high quality access control by checking the ACLs on all the server's resources at regular intervals. Remember, in Windows 2000 you need to check ACLs on file system objects *and* on Active Directory objects.

■ **Communications security.** You can provide additional communications security for the issuing CAs connected to your production network by installing them on a separate subnet, behind a dedicated firewall, filtering out all non-PKI related traffic.

You can use the Security Configuration and Analysis tool (SCA—it comes with Windows 2000) to audit the security settings on Windows 2000 Servers. You can automate the SCA Analysis and run it at regular intervals in batch mode (using *secedit.exe*).

Case Study: Trey Research's CA Specification

Trey Research decided to integrate four of their CAs with the Active Directory and to keep the standard Enterprise policy module on all of them. The four CAs will all have CRLDPs defined that point to the Active Directory and to a Web directory from which partners can get the latest CRLS.

The CA located on the DMZ and the two root CAs will be installed in standalone mode.

To provide access to the CRLDPs and root certificates of the offline root CAs, the CRLDP and AIA pointers will be changed in the policy-settings of both root CAs. The CRLDPs will be pointed to a location that is always online. AIA (Authority Information Access) pointers are X.509 extensions that point to a place where the certificate of a certificate's issuing CA can be found.

All CA servers will be installed on dedicated servers in a high-security room. Only CA administrators will be able to log on locally; users will need to use smart-card authentication to access the servers. The IT department will harden the CA servers by creating a checklist of Windows 2000 related security settings that will be applied and regularly checked using *secedit.exe*.

All issuing CAs will store their private key on smart cards that will be stored in a highly secured area.

The IT department will create a customized Web page where partners can enroll for a client authentication certificate. Access will be secured using digest authentication. The same Web page will contain a link to a page from which partners can download Trey Research's CRLs, user certificates, and root certificates.

Trey Research will set CRL lifetime to one month, and will shorten it to one week when more certificates are issued. The root CA certificate has a lifetime of two years; subordinate CAs certificates one year.

Only the certificate templates that are really used will be loaded on the CAs. To control which users can get which certificate-types, special Windows 2000 groups will be created and set in the ACLs of the certificate templates.

Defining Public Key Policy Settings (GPO)

Windows 2000 users and computers are subject to the Enterprise policies kept in the Active Directory. Group Policy Objects (GPOs) facilitate the distribution of system and user-related parameters within the corporate Windows 2000 environment. You can apply them at the domain, organizational unit, site, or computer level.

Windows 2000 GPO objects include these PKI-related entries:

- **Certificate Trust Lists.** CTLs, containing certificates of CAs external to the corporate PKI hierarchy, are used to provide networked trust. You can fine-tune Windows 2000 CTLs based on certificate type and validity period. Certificate *type* allows you to specify that certificates coming from a particular CA are trusted only for some uses (such as secure e-mail). *Validity period* allows you to specify that certificates coming from a particular CA are trusted only if they have been issued within a certain time interval. Note that in Windows 2000 networked trust is set using GPOs at the Active Directory level *not* on the CA level.

- **Automated certificate enrollment and renewal.** Windows 2000 administrators can enroll machine accounts automatically for a certificate, which can be useful for IPsec authentication based on certificates. Accounts set in this list also profit from automatic certificate renewal.

- **Trusted root Certification Authorities.** This is a list of trusted root CAs that contains the certificates of internal root CAs that should be trusted by any entity in a Windows 2000 domain. If you install an Enterprise CA in your domain, its certificate is automatically added to the list of *Trusted Root CAs*. If external entities need the root certificate of one of your internal CAs, you'll need another location or means to distribute it.

- **Data recovery agents.** These settings are used to recover Encrypting File System (EFS) data. A Windows 2000 domain administrator can grant the EFS data recovery privilege to a limited number of Windows 2000 accounts by including them in the Data Recovery Agent GPO entry.

Remember that you can set Windows 2000 GPO settings at the machine, site, domain, and organizational unit (OU) level. In other words, you can define different CTLs for different OUs, as well as different recovery agents, trusted root Cas, and automated enrollment settings.

From the Trenches: Implementing EFS Recovery on Top of PKI

The new Windows 2000 Encryption File System (EFS) feature allows you to encrypt files and folders on the file-system level. Based on a hybrid cryptographic solution that combines symmetric and asymmetric ciphers, EFS handles client-side encryption on the desktop and on laptop systems operating in network, standalone, or offline modes.

A key EFS feature is recovery of encrypted files or folders. A Windows 2000 account (called a *recovery agent*) other than the original owner of the data can decrypt and recover the data if (and only if):

- The recovery agent's public key was used to encrypt the session key that was used to encrypt the data
- The resulting encrypted session key is part of an NTFS file stream that is linked to the encrypted data

You use Windows 2000 group policy objects (GPOs) to make recovery agents available to the EFS system on client computers. The GPO's Encrypted Data Recovery Policy (EDRP) entry lists the recovery agents. As with any other GPO entry, you can set the EDRP on the machine, site, domain, and organizational unit levels.

Here is an example: an EDRP policy is defined on the domain level. If a laptop (belonging to the above domain) logs on to the Windows 2000 domain, the domain GPO settings are applied to it, and thus: the recovery agents are in place. Once applied, the GPO settings stay active, even when the system is working in offline mode.

You should carefully remember these two characteristics of the EDRP:

- The default recovery agent is the administrator account. By default the administrator can decrypt all data encrypted in the domain. In many environments this is fine; in others it should be changed.
- A user's private key is stored in a secured part of the user's profile (the protected store). In a Windows 2000 environment users can access their private key if they've successfully authenticated to a machine or to a domain.

Suppose Jerry installs Windows 2000 Professional; creates a user account *Jerry*, and encrypts some files and folders while he's logged on as *Jerry*. Later, for some reason, he has to reinstall the operating system, so he recreates a user account *Jerry*, but when he tries to access the previously encrypted files and folders, the operating system generates an error and the access fails. What happened?

When Jerry created his second user account, he got a new SID (a security identity). By definition a SID is unique. The SID linked to the new user account is different from Jerry's original SID. And thus, using the new SID Jerry can no longer access his encrypted files. Instead of simply creating a new account, he should have exported his private key to a floppy before reinstalling, then imported it from the floppy after reinstalling. Or he could have decrypted the data with the old SID then re-encrypted it with the new SID.

Defining the Security Policy, Certificate Policies, and the Certificate Practice Statement

The majority of the guidelines in this chapter focus on the technical aspects of the PKI-infrastructure design and planning. An important non-technical aspect often forgotten by technically-oriented planners is defining the Security Policy, Certificate Policies (CPs), and Certificate Practice Statements (CPS).

The *Security Policy* (SP) is a high-level document created by the corporate IT group. It defines a set of rules regarding the use and provision of security services within the organization, and should reflect your organization's business- and IT-strategy. As a sort of context definition for corporate security services, it should answer these types of PKI questions:

- What applications should be secured with certificates?
- What kind of security services should be offered using certificates?

A *Certificate Policy* (CP) is linked to a certificate-type that is issued by a CA. It focuses on certificate characteristics such as usage, enrollment procedure, liability issues, etc. It should answer questions such as:

- What type of applications can the certificate be used for?
- How can a user enroll for the certificate?
- How are users identified when they request a certificate?
- What is a certificate's lifetime?
- How is renewal defined? Is a new key pair generated at every certificate renewal?
- What key lengths and ciphers are used to generate the certificate?
- Where is the private key stored?
- What about liability when the issuing CA is compromised or when users lose their private keys?

The *Certificate Practice Statement* (CPS) translates Certificate Policies (CPs) into operational procedures on the CA level. The CP focuses on a certificate; the CPS focuses on a Certification Authority (CA). A CPS answers questions such as:

- What policy is linked to the CA?
- How are certificates issued? Are they issued directly to users, or into a directory?
- Who can administer the CA? What subtasks are delegated to the different administrators?
- How is certificate revocation handled? When is a certificate revoked (conditions)? Where are CRLs published? How often are the CRLs updated?

- How is the access to the CA physically and logically secured?
- Who is responsible for backing up the CA?
- What about the quality of the CA-certificate and private key? What's the lifetime of the keys and the certificate? Where is the private key stored?

PKI Maintenance and Administration

CA Administration

The primary Certificate Server administration interface is a Microsoft Management Console (MMC) snap-in. You can use it to stop and start CA service, revoke certificates, issue CRLs, add certificate templates, back up and restore the CA, and look at the CA database contents. You can set permissions on the level of the CA container, which allows you to delegate CA-related administrative tasks.

CA-Directory Backup-Restore

Certificate Server and the Active Directory both have an integrated backup-restore utility. Remember that in a PKI the backup-restore of the directory containing certificates and CRLs is much more important than the backup-restore of the CA and its database.

CA Certificate Renewal

Like any certificate, the CA certificate has a lifespan, and when it expires the CA cannot issue any new certificates. At regular intervals, you must renew the certificates of the root and the subordinate CAs.

To prevent "orphaned" certificates, the Certificate Server makes sure that all certificates issued by the CA expire before the CA's certificate expires. For example: if a request is sent to create a certificate with a 2-year lifetime and CA's certificate is about to expire in 1 year, the CA generates a certificate with a lifetime slightly shorter than 1 year.

To renew a CA certificate, you simply run a renewal wizard from the CA snap-in. You are asked if you want to reuse the same key pair or generate a new one. This is an important choice. Generating a new key pair has these advantages:

- **Better security.** A CA is the most critical PKI component; reusing keys gives hackers more time to derive and compromise your CA's private key.
- **Generating a new CRL.** CRLs are signed with the CA's private key, so if you regenerate the CA's private key a new CRL is generated. This helps you deal with big CRLs.

From the Trenches: Integrating Exchange Advanced Security with MS PKI to Provide S/MIME-based Secure E-mail

Exchange 5.5 and Exchange 2000 come with an Advanced Security extension. It is based on the Key Management Service (KMS) which enables an Exchange user to use S/MIME to sign and seal e-mail messages. Here is how the KMS integrates with Windows 2000 PKI services.

Exchange 5.5 Service Pack 1 introduced a way to integrate the KMS service with Microsoft's Certificate Server. Integration (standard in Exchange 2000) allows the KMS to act as a kind of Registration Authority (RA), handling all administrative tasks, while the CA handles the real certification tasks. Integrating the KMS with the CA increases scalability. You can link an Exchange KMS into a CA hierarchy, and an Exchange organization can contain more than one KMS service. Because the KMS services are linked to a CA, they can see each other.

There are a few issues with the Exchange 5.5 SP 1 implementation. First, the KMS is always linked to only one CA: if this one goes down, there's no way to issue or to revoke certificates. The implementation also requires that you install a special policy module on the CA-side to enable communication between the KMS and the CA. Once you install it, the CA can issue only KMS certificates.

With Exchange 5.5 SP 3 you can install the Exchange 5.5 KMS on a Windows 2000 platform. This lets you take advantage of the new CA GUI and of its ability to support CA hierarchies with more than two levels. You still have to install the Exchange policy module on the Windows 2000 CA to enable communication between the KMS and the CA.

Exchange 2000 resolves these issues. The Exchange 2000 KMS integrates seamlessly with the Windows 2000 PKI, Exchange 2000 running on Windows 2000 does not need the special policy module, the Windows 2000 CA can issue more than just Exchange certificates, and the KMS is no longer bound to just one CA. Because CA location information is published in the Active Directory, the Exchange 2000 KMS can look for another CA in the Active Directory if the primary CA is unavailable. You can also take advantage of all the other advanced PKI features in Windows 2000— Active Directory integration, advanced CRL checking (CRLDPs), certificate templates, and so on.

Conclusion

Because it is based on open standards, the PKI software included with Windows 2000 offers flexibility and scalability in the planning and deployment of public-key based security solutions within the enterprise.

If you're planning to implement a Windows 2000-based PKI, remember that about half of the planning, design, and administration work related to a PKI is non-technical, in that it deals with core business needs and your specific security requirements for information and network communication. The technology is important, but you have to design an infrastructure that *meets your needs*. Remember too that a PKI is an *infrastructure*, not simply a piece of software. In addition to applications it also to some extent affects everything and everybody that deals with your corporate IT-infrastructure—from end users to the CIO.

Index

G

System Requirements

In order to run the tools, utilities, and scripts included on the CD, you need a computer with Windows 2000 Server installed. Here are the minimum system requirements for installing Windows 2000 Server. (Note that Windows 2000 Server supports up to four CPUs on one machine.)

- 133 MHz or higher Pentium-compatible CPU
- 256 MB of RAM recommended minimum (128 MB minimum supported; 4 GB maximum)
- 2 GB hard disk with a minimum of 1.0 GB free space (Additional free hard-disk space is required if you are installing over a network.)

In order to use or view the various documents, spreadsheets, and templates included on the CD, you need a computer with Windows 95 or later, or Windows NT or later (including Windows 2000) installed. You also need the following software, depending on which document you want to use or view:

- Microsoft Word 95 or later (Word documents can also be viewed using WordPad, which is a standard feature in Windows 2000)
- Microsoft Excel 95 or later
- Microsoft Project 98 or later
- Visual Basic (if you want to alter any of the source files included in the **sources** subfolder within the **Capacity Planning Tools** folder on the CD)
- Adobe Acrobat Reader (included on the CD that accompanies this book)

Powerhouse resources to minimize costs while maximizing performance

Deploy and support your enterprise business systems using the expertise and tools of those who know the technology best—the Microsoft product groups. Each RESOURCE KIT packs precise technical reference, installation and rollout tactics, planning guides, upgrade strategies, and essential utilities on CD-ROM. They're everything you need to help maximize system performance as you reduce ownership and support costs!

Microsoft® Windows® 2000 Server Resource Kit
ISBN 1-57231-805-8
U.S.A. $299.99
U.K.   £189.99 [V.A.T. included]
Canada $460.99

Microsoft Windows 2000 Professional Resource Kit
ISBN 1-57231-808-2
U.S.A. $69.99
U.K.   £45.99 [V.A.T. included]
Canada $107.99

Microsoft BackOffice® 4.5 Resource Kit
ISBN 0-7356-0583-1
U.S.A. $249.99
U.K.   £161.99 [V.A.T. included]
Canada $374.99

Microsoft Internet Explorer 5 Resource Kit
ISBN 0-7356-0587-4
U.S.A. $59.99
U.K.   £38.99 [V.A.T. included]
Canada $89.99

Microsoft Office 2000 Resource Kit
ISBN 0-7356-0555-6
U.S.A. $59.99
U.K.   £38.99 [V.A.T. included]
Canada $89.99

Microsoft Windows NT® Server 4.0 Resource Kit
ISBN 1-57231-344-7
U.S.A. $149.95
U.K.   £96.99 [V.A.T. included]
Canada $199.95

Microsoft Windows NT Workstation 4.0 Resource Kit
ISBN 1-57231-343-9
U.S.A. $69.95
U.K.   £45.99 [V.A.T. included]
Canada $94.95

mspress.microsoft.com

Gain work-ready expertise as you prepare for the Microsoft Certified Professional (MCP) exam.

Learn by doing—learn for the job—with official Microsoft self-paced training kits. Whether you choose a book-and-CD TRAINING KIT or the all-multimedia learning experience of an ONLINE TRAINING KIT, you'll gain hands-on experience building essential systems support skills—as you prepare for the corresponding MCP exam. It's Microsoft Official Curriculum—how, when, and where you study best.

Microsoft® Certified Systems Engineer Core Requirements Training Kit
ISBN 1-57231-905-4

MCSE Training Kit, Microsoft Windows® 2000 Server
ISBN 1-57231-903-8

MCSE Online Training Kit, Microsoft Windows 2000 Server
ISBN 0-7356-0954-3
COMING SOON

MCSE Training Kit, Microsoft Windows 2000 Professional
ISBN 1-57231-901-1

MCSE Online Training Kit, Microsoft Windows 2000 Professional
ISBN 0-7356-0953-5
COMING SOON

MCSE Training Kit, Microsoft Windows 2000 Active Directory™ Services
ISBN 0-7356-0999-3

MCSE Online Training Kit, Microsoft Windows 2000 Active Directory Services
ISBN 0-7356-1008-8
COMING SOON

Microsoft SQL Server™ 7.0 Database Implementation Training Kit
ISBN 1-57231-826-0

Microsoft SQL Server 7.0 Database Implementation Online Training Kit
ISBN 0-7356-0679-X

Microsoft SQL Server 7.0 System Administration Training Kit
ISBN 1-57231-827-9

Microsoft SQL Server 7.0 System Administration Online Training Kit
ISBN 0-7356-0678-1

MCSE Training Kit, Networking Essentials Plus, Third Edition
ISBN 1-57231-902-X

MCSE Online Training Kit, Networking Essentials Plus
ISBN 0-7356-0880-6

Upgrading to Microsoft Windows 2000 Training Kit
ISBN 0-7356-0940-3

MCSE Training Kit, Microsoft Windows 2000 Network Infrastructure Administration
ISBN 1-57231-904-6
COMING SOON

***Microsoft*®**

mspress.microsoft.com

MICROSOFT LICENSE AGREEMENT

Book Companion CD

IMPORTANT—READ CAREFULLY: This Microsoft End-User License Agreement ("EULA") is a legal agreement between you (either an individual or an entity) and Microsoft Corporation for the Microsoft product identified above, which includes computer software and may include associated media, printed materials, and "on-line" or electronic documentation ("SOFTWARE PRODUCT"). Any component included within the SOFTWARE PRODUCT that is accompanied by a separate End-User License Agreement shall be governed by such agreement and not the terms set forth below. By installing, copying, or otherwise using the SOFTWARE PRODUCT, you agree to be bound by the terms of this EULA. If you do not agree to the terms of this EULA, you are not authorized to install, copy, or otherwise use the SOFTWARE PRODUCT; you may, however, return the SOFTWARE PRODUCT, along with all printed materials and other items that form a part of the Microsoft product that includes the SOFTWARE PRODUCT, to the place you obtained them for a full refund.

SOFTWARE PRODUCT LICENSE

The SOFTWARE PRODUCT is protected by United States copyright laws and international copyright treaties, as well as other intellectual property laws and treaties. The SOFTWARE PRODUCT is licensed, not sold.

1. GRANT OF LICENSE. This EULA grants you the following rights:

a. **Software Product.** You may install and use one copy of the SOFTWARE PRODUCT on a single computer. The primary user of the computer on which the SOFTWARE PRODUCT is installed may make a second copy for his or her exclusive use on a portable computer.

b. **Storage/Network Use.** You may also store or install a copy of the SOFTWARE PRODUCT on a storage device, such as a network server, used only to install or run the SOFTWARE PRODUCT on your other computers over an internal network; however, you must acquire and dedicate a license for each separate computer on which the SOFTWARE PRODUCT is installed or run from the storage device. A license for the SOFTWARE PRODUCT may not be shared or used concurrently on different computers.

c. **License Pak.** If you have acquired this EULA in a Microsoft License Pak, you may make the number of additional copies of the computer software portion of the SOFTWARE PRODUCT authorized on the printed copy of this EULA, and you may use each copy in the manner specified above. You are also entitled to make a corresponding number of secondary copies for portable computer use as specified above.

d. **Sample Code.** Solely with respect to portions, if any, of the SOFTWARE PRODUCT that are identified within the SOFTWARE PRODUCT as sample code (the "SAMPLE CODE"):

i. **Use and Modification.** Microsoft grants you the right to use and modify the source code version of the SAMPLE CODE, *provided* you comply with subsection (d)(iii) below. You may not distribute the SAMPLE CODE, or any modified version of the SAMPLE CODE, in source code form.

ii. **Redistributable Files.** Provided you comply with subsection (d)(iii) below, Microsoft grants you a nonexclusive, royalty-free right to reproduce and distribute the object code version of the SAMPLE CODE and of any modified SAMPLE CODE, other than SAMPLE CODE (or any modified version thereof) designated as not redistributable in the Readme file that forms a part of the SOFTWARE PRODUCT (the "Non-Redistributable Sample Code"). All SAMPLE CODE other than the Non-Redistributable Sample Code is collectively referred to as the "REDISTRIBUTABLES."

iii. **Redistribution Requirements.** If you redistribute the REDISTRIBUTABLES, you agree to: (i) distribute the REDISTRIBUTABLES in object code form only in conjunction with and as a part of your software application product; (ii) not use Microsoft's name, logo, or trademarks to market your software application product; (iii) include a valid copyright notice on your software application product; (iv) indemnify, hold harmless, and defend Microsoft from and against any claims or lawsuits, including attorney's fees, that arise or result from the use or distribution of your software application product; and (v) not permit further distribution of the REDISTRIBUTABLES by your end user. Contact Microsoft for the applicable royalties due and other licensing terms for all other uses and/or distribution of the REDISTRIBUTABLES.

2. DESCRIPTION OF OTHER RIGHTS AND LIMITATIONS.

- **Limitations on Reverse Engineering, Decompilation, and Disassembly.** You may not reverse engineer, decompile, or disassemble the SOFTWARE PRODUCT, except and only to the extent that such activity is expressly permitted by applicable law notwithstanding this limitation.

- **Separation of Components.** The SOFTWARE PRODUCT is licensed as a single product. Its component parts may not be separated for use on more than one computer.

- **Rental.** You may not rent, lease, or lend the SOFTWARE PRODUCT.

- **Support Services.** Microsoft may, but is not obligated to, provide you with support services related to the SOFTWARE PRODUCT ("Support Services"). Use of Support Services is governed by the Microsoft policies and programs described in the user manual, in "on-line" documentation, and/or in other Microsoft-provided materials. Any supplemental software code provided to you as part of the Support Services shall be considered part of the SOFTWARE PRODUCT and subject to the terms and conditions of this EULA. With respect to technical information you provide to Microsoft as part of the Support Services, Microsoft may use such information for its business purposes, including for product support and development. Microsoft will not utilize such technical information in a form that personally identifies you.

- **Software Transfer.** You may permanently transfer all of your rights under this EULA, provided you retain no copies, you transfer all of the SOFTWARE PRODUCT (including all component parts, the media and printed materials, any upgrades, this EULA, and, if applicable, the Certificate of Authenticity), **and** the recipient agrees to the terms of this EULA.

- **Termination.** Without prejudice to any other rights, Microsoft may terminate this EULA if you fail to comply with the terms and conditions of this EULA. In such event, you must destroy all copies of the SOFTWARE PRODUCT and all of its component parts.

3. **COPYRIGHT.** All title and copyrights in and to the SOFTWARE PRODUCT (including but not limited to any images, photographs, animations, video, audio, music, text, SAMPLE CODE, REDISTRIBUTABLES, and "applets" incorporated into the SOFTWARE PRODUCT) and any copies of the SOFTWARE PRODUCT are owned by Microsoft or its suppliers. The SOFTWARE PRODUCT is protected by copyright laws and international treaty provisions. Therefore, you must treat the SOFTWARE PRODUCT like any other copyrighted material **except** that you may install the SOFTWARE PRODUCT on a single computer provided you keep the original solely for backup or archival purposes. You may not copy the printed materials accompanying the SOFTWARE PRODUCT.

4. **U.S. GOVERNMENT RESTRICTED RIGHTS.** The SOFTWARE PRODUCT and documentation are provided with RE-STRICTED RIGHTS. Use, duplication, or disclosure by the Government is subject to restrictions as set forth in subparagraph (c)(1)(ii) of the Rights in Technical Data and Computer Software clause at DFARS 252.227-7013 or subparagraphs (c)(1) and (2) of the Commercial Computer Software—Restricted Rights at 48 CFR 52.227-19, as applicable. Manufacturer is Microsoft Corporation/One Microsoft Way/Redmond, WA 98052-6399.

5. **EXPORT RESTRICTIONS.** You agree that you will not export or re-export the SOFTWARE PRODUCT, any part thereof, or any process or service that is the direct product of the SOFTWARE PRODUCT (the foregoing collectively referred to as the "Restricted Components"), to any country, person, entity, or end user subject to U.S. export restrictions. You specifically agree not to export or re-export any of the Restricted Components (i) to any country to which the U.S. has embargoed or restricted the export of goods or services, which currently include, but are not necessarily limited to, Cuba, Iran, Iraq, Libya, North Korea, Sudan, and Syria, or to any national of any such country, wherever located, who intends to transmit or transport the Restricted Components back to such country; (ii) to any end user who you know or have reason to know will utilize the Restricted Components in the design, development, or production of nuclear, chemical, or biological weapons; or (iii) to any end user who has been prohibited from participating in U.S. export transactions by any federal agency of the U.S. government. You warrant and represent that neither the BXA nor any other U.S. federal agency has suspended, revoked, or denied your export privileges.

6. **NOTE ON JAVA SUPPORT.** THE SOFTWARE PRODUCT MAY CONTAIN SUPPORT FOR PROGRAMS WRITTEN IN JAVA. JAVA TECHNOLOGY IS NOT FAULT TOLERANT AND IS NOT DESIGNED, MANUFACTURED, OR INTENDED FOR USE OR RESALE AS ON-LINE CONTROL EQUIPMENT IN HAZARDOUS ENVIRONMENTS REQUIRING FAIL-SAFE PERFOR-MANCE, SUCH AS IN THE OPERATION OF NUCLEAR FACILITIES, AIRCRAFT NAVIGATION OR COMMUNICATION SYSTEMS, AIR TRAFFIC CONTROL, DIRECT LIFE SUPPORT MACHINES, OR WEAPONS SYSTEMS, IN WHICH THE FAILURE OF JAVA TECHNOLOGY COULD LEAD DIRECTLY TO DEATH, PERSONAL INJURY, OR SEVERE PHYSICAL OR ENVIRONMENTAL DAMAGE. SUN MICROSYSTEMS, INC. HAS CONTRACTUALLY OBLIGATED MICROSOFT TO MAKE THIS DISCLAIMER.

DISCLAIMER OF WARRANTY

NO WARRANTIES OR CONDITIONS. MICROSOFT EXPRESSLY DISCLAIMS ANY WARRANTY OR CONDITION FOR THE SOFTWARE PRODUCT. THE SOFTWARE PRODUCT AND ANY RELATED DOCUMENTATION ARE PROVIDED "AS IS" WITHOUT WARRANTY OR CONDITION OF ANY KIND, EITHER EXPRESS OR IMPLIED, INCLUDING, WITHOUT LIMITATION, THE IMPLIED WARRANTIES OF MERCHANTABILITY, FITNESS FOR A PARTICULAR PURPOSE, OR NONINFRINGEMENT. THE ENTIRE RISK ARISING OUT OF USE OR PERFORMANCE OF THE SOFTWARE PRODUCT REMAINS WITH YOU.

LIMITATION OF LIABILITY. TO THE MAXIMUM EXTENT PERMITTED BY APPLICABLE LAW, IN NO EVENT SHALL MICROSOFT OR ITS SUPPLIERS BE LIABLE FOR ANY SPECIAL, INCIDENTAL, INDIRECT, OR CONSEQUENTIAL DAMAGES WHATSOEVER (INCLUDING, WITHOUT LIMITATION, DAMAGES FOR LOSS OF BUSINESS PROFITS, BUSINESS INTERRUP-TION, LOSS OF BUSINESS INFORMATION, OR ANY OTHER PECUNIARY LOSS) ARISING OUT OF THE USE OF OR INABILITY TO USE THE SOFTWARE PRODUCT OR THE PROVISION OF OR FAILURE TO PROVIDE SUPPORT SERVICES, EVEN IF MICROSOFT HAS BEEN ADVISED OF THE POSSIBILITY OF SUCH DAMAGES. IN ANY CASE, MICROSOFT'S ENTIRE LIABIL-ITY UNDER ANY PROVISION OF THIS EULA SHALL BE LIMITED TO THE GREATER OF THE AMOUNT ACTUALLY PAID BY YOU FOR THE SOFTWARE PRODUCT OR US$5.00; PROVIDED, HOWEVER, IF YOU HAVE ENTERED INTO A MICROSOFT SUPPORT SERVICES AGREEMENT, MICROSOFT'S ENTIRE LIABILITY REGARDING SUPPORT SERVICES SHALL BE GOV-ERNED BY THE TERMS OF THAT AGREEMENT. BECAUSE SOME STATES AND JURISDICTIONS DO NOT ALLOW THE EXCLUSION OR LIMITATION OF LIABILITY, THE ABOVE LIMITATION MAY NOT APPLY TO YOU.

MISCELLANEOUS

This EULA is governed by the laws of the State of Washington USA, except and only to the extent that applicable law mandates governing law of a different jurisdiction.

Should you have any questions concerning this EULA, or if you desire to contact Microsoft for any reason, please contact the Microsoft subsidiary serving your country, or write: Microsoft Sales Information Center/One Microsoft Way/Redmond, WA 98052-6399.

Proof of Purchase

0-7356-0860-1

Do not send this card with your registration.
Use this card as proof of purchase if participating in a promotion or
rebate offer on *Microsoft Book Title*. Card must be used in conjunction with
other proof(s) of payment such as your dated sales receipt—see offer details.

Building Enterprise Active Directory™ Services: Notes from the Field

WHERE DID YOU PURCHASE THIS PRODUCT?

CUSTOMER NAME

Microsoft®

mspress.microsoft.com

Microsoft Press, PO Box 97017, Redmond, WA 98073-9830

OWNER REGISTRATION CARD   *Register Today!*   0-7356-0860-1

Return the bottom portion of this card to register today.

Building Enterprise Active Directory™ Services: Notes from the Field

FIRST NAME   MIDDLE INITIAL   LAST NAME

INSTITUTION OR COMPANY NAME

ADDRESS

CITY   STATE   ZIP

(   )

E-MAIL ADDRESS   PHONE NUMBER

U.S. and Canada addresses only. Fill in information above and mail postage-free.
Please mail only the bottom half of this page.

For information about Microsoft Press®
products, visit our Web site at
mspress.microsoft.com